THEORY AND INTERPRETATION OF NARRATIVE
James Phelan, Peter J. Rabinowitz, and Robyn Warhol, Series Editors

After Testimony

The Ethics and Aesthetics of
Holocaust Narrative for the Future

Edited by
JAKOB LOTHE,
SUSAN RUBIN SULEIMAN,
and JAMES PHELAN

THE OHIO STATE UNIVERSITY PRESS · COLUMBUS

Chapter 15 adapted from *Multidirectional Memory: Remembering the Holocaust in the Age of Decolonization* by Michael Rothberg. Copyright © by the Board of Trustees of the Leland Stanford Jr. University. All rights reserved. Used with the permission of Stanford University Press, www.sup.org.

Library of Congress Cataloging-in-Publication Data

After testimony : the ethics and aesthetics of Holocaust narrative for the future / Edited by Jakob Lothe, Susan Rubin Suleiman, and James Phelan.
    p. cm.—(Theory and interpretation of narrative)
Includes bibliographical references and index.
 ISBN 978-0-8142-5182-9 (pbk. : alk. paper)—ISBN 978-0-8142-1176-2 (cloth : alk. paper)—ISBN 978-0-8142-9277-8 (cd)
 1. Holocaust, Jewish (1939–1945), in literature. 2. Holocaust, Jewish (1939–1945), in motion pictures. 3. Holocaust, Jewish (1939–1945)—Historiography. I. Lothe, Jakob.
II. Suleiman, Susan Rubin, 1939– III. Phelan, James, 1951– IV. Series: Theory and interpretation of narrative series.
 PN56.H55A37 2012
 809'.93358405318—dc23

Cover design by Mia Risberg
Text design by Juliet Williams
Type set in Adobe Minion Pro
Printed by Sheridan Books, Inc.

9   8   7   6   5   4   3   2   1

CONTENTS

ILLUSTRATIONS

ACKNOWLEDGMENTS

The editors and contributors owe their collaboration on this volume to the Centre for Advanced Study (CAS) at the Norwegian Academy of Science and Letters in Oslo. The editors and many of the contributors were members of an international research project on narrative theory and analysis, proposed and led by Jakob and hosted and funded by CAS during the 2005–6 academic year. CAS supported not just the project but also a three-day conference in Berlin in June 2007, where drafts of all the projected essays in this book were discussed in detail. We are most grateful to Professor Willy Østreng, who was director of the Centre at the time we were there, and to the administrative staff of CAS, for their friendliness, encouragement, and assistance. Moreover, CAS generously contributed funding to offset the publication costs of this volume. We have also benefited from the collegial intellectual atmosphere fostered at CAS by the other members of the research team: Daphna Erdinast-Vulcan, Anniken Greve, Jeremy Hawthorn, J. Hillis Miller, Beatrice Sandberg, Anette H. Storeide, and Anne Thelle. In addition, we express our gratitude to the following distinguished scholars who also participated in the project, offering wise advice and agreeing to contribute to the volume: Sidra deKoven Ezrahi, Marianne Hirsch, Irene Kacandes, Philippe Mesnard, Michael Rothberg, and Janet Walker. We are also grateful for the valuable proofreading and other technical help provided by Jim's research assistant, Brian McAllister. Finally, Jakob and Jim want to express their special gratitude to Susan, whose extensive knowledge of Holocaust narrative was indispensible at every turn and was especially invaluable as we wrote the introduction.

"After" Testimony

Holocaust Representation and Narrative Theory

JAKOB LOTHE,
SUSAN RUBIN SULEIMAN,
and JAMES PHELAN

In a few years, there will be no living survivors of the Holocaust. Although many commentators have acknowledged this fact, few have made sustained efforts to draw out its full implications. Will the disappearance of the last witness affect the way public discourse deals with the Holocaust? Will the Holocaust become, perhaps for the first time, truly "past history"? How will writers and filmmakers who may have no personal connection to the event engage with that history: what kinds of stories will they tell, and will they succeed in their effort to keep the public memory of the event from being lost? Indeed, what has allowed some narratives of the Holocaust produced over the past half-century to survive and become "classics"? And will these same properties ensure their survival in the future? What can we learn from the recent history of Holocaust narratives, both fictional and nonfictional?

These were among the starting questions for the research project that forms the basis for this book, and implicit in them are some more specific issues that we believe will be crucial for the new period of Holocaust narrative and Holocaust criticism.[1] When we ask, "What kinds of stories?" or "How do stories live beyond their immediate moment, and what can we learn from previous works?" we are in part asking questions about aesthetics. But since these questions concern the Holocaust, we are also necessarily asking about the relation between aesthetics and ethics, and about the relation between aesthetics and transmission. At least since Theodor W. Adorno's famous (and often misunderstood) claim that "writing poetry after Ausch-

1

witz is barbaric,"[2] scholars and others have been justifiably concerned with the ethics of aestheticizing the Holocaust. At the same time, one of the lessons of the past half-century is that the narratives that endure, and that have the greatest chance of transmitting the story to future generations, all possess a significant aesthetic dimension. Responding to this characteristic feature of Holocaust narratives, the essays in this volume all address in some way the interrelation of ethics and aesthetics. Some also address, implicitly or explicitly, the issue of politics, whether in relation to the role of Holocaust narrative in the political and social history of Israel or in relation to the representation of Nazi perpetrators in fiction. Because the political uses of Holocaust narrative, both in Israel and elsewhere, have been amply discussed and debated in recent years, they are not the principal subject of this volume. At the same time, the essays are informed by our contributors' awareness of what the last few decades of cultural theory have convincingly demonstrated; namely, that the aesthetic and the political—whether defined in terms of gender, class, race, or nation—are deeply intertwined.

These sixteen wide-ranging essays comprise discussions of literary works (from early testimony to contemporary memoirs and fiction, with a heavy emphasis on the latter), biography, film, and photography, and they represent narratives from numerous national and cultural locations—Germany, England, France, Hungary, Italy, Poland, Israel, Japan, Norway, and the United States. We have included discussions of some works that have long been in the Holocaust canon, but we have particularly emphasized outstanding works of literature and film that are not (or not yet) well known internationally, including very recently published works.

The word "after" in our title merits further discussion. As we have suggested, it refers first of all to the historical fact that we are nearing an age "after testimony," an age where first-person accounts by Holocaust survivors will no longer be forthcoming. But "after" also has another meaning, referring not to chronology but to artistic creation: a painting "after" Michelangelo is one that situates itself self-consciously in a position of imitation or homage. Using the word in conjunction with "testimony," we shift its meaning slightly: the phrase seeks not to describe artistic imitation but rather to suggest that all works dealing with the Holocaust must in some way come to terms with the historical reality that the accounts of survivors have tried to communicate. In that broad sense, all works relating to the Holocaust that deserve our attention, even the most speculative or experimental novels or films, are bound by a certain obligation to the history referred to in those testimonies. But to come "after" also implies an obligation to the future: in that respect, this volume is turned toward thinking about the future of Holocaust narrative and about the afterlife of Holocaust narratives in different cultures.

The Question of Aesthetics in Holocaust Literature and Criticism
A Brief Overview

In the years immediately following World War II and the return of survivors from Nazi concentration and labor camps, the overwhelming need appeared to be to testify, independently of considerations of art or artfulness. As many witnesses stated, they lived only for the day when they could tell the world about the unimaginable horrors they had experienced—and many also feared that no one would believe them or, worse still, that no one would care. In *The Drowned and the Saved,* Primo Levi tells of a recurrent nightmare that he and many other survivors experienced (and that he had already mentioned in his first book, *Survival in Auschwitz*), of attempting to tell their stories but finding that no one believed them, not even their own families (12). Indeed, despite the large number of testimonies that were published in the years immediately following the war, their reception was not encouraging. Levi's own *Se questo è un uomo* (*If This Is a Man* [*Survival in Auschwitz*]), first published in 1947, did not attain a wide readership until its reprinting in 1958 and did not attain the primary place it has today in the Holocaust canon until the 1960s. The historian Annette Wieviorka has shown that in France, the first large wave of testimonies was soon followed by responses of "no more!" (*Déportation et génocide*). What Wieviorka later called "the era of the witness" did not actually begin until the early 1960s, when the Eichmann trial in Jerusalem inaugurated the era of Holocaust awareness that is still with us and that has brought us countless survivor accounts, both written and oral, as well as innumerable works of fiction and film by both survivors and others born after the events of the Holocaust.

Not surprisingly, critical works about Holocaust literature did not emerge until the 1970s, by which time a considerable body of Holocaust writing, both fictional and nonfictional, was available for discussion. However, the question of aesthetics—and its relation to ethics, for the two were seen from the very start as inextricably connected in this domain—arose earlier. Adorno's pronouncement in 1949 about the "barbarity" of writing poetry after Auschwitz influenced much of the critical discourse to follow. Fifteen years later, in an article in *Commentary* that was among the first critical discussions of

Holocaust literature published in English, A. Alvarez seemed to be responding to Adorno when he defended art as a *means* to greater ethical consciousness: "from the fragile, tentative, individual discriminations of art emerge
precisely those moral values which, if understood and accepted, would make
totalitarian atrocities impossible" (65). Alvarez, relying on modernist criteria of irony and understatement, considered Elie Wiesel's *Night*—which
was already acquiring a foundational status in Holocaust literature after its
translation into English in 1961—as less than an artistic success, because it
indulged too much in "rhetoric." Alvarez much preferred the bitterly ironic
works of Tadeusz Borowski and Piotr Rawicz, both of them camp survivors
who had published acclaimed fictional works based on their own wartime
experiences.[3] One could argue that Wiesel was simply using aesthetic strategies that Alvarez did not value, for *Night* is a highly stylized work in many
ways. However one evaluates these individual works, the larger point is that
discussions of aesthetic success and its relation to ethical, even historical,
awareness (Alvarez sees great art as somehow being able to prevent further
atrocities) were present in critical reflections on Holocaust writing from the
very start.

Perhaps even more significantly, questions of aesthetics also preoccupied
many survivors who were seeking ways to write about their experiences—
even as those experiences provided a warrant for their turn to aesthetics.
Jorge Semprun, a survivor of Buchenwald and the author of several acclaimed
novels and memoirs about the Holocaust, has explained that he refrained for
many years after the war from writing anything at all. He did not want to
write a "straight" testimony, for he was convinced of the paradox that only
the artifice of literary writing, which allows for invention and for various
kinds of "poetic license" in addition to factual reporting, could convey the
truth of that experience.[4] Wiesel, who is known for a statement that is quoted
almost as often as Adorno's, "A novel about Auschwitz is not a novel, or else it
is not about Auschwitz," has nevertheless written novels in which Auschwitz
figures prominently, represented in the memory of the survivor protagonist.[5]
Still, whether provocatively defending the right to artifice like Semprun, or
adopting a more ambivalent stance like Wiesel—or like Charlotte Delbo,
who, in her highly poetic memoir *None of Us Will Return,* often reflects on
the impossibility of fully conveying the truth of the camp in language—writers who are also survivors can rely on the authority of their lived experience
to vouchsafe their "right" to aesthetic expression. Sara Horowitz has pointed
out that in debates about aesthetics and Holocaust representation, many who
acknowledge that testimonial writing can have an aesthetic dimension also
argue that the aesthetic dimension of fiction about the Holocaust renders it

unreliable and open to suspicion.[6] The authority of a survivor allays some of that suspicion.

Lawrence Langer was the first literary scholar to offer, unapologetically, a book-length study of Holocaust writing as art—what he called a literature of atrocity. In *The Holocaust and the Literary Imagination* (1975), Langer argued vigorously against theorists like Adorno (as he was understood at the time) or George Steiner, who in his 1967 book *Language and Silence* had expressed deep distrust of anything that could be construed as an aestheticizing of the horrors of the Holocaust. Langer, contesting the idea (which he attributed to Steiner) that since language is incapable of capturing those horrors, silence about them is preferable (a version of Wittgenstein's famous dictum that "about that which cannot be spoken of, one must be silent"), proposed to study precisely the "aesthetics of atrocity" (22). He took as his corpus literary works by writers who had lived through the Holocaust, either as survivors of persecution (ranging from camp survivors like Wiesel or Semprun to children who had lost their parents or their whole families, like Yakov Lind or André Schwarz-Bart) or as bystanders or even soldiers in the German army (like Heinrich Böll). These writers, Langer argued, had produced memorable literary works based on their own experiences, succeeding in transmuting a horrendous, incomprehensible reality into verbal art.

Langer did not study literary works by writers who had no personal memory of World War II and the Holocaust, for the simple reason that there were no such works to speak of when he was writing his book. In addition, a number of great books by survivors had not yet been written. For example, Semprun, whose autobiographical novel about deportation, *Le grand voyage* (1963), had been immediately translated and was included in Langer's and other studies, published a beautiful memoir about Buchenwald only much later, sixty years after the events (*L'écriture ou la vie* 1994 [*Literature or Life*]). The Hungarian Auschwitz survivor Imre Kertész's brilliant autobiographical novel *Fatelessness* (*Sorstalanság*) was published in Hungary in 1975, but was not translated into English until 1992 and did not become widely known until after Kertész had been awarded the Nobel Prize in Literature in 2002. The unavailability or international invisibility of works written in "minor" languages—including works that later become internationally canonized—affects Holocaust literature as it does any other.

After Langer's pioneering work, Sidra DeKoven Ezrahi and James Young (who studied with Ezrahi in Israel) wrote extensive studies in the 1980s that have become standard references for students of Holocaust literature.[7] We see here a phenomenon of generations that concerns critics rather than writers: neither Ezrahi, born in the United States during World War II, nor

Young, born almost a decade after the war ended, has a personal biographical connection to the Holocaust. Indeed, Young prefaces his book by noting that it arose from his realization "that none of us coming to the Holocaust afterwards can know these events outside the ways they are passed down to us" (vii). Young's work subsequently moved on to the study of Holocaust memorials in Europe and the United States, and to the complex issues of visualization and transmission they involve.

The study of Holocaust memory has now become an immense field in its own right (part of an even larger field of memory studies inaugurated in 1984 by the collective project directed by Pierre Nora, *Les lieux de mémoire*), and much of it is concerned with what Marianne Hirsch has called postmemory, which is precisely a "passed down" memory inherited by those who were born after the events and can have no personal recollection of them.[8] The issues raised by transmission culminate in problems of pedagogy, as the Holocaust becomes an institutionalized area of study in both secondary and higher education. The collective volume published in 2004 by the Modern Language Association, *Teaching the Representations of the Holocaust,* coedited by Hirsch and Irene Kacandes, is simultaneously an excellent guide for teachers, an assessment of the contemporary state of Holocaust studies, and a wide-ranging examination of current and recurrent issues of Holocaust representation in different media and genres, especially history, prose fiction, photography, and film.

Meanwhile, the question of aesthetics in Holocaust representation has continued to be posed in renewed and challenging ways. In 1982, *Probing the Limits of Representation,* the important collective volume edited by Saul Friedländer (who is a child survivor of the Holocaust and the author of the beautiful memoir *When Memory Comes,* in addition to his acclaimed work as a historian of Nazi Germany and the Holocaust) brought together historians and literary scholars to "probe the limits of representation." In 1992, the collaborative work by Shoshana Felman and Dori Laub, *Testimony,* brought together the perspectives of a practicing psychoanalyst (Laub too is a child survivor of the Holocaust) and of a deconstructionist critic to examine some of the ways in which witnessing functions in therapeutic as well as artistic settings. Rounding off the progression of influential works that happened to appear at ten-year intervals, in 2002 an exhibition organized by the Jewish Museum in New York became a *cause célèbre* for several weeks, prompting numerous and conflicting responses in the press as well as some demonstrations outside the museum. Titled "*Mirroring Evil: Nazi Imagery/Recent Art,*" the exhibition (curated by Norman L. Kleeblatt and accompanied by a catalog with the same title) presented visual works and installations by thirteen artists from the United States, Europe, and Israel, all of them born in the 1950s or later; all the works focused in controversial ways on figures of Nazis. As Sidra DeKoven Ezrahi wrote in her catalog essay (one of six essays by well-known scholars of the Holocaust), this was perhaps "the most daring exhibit ever mounted by the Jewish Museum"—not only because of the transgressive presence of this crowd of "Nazis" within the museum's walls but also because of the unusually demanding personal engagement that was required on the part of the spectator ("Acts" 17–18). Indeed, the visitor to the exhibition was constantly challenged to judge the appropriateness as well as the aesthetic success or failure of works ranging from a Lego model of a concentration camp to a pseudo-kitschy visual biography of Hitler's mistress Eva Braun. As Ezrahi points out, there were no "correct" ways to confront this work, which illustrated in particularly striking fashion the indissociability of aesthetic from moral issues in art about the Holocaust.

An important recent approach to Holocaust literature and film puts the Holocaust in relation with other traumas, whether personal or historical. *In Present Pasts* (2003), Andreas Huyssen shows how discussions and debates about Holocaust memorials have influenced the construction of other memorial sites unrelated to the Holocaust, such as the Memory Park in Buenos Aires or the projected 9/11 memorial in New York City. Janet Walker, in her 2005 book *Trauma Cinema,* argues that trauma theory can productively span both historical documentaries about the Holocaust and films about incest. Michael Rothberg, in his 2009 book *Multidirectional Memory,* examines and theorizes the ways in which postcolonial literature and the literature of decolonization intersect with Holocaust writing and film.[9] Other recent works reconnect in new ways with the reflections and debates about aesthetics that have been a constant preoccupation of Holocaust criticism. Thus Brett Kaplan states on the very first page of her 2007 book *Unwanted Beauty* that her subject is the highly fraught one of "aesthetic pleasure in complex and multivalent texts" about the Holocaust. The apparently contradictory notion that beauty in Holocaust works is both "unwanted" and beneficial to deeper understanding is one that Kaplan shares with a number of other recent theorists—such as Ernst Van Alphen, whose 1997 book *Caught by History* argued strongly for the value of innovative contemporary art about the Holocaust—and indeed with a whole line of earlier critics as we have tried to suggest.

Berel Lang, in his introduction to one of the first major collective volumes about Holocaust literature, *Writing and the Holocaust* (1988), wrote that the main premise behind that collection of essays was "that there is a significant relation between the moral implications of the Holocaust and the means of literary expression. . . . .What constraints, whether in the use of fact or in the reach of the imagination, are imposed on authors or readers by the subject of the Holocaust? How does that subject shape the perspectives from which it is viewed . . . ? Is the enormity of the Holocaust at all capable of literary representation?" (2–3). These questions are still relevant today, but our questions in this volume focus not on "whether" Holocaust representation is possible, or ethically permissible, for the former question has been settled once and for all by the huge number of works that continue to be produced about the Holocaust, and the latter question is argued all over again each time some "trespass" occurs, as exhibitions such as "Mirroring Evil" and myriads of other controversial films, literary works, and public events testify. The question, therefore, is not whether but *how: how is it done, how has it been done most effectively,* so that it can reach readers who have neither personal nor familial nor historical nor geographical connections to the event? In a sense, this is the question that literary interpreters are always asking about works of literature, whether they deal with the Holocaust or any other subject. But the stakes involved are higher when it comes to literature that deals with historical events that still matter to readers. The Holocaust is one such event, perhaps the principal such event of the twentieth century.

The Contributions of Narrative Theory

The area of literary studies that has devoted the most rigorous attention to questions about the techniques of representation, especially representation through storytelling, is narrative theory. Narrative theory begins not with the development of its well-known toolbox of analytical concepts but with the observation that storytelling is a distinctive way of making sense of our experiences of the world, particularly our experiences of time, process, and change. Narrative, whether fictional or nonfictional, whether in print, paint, or pixels, has the capacity to offer us explanations about our experiences that often elude other modes such as expository descriptions, abstract arguments, or statistical analyses. Narrative depends on both selection (any narrative implicitly says "out of all the events that happened during this period and all the people involved in those events, these are the ones that matter most") and detailed attention to what is selected. At the same time, narrative combines its focus on concrete details with an interest in their broader significance: narrative implicitly or explicitly thematizes its characters and events. Furthermore, narrative engages us on multiple levels—intellectually, emotionally, ethically, aesthetically. In addition, narrative is a highly flexible mode of expression, one that is open to all kinds of subject matter and that can bend its usual forms in order to meet the special demands of extraordinary experiences.

Narrative theory sees questions about the *what* of representation (events, characters, and their settings) as closely related to questions about the *how* (who tells the tale, whose perspective is employed, how the events are ordered, and so on). Furthermore, over the last forty years, the field has sought to be responsive to both narrative's explanatory power and its flexibility. As a result, narrative theorists have developed a very rich set of concepts for analyzing just about all elements of narrative, even as they have developed several distinct and productive approaches (structuralist, rhetorical, feminist, cognitive) to the various deployments of those elements. Thus the field has both expanded its capacity to analyze the formal dimensions of narrative and found ways to connect those analyses with narrative's other dimensions. Contemporary narrative theorists are interested, for example, not just in identifying distinct combinations of vision (who sees or perceives) and voice (who speaks) but also in analyzing the ethical, affective, and aesthetic consequences of a given narrative's deploying a particular combination in a particular context.

We are aware that any mode of representation, even one as powerful as narrative, will at times seem inadequate to our efforts to respond to the Holocaust. *In Reading the Holocaust,* Inga Clendinnen notes that all her studying and thinking about the event gave her no sense of "accumulating comprehension. . . . I could not frame the kinds of questions that would let me make the human connections—connections with both perpetrators and victims—which lie at the root of all purposeful inquiry" (3). This critical humility is one of the reasons why Clendinnen's study is a significant contribution to attempts to grapple with the apparent incomprehensibility of the Holocaust. The narrative artists whose work is discussed in this volume frequently demonstrate a similar kind of humility. These authors approach the topic of the Holocaust with trepidation, yet they also show remarkable courage and perseverance in their efforts to come to terms with something that may remain at least partly incomprehensible even after years of study. Narrative proves to be a great resource in these attempts, even, paradoxically, when it comes up against the limits of its ability to explain. Precisely because it is such a powerful mode of exploration and explanation, narrative can take those involved in its production—author, narrator, character, reader— to a point where the comprehension of experience threatens to disintegrate into fragments. At the same time, in many Holocaust narratives the author's and narrator's motivation to narrate seems to be prompted partly by such a quality of loss and absence—a blank that, because it both suspends conventional causality and draws attention to the underlying but ultimately elusive events of the Holocaust, demands to be filled in, or rather, since that is not possible, identified, addressed, and explored.

As the following essays demonstrate, authors writing about the Holocaust often subject conventional forms of narrative to unusual and even extreme transformations: they distort chronology, offer fragmented stories, leave conspicuous gaps in what would otherwise be coherent accounts, and experiment with relations between vision and voice and between representations of individual and collective consciousness. They also adapt familiar techniques such as unreliable narration to their distinctive purposes. Even as these techniques emphasize their authors' difficulty in coming to terms with the Holocaust, they simultaneously challenge—and often place a considerable interpretive burden on—their audiences. In this way, the authors' efforts to find the appropriate aesthetic forms of representation raise questions about the ethics of their relationship to their audiences. The authors inevitably address an ethics of the told (in their attention to the specific experiences of perpetrators, victims, bystanders, and others), while their techniques also direct attention to the ethics of their telling.

The traumatic events of the Holocaust are not only unusually difficult to comprehend; they are also ones in which the links among history, memory, and narrative are particularly strong and insistent. As Dominick LaCapra writes in *History and Memory after Auschwitz*, "the traumatic event has its greatest and most clearly unjustifiable effect on the victim, but in different ways it also affects everyone who comes in contact with it: perpetrator, collaborator, bystander, resister, those born later" (8–9). There is, notes LaCapra, an "effect of belatedness" (9) linked to the Holocaust, an effect observable in several of the narratives discussed in this volume, underlying and influencing the ways in which they are presented. One aspect of this belatedness is that at a point in time when the last survivors are passing away, we realize there is still too much we do not know. A related aspect is that only recently, after a period of latency, has it become possible to identify and analyze significant elements of the Holocaust, not least elements pertaining to perpetrators and bystanders, that were earlier too painful to talk about. As a way to respond to both aspects of this belatedness, many authors have turned to the resources of narrative fiction, and their work has a prominent place in this collection.

The contributors to this volume would all agree with Lang's point that "there is a significant relation between the moral implications of the Holocaust and the means of literary expression," but they work by induction in order to explore the specific relations proposed and developed in the narratives they analyze. The contributors all draw on one or more concepts from narrative theory—ranging from focalization to the fiction/nonfiction distinction and from generic plot structures such as the bildungsroman to the ethics of unreliable narration—as they pursue their particular inquiries, but these concepts enable rather than control the move from the details of representation to the larger conclusions about their ethics and aesthetics. The role of narrative theory in these essays is not to determine their conclusions but rather to provide ways of seeing and meeting the challenges implicit in the various ways that the narratives under discussion come to terms with the extraordinary events of the Holocaust.

The Shape of This Book

As noted above, this collection addresses a broad spectrum of Holocaust narratives and a correspondingly broad set of issues about the aesthetics and ethics of representation. At the same time, the essays speak with and to each other in various explicit and implicit ways. We have organized them into three distinct groups that reflect some overarching interests among the contributors, but we see the boundaries between the groups as permeable rather than rigid. The essays in the first group, "The Powers and Limits of Fiction," all focus on how writers have adapted the resources of fictional narrative in their efforts to address one or more aspects of the Holocaust. Those in the second group, "Intersections/Border Crossings," all examine how artists have found it necessary to cross traditional boundaries—between testimony and imagination, the verbal and the visual, or some other conventional divide— in their efforts to represent distinctive experiences of the Holocaust. The essays in the third group, "The Holocaust and Others," all discuss the relationship between the Holocaust and another significant historical event or another cultural context.

The opening essay, J. Hillis Miller's "Imre Kertész's *Fatelessness*: Fiction as Testimony," poses some of the key questions discussed in the volume overall: Is it possible to bear witness to the Holocaust in a work of fiction, even autobiographical fiction? If so, how? Miller's careful reading of Kertész's use of character narration for ironic and other effects answers the question in the affirmative and opens *Fatelessness* to other readers. As Miller notes in a concluding point, this autobiographical fiction may "contribute to the creation of a community of readers who may, if not know, at least not forget, Auschwitz" (49). The questions Miller raises about the efficacy of fiction as a response to the Holocaust appear in different ways in the other essays of part I. In "Challenges for the Successor Generations of German–Jewish Authors in Germany," Beatrice Sandberg considers the difficult challenges faced by the successor generations of Jewish writers in Germany. One such challenge—forcibly present in the work of Esther Dischereit—is the problem of identity and narration in postwar societies in which the perception of the past gradually changes. As the narratives discussed by Sandberg helpfully remind us, Germany does not dispose of a common memory, since the population has to live with a traumatized memory of the war in general and the Holocaust in particular.[10] Sandberg's essay highlights the fact that, although all post-Holocaust Germans can be said to have traumatized memories, the nature and consequences of the remembered trauma are different for Jews than for non-Jews. Variants on this problem are observable in many countries, including France, where, as Philippe Mesnard shows in "Recent Literature Confronting the Past: France and Beyond ," novelists born decades after the war but writing about that period reproduce specific narrative schemas that fit into the wider movement of memorialization in which the Holocaust occupies a central place.

Not surprisingly, the perpetrators of the Holocaust have offered little testimony about their participation in it, but fiction writers have combined history with acts of the imagination to represent the perpetrators' perspective. These representations often involve the interplay of reliable and unreliable narration, as Susan Rubin Suleiman and James Phelan demonstrate in their respective essays, "Performing a Perpetrator as Witness: Jonathan Littell's *Les Bienveillantes*" and "The Ethics and Aesthetics of Backward Narration in Martin Amis's *Time's Arrow*." Amis's and Littell's novels set out to capture, albeit in very different ways, the psychology and motivations of those who participated actively in the Nazi genocide. While Suleiman analyzes the layered aesthetic and ethical performances of Littell and his first-person narrator, a former SS officer who looks back on his participation in the Holocaust and World War II, Phelan examines the aesthetic and ethical consequences of Amis's decision to use "backward" narration to tell the story, from death to earliest consciousness, of his chosen protagonist, a Nazi doctor who worked at Auschwitz.

The first three essays of the second part, "Intersections/Border Crossings," shift the focus from fiction to nonfiction as they discuss examples of testimony, biography, and family memoir. In "The Face-to-Face Encounter in Holocaust Narrative," Jeremy Hawthorn analyzes testimonies by Holocaust survivors (including Charlotte Delbo and Primo Levi) and a fictionalized account by Auschwitz survivor Tadeusz Borowski, all of which include representations of dramatic one-to-one interactions between a victim and one or more perpetrators or others. Hawthorn finds a range of human behavior in these encounters, but each point on the range deepens the reader's understanding of their sometimes complex, sometimes brutally simple, ethical dimensions. In "Knowing Little, Adding Nothing: The Ethics and Aesthetics of Remembering in Espen Søbye's *Kathe, Always Lived in Norway,*" Anniken Greve discusses Søbye's biography of a young Jewish girl born and bred in Oslo, who was deported to Auschwitz at the age of fifteen and killed on arrival. Emphasizing Søbye's distance from the events he recounts, Greve argues that, paradoxically, it is fundamental to the biography's recognition of Kathe Lasnik's individuality that she remains largely unknown to the reader. Different solutions for dealing with gaps in the historical record are explored in Irene Kacandes's "'When facts are scarce': Authenticating Strategies in Writing by Children of Survivors." After discussing a number of such strategies, Kacandes concludes that memoirs of children of survivors provide valuable examples of attempts to use our imagination to advance our understanding about what the persecuted experienced and how they felt about that experience.

The last four essays of part II move beyond verbal narrative to consider various intersections between the verbal text and visual image. In the context of the concerns of this volume, a significant question about visual images is whether—and if so, to what extent and in what ways—they possess a narrative dimension. The same question can be asked about other visual objects such as memorials—does an abstract memorial like Peter Eisenman's 2005 *Memorial to the Murdered Jews of Europe* in Berlin, a photograph of which we feature on our cover, contain a narrative element? One could certainly suggest several narratives implied by the labyrinthine design of the gray stones that cover close to an acre of ground in the center of the city, and even more so by the photograph of a single human figure with a red umbrella among the stones. But the designers of the memorial also included a more explicit form of narration by supporting the stones with an underground Information Center that presents the historical narrative of the Nazi regime's racist policies from 1933 to 1945 and then focuses on individual families and life stories to convey the experience of persecution.

Photographs often possess an intrinsic narrative element, especially when they evoke historically or affectively significant sites or personages. As viewers we tend to link a photo of, say, the gate of Auschwitz, with its infamous inscription "Arbeit macht frei" ("Work liberates you"), to what happened to the many prisoners who went through that gate. Moreover, as Marianne Hirsch has shown in *Family Frames: Photography, Narrative, and Postmem-*

ory, family photographs—not least one of a child, woman, or man murdered by the Nazis—may preserve ancestral history and perpetuate memories. In her contribution to this volume, "Objects of Return," Hirsch traces the role of objects and photographs in reviving memory and analyzes the plot engendered by return journeys to lost homes as well as the promises of revelation such journeys hold out—and ultimately do not fulfill. Jakob Lothe, in "Narrative, Memory, and Visual Image: W. G. Sebald's *Luftkrieg und Literatur* and *Austerlitz*," demonstrates that the incorporation of visual images into written narratives about the Holocaust, whether fictional or nonfictional, can have wide-ranging thematic, aesthetic, and ethical consequences. Lothe considers *Austerlitz* as a strangely compelling fiction whose oblique rendering of the Holocaust insists on this particular event's historical veracity while at the same time demonstrating the crisis and unavoidable shortcomings of human memory.

Unsurprisingly, filmic narratives of the Holocaust have predominantly adopted a documentary approach. Yet, as Anette H. Storeide and Janet Walker show, the "documentary" element of these narratives is frequently shaped in the service of ethical and political ends. As Walker observes in *Trauma Cinema*, "the more closely one studies the documentary and fictional modes, the more obvious it becomes that 'pure documentary' and 'pure fiction' are heuristic categories" (24). In her essay in this volume, "Moving Testimonies: 'Unhomed Geography' and the Holocaust Documentary of Return," Walker maps the transposition and transmission of Holocaust testimonies generationally, across a geographical distance, and into the audiovisual space of the moving image. Storeide, in her essay "*Which* Narrative of Auschwitz? A Narrative Analysis of Laurence Rees's Documentary *Auschwitz: The Nazis and 'the Final Solution*,'" assesses Rees's effort to establish a widely accepted narrative of Auschwitz sixty years after the Holocaust. Focusing on the combination of documentary strategies and dramatized scenes, Storeide interprets Rees's documentary as a "docudrama" and points out both its successes and its limitations.

As the essays in the third group show, our understanding of the Holocaust is inevitably, and increasingly, colored by other significant historical events and by cultures and societies not directly involved in the crime committed by the Nazis. In "From Auschwitz to the Temple Mount: Binding and Unbinding the Israeli Narrative," Sidra DeKoven Ezrahi, taking her cue from Adorno's often-quoted statement, considers aspects of "the barbaric" by exploring forms of border crossing in the context of recent Israeli politics. She traces a move in public rhetoric from a narrative of boundaries to a narrative of sacrifice and then elaborates a model of self–other relations that is based not on rigid categories leading to violence but rather on a variety of negotiated, ultimately comic possibilities. She finds these possibilities exemplified in the Hebrew poetry of Dan Pagis, in the fiction of David Grossman, and, most pointedly, in her revisionist reading of a central text in the Hebrew Bible, the *Akeda* or binding of Isaac. Grossman's work is examined in a somewhat different perspective relating to Israeli society by Daphna Erdinast-Vulcan, in "The Melancholy Generation: David Grossman's *Book of Interior Grammar.*" Erdinast-Vulcan argues that though ostensibly not "about" the Holocaust, Grossman's 1991 novel in fact challenges the normalizing drive of a post-Holocaust society that needed to suppress its recent traumatic past and reinvent itself in order to survive.

The two last essays of the volume explore different yet related aspects of memory and memorialization. In "Fractured Relations: The Multidirectional Holocaust Memory of Caryl Phillips," Michael Rothberg shows how the contemporary novelist and travel writer Caryl Phillips uses various narrative means to bring together the histories of the Holocaust, slavery, and colonialism. Rothberg argues that Phillips's project is not to establish an equation between black and Jewish history but rather to highlight similar structural problems within those histories and in the missed encounters between them, thus producing a version of "multidirectional memory." Anne Thelle also links the Holocaust, an event that occurred at the center of Europe, to another culture. In "Hiroshima and the Holocaust: Tales of War and Defeat in Japan and Germany—A Contrastive Perspective," Thelle analyzes the ways in which Japan's narratives of the bombing of Hiroshima have contributed to a repression of other war narratives, like those of Japanese wartime aggression. She argues that Japan's embrace of the narrative of victimization has significantly influenced its self-understanding and postwar identity, and has resulted in a radical difference in the world's perceptions of Japanese and of German aggression during World War II.

We offer this diverse yet unified collection as a contribution to the ongoing current reflections on the Holocaust's implications for contemporary history and for contemporary thinking about culture and aesthetics. Geoffrey Hartman has noted that there can be "no statute of limitations" on research or interpretation involving the Holocaust: closure in this area is neither possible nor desirable, at least not now or in the foreseeable future (*Longest Shadow* 4). In the realm of artistic representation, this absence of closure allows for invention and renewal as antidotes against the clichés and triteness that threaten Holocaust art as much as any other: "even so estranging an event as the Shoah may have to be estranged again, through art," Hartman writes (53). We agree. Hartman's work—he was a well-known scholar of English Romantic poetry before he turned his attention to problems of Holocaust representation and Holocaust memory—demonstrates another important truth about many of the essays in this book: one need not be a "Holocaust specialist" in order to become passionately engaged in the problems posed by Holocaust representation.[11] And just as the Holocaust has become ever more part of a "global memory," an event whose significance goes far beyond any single group or nation, we believe that Holocaust narratives can become the ground for ever-widening reflections on the relation between ethics and cultural production.

Notes

1. The project first took shape as part of a yearlong international research group on narrative theory and analysis, led by Jakob Lothe at the Centre for Advanced Study in Oslo. Some members of the group had already worked extensively on problems relating to the Holocaust; others were just starting. As the project developed into a collective volume, we invited some of the most distinguished contemporary scholars of the Holocaust to contribute to the book; the full group met for a three-day conference in Berlin in June 2007, where drafts of all the projected essays were discussed in detail, and where the group also discussed the overall design of the volume. We are pleased to know that other scholars are also addressing the questions associated with "after testimony." A conference held in Paris in June 2009, for example, focused on how to write the history of Holocaust literature with the passage "from witnesses to inheritors" ("Des témoins aux héritiers: une histoire de l'écriture de la Shoah" conference organized by the Centre National de la Recherche Scientifique and the École des Hautes Études en Sciences Sociales, June 5–6, 2009). The proceedings will be published, edited by Luba Jurgenson and Alexandre Prstojevic.

2. Adorno first wrote the sentence in 1949 in his essay "Cultural Criticism and Society," published in 1951. The lapidary style and categorical tone of the statement no doubt contributed to its ubiquity in later critical discourse; Adorno himself reiterated and qualified his assertion several times in subsequent years. For a careful reading of these iterations, see Rothberg, *Traumatic Realism*, 34–56.

3. Borowski's collection of short stories, *This Way for the Gas, Ladies and Gentlemen*, was published in English (translated from Polish) in 1967, but the title story that Alvarez comments on had appeared in *Commentary* in July 1962; the work has been part of the Holocaust canon for many years. Rawicz's *Blood from the Sky* (*Le sang du ciel*), published in French in 1961 and in English in 1964, dropped out of sight for many years but is now the object of serious study in France.

4. See Semprun, *L'écriture ou la vie* (*Literature or Life*), which contains the fullest exposition of his views about the necessity of artifice. Semprun's first work was the autobiographical novel *Le grand voyage* (*The Long Voyage*), published in 1963.

5. See, for example, *Dawn* and *The Accident*. While the action of these novels takes place after the war, the hero (very much modeled on Wiesel himself) is haunted by his memories of the camp. The statement about novels and Auschwitz, first made in 1975, has been widely quoted (e.g., in Horowitz, *Voicing the Void*, 15), and reiterated by Wiesel

himself with some variations. In his essay collection *A Jew Today,* Wiesel goes so far as to say that "there is no such thing as Holocaust literature . . . the very term is a contradiction" (197). He implies that survivors can at least attempt to communicate their experience, but that those who have not lived through it cannot possibly imagine or "reinvent" it (198). This is of course a highly debatable assertion.

6. *Voicing the Void,* 5–7. Horowitz's introductory chapter offers a wide-ranging discussion of some of the same issues we are concerned with here.

7. Ezrahi, *By Words Alone* (1980); Young, *Writing and Rewriting the Holocaust* (1988). It is noteworthy that the first serious studies of Holocaust literature were all written in English, despite the fact that the works they discussed were most often translated from European languages. The academic study of Holocaust literature has taken considerably longer to become established in some of the countries where the most important literary works were written. In France, it is only in the last decade or so that scholars have started devoting serious attention to Holocaust literature, and there are no university departments devoted to Holocaust studies. In Germany, Holocaust studies have been predominantly historical, but research centers such as Kulturwissenschaftliches Institut Essen (http://www.kwi-nrw.de/home/kwi.html) focus on narrative memories of the war and on the Holocaust in Germany, as well as in a European comparative perspective. The Arbeitsstelle Holocaust-Literatur at Giessen University has done important work charting and defining the concept of "Holocaust Literature," and the research activities of the Simon Dubnow Institute for Jewish History and Culture at Leipzig University include studies of literary Holocaust memory (http://www.dubnow.de/index.php?id=2&L=1).

8. Hirsch, *Family Frames* and a forthcoming book of essays, *The Generation of Postmemory.* On Holocaust memory, see (among many others) Bal et al., eds., *Acts of Memory;* Hartman, *The Longest Shadow,* and Hartman, ed., *Holocaust Remembrance;* Huyssen, *Present Pasts;* Langer, *Holocaust Testimonies;* Robin, *La mémoire saturée;* Suleiman, *Crises of Memory and the Second World War;* Wieviorka, *Era of the Witness* (*L'ère du témoin*); Zelizer, *Remembering to Forget;* Levi and Rothberg, eds., *The Holocaust,* especially 189–226.

9. Both trauma studies and postcolonial studies would deserve extensive discussion insofar as they have appropriated—and been appropriated by—Holocaust studies.

10. Looming large in Holocaust studies, the issue of traumatized memory offers rich and varied illustrations of the reciprocal relationship between memory and narrative. One indication of the complexity of traumatized memory of the Holocaust is that for the individual concerned, it can be linked to and prompted by memories of all those involved in the event, including perpetrators, victims, and bystanders. See Hilberg, whose 1992 book makes systematic use of this tripartite distinction; Vetlesen, especially 1–13 and 235–57; and the studies of Holocaust memory referred to above.

11. Hartman, born in 1930 in Frankfurt, is a child survivor of the Holocaust who was sent on a children's transport to England when he was nine years old. He has explained that he chose deliberately to be "future-oriented" (*Longest Shadow,* 19) rather than dwell on his past experiences; it was not until the late 1970s, after he had been teaching English at Yale for many years, that he became involved in Holocaust studies, becoming a founder and director of Yale's Fortunoff Videoarchive of Holocaust Testimonies.

Works Cited

Alvarez, A. "The Literature of the Holocaust." *Commentary* 38 (November 1964): 65–69.

Bal, Mieke, Jonathan Crewe, and Leo Spitzer, eds. *Acts of Memory: Cultural Recall in the Present.* Hanover, NH: University Press of New England, 1999.

Borowski, Tadeusz. *This Way for the Gas, Ladies and Gentlemen.* Translated by Barbara Vedder. New York: Viking Press, 1967.

Clendinnen, Inga. *Reading the Holocaust.* Cambridge: Cambridge University Press, 2002.

Delbo, Charlotte. *None of Us Will Return.* In *Auschwitz and After,* translated by Rosette Lamont. New Haven: Yale University Press, 1995.

Ezrahi, Sidra DeKoven. "Acts of Impersonation: Barbaric Spaces as Theater." In *Mirroring Evil: Nazi Imagery/Recent Art,* edited by Norman L. Kleeblatt, 17–38. New York: The Jewish Museum; and New Brunswick: Rutgers University Press, 2001.

———. *By Words Alone: The Holocaust in Literature.* Chicago: University of Chicago Press, 1980.

Felman, Shoshana and Dori Laub. *Testimony: Crises of Witnessing in Literature, Psychoanalysis, and History.* New York and London: Routledge, 1992.

Friedländer, Saul, ed. *Probing the Limits of Representation: Nazism and the "Final Solution."* Cambridge, MA: Harvard University Press 1982.

———. *When Memory Comes.* Translated by Helen R. Lane. New York: Farrar, Straus and Giroux, 1979.

Hartman, Geoffrey. *The Longest Shadow: In the Aftermath of the Holocaust.* New York: Palgrave Macmillan, 2002 [orig. ed. Indiana University Press, 1996].

———, ed. *Holocaust Rembrance: The Shapes of Memory.* Oxford: Blackwell, 1994.

Hilberg, Raul. *Perpetrators, Victims, Bystanders: The Jewish Catastrophe, 1933–1945.* New York: Aaron Asher Books, 1992.

Hirsch, Marianne. *Family Frames: Photography, Narrative, and Postmemory.* Cambridge: Harvard University Press, 1997.

———. *The Generation of Postmemory: Visual Culture After the Holocaust.* New York: Columbia University Press, 2012.

Hirsch, Marianne and Irene Kacandes, eds. *Teaching the Representation of the Holocaust.* New York: Modern Language Association, 2004.

Horowitz, Sara R. *Voicing the Void: Muteness and Memory in Holocaust Fiction.* Albany: State University of New York Press, 1997.

Huyssen, Andreas. *Present Pasts: Urban Palimpsests and the Politics of Memory.* Stanford: Stanford University Press, 2003.

Kaplan, Brett. *Unwanted Beauty: Aesthetic Pleasure in Holocaust Representation.* Urbana: University of Illinois Press, 2007.

Kertész, Imre. *Fatelessness.* Translated by Tim Wilkinson. New York: Knopf, 2003. [First published in English as *Fateless,* translated by Christopher C. Wilson and Katharine M. Wilson. Evanston: Northwestern University Press, 1992].

LaCapra, Dominick. *History and Memory after Auschwitz.* Ithaca: Cornell University Press, 1998.

Lang, Berel, ed. *Writing and the Holocaust.* New York: Holmes and Meier, 1988.

Langer, Lawrence. *The Holocaust and the Literary Imagination.* New Haven: Yale University Press, 1975.

———. *Holocaust Testimonies: The Ruins of Memory.* New Haven: Yale University Press, 1991.

Levi, Neil and Michael Rothberg, eds. *The Holocaust: Theoretical Readings.* Edinburgh: Edinburgh University Press, 2003.

Levi, Primo. *The Drowned and the Saved.* Translated by Raymond Rosenthal. New York: Summit Books, 1988.

———. *Se questo è un uomo.* 1947; rept. Torino: Giolio Einaudi editore, 1958.

———. *Survival in Auschwitz* [*If This Is a Man*]. Translated by Stuart Woolf. New York: Collier Books, 1969.

Nora, Pierre. *Les lieux des mémoires.* 3 vols. Paris: Gallimard: 1984-1992.

Rawicz, Piotr. *Blood from the Sky.* Translated by Peter Wiles. New York: Harcourt Brace and World, 1964.

Robin, Régine. *La mémoire saturée.* Paris: Stock, 2003.

Rothberg, Michael. *Multidirectional Memory: Remembering the Holocaust in the Age of Decolonization.* Stanford: Stanford University Press, 2009.

———. *Traumatic Realism: The Demands of Holocaust Representation.* Minneapolis: University of Minnesota Press, 2000.

Semprun, Jorge. *L'écriture ou la vie.* Paris: Gallimard, 1994.

———. *Le grand voyage.* Paris: Gallimard, 1963.

Steiner, George. *Language and Silence: Essays 1958–1966.* London: Faber, 1967.

Suleiman, Susan Rubin. *Crises of Memory and the Second World War.* Cambridge, MA: Harvard University Press, 2006.

Van Alphen, Ernst. *Caught by History: Holocaust Effects in Contemporary Art, Literature, and Theory.* Stanford: Stanford University Press, 1997.

Vetlesen, Arne Johan. *Evil and Human Agency: Understanding Collective Evildoing.* Cambridge: Cambridge University Press, 2005.

Walker, Janet. *Trauma Cinema: Documenting Incest and the Holocaust.* Berkeley: University of California Press, 2005.

Wiesel, Elie. *A Jew Today.* Translated by Marion Wiesel. New York: Random House, 1978.

———. *La nuit.* Paris: Minuit, 1958.

———. *Night; Dawn; The Accident: A Trilogy.* Various translators. New York: Hill and Wang, 2004.

Wieviorka, Annette. *Déportation et génocide.* Paris: Plon, 1992.

———. *Era of the Witness.* Translated by Jared Stark. Ithaca: Cornell University Press, 2006.

Young, James. *The Texture of Memory: Holocaust Memorials and Meaning.* New Haven: Yale University Press, 1993.

———. *Writing and Rewriting the Holocaust: Narrative and the Consequences of Interpretation.* Bloomington: Indiana University Press, 1988.

Zelizer, Barbie. *Remembering to Forget: Holocaust Memory through the Camera's Eye.* Chicago: University of Chicago Press, 1998.

PART I

The Powers and Limits of Fiction

CHAPTER 1

Imre Kertész's *Fatelessness*

Fiction as Testimony

J. HILLIS MILLER

> . . . the survivors bore witness to something it is impossible to bear witness to.
>
> —Giorgio Agamben, *Remnants of Auschwitz:*
> *The Witness and the Archive*

> A novel about Auschwitz is not a novel—or else it is not about Auschwitz.
>
> —Elie Wiesel, preface to *Day*

> We read books on Auschwitz. The wish of all, in the camps, the last wish: know what has happened, do not forget, and at the same time never will you know.
>
> —Maurice Blanchot, *The Writing of the Disaster*[1]

Preliminary Statement of the Problem
How to Testify to Auschwitz in a Work of Fiction

Imre Kertész is a Hungarian Jew who was born in Budapest on November 6, 1929. At age fourteen he was deported to the death camps along with hundreds of thousands of other Hungarian Jews, most of whom died in the camps. Like the hero of his novel *Fatelessness*, Kertész probably survived by lying about his age, since all those under sixteen were immediately gassed and cremated. Those old enough and strong enough were separated out at the initial *Selektion* and sent to work camps instead. Kertész was imprisoned at Buchenwald. After the liberation of the camps Kertész returned to Budapest and became a writer. His first novel, *Sorstalanság (Fatelessness)*[2] was published in 1975, that is, twenty years after his liberation from the camps, though the novel had been completed earlier. Kertész has insisted that the novel is not autobiographical and that it is not even a novel. Nevertheless, the story it tells of a fifteen-year-old boy from Budapest who is transported to Auschwitz and survives there obviously bears some relation to Kertész's own experience. It also looks like a novel to me, whatever Kertész says. It employs sophisticated novelistic techniques, and it is apparently not just a transcription of history. *Fatelessness* was first translated into English, as *Fateless,* in 1992, and then, in a translation by Tim Wilkinson, as *Fatelessness* in 2004. I cite the latter translation in this essay. A film based on *Fatelessness,* titled *Fateless,* was made in Hungary in 2005, with a script by Kertész. Kertész has published in Hungarian many other works since then, many of which have been translated into English. His best known other work is probably *Kaddis a meg nem született gyermekért* (1990) (*Kaddish for an Unborn Child* [2004]). Kertész's work was initially not greatly successful in Hungary. He moved to Germany and now resides in Berlin, though he continues to write in Hungarian. In 2002 Kertész was awarded The Nobel Prize in Literature.

The central questions of this essay are the following: Is it possible to bear witness to the Holocaust in a work of fiction? If so, just how might that be done, by what narrative procedures? Does *Fatelessness* succeed in performing that work of testimony? What, if anything, should I do after reading *Fatelessness*? Is a critical analysis of the novel's narrative procedures an appropriate response, or would some other action be better to perform? Just what does critical or narratological analysis contribute by mediation to what might be called the performative force of *Fatelessness*? I mean by "performative force" the novel's ability to do something with words, for example, possibly to bear witness to Auschwitz.[3]

The writing of *Fatelessness,* like the writing of any novel about Auschwitz, was subject to a double obstacle, or even what might be called a double double bind or double blind alley, a complex "aporia." "Aporia" means in Greek a dead end or no thoroughfare. An aporia is an impasse in an argument in which two conclusions follow from the premises, but contradict one another, though neither can be chosen over the other. The aporia in this case perhaps blocks the project of bearing witness to Auschwitz in a novel or indeed in any other form of words, even the most factual or autobiographical. Kertész, like anybody who writes about the Holocaust, was confronted with these obstacles. The narrative form *Fatelessness* took was, this essay argues, his way of dealing with this double obstacle and making his way forward in spite of it. Here are the aporias I have in mind:

First aporia: The facts of Auschwitz are, it may be, inherently unthinkable and unspeakable, by any means of representation. One must be careful, however, in using such terms, because if they are taken in one possible way, they assimilate Auschwitz, illicitly, to a species of negative theology. They imply that just as God is unthinkable and unsayable, so is Auschwitz. Taken another possible way, saying Auschwitz is unthinkable and unsayable falls into the hands of the Nazis and into the hands of the deniers, the revisionists. The Nazis taunted their victims by telling them that what the SS was doing was so awful that no one would believe the few who might survive to bear witness. It would be easy to pass it off as Allied propaganda (Simon Wiesenthal, cited in Levi, *The Drowned* 11–12). The bare facts of Auschwitz, the *Selektion,* the deadly gas, the crematoria, the approximate number of those murdered, the starvation and forced labor, can be said in so many words. Those facts are irrefutable because they are backed up by so much documentary evidence. Nevertheless, as almost every survivor agrees, bearing witness to the actual experience of the camps presents big linguistic, and more than just linguistic, difficulties. Episodes at the end of *Fatelessness,* discussed later, dramatize these difficulties.

Jean-François Lyotard succinctly identifies a core aspect of Auschwitz that resists being said and transmitted to others: "To have 'really seen with his own eyes' a gas chamber would be the condition which gives one the authority to say that it exists and to persuade the unbeliever. Yet it is still necessary to prove that the gas chamber was used to kill at the time it was seen. The only acceptable proof that it was used to kill is that one died from it. But if one is dead, one cannot testify that it is on account of the gas chamber" (Lyotard, cited in Agamben 35). Kertész's hero comes up against this impasse when he confronts an Auschwitz denier on his return to Budapest, as I shall show. This impasse may be at least part of what Agamben means when he says that witnesses to Auschwitz must bear witness to something to which it is impossible to bear witness. That does not mean, however, that such bearing witness should not be attempted, in the teeth of its impossibility. *Fatelessness* tries to do that.

Matters are not quite so simple as Lyotard says, however. One significant class of prisoners was the *Sonderkommandos,* or "Special Squads." These were prisoners, usually Jews, who were, horrifyingly, conscripted by the SS to perform the dirty work of the gas chambers, that is, to kill and then cremate their fellow prisoners, sometimes their own relatives or friends. Though the SS made a point of periodically sending the *Sonderkommando* teams themselves to the gas chambers and replacing them with a new batch, so that no witness would remain, nevertheless a few did leave written records or did survive to testify to their inhuman experience. These survivors had seen the gas chambers at their work of extermination with their own eyes and so could bypass Lyotard's aporia.

Second aporia: Turning the Nazi genocide into a fiction of any kind, "aestheticizing" it, is inherently a deeply suspect operation, perhaps a form of putting the reader under anesthetic. On the one hand, the more successful the novel is as a novel, the further away it may be from Auschwitz. Perhaps. That is what Elie Wiesel says in my second epigraph. On the other hand, Imre Kertész may have been right when he said more than once in a recent oral communication that all testimony to Auschwitz, even the most overtly autobiographical, is "fiction."[4] He certainly did not mean that the Holocaust is a fiction in the sense meant by Holocaust deniers who say the Shoah never happened. Quite the reverse. It is crucial to be clear about this. I think Kertész meant that any narrative of the Holocaust is a selective and ordered sequence. I extrapolate on my own from what Kertész said to affirm that any narrative of a concentration camp experience by a survivor, from the most autobiographical to the most fictional transposition, is a putting together of somewhat arbitrarily chosen details to make a story out of them. This "putting together" is not inherent in the details themselves. Any narrating puts the facts in constructed form, though the facts remain facts. I would express this by saying that Auschwitz narratives, whether autobiographical or fictional, are not just an ordering of facts but an interpretation of them, a passing judgment on them—in short, a bearing witness to them.

This essay centers on the claim that the form of storytelling Kertész employs in *Fatelessness* made it possible for him to bear witness to Auschwitz more effectively than he could otherwise have done and that the novel itself dramatizes within itself the reasons for this.

Performing a "rhetorical reading" or a "narratological reading" of a novel like *Fatelessness,* with close attention to the text, to the way it operates its performative magic of testifying to Auschwitz, may just compound that possible shame of writing fiction about Auschwitz. I distinguish between the two forms of reading I have just named. A rhetorical reading, in the sense I mean it, especially attends to patterns of tropes, to the function of recurrent terms, to stylistic features such as irony. A narratological reading concerns itself with narrators, points of view, plot structure, and other matters of narrative form. My reading somewhat uneasily combines these two. They cannot in any case be sharply divided. Either form or any combination may be subject to the obstacle Maurice Blanchot identifies in *The Writing of the Disaster:* "all theories, however different they may be, constantly change places with one another, distinct each from the next only because of the writing which supports them and which thus escapes the very theories purporting to judge it" (80).

How can we in good conscience perform either sort of theory-based analysis, or any combination, with something so serious as bearing witness to Auschwitz? On the one hand, analytical commentary, with its scrupulous distinctions, such as I am performing here, is perhaps just a way to protect oneself from the affective force of *Fatelessness,* so disabling its testimonial force, anesthetizing oneself as reader. The story this novel tells is certainly hard to take. The reader resists confronting it directly. On the other hand, can a critical analysis of a novel that bears witness to Auschwitz be itself a form of testimony or at least a form of testimony's effective transmission, in defiance of Paul Celan's assertion, mentioned again below, that no one bears witness for the witness (179)?

Impediments to Bearing Witness to Auschwitz

The obstacles to testifying to Auschwitz are inscribed in the novel itself in the displaced form of difficulties Kertész's protagonist, Gyuri,[5] has in getting his experiences understood by those he encounters on his way home after being liberated and when he first arrives back in Budapest. These encounters dramatize the problems Kertész himself may have felt he faced in trying, a good many years after his experience in the camps, to write a novel that would work as a successful testimony to Auschwitz. Though these episodes come at the end of the novel, I need to discuss them now in order to establish the problem of bearing witness to Auschwitz as Kertész's protagonist experienced that problem. I hope the reader will forgive my metalepsis, putting the cart before the horse. My procedure may be especially unforgivable, and therefore in need of forgiveness, because Kertész himself follows such a strict chronological order in his own narration. The logic of my own argumentation, the story I am telling, is different, however, from that of the novel itself. Expressing cogently my reading of the novel necessitates turning at this point to the end of Gyuri's story.

My hypothesis is that the choice of writing a work of fiction rather than a memoir, and the choice of the narrative strategies Kertész employs in *Fatelessness,* were his solutions to an experience of blank incomprehension such as he ascribes to Gyuri when he comes home from Buchenwald after its liberation. I must now show how that encounter with incomprehension is dramatized by displacement to a fictional protagonist. After that, I shall then move on to consideration of the function of irony and other stylistic features in the novel and then to the way Kertész's narrative strategies are employed in the climactic episode of the novel, its *peripeteia* or turning point: Gyuri's almost becoming what was called at Auschwitz, a *Muselmann,* that is, someone near death from starvation, overwork, and abuse. That episode includes another example of the way Gyuri's cool irony serves an essential narrative function in this fictional testimony. I shall return finally to an explanation of the title and the title's relation to Kertész's choice of a strictly chronological narration as the right way to testify to the Shoah. These three sections are approaches from different perspectives to giving an account of *Fatelessness.*

At the end of the novel, Gyuri, having miraculously survived until the liberation of the camps, makes his way back home to Budapest, penniless and still wearing his prison uniform. Along the way and when he reaches his native city, he has four confrontations that bring home to him the difficulties of communicating what he has experienced, five if you count the meeting with his mother he is starting toward as the novel ends and which he anticipates as though it were fated to happen in a certain way. The reader is not told how that reunion comes off, though Gyuri says, "My mother was waiting, and would no doubt greatly rejoice over me" (262).

The first encounter takes place on the way home, in an unnamed city where Gyuri hears "a lot of Hungarian being spoken as well as Czech" (240). As Gyuri waits for the next train, a stranger in the street approaches him and asks whether he "personally, however, did not ascertain this [the existence of the gas chambers] with your own eyes." When he answers, truthfully, "no," since, as he says, he would be dead if he had, the stranger says, "I see," and walks away "unless I was very much mistaken, satisfied in some manner" (242). "Unless I was very much mistaken" is one of those either/or reservations characteristic of Gyuri's narration. The significance of these is discussed below. The implication is that the man who interrogates Gyuri is an Auschwitz denier whose refusal to believe will now be confirmed. That implication is less explicit in the film version, since the sentence I have just quoted about his interlocutor's satisfaction is, naturally, missing, as it is part of the narrator's report of Gyuri's thoughts. You cannot film thoughts or internal monologue, except by the extremely awkward and anti-cinematic device of a disembodied voiceover. In the film we have only the denier's facial expression to go by.

The second confrontation is with Bandi Citrom's sister and mother in their apartment on Forget-me-not Road. Bandi was Gyuri's only true friend in the camps, though he abandons Gyuri when the latter is on the way to becoming a *Muselmann.* Bandi had spoken with nostalgia about what a wonderful place Forget-me-not Road is, though Gyuri finds it shabby enough when, even before going home, he goes to Bandi Citrom's house to see if Bandi has survived and made it home. The painful confrontation with Bandi's sister and mother reveals that Bandi has not returned and that almost certainly he has died in the camp. Gyuri makes no attempt to tell Bandi's sister and mother what the camps were like.

The third confrontation is a most unsatisfactory conversation with a journalist. Gyuri meets this reporter on a tramcar on his way home from Bandi Citrom's house. This man tries, unsuccessfully, to get Gyuri to acquiesce to a whole set of clichés about the camps, for example, "Can we imagine a concentration camp as anything but a hell?" (248). The journalist is greatly annoyed when Gyuri says he knows nothing about hell, but the difference, he guesses, is that it is impossible to be bored in hell, whereas he was sometimes bored, even in Auschwitz. He tells the journalist that his primary feeling, now that he is back home in Budapest, is "hatred." Hatred of whom? "Everyone." The journalist asks, "Did you have to endure many horrors?" To which Gyuri replies, "it all depended what he considered to be a horror" (247). Finally, the journalist says, "No, it's impossible to imagine it" (250), with which the narrating Gyuri remembers being in silent agreement. He soon ends the conversation, though the journalist wants to help him write and publish his memories of the camps.

The implication is that journalistic clichés about the camps are not a successful bearing witness, while the narrative strategies Kertész uses in *Fatelessness* may possibly succeed, for example, in the passage the reader is at that moment reading. Writing a novel about Auschwitz rather than a factual account within the constraints of journalistic conventions is here implicitly defended as the right way to bear witness, in blank contradiction to what Wiesel was later to assert, as cited in the second of my epigraphs for this essay.

The fourth encounter is an equally unsatisfactory meeting with two members of what is left of Gyuri's original community. His father has died at Mauthausen, and his stepmother has remarried. An impassioned speech from Gyuri only angers his Uncle Fleischmann and his Uncle Steiner. (They are apparently not blood relatives, but are called "uncles" because they are intimate friends and neighbors of his family.) Uncle Fleischmann asks him about his plans for the future. Gyuri answers that he has not given it much thought, whereupon Uncle Steiner tells him that he "must put the horrors behind you. . . . in order . . . to be able to live" (256). "Live freely," adds Uncle Fleischmann. Gyuri reacts negatively to these suggestions. For one thing, he says, he would be unable to forget unless he were to suffer some injury or disease that would affect his mind. Moreover, he does not want to forget.

This painful confrontation is the climax of Gyuri's discovery that though he feels an obligation to testify to his experiences, a direct account of them seems to convey nothing. It confirms, rather, the second half of Blanchot's contradictory injunction in my third epigraph: "know what has happened, do not forget, and at the same time never will you know." Gyuri's explanatory speech to his uncles just makes them angry. His visit to them is broken off in the recognition that they have understood nothing and did not want to understand anything: "But I could see they did not wish to understand anything, and so, picking up my kit bag and cap, I departed in the midst of a few disjointed words and motions, one more unfinished gesture and incomplete utterance from each" (261). This is the hyperbolic climax of Gyuri's experience of the difficulty of testifying to Auschwitz.

Ironic Narration as Witnessing

The narrative strategies of *Fatelessness* repay with interest minute rhetorical and narratological analysis. Just what is that interest? It comes back as a kind of supplementary repayment, a plus value, for close attention to the words on the page. That plus value may include a deeper understanding of what is at stake in trying to bear witness to Auschwitz in a fictional work.

As I said above, a powerful film of *Fatelessness,* with a script by Kertész, called *Fateless,* is available on DVD. Space limitations here forbid the extended analysis this admirable film deserves. Moving and disturbing as the cinematic version is, however, partly through putting before the viewer's eyes the atrocities and sufferings the reader of the novel must imagine on the basis of the words on the page, the film has great difficulty finding graphic equivalents for the verbal complexities of Gyuri's narration in the novel proper. These are essential to the novel's meaning. As is always the case, the juxtaposition of novel and film has great value as a means of identifying distinctive features in each medium by way of differences between one and the other.

The film makes intermittent and quite effective use of the protagonist's speech in voice-over. That disembodied voice repeats some important things that are said by the first-person narrating-I or by the experiencing-I in the novel. Nevertheless, only part of this level of discourse is given. The pervasive irony of the novel is more or less missing, naturally, from the film. I say this is natural because irony is essentially a linguistic effect, not a visual one, though of course something somewhat like irony can arise from the juxtaposition of images. What is given in the novel as Gyuri's sharp vision of things, a vision that makes him a kind of camera eye, becomes in the film the actual "camera eye" vision, often a vision of Gyuri's silent and more or less impassive face, seen, naturally, from the outside, something the novel nowhere presents. The explicit theme of the *Muselmann,* so important in the novel and in my reading of it later in this essay, is absent, oddly, from the film, though the film powerfully presents Gyuri's near-death in a way that closely follows the novel.

I have seen the Hungarian original of the novel. It was available online in 2007, though the site is now unavailable. Happily, I downloaded it in time. The Hungarian original has been helpful to my reading, even though I do not know Hungarian. My ignorance means that it is an act of chutzpah to pretend to be able to talk intelligently about this novel. A painful inability by Gyuri to understand what is being said around him in the camps, since so many different languages are spoken there, is one of the ways the survival of community is endangered in *Fatelessness.* To compare great things with small, my inability to read *Fatelessness* in the original Hungarian may possibly give me a vague idea of what it must have been like for Kertész (or Gyuri) to be surrounded by a Babel of languages he did not understand. The difference, and it is a huge difference, is that a failure to understand in Auschwitz was likely to be a matter of life or death, whereas nothing more is at stake in my linguistic inability than my scholarly competence to write about *Fatelessness* at all.

Kertész's solutions to the aporias I have identified included his choice of a first-person mode of narration and his use of irony as the basic form of discourse in that narration. The narratological presupposition of *Fatelessness* is to tell in the first person the story of a fifteen-year-old Hungarian Jewish boy's experiences of arrest in Budapest in 1944, near the end of World War II; his deportation to Auschwitz along with hundreds of thousands of other Hungarian Jews, most of whom died; and then his survival in the labor camps at Buchenwald and Zeitz, that is, the Wille subcamp of Buchenwald, nearby to the town of Zeitz. Zeitz was a labor camp for work in the synthetic oil factory in that town. The story that Kertész's hero tells matches closely many details about life in the camps given, for example, in the overtly autobiographical accounts by Primo Levi in *Survival in Auschwitz* and by Elie Wiesel in *Night.*

Gyuri is presented as a "cool," detached, ironic, more or less affectless teenager, who nevertheless (or perhaps as a result) has an extremely sharp eye for details of what he witnesses, for example, what other people look like. He also has an extraordinary ability to put in retrospect what he has seen into words, a sharp intelligence devoted to figuring things out for himself, and a quiet "stubbornness" (138) that contributes to his extremely unlikely, and in

many ways fortuitous, survival. "Stubbornness" is an important word in the
novel, as I shall show.

Gyuri's experiences are narrated in strict chronological order. No confusing time shifts for Kertész. The novel narrates one vivid present after another,
in "fateless" sequence. I shall identify later the significance of this narratological choice. The past is rarely explicitly remembered in the present by the
protagonist whose story the narrator is telling, the experiencing-I, and the
future is almost completely unpredictable to him.

I call the hero *then* "the protagonist," or "the experiencing-I," and the
hero *now* narrating his past experiences "the narrator," or "the narrating-I,"
in this first-person novel. Protagonist and narrator are two aspects of the
same person, separated by the gulf between the unidentified present of the
narration and the past of what is narrated. They are also separated by the fact
that the narrator knows that Gyuri survived to return to Budapest, while the
protagonist lived from moment to moment in danger of imminent death.
The narrator is granted, apparently, the ability to remember everything, as is
a common convention of first-person novels. These differences between the
narrating-I and the experiencing-I require distinguishing, as with most first-
person novels, the language of the protagonist *then* from the language of the
narrator *now*. Sometimes, however, that may be difficult or even impossible
to do. This is parallel to the ambiguities of telling whose language is being
used in free indirect discourse: that of the protagonist or that of the narrator who speaks in the third-person past tense on the protagonist's behalf.
Periodic use of the present tense in *Fatelessness* (as in the opening sentence:
"I didn't go to school today" [3]) plays an important role in reinforcing the
experiencing-I's absorption in the present moment when the events now
narrated in retrospect actually took place.

Gyuri is granted by Kertész an extremely active mind. That activity is
devoted to interpreting what he sees, hears, and feels, even when starvation
and infections bring him to the brink of death, almost to the state of the
Muselmänner in the camps. The basic narrative assumption of *Fatelessness*
is that Gyuri has no understanding of the details of what he sees and hears
until he figures them out firsthand for himself. He is fooled into thinking
he is leaving Hungary for work, not to be starved, beaten, and most probably gassed and cremated. Many other deportees were similarly fooled. The
reader knows, the retrospectively narrating Gyuri knows, and Kertész knows,
but the experiencing Gyuri does not at first know, that the strange smell at
Auschwitz is the burning bodies of the gassed in the crematoria. He thinks at
first that those chimneys with billowing black smoke are tanneries. He does
not understand at first that those sent to the right-hand group in the initial

Selektion at Auschwitz will be immediately gassed and cremated, including boys in the group arrested with him who are too fat or who have poor eyesight or weak muscles. However, Gyuri figures all this out by the end of his first day in Auschwitz. His understanding is based on the evidence of his senses and on what he hears other prisoners say. Part of the force of the novel depends on presenting these unspeakable atrocities as an understanding of them gradually replaces the ignorance and innocence of an intelligent and observant teenager. The reader knows these atrocities already in a general way, but seeing them in this new form, through the eyes of someone who was from moment to moment in mortal danger and who only gradually realized this, brings these "horrors" home to the reader, proves them on his or her pulses, in a particularly unforgettable way.

Fatelessness is told throughout in a mode of ironic understatement that matches Gyuri's detached observation. Irony is an aspect of Gyuri's teenage "coolness" (Eszter). The irony is related to another salient stylistic feature of *Fatelessness*. This feature is a cognitive or discursive counterpart to the distressing performative uncertainty of that trope that is not a trope: irony. Irony is a way of doing something with words, but that something is to put the reader in a suspended condition of uncertainty. If irony says two incompatible things at once, cutting both ways, Gyuri's explicit judgments, though they are based on his stubborn innate commitment to seeing clearly and to understanding correctly, also are an enunciation in cognitive terms of ironic suspension or parabasis. Gyuri registers his cognitive uncertainty as part of his truth-telling testimony.

Gyuri is systematically unwilling or unable to make any straightforward, unequivocal judgment about anything he sees. He is, moreover, too honest to pretend otherwise. Even though he says more than once "no two ways about it" (154), as if to put an end to his "either/or," his judgments are characteristically accompanied by an often extraordinary series of qualifications, provisos, revisions, contradictions, and assertions of uncertainty. For Gyuri, there are "two ways about" more or less anything he sees. Here is one example among many: "I noticed that the emotion gratified them, gave them some sort of pleasure, the way I saw it. Indeed—and I could have been mistaken of course, though I don't think so . . ." (213). This qualified assertion is movingly ironic because it comes as part of an episode in which one of the doctors who are treating Gyuri in the camp hospital gets him to tell the story of how he was arrested and sent to Auschwitz. The doctor then passes that story on to other doctors and patients. The emotion in question is pity: "In the end, I found that people on all sides were looking at me, heads shaking, and with a most singular emotion on their faces, which was a little embarrassing because, as best I could tell, they were feeling sorry for me. I felt a strong urge to tell them there was no need for that after all, at least not right at that moment, but I ended up saying nothing, something held me back, somehow I couldn't find it in my heart to do so, because . . ." (213). Then follows the passage already cited: "I noticed the emotion gratified them," and so on.

Gyuri doesn't say anything not because he thinks pity for him is justified, but for the strange and ironically dissonant reason that he cannot bring himself, in this concentration camp hospital, to deprive the doctors, orderlies, and patients of the pleasure of feeling sorry for him. He is not even sure that he is right about the emotion he thinks they are feeling, but he says they were feeling sorry for him "as best I could tell." In saying this, Gyuri is being true to one important law of this first-person narration. This law decrees that no direct access is possible to the minds of other people, such as an omniscient or telepathic third-person narrator might have.

The sequence is a good example of the ironic disjunction between the language of the experiencing-I and the language of the narrating-I. It also exemplifies the difficulties of distinguishing with certainty between those two languages, particularly in a narrative that is ironic through and through. The statement "I noticed that the emotion gratified them, gave them some kind of pleasure, the way I saw it" must be, the reader thinks—if she thinks about it at all—the narrating-I reporting in the past tense what the experiencing-I noticed and saw. The statement "I could have been mistaken of course, though I don't think so," the reader assumes, must be the narrating-I's present judgment on the accuracy of the experiencing-I's judgment. But is this absolutely certain, plausible as it seems? "I noticed that the emotion gratified them," and the rest, could be either the narrating-I putting words in the experiencing-I's mouth, or it could be a transposition into the past tense of Gyuri in the past thinking to himself in the present tense: "The way I see it, the emotion gratifies them, gives them some sort of pleasure. I could be mistaken of course, though I don't think so." After all, the narrating-I has earlier in the sentence told in the past tense about the pity that the experiencing-I discerned in those who had just heard his story, "as best I could tell." That seems clearly to be a reporting of the experiencing-I's evaluation. Still, "I don't think so" seems indubitably a statement of the narrating-I's judgment in the present of what the experiencing-I saw and judged in the past. This linguistic mixture corresponds to the psychological or phenomenological mixture within any person's consciousness at a given moment of features that belong to the past and features that belong to her or his present memory of the past. It is hard to tell, in a given sample of first-person narration, whether the words on the page reflect the experiencing-I's transformation of perhaps initially wordless thoughts, feelings, and observations (if there are such things) into words that accompanied them, in the endless dialogues that we carry on with ourselves all the time, or whether the narrating-I has given language to what was originally, *then,* a wordless event of experiencing.

Gyuri's ironic understatement functions powerfully to generate pity in me too. What has happened to Gyuri is truly atrocious. The Aristotelian tragic emotions of pity and fear are appropriate responses—pity for Gyuri and fear that a similar fate might in some unforeseen way happen to me. Something not entirely dissimilar has happened even today for those who have been unjustly imprisoned in Guantánamo Bay or who have been subjected to "extraordinary rendition" and then torture in a foreign jail. Kertész has given a name by displacement to the emotion the reader should feel when reading *Fatelessness,* though he has also warned the reader against taking too much pleasure in that feeling of pity.

James Phelan, in *Living to Tell about It,* identifies three main functions of narrators: reporting, interpreting, and evaluating. Gyuri as the narrating-I certainly performs all those functions, but it is not always easy to be sure just which Gyuri is doing the performing of these linguistic acts, or whose language the reader is encountering. Kertész's narrating-I in this novel appears to be that happy thing, a reliable narrator. He is restricted, however, to reporting, interpreting, and evaluating Gyuri's experiences in the camps from Gyuri's perspective. This exemplifies another of Phelan's narratological terms: "restricted narration." Kertész's narrator can only show the way events appeared to other characters by means of what they say. Direct access to the minds of others is forbidden. This means that both Gyuris may conceivably be mistaken. The narrating-I may conceivably have forgotten something important. The reader has no way to know for sure since no other perspective is given. We do not have access to any outside confirmation of the testimony the narrating Gyuri proffers.

There is no way out of this uncertainty within a first-person narration. Testimony is a performative enunciation, not a constative one. Any testimony is, like that of a witness in a court case, implicitly prefaced by a performative oath: "I swear this is what I saw with my own eyes and heard with my own ears." The one who hears the testimony, a jury member, for example, must believe, without being able to prove, that the witness thinks he or she is telling the truth. Even if what the witness says is demonstrably wrong, that does not mean she does not think she is right. The possibility of forgetting what the camps are like, even by a survivor, is named in the last sentence of the novel, in a moving conclusion, to which I shall return.

For Gyuri, in any case, I mean that for both the experiencing-I and the narrating-I, in their often inextricable entanglement or superimposition, there often are "two ways about" anything he experiences. A frequent locution is something like "from another angle, though," or "from yet another angle, though" (135, 250). The ironic suspension of certain knowledge characteristic of Gyuri's narration is expressed in these locutions.

The *Muselmann* and His Witnessing Survivor

I want now to identify an additional important feature of *Fatelessness* as a fictional bearing witness to Auschwitz. Everything I have written so far has been preparation, staging, *mise-en-scène,* for this section of my argument. The denouement of Gyuri's story, its resolution or untying, is his return home, his four encounters with uncomprehending people who have not been in the camps, his development of his concept of "fatelessness," and his turning away in silence from his "uncles," when they do not understand, to make his way toward his mother. The *peripeteia,* or turning point, of *Fatelessness* is the moment, earlier in the narrative, when Gyuri returns to life, so to speak, after almost becoming a *Muselmann.* I say "almost" because once one becomes veritably a *Muselmann,* as witnesses testify, return is almost impossible and rarely occurs. Gyuri retains his lucid vigilance even in this extremity, when he is nearest to death, as, we are told, the true *Muselmänner* did not. This stubborn, unquenchable lucidity and Gyuri's return from the *Muselmann* condition are two of the quasi-miraculous features of *Fatelessness,* along with all the other "miracles" that allow him to become a survivor, against all odds.

Just what is a *Muselmann*? It is a name given by prisoners in the camps to those other prisoners who, through starvation, overwork, beatings, and repeated abuse, both physical and verbal, by the SS guards, became reduced to walking corpses, zombies, "mummy-men," dead–alive nonhuman persons who had lost the will to live. Such prisoners may have been called *Muselmänner* because they swayed their upper bodies rhythmically back and forth as they stood in place, or stumbled forward, or crouched on the ground, like Muslims at prayer time. Those who came back from this living death, however, claim that they made this movement to avoid getting pneumonia. Almost all of the *Muselmänner* were gassed or simply died of starvation or abuse, but a few survived. Giorgio Agamben, at the end of *Remnants of Auschwitz* (166–71), cites some of the moving testimony of those who can say, "I was a *Muselmann.*" Filiksa Piekarska, for example, writes, "I personally was a *Muselmann* for a short while. . . . I completely collapsed as far as my psychological life was concerned. The collapse took the following form: I was overcome by a general apathy; nothing interested me; I no longer reacted either to external or internal stimuli; I stopped washing, even when there was water; I no longer even felt hungry" (cited in Agamben 166). The other survivors of the camps testify that those who were not *Muselmänner* left the *Muselmänner* strictly alone, as if nothing more could be done to help them. They were outside the human community.

Agamben argues, in his admirable chapter "The *Muselmann*," in *Remnants of Auschwitz* (41–86), that perhaps even worse than the millions of murders in the gas chambers was the reduction of so many living human beings, before they were actually killed, to the dead–alive, human–inhuman state of the *Muselmänner*: "The *Muselmann* is not only or not so much a limit between life and death; rather, he marks the threshold between the human and the inhuman. . . . There is thus a point at which human beings, while apparently remaining human beings, cease to be human" (55).

The *Muselmann* chapter of Agamben's *Remnants of Auschwitz* is centrally devoted to developing what he calls "Levi's paradox." It is a version of the paradox I cited from Lyotard at the beginning of this essay. On the one hand, Levi asserts categorically that "We survivors are not only an exiguous but also an anomalous minority: we are those who by their prevarications or abilities or good luck did not touch bottom. Those who did so, those who saw the Gorgon, have not returned to tell about it or have returned mute, but they are the 'Muslims,' the submerged, the complete witnesses, the ones whose deposition would have a general significance. They are the rule, we are the exception" (*The Drowned* 83–84).

"No one," as Paul Celan says, "bears witness for the witness" (179). No one but the *Muselmänner* can testify to what it was like to be a *Muselmann*. On the other hand, the *Muselmänner* could not, cannot, speak for themselves. Only those who did not fully become *Muselmänner* and survived can bear witness by proxy for these exclusively privileged witnesses. But the *Muselmänner* had nothing to say for themselves any more than did those who were gassed and cremated. It is impossible to bear witness for them. That is what Agamben means by saying that "the survivors bore witness to something it is impossible to bear witness to" (13). Here is Levi's formulation of this in *The Drowned and the Saved*:

We who were favored by fate tried, with more or less wisdom, to recount not only our own fate but also that of the others, indeed of the drowned [Levi's word here for the *Muselmänner*]; but this was a discourse "on behalf of third parties," the story of things seen at close hand, not experienced personally. The destruction brought to an end, the job completed, was not told by anyone, just as no one ever returned to describe his own death. Even if they had paper and pen, the drowned would not have testified because their death had begun before that of their body. Weeks and months before being snuffed out, they had already lost the ability to observe, to remember, to compare and express themselves. We speak in their stead, by proxy. (83–84)

This speaking by proxy, however, is impossible. It is an absurd project. As Agamben says, "And yet to speak here of a proxy makes no sense; the drowned have nothing to say, nor do they have instructions or memories to be transmitted. They have no 'story' . . . , no 'face,' and even less do they have 'thought.' . . . Whoever assumes the charge of bearing witness in their name knows that he or she must bear witness in the name of the impossibility of bearing witness" (34). Agamben's book ends with the claim that the survivors who can say "I was a *Muselmann*" do not refute Levi's paradox but utter its most extreme and verifying formulation: "I, who speak, was a *Muselmann,* that is, the one who cannot in any sense speak" (165). As Agamben asserts, Levi's paradox "implies two contradictory propositions: 1) 'the *Muselmann* is the non-human, the one who could never bear witness,' and 2) 'the one who cannot bear witness is the true witness, the absolute witness'" (150).

The hero of *Fatelessness* suspends, or, rather, expresses in a unique way, Levi's paradox by combining in one person both the narrator, the narrating-I, and the protagonist, the experiencing-I, both the "complete witness," the *Muselmann,* and the proxy who bears witness for what it is impossible to bear witness to. Kertész's evasion of Levi's paradox is perhaps one that is only possible, for him at least, by way of a particular exploitation of the conventions of fictional representation. Kertész's genius, I claim, was to understand that and to give *Fatelessness* the form of a first-person novel. Like all first-person novels, the narrative language of *Fatelessness* combines two persons, the Gyuri who had the experience of the camps and the narrating Gyuri who has survived that experience to tell the tale. It is as though Kurtz and Marlow, in Conrad's *Heart of Darkness,* were combined in one person. Or rather, the experiencing Gyuri is already doubled into the almost *Muselmann* and the lucid vigilance that is still aware of what is happening to him and that can therefore survive into a future remembering. That doubling is then doubled again by the narrating-I in the present looking back and reporting on what the experiencing Gyuri experienced. What distinguishes Gyuri, as I have already emphasized, is his extremely sharp eyes, ears, nose, and touch, his observation of sights, sounds, and tactile sensations, along with his exceptional ability to turn all these into succinct, vivid language that carries them over to the reader.

Essential to the meaning of *Fatelessness* is that Gyuri, in defiance of the standard descriptions of the *Muselmänner* and even against physiological probability, retains his remarkable lucidity even when he almost becomes a *Muselmann.* He is able to tell the reader in retrospect just what it felt like to be almost a *Muselmann.* That wakeful vigilance is mirrored, at least for sight and sound, and without the ironic narrator's commentary, by the camera eye and the recording microphone in the film version of *Fatelessness.*

The *Muselmänner* first appear in *Fatelessness* soon after Gyuri arrives at Zeitz. His description of them is as vivid and specific as any other testimonies to their existence in the camps that we have. Describing certain of the prisoners from Riga, Gyuri shifts from the present tense, a kind of eternal present maintained in existence by testimony, to the past tense, in the midst of a sentence, and then back to the present tense, at least in the translation. He also uses his characteristic ironic understatement, for example, "a little disconcerting," as well as his gift for startling but apt metaphor:

> Among them one can see those peculiar beings who at first were a little disconcerting. Viewed from a certain distance, they are senilely doddering old codgers, and with their heads retracted into their necks, their noses sticking out from their faces, the filthy prison duds that they wear hanging loosely from their shoulders, even on the hottest summer's day they put one in mind of winter crows with a perpetual chill. As if with each and every single stiff, halting step they take one were to ask: is such an effort really worth the trouble? (138)

Gyuri's new Hungarian friend, Bandi Citrom, warns him away from the *Muselmänner.* "You lose any will to live just looking at them," he says (138). In the next chapter, chapter 7, many pages later, Gyuri recounts his own transformation almost into a *Muselmann* and his quasi-miraculous recovery from that state. Note that I say "almost." If he had gone all the way, he would not have returned to tell his tale. Gradually reduced to lassitude, weakness, and semiconsciousness, he stops washing or in other ways taking care of himself. He gets, in short, almost in the state of those *Muselmänner* he had looked at so curiously when he first entered the work camp:

> I can report that, after so much striving, so many futile attempts and efforts, in time I too found peace, tranquility, and relief. For instance, cer-

tain things to which I had attributed some vast, practically inconceivable
significance, I can tell you, lost all importance in my eyes. Thus, if I grew
tired while standing at *Appell,* for example, without so much as a look at
whether it was muddy or there was a puddle, I would simply take a seat,
plop down, and stay down, until my neighbors forcibly pulled me up. Cold,
damp, wind, or rain were no longer able to bother me; they did not get
through to me, I did not even sense them. Even my hunger passed; I continued to carry to my mouth anything edible I was able to lay my hands on,
but more out of absentmindedness, mechanically, out of habit, so to say. As
for work, I no longer even strove to give the appearance of it. If people did
not like that, at most they would beat me, and even then they could not
truly do much harm, since for me it just won some time: at the first blow
I would promptly stretch out on the ground and would feel nothing after
that, since I would meanwhile drop off to sleep. (171–72)

Bandi Citrom tells Gyuri he is "letting himself go" and forcibly washes
him. Bandi can tell from Gyuri's face, however, when he asks him, "did I
maybe not want to get home," that Gyuri is becoming, or has already become,
a *Muselmann.* True to the "opinion he had once expressed about Muslims"
(173) and true to what other survivors say about the way the *Muselmänner*
were ignored, given up for lost, Bandi Citrom abandons Gyuri henceforth.
After Citrom turns him over to the infirmary, they never see one another
again. The rest of the chapter describes with extreme precision Gyuri's experiences in various infirmaries and hospitals inside Zeitz and eventually back
again in Buchenwald.

A good example of the superimposition of the two experiencing Gyuris
is a passage in which he describes himself lying outdoors in the rain after
his return to Buchenwald, waiting to be taken to the hospital. On the one
hand, he is practically in a *Muselmann* state: "it seemed I must have lain
there in that way for some time, and I was getting on just fine, peacefully,
placidly, incuriously, patiently, where they had set me down" (186). On the
other hand, Gyuri, even in that extremity, has a clear and precise vision of
what he can see above him: "the low, gray, impenetrable sky, for instance, or
to be more precise the leaden, sluggishly moving wintry cloud-cover, which
concealed it from view" (186, my italics). This sky is shown in the film version as a shot of what Gyuri sees as he lies peacefully on the cold, wet ground.
The passage in the novel goes on to name, in a style that shifts from realistic
description toward allegorical picture, the way the leaden sky is intermit-
tently "parted by an unexpected rent, with a more brilliant gap arising in it
here and there for a fleeting moment, and that was like a sudden intimation

of a depth out of which a ray was seemingly being cast on me from above" (186). That ray seems to Gyuri like "a rapid, searching gaze, an eye of inde- terminate but unquestionably pale hue—similar to that of the doctor before whom I had once passed, back in Auschwitz" (186). The sky's metaphoric gaze reminds Gyuri of the searching gaze of the doctor in the *Selektion* at Auschwitz. That doctor probably knew that Gyuri was lying when he said he was sixteen, but he saved him from immediate gassing nevertheless.

Sure enough, this moment is followed a couple of pages later by Gyuri's arrival in a handcart with other dead–alive *Muselmänner* inside Buchenwald. He gets a whiff of the familiar turnip soup of the camp, weeps a few tears from his dried-out eyes, and, in a moment that is especially emotional for the reader too, recovers, senselessly, his will to live. This is without doubt the turning point of the novel. Gyuri describes it with characteristic irony: "Despite all deliberation, sense, insight, and sober reason, I could not fail to recognize within myself the furtive and yet—ashamed as it might be, so to say, of its irrationality—increasingly insistent voice of some muffled craving of sorts: I would like to live a little bit longer in this beautiful concentration camp" (189).

In the topsy-turvy world of those who have been reduced to the condi- tion of *Muselmänner*, the natural will to live is unnatural. What would be most natural, sensible, and reasonable would be the will to die. Two pages earlier, as he and other prisoners lay there in the rain, a camp guard had quiz- zically asked one of Gyuri's fellow prisoners, the man whose refrain is still, in his extremity, "I p . . . pro . . . protest," "*Was? Du willst noch leben?*" ("What? You still want to live?") (187). The return of Gyuri's will to live is the novel's moment of reversal. It marks the instant of Gyuri's exit from an almost- *Muselmann* state that has always been shared with another Gyuri, the one who, even in his extremity, can see his condition and his surroundings with sober, ironic clarity, can look up in the rain toward the gaze of the distant judging sky, and later on, as the narrating I, can report in precise language what he so vividly remembers.

Gyuri is able to solve Levi's paradox or at least to live his life in an acute demonstration that it is impossible to solve. During all of chapter 7, Gyuri is both almost the complete witness and the proxy witness who testifies on that witness's behalf. This is so even though it remains impossible to bear witness to the experience of either being gassed or having become one of the "drowned," to have seen the lethal Gorgon's face that turns the viewer to stone (to echo Levi's figures in *The Drowned and the Saved*), to have crossed the border into the state from which there is no return, the state of the *Muselmänner*.

The genius of *Fatelessness* is the way in which Kertész has been able to combine in one person the *Muselmann* and his proxy witness in a novel that bears witness to something to which it is impossible to bear witness. That "something" has as one of its components "the conflagration of community." Bearing witness depends on the survival of community along with the legal and conventional forms of obligation and togetherness, or *Mitsein,* that community entails. No community, no bearing witness. The Nazis deliberately destroyed, as best they could, Jewish communities both in the ghettos and then in the extermination camps. Nevertheless, *Fatelessness* and other testimonies report the continuation even in the camps of, for example, clandestine groups of Orthodox Jews who held secret services.

Gyuri experiences, however, the paradox of being treated as an outsider, as a Gentile, by Jewish groups in the camps, for example, because he does not know Yiddish: "*Di bisht nisht kai yid, d'bisht a shaygets*" ("You're not a Jew, you're a Gentile kid") (139–40). The diversity of languages in the camps made difficult the establishment of even fragile communities among the prisoners, many of whom had to betray friends for a scrap of bread if they were to survive a little longer. When Gyuri returns to Budapest, he finds that the community of family and neighbors he had left behind no longer exists.

Fatelessness itself, however, it might be argued, creates the community of its readers, those who across several languages and in different national locations nevertheless come together in their shared experience of this novel's testimony to Auschwitz. Unless we forget. I shall return at the end of this essay to my sense of this community's limitations. It is no substitute for what we have traditionally meant by a community, that is, people who live together in the same place and know one another by name.

The Meaning of the Title
The Necessity of a Strictly Chronological Narrative

Gyuri at the end of his unsatisfactory encounter with his "uncles" develops what might be called a striking emblem for the temporal series of events that make up a human life. Gyuri's impassioned speech to his uncles about fate just makes them violently angry when they understand that he is accusing them of being responsible in some measure for what has happened, rather than agreeing that they have been passive and innocent victims. Gyuri transposes that to an affirmation of his own responsibility for his fate. Since this speech and the coda that follows it are the dénouement of the novel, it must be read with care, micrologically, with close attention to detail. The figure of a step-by-step movement through time, with a new decision being required at every moment, suggests why Kertész employs a strictly chronological method of narration in *Fatelessness*. It is another example of the way narrative form follows function and contributes essentially to meaning in this novel, as in literary texts in general, and as in this chapter.

Just as those in the lines waiting for the *Selektion* at Auschwitz move forward step by step toward "the point where it is decided whether it will be gas immediately or a reprieve for the time being" (257), so he and all the rest of us human beings, Gyuri says to his uncles, move moment by moment, and step by step, through life. This comparison is shocking to his "uncles" and to his so-called "aunt," the wife of Uncle Fleischmann. They saw their life in Budapest during the Nazi occupation as a series of happenings that just "came about." Gyuri argues that each of those moments was both determined by its contingent contexts, in that sense "fated," and at the same time free, so that we are responsible for what we make of whatever situation in which we find ourselves. Each moment is detached from the ones before and after, and each is the opportunity for endless new possibilities. "There are only given situations and new givens inherent in them" (259). "It was not quite true," Gyuri reports himself as having said, "that the thing 'came about'; we had to go along with it too. Only now, and thus after the event, looking back, in hindsight, does the way it all 'came about' seem over, finished, unalterable, finite, so tremendously fast, and so terribly opaque. And if, in addition one knows one's fate in advance, of course" (257). Only by way of the falsifications of hindsight or of an impossible foresight does one's life congeal into a "fate": "whether one looks back or ahead, both are flawed perspectives, I suggested" (258).

Life as it is actually lived, from minute to minute, is always open to an unpredictable future that might radically change the past: "Every one of those minutes might in fact have brought something new. In reality it didn't, naturally, but still, one must acknowledge that it might have; when it comes down to it, each and every minute something else might have happened other than what actually did happen, at Auschwitz just as much as, let's suppose, here at home, when we took leave of my father" (258). His father was, at the beginning of the novel, ordered to a labor camp, where he died. His family, for example, might have hidden him and have helped him escape to another country. His uncles are angered at what Gyuri says and ask what they could have done on behalf of his father. "Nothing, naturally," he answers, "or rather anything, . . . which would have been just as senseless as doing nothing, yet again and just as naturally" (258).

Note the three uses of "naturally" (*természetesen* in Hungarian) in the two citations just made from what Gyuri says to his uncles. As I have shown in the longer analysis of *Fatelessness* in my *The Conflagration of Community,* of which this essay is a revised extract, "naturally" is a frequent word in *Fatelessness. Természetesen* means "naturally," but the word takes on an antithetical meaning in Gyuri's ironic and repeated usage, since he often uses it to name something quite unnatural by ordinary measures, such as life in a concentration camp. The word appears only a couple of times in the film, much less often than it appears in Gyuri's narration in the novel.

It is on the basis of a quite specific and quite sophisticated theory of human time and freedom that the reader can understand the meaning of the novel's strange title. What Kertész has Gyuri say is perhaps influenced, however indirectly, by Sartrean existentialism, but with a twist toward "postmodern" undecidability, as in what Gyuri says about being neither winner nor loser, about cause and effect, and about being both wrong and right. Just what does it mean, "fatelessness" ("*sorstalanság*")? Gyuri tries to answer this question in what he says to his uncles:

> Why did they not wish to acknowledge that if there is such a thing as fate, then freedom is not possible? If, on the other hand—I swept on, more and more astonished myself, steadily warming to the task—if there is such a thing as freedom, then there is no fate; that is to say—and I paused, but only long enough to catch my breath—that is to say, then we ourselves are fate, I realized all at once, but with a flash of clarity I had never experienced before. . . . It was impossible, they must try and understand, impossible to take everything away from me, impossible for me to be neither winner nor loser, for me not to be right and for me not to be mistaken that I was neither the cause nor the effect of anything; they should try to see, I almost pleaded, that I could not swallow that idiotic bitterness, that I should merely be innocent. But I could see they did not wish to understand anything. . . . (259–61)

This passage comes just before the end of the novel. It is the nearest the reader comes to a conceptual explanation for the either/or; both/and; neither/nor; maybe this/maybe that, ironic rhetoric that characterizes Gyuri's discourse throughout the novel. It also helps to explain Kertész's choice of a chronological recounting of Gyuri's life. Anything positive that can be said can also be plausibly negated, as in the antinomies of freedom and fate.

Surely Efraim Sicher oversimplifies, in his otherwise fine book, *The Holocaust Novel,* to say that Gyuri "followed a fate given to him, minute by minute, day after day, step by step" (48). This could too easily be read as a return to the religious explanation offered by Gyuri's Uncle Lajos. That explanation is clearly repudiated by Gyuri's irony. Uncle Lajos, at the beginning of the novel, tells Gyuri, "You too . . . are a part of the shared Jewish fate." This fate, says Uncle Lajos, was one of "unbroken persecution that has lasted for millennia." This suffering must be accepted "with fortitude and self-sacrificing forbearance," because "God has meted it out to them for their past sins" (20). It is true that Gyuri says at one point in his eloquent but, as he puts it, "a little incoherent" speech to his uncles that "I too had lived through a given fate. It had not been my own fate, but I had lived through it, and I simply couldn't understand why they couldn't get it into their heads that I now needed to start doing something with that fate, needed to connect it to somewhere or something; after all, I could no longer be satisfied with the notion that it had all been a mistake, blind fortune, some kind of blunder, let alone that it had not even happened" (259). Note that Gyuri says this was not "his fate," even though it had been "given."

Gyuri does not want to break off his life in some impossible way and start life afresh, as his uncles counsel, but to go forward step by step in continuity with what has happened: "we can never start a new life, only ever carry on the old one" (259). This means accepting responsibility for the steps you have already taken and going forward on the basis of those. Gyuri's ultimate resolution is expressed in a Blanchotian or Beckettian aporetic formulation: "I was already feeling a growing and accumulating readiness to continue my uncontinuable life" (262). Gyuri's attempt to convey to his uncles that they were not passive victims but to some degree responsible for what has happened just makes them violently angry: "'So it's us who are the guilty ones, is it? Us, the victims!' I tried explaining to them that it wasn't a crime; all that was needed was to admit it, meekly, simply, merely as a matter of reason, a point of honor, if I might put it that way" (260).

Gyuri's impassioned demand that his uncles recognize that no one is just an innocent victim, that we are all responsible for our fates, even if our fate is to be sent to Auschwitz, is met with incomprehension by Gyuri's uncles, expressed in a sentence already cited: "But I could see they did not wish to understand anything" (261). The uncles are clearly proxies for you and me, dear reader. Do we too not wish to understand anything, or are we able to accept Kertész's belief that we are responsible for our fates, even though we cannot rationally comprehend the mixture of freedom and fate in our lives?

An equivocation, one can see, exists in the word "fate," as Kertész uses it and as it is traditionally used. "Fate" can either mean, as in the Homeric

epics or in Uncle Lajos's discourse, a transcendent, divine force that predes-
tines people to live their lives in a certain way, or it can mean no more than
that in retrospect, one can see that things happened as they did happen, in a
combination of contingencies and free steps taken one by one, from moment
to moment. This happens according to the theory of human time Gyuri
so eloquently expresses. He took steps in response to the options that the
contingencies he encountered allowed, such as getting arrested and finding
himself deported to Auschwitz just because he happened to be on a certain
bus at a certain time. Gyuri seems to be using more this second sense of fate
than Uncle Lajos's when he says: "I took the steps, no one else, and I declared
that I had been true to my given fate throughout" (259). This means, as he
says on the next page, that "we ourselves are fate."

"Fatelessness" in the title of Kertész's novel refers, in my judgment, to
Gyuri's experience that things happen as they do happen, in a mixture of
randomness and steps taken as free responses, within the limits of the given
situation, to what happens. We do not have preordained fates. An example is
the steps Gyuri takes to keep himself alive in the three camps. His survival is
the result of an astonishing series of quite implausible or even "miraculous"
events. Why did the doctor believe his lie when he said he was sixteen, not
fifteen, as he actually was, at the preliminary *Selektion* at Auschwitz? Why,
when he was near death from abscesses on his knee and hip at Zeitz, was
he more or less tenderly cared for at a succession of hospitals rather than
just allowed to die, since he would be of no more use for work? Why did
the *Pfleger* (male nurse), Bohoosh, from the building next to the hospital at
Buchenwald where Gyuri lies near death, choose to keep Gyuri alive by bringing him bread and tinned sausage for no recompense and at great danger to
himself? These events, and many others equally crucial to Gyuri's survival,
against all odds, just do not make sense. Gyuri makes only highly tentative
attempts to explain them. In one place, when he has reached comparative
safety in a hospital bed in the surgical ward in Buchenwald, where he is actually given fairly good medical attention, he says, "after all, if I took a rational
view of things, I could see no reason, I was incapable of finding any known
and, to me, rationally acceptable cause for why, of all places, I happened to
be here instead of somewhere else" (207). "I have to say," he comments near
the end of his account, "that over time one can become accustomed even to
miracles" (225). That Gyuri survives at all justifies the term "miracle" when
so many millions, in just his situation, died.

The human condition, Gyuri's experience confirms, is one of fatelessness.
You cannot blame anything on fate, at least in the sense of a benign or malign
force pulling strings behind the scenes. Gyuri's ultimate wisdom, perhaps, is

that every positive judgment has an equally plausible counterjudgment and that, as he says of his day-to-day existence in Zeitz, "The main thing was not to neglect oneself; somehow there would always be a way, for it had never yet happened that there wasn't a way somehow. . . . For example, your first device is stubbornness" (136, 138). "Stubbornness" (*makacsság* in Hungarian) is the name Gyuri gives to taking such steps as you can take, even when you are moving forward in the line toward the moment of the *Selektion*. "Stubbornness" is the best explanation Gyuri can give, for example, of Bohoosh's kindness, since that kindness is a recalcitrant and extremely risky defiance of camp rules.

If there are no atheists in foxholes, there appear to be relatively few true believers in God, in Kertész's view, in concentration camps. The camps appear to have tended to take away, to some considerable degree, shared religious belief as a form of community togetherness, along with the rest of such forms. In the film, Gyuri joins in the prayer for the dead when the prisoners stand at attention watching the escaped and recaptured prisoners dangle from the gallows, but this does not occur in the novel. The narrator in the novel says, rather, "for the first time, I now somewhat regretted that I was unable to pray, if only a few sentences, in the language of the Jews" (162). Vladek, in Art Spiegelman's *Maus*, hears in Auschwitz someone in extremity calling on God. He comments to Artie, when telling the story in retrospect, "But here God didn't come. We were all on our own" (189). *Fatelessness* seems to be saying something similar, in its own way. "Apart from the last few twitches of the hanged men, nothing moved, nothing wavered at these words [the Kaddish]" (162). That may be one reason why, as Sicher comments, Kertész "has not been easily accepted in the canon of Hungarian literature, where critics have not always welcomed his pessimistic self-irony" (51).

"Pessimistic self-irony" does not quite seem to me an adequate descriptive summing up of Gyuri's attitude. *Fatelessness* ends, as does Albert Camus' *The Stranger*, with an appeal to happiness, clearly echoed by Kertész, that seems to me moving and plausible, not pessimistic or self-ironizing. I suppose "self-irony" means "self-deprecating" irony, irony directed at oneself. Gyuri's persistent attitude or tone, surfacing explicitly at the end, is rather of irony against, for example, the journalistic clichés that assume the camps were unmitigated "hell," that no one was ever bored or ever happy there. Anticipating his future postwar life fulfilling his mother's hopes for him to be "an engineer, a doctor, or something like that" (262), Gyuri says, in a powerfully counterintuitive formulation, that not "fate" but "happiness" will be watching over his future, as it has watched over him in the camps:

No doubt that is how it will be, just as she wished; there is nothing impossible that we do not live through naturally, and keeping a watch on me on my journey, like some inescapable trap, I already know there will be happiness. For even there, next to the chimneys, in the intervals between the torments, there was something that resembled happiness. Everyone asks only about the hardships and the "atrocities," whereas for me perhaps it is that experience which will remain the most memorable. Yes, the next time I am asked, I ought to speak about that, the happiness of the concentration camps. (262)

That, however, is not quite the end. Two characteristically qualifying sentences follow, given a separate final paragraph to themselves: "If indeed I am asked. And provided I myself don't forget" (262). Such is the fragility of testimony, based as it is on the vagaries of memory and on being in a situation in which one is called on to bear witness.

Coda

I claim to have shown that Kertész's fictional testimony to the Shoah is made possible by the specific narrative devices he brilliantly employs in *Fatelessness*: the ironic discourse of the narrator, the combining of narrator and protagonist, the narrating-I and the experiencing-I, within the same imaginary personage, and the double doubling of the I in the *Muselmann* episode and throughout. Gyuri's ironic testimony to his experiences in the camps somewhat paradoxically not only distances the events being narrated but also allows the reader to see them more sharply and vividly than a sentimental or melodramatic telling might have done. The combining in one voice of the narrating-I and an already doubled experiencing-I means that the *Muselmann* and the proxy witness who survives the *Muselmann* can be combined in a single, ironic, doubly doubled vision. This provides a fictional solution to Levi's paradox. The strictly chronological narration, finally, corresponds to the concept of fatelessness as a series of step-by-step decisions in given circumstances.

My commentary in turn is not so much a bearing witness for the witness as it is a facilitating of reading by what might be named a "calling attention" to the testimonial work the novel enacts. My chapter, however, also has a dimension of performative testimony. It is a declaration of what has happened to me when reading and rereading the novel. A reading in the sense of analytic commentary, if it works, can help open a literary work to other readers. It will thereby perhaps contribute to the creation of a community of readers who may, if not know, at least not forget, Auschwitz. I would not, however, put too much stress on this idea of "a community of readers." Such a community, if it exists, is fairly abstract, since it is made up of people who, for the most part, do not know one another. A "community of readers," as I said earlier, is quite different from a traditional community of people living together from generation to generation in the same place and sharing the same culture, such as the Jewish communities the Nazis so systematically destroyed.

Notes

1. Maurice Blanchot (1907–2003) was one of the most important French critics and fiction writers of the twentieth century. One of Blanchot's characteristic locutions, as many of his critics have noted, takes the form of "X without X." In the case of my third epigraph, Blanchot affirms that we have knowledge without knowledge of Auschwitz. My citation is taken from a section about the Shoah in a late aphoristic work by Blanchot, *L'Écriture du désastre* (131) (*The Writing of the Disaster* [82]). Here is the French original: "Nous lisons les livres sur Auschwitz. Le vœu de tous, là-bas, le dernier vœu: sachez ce qui s'est passé, n'oubliez pas, et en même temps jamais vous ne saurez." A somewhat different version of my essay has been published as "Imre Kertész's *Fatelessness: Fiction as Testimony*," in my *The Conflagration of Community: Fiction before and after Auschwitz* (Chicago: The University of Chicago Press, 2011), 177–227. I am grateful for permission to reuse this essay in my book.

2. See the Works Cited for references to an online edition of *Sorstalanság* (Kertész, accessed spring 2007, no longer available); an online bibliography of works by and about Kertész (*A Bibliography*, accessed spring 2007); an online essay by Susan Eszter on irony in *Fatelessness* (Eszter, accessed spring 2007); and a collection of essays about Kertész's work (Vasvari and Tötösy de Zepetnek, eds.).

3. I am extremely grateful to Susan Rubin Suleiman, Jakob Lothe, and James Phelan for their careful reading of the first version of this essay and for the helpful suggestions and corrections they made. Some important work in the abundant and growing secondary literature in Holocaust studies has focused on the question of how to represent the "unspeakable" Shoah, though usually without my emphasis on the performative aspect of such representation. Examples are Sidra DeKoven Ezrahi, *By Words Alone;* Thomas Trezise, "Unspeakable"; and Erin McGlothlin, "Narrative Transgression in Edgar Hilsenrath's *Der Nazi und der Friseur*." These essays and Naomi Mandel's book *Against the Unspeakable* have helped me get some sense of current thinking on questions of the "unspeakable" and on consequent challenges to representing the Holocaust. I am grateful for these references to the anonymous reviewer of this essay for The Ohio State University Press. Naomi Mandel, for example, argues persuasively that claiming the Holocaust is "unspeakable" may be a copout, a way to avoid talking or writing about it at all.

4. He said this quite emphatically in the generous conversation he held in Berlin on

June 29, 2007, with members of the Oslo research group on narratology that sponsored this present essay.

5. *Fatelessness*'s protagonist's formal name is György Köves, but his family calls him, "Gyuri." I shall refer to him as Gyuri (pronounced something like "Jury"), since that probably corresponds best to what we are to imagine was his most commonly used name, perhaps the name by which he referred to himself. The English subtitles in the film transcribe his familiar name as Gyurka, but I shall use the name as it is given in Tim Wilkinson's translation.

Works Cited

Agamben, Giorgio. *Remnants of Auschwitz: The Witness and the Archive.* Translated by Daniel Heller-Roazen. New York: Zone Books, 2002.

A Bibliography of Works by and about Imre Kertés. Compiled by Tötösy de Zepetnek. http://clcwebjournal.lib.purdue.edu/library/imrekerteszbibliography(totosy).html. Accessed spring 2007.

Blanchot, Maurice. *L'Écriture du désastre.* Paris: Gallimard, 1980.

———. *The Writing of the Disaster.* New ed. Translated by Ann Smock. Lincoln and London: University of Nebraska Press, 1995.

Camus, Albert. *The Stranger.* New York: Vintage, 1961.

Celan, Paul. *Breathturn.* Translated by Pierre Joris. Los Angeles: Sun & Moon Press, 1995.

Eszter, Susan. "The Narrative of Irony—Imre Kertész' *Fatelessness.*" http://www.google.ca/search?hl=en&q=Imre+Kertesz+irony&btnG=Google+Search&meta=. Last accessed January 14, 2010, no longer available.

Ezrahi, Sidra DeKoven. *By Words Alone: The Holocaust in Literature.* Chicago: University of Chicago Press, 1980.

———. "Representing Auschwitz." *History and Memory* 7, no. 2 (Winter 1996): 121–54.

Kertész, Imre. *Fatelessness.* Translated by Tim Wilkinson. New York: Vintage, 2004.

———. *Kaddish for an Unborn Child.* Translated by Tim Wilkinson. New York: Vintage International, 2004.

———. *Sorstalanság.* http://www.irodalmiakademia.hu/scripts/DIATxcgi?infile=diat_vm_talalatok.html&locator=/dia/diat/muvek/html/KERTESZ/kertesz00004/kertesz00004.html&oid=77770&session=1886835562. Accessed spring 2007.

———. *Fateless.* 2005. Hungarian Motion Picture Ltd. DVD (2006) distributed by ThinkFilm. ASIN: B000EQ5Q2W. A film in Hungarian titled *Sorstalanság,* with English subtitles. Script by Imre Kertész. Directed by Lajos Koltai. Starring Marcell Nagy and Béla Dóra, with Bálint Péntek, Áron Dimény, and Péter Fanciskai. Cinematography by Gyula Pados. Musical score by Ennio Morricone. Produced by Alexandra Stolle, Andras Hamori, Bernd Helthaler, Endre Sik, and Erika Tarr.

Levi, Primo. *The Drowned and the Saved.* Translated by Raymond Rosenthal. New York: Vintage, 1989.

———. *Survival in Auschwitz: The Nazi Assault on Humanity.* New York: Simon and Schuster; A Touchstone Book, 1996.

Mandel, Naomi. *Against the Unspeakable: Complicity, the Holocaust, and Slavery in America.* Charlottesville: University of Virginia Press, 2006.

McGothlin, Erin. "Narrative Transgression in Edgar Hilsenrath's *Der Nazi und der Friseur* and the Rhetoric of the Sacred in Holocaust Discourse." *The German Quarterly* 80, no. 2 (Spring 2002): 220–39.

Phelan, James. *Living to Tell about It: A Rhetoric and Ethics of Character Narration.* Ithaca: Cornell University Press, 2005.

Sicher, Efraim. *The Holocaust Novel.* New York and London: Routledge, 2005.

Spiegelmann, Art. *Maus: A Survivor's Tale.* New York: Pantheon, 1997.

Trezise, Thomas. "Unspeakable." *The Yale Journal of Criticism* 14, no. 1 (Spring 2001): 36–66.

Vasvari, Louise O. and Steven Tötösy de Zepetnek, eds. *Imre Kertész and Holocaust Literature.* West Lafayette, IN: Purdue University Press, 2005.

Wiesel, Elie. *The Night Trilogy: Night; Dawn; Day.* Translated by Marion Wiesel et al. New York: Hill and Wang, 2008.

CHAPTER 2

Challenges for the Successor Generations of German–Jewish Authors in Germany

BEATRICE SANDBERG

Introduction

In the course of the last twenty years the situation for writers who deal with the consequences of National Socialism in general, and the Shoah specifically, has changed considerably. In what follows I shall examine some narratives by three writers from the "successor generation" who, in spite of the fate of their families, have chosen to live their lives in Germany as Jewish–German writers: Esther Dischereit, Rafael Seligmann, and Maxim Biller. To put their work in context, however, I shall begin with some brief remarks about some German–Jewish writers from the eyewitness generation who also wrote about their experiences decades earlier in ways that met with similar resistance from both publishers and readers who habitually brought sharply defined attitudes and expectations to bear on anything written about this most painful and sensitive of topics. Finally we shall look at a Jewish writer from Switzerland, Charles Lewinsky, whose life was of course not affected by the Holocaust in the same way as those of his coreligionists in Germany. Does his novel, which deals with four generations of a Jewish family, represent an effort to compensate, in some small way, the Jews for the families they had lost and for all the missing life histories attached to them? Is this perhaps a work that could only be written outside Germany itself?

In the writings of Jewish authors living in Germany, the consequences of the Shoah are still present as traces, often hidden and yet sometimes erupting in unexpected ways. They all focus on problems of identity arising from living in Germany, from struggling with their fate as Jews, living as a small minority among "ordinary" people and often being confronted with the Holocaust and the effects of the genocide. Many descendants feel they are still suffering from the *morbus Auschwitz*—as Grete Weil (1906–99), a German–Jewish author who escaped from the Nazis by hiding in Amsterdam, called it—the guilt of the survivors: "I suffer from Auschwitz as others suffer from TB or cancer. I am just as difficult to put up with as anyone with an illness."[1] In her narratives she insists that Auschwitz is something that affected not only the victims but an entire civilization. On her return to Germany she observed that the country was just as broken as she was. Fifty years on, there are others who still feel the same way and seek to express their struggle to achieve a meaningful life through various modes of writing. Esther Dischereit belongs to the younger generation who have to deal with the difficulties of living in Germany with the heritage of their Jewishness after the Shoah; at the same time she confesses to being tired of constantly having to satisfy the expectation that she should "wear the incarnation of suffering on her face" (*Joëmis Tisch* 68). Others from that generation dislike in turn the earnestness of most representations of the past and the kind of unnatural sternness they encounter. The desire to be allowed to use humor in their treatment of the Holocaust crops up repeatedly in the works of Rafael Seligmann and Maxim Biller. In their attempts to achieve greater normality in the coexistence between Germans and German Jews, they seek to push at the limits and even break through the pain barriers that generally circumscribe the topic of the Holocaust.

The Eyewitness Generation and the Problems of Representation and Narratability

It would be to mistake the situation to assume that the use of humor is simply an affront inflicted on the first generation of survivors by their disrespectful successors. In fact there are literary precedents for this way of dealing with the topic of Jewish persecution in the works of some of the survivor generation itself, such as Jurek Becker, George Tabori, and Edgar Hilsenrath. Hilsenrath, a survivor of a Jewish ghetto in the Ukraine, emigrated first to Israel in 1945, then went to the United States in 1951, and returned to Germany in 1975. His novel *Der Nazi und der Friseur* (*The Nazi and the Barber: A Tale of Vengeance*), written in 1968–69, published in the United States in 1971, and translated into eighteen languages, was rejected by over sixty publishers in Germany before a small publishing house in Cologne finally accepted it for printing in 1977—only to withdraw it subsequently. Today it is considered to be one of the most significant works of German postwar literature. Hilsenrath's first novel *Nacht* (1964, translated as *Night* in 1966) is a brilliant example of how "to express the inexpressible" in absolutely sober language, but it also illustrates the arbitrariness of a book's fate and the inadequacy of a book's initial reception by critics and readers. Nowadays experts regard *Nacht* as a book that deserves to be as well known as the "standard" early literary treatments of the Holocaust. Hilsenrath, who is still alive and living in Berlin, now appears at long last to be enjoying a degree of recognition.

The reason for the rejection of *Der Nazi und der Friseur* by German publishers lay in Hilsenrath's use of satire, black humor, and the grotesque when treating the topic of the SS and the Jews. The novel reveals the banality of fascism at the same time as it perverts guilt and atonement and pokes fun at justice. The grotesque (and the provocation it generates) was for Hilsenrath the appropriate aesthetic category to characterize the exceptional situation and the absolute debasement of human beings in the concentration camps. Similar debates about the use of such elements as the grotesque and farce sprung up at about the same time in the United States in relation to George Tabori's drama *The Cannibals* (1965). Reflecting on those controversies, Michael Hofmann has emphasized the need for a discussion about the question of the adequacy of particular genres or forms in Holocaust literature. Hofmann argues, rightly in my view, that elements of farce can contribute successfully to the aesthetics and poetics of provocation by accentuating the consequences of the rupture of civilization that the Holocaust represents. He is also convinced "that the literary methods used . . . convey specific insights relating to the overcoming of conventional narrative strategies" (232). For most Jewish survivors, however, in the 1960s it was definitely too early to use these literary means to deal with the Holocaust in Germany. Even now, forty years later, the younger German–Jewish writers mentioned above are still meeting resistance from critics who disapprove of any such approach to the subject.

The persistence of these antagonisms—of authenticity versus fictionalization, gravity versus grotesque humor—suggests, contrary to what one might suppose, that what many readers regard as the acceptable literary means of representing the Holocaust seems not to depend simply on historical distance from the events. Rather, there is a series of elements that combine to make the impossible possible at a given point in time or, conversely, to lend authenticity to the seemingly inauthentic at some other point when we least expect it. The demand generally placed on the first generation of survivors was for authenticity and documentary reliability when recounting personal experiences in the concentration camps and in the ghettos. Fictional treatments were not considered to be appropriate to the gravity of the topic. Over the years there has been no shortage of attempts to constrict and constrain writing after the Holocaust, but many of the survivors themselves did not in fact write in accordance with them, and many rejected the verdicts of critics and publishers.

A good example of this kind of recalcitrance is to be found in the work of the Austrian–Jewish writer Fred Wander who was born in Vienna in 1917 and died there in August 2006. Having spent over two years in various camps, Wander found that his only thought was to tell those outside what had happened once it was all over, but this proved much more difficult than he had imagined. Jorge Semprun encountered similar difficulties, whereas Primo Levi, a fellow sufferer with whom Wander was familiar and to whom he refers repeatedly, began to write about his experiences shortly after his return. Semprun and Wander, on the other hand, both had to wait many years before finding an adequate form in which to write about the past. The releasing factor for Wander's writing was the painful death of his own eight-year-old daughter, Kitty, which reminded him of the death of a young boy in the camp, an event that clearly had a powerful effect on him but that needed the death of Kitty to force its way to the surface again. The novel *The Seventh Well* from 1971[2] is dedicated to Kitty's memory. Wander here hides his own experiences behind the fate of his comrades in a fictionalized narrative while at the same time displaying his learning process about *how* to narrate such painful experiences. Wander has also insisted that narrating was, for him at least, the most important survival strategy in the camps. To narrate meant to be alive, to communicate with another person, not to be alone. Wander quotes Hannah Arendt's observation that suffering becomes bearable when one can at least tell about it (*Das gute Leben* 341). Narrating about the past or even inventing fantastic histories from their former lives helped the prisoners to carry on believing in life and maintaining hope in a seemingly hopeless situation. That is also the reason why both Wander and Kertész were able to describe moments of happiness in the camps, something that was difficult for many readers of Holocaust literature to accept. Both writers were aware of posterity's categorical expectations about how victims were supposed to write about their experiences: in a nonfictional mode and without any "alleviating" means such as humor. Yet in defiance of these expectations they both insisted on choosing their own means. Thus their autobiographical writing involves the interplay of more or less authentic memories with consciously fictional elements. This technique deliberately reflects on the constructed nature of the text and on the impossibility of writing about a horrifying past without some means of protection for the writer. Thus Wander introduces the medium of a narrator who tells about the sufferings in the camp; only by processing things in this way can he even begin to express something of his own pain. He does not regard truth as something opposed to fiction or necessarily requiring a documentary approach. In his autobiography *Das gute Leben* (*The Good Life*), first published in 1996 and later rewritten and supplied with the subtitle "Happiness amidst Horror" (2006), Wander says little about the time he spent in the concentration camps, arguing that only by fictionalizing them was he able to write about certain areas of experience. For his generation *authenticity* had already become linked to "memory's truth" in the sense referred to by Salman Rushdie and many other critics as *subjective truth*.[3]

Dealing with Conflicts of Identity and Representation

For the members of the successor generation the Shoah has become a past historical event. Hartmut Steinecke summarizes his findings on the second generation of German–Jewish writers as follows: "For Jewish writers born after the Shoah ('the second generation'), this event no longer occupies the central position in their texts. The Shoah is still an important event for them, especially its role in contemporary society and in the question of their own identity" (246).[4]

These writers have to deal with specific private problems personally and when meeting the public. Having lost members of their family, they also suffer from a loss of tradition. They feel marginalized by society, and this may be the reason why they do not feel any national affiliation. At times they have to listen to the reproach that they can rely on an "Auschwitz-bonus" (an expression used by Maxim Biller, "Harlem Holocaust" 114) as an aid to getting their work published. At the same time they must be wary of being sucked in by the Shoah-Business through participation in public events and commemorations.[5]

Even though they no longer focus on the Shoah as a main subject, it remains an important element in their self-perception and their public identity. Not only are they met with compassion and pity when people hear of their family fate, but they are often burdened with the knowledge that their parents felt a kind of "survivor's guilt" that could make them try to hide their Jewishness or even make them become invisible. At the same time, their German neighbors and acquaintances could feel uneasy about living together with descendants of Holocaust victims without knowing how to behave toward them in an unbiased way in everyday life.[6] We know that Germans scarcely dared to use the word "Jew" for fear of being accused of harboring anti-Semitic prejudice. In German literary studies, the term *sprachliche Vermeidungsstrategien* ("linguistic strategies of evasion") indicates this kind of gap of silence on both sides.[7]

There is one more element that distinguishes the eyewitness literature of the first generation from the literature of succeeding generations. Whereas most of the survivors wanted to contribute to collective memory by communicating their experiences, the following generations often have quite different motivations for their writing. "Holocaust memory" is something imposed on them by their surroundings, above all by their family. They thus have to deal with an (often) involuntary attribution of identity as Jews and Jewish victims. Their narrative strategies focus on finding their own place in society, by either accepting the obligation to commemorate as part of the Shoah community, or refusing to do so by trying to establish an independent existence and showing their rejection of the prescribed role through various forms of opposition. No matter which way they turn, they have to fight against inner and outer obstacles when choosing their manner of writing. Writing gives them the chance to reveal and to deal with the aftereffects of the historical Holocaust, even as the Holocaust itself is slowly disappearing beyond the horizon of directly lived experience.

When narrating family histories or stories told by survivors or friends, the successor generation, lacking any direct, personal experience of the Shoah, are forced to use the means of fiction. They may deploy genres such as the grotesque and farce, or they may play on the whole scale of stereotypes and incorporate the most awful prejudices into their texts as Maxim Biller and Rafael Seligmann do. If non-Jewish authors had used the same kind of literary vocabulary, they would have been placed on trial. In fact, no German publisher was willing to print *Rubinsteins Versteigerung* (*The Auctioning of Rubinstein*), even though Seligmann was already well known as a journalist. Eventually he published the book at his own cost.[8] Compared to the almost universal rejection of Hilsenrath's book, however, the positive responses of the readers to this highly provocative novel indicate that a change of attitude has taken place, but what are the long-term consequences of breaking taboos? Does it mean that increasing historical distance will remove the inner and outer barriers that define the Shoah as an extraordinary matter that needs to be dealt with by extraordinary means? I think we will see a wide spectrum of different approaches in the future, depending on the authors' inner and outer relation to the issues they are dealing with. Until now, there seems to be one almost impassable frontier, which is to write about life in the camps in the voice of a first-person narrator, although even here there have been a few exceptions. Binjamin Wilkomirski, alias of the Swiss musician Bruno Doessekker, pretended that he had experienced a childhood in the camps, a statement that turned out to be false. *La vita è bella* (1997) (*Life Is Beautiful*), a film depicting a child who survived in a concentration camp thanks to the help of the inmates, was written by the son of a concentration camp prisoner, Roberto Benigni, who also plays the part of the father in the film. In Germany, Gila Lustiger, daughter of an Auschwitz survivor and historian, wrote a novel in 1987 titled *Die Bestandsaufnahme* (*The Inventory*). Using a first-person narrative perspective, she deployed the means of sarcasm and empathy, a choice that met with a good deal of criticism. This shows that it will indeed be possible for later generations to write Holocaust narratives and films in the first person without having any firsthand knowledge of life in the camps, but it also shows how difficult it is to do so in a convincing or satisfactory way.

These problems, and other related ones, are the issues that Esther Dischereit (b. 1952 in Heppenheim), Rafael Seligmann (b. 1948 in Israel), and Maxim Biller (b. 1960 in Prague) focus on in their writing. Their social and cultural experiences vary, and so do their approaches to the strategies of representation. Each of them depicts characters, often represented as first-person narrators, struggling with the problem of identity when writing about the difficulty of being Jewish authors writing in German or German authors of Jewish origin who live in Germany.[9]

Esther Dischereit
The Impossible Identity

The first author I will consider in more detail is Esther Dischereit, born in 1952 in Heppenheim. Her Jewish mother had managed to stay alive during the war while remaining in Germany, having survived out of sheer defiance, as she maintained. Dischereit was brought up by her mother and was instructed in Jewish religion and customs in a Hebrew School of the Jewish Community until her mother died. She trained as a teacher, but in the 1960s she became engaged in politics on the extreme left ("Red Cells") and lost her job. Since then she has been active on the Left and worked as a publicist. She went to West Berlin and moved to Eastern Germany in 1989. In 1995 she became a Fellow of the Moses Mendelssohn Center in Potsdam, where she also teaches in the area of European-Jewish Studies. She is known in the United States because of her visits to various universities, including Boston, Berkeley, Ithaca, and Amherst. She also travels a great deal in Germany, giving lectures on her topic—living in Germany as a Jewish–German writer—a topic that she cannot leave behind.

"No Exit from This Jewry" is the title of one of Esther Dischereit's essays from 1994, written in English and published in German in 1998. Here she exposes the difficulty of accepting that to be a Jew is something normal, because everything that belongs to normality for the majority—relatives, tradition, heritage, belief—was destroyed for the Jews in the Shoah. Dischereit is a representative of the second generation of German Jews who decided to stay in the country but who struggle to live an ordinary life. She focuses unremittingly on the problem of identity, using her own acute methods. Her main instrument as a writer is language, and because she is writing in German, she has a language problem. As many writers have complained, Nazism compromised the German language. There are words that simply cannot be used any longer according to Dischereit. Words such *Rampe* ("platform") or *Jude* ("Jew") can never be ordinary words again in the way that *puppet, boy, little,* or *sweet* can (*Übungen* 19ff.). German thus remains a foreign language to her, but so does Hebrew. Writing German as a Jew feels like undressing in public, Dischereit says. The label *Jew* feels as if it contradicts the term *German;* there is a dissonance between them that cannot be resolved. Correspondingly, Jews do not belong to German culture; they never did, Dischereit maintains, analyzing statements such as "the Jews have enriched German culture." If they "enriched" German culture, then they never were part of it, but something outside. Like Katja Behrens, another female writer, she stresses her firm conviction that there never was a Jewish–German symbiosis[10] and she therefore refers to the "Jewishness" of her stories.

These are only a few of the many problems Dischereit confronts when examining her relationship between "the German" and her deeply problematic identity. She has no hope that she will find a new identity through writing, because "the mark of Cain, forgotten under the waters of Socialism, is still on my skin" (*Joëmis Tisch* 9). An additional issue is her lack of memories, childhood memories, family memories, and narratives transferred within the family—elements, as we all know, that help to establish and to stabilize personal identity. Dischereit feels exposed in both directions, to a German and a Jewish identity, but she sees a lack of understanding on both sides:

> I declare that I am Jewish and I am not sure whether I am not lying. After
> all, I had not worried for decades about the fact that, or the question of

whether, I was one. My daughter declares that she is not a Jew, and knows that she too is lying. 'I am not a diaspora Jew, no, not me. I am a German and proud of it,' says a young friend, and she too is lying. Just as I am perhaps a "Jew in spite of myself," which is possible, she has become a 'German in spite of herself.' (*Übungen* 48)

In addition, Dischereit observes a certain feeling of rivalry among the Jews in Germany toward American, Israeli, and other Jews. They are rivals in Jewishness (*Übungen* 46), because German Jews presume that American and Israeli Jews do not share the same problems with their Jewish identity as they do, believing that the others are able simply to take their ethnic distinctness for granted. In her eyes, Israeli Jews seem to represent the prototype of this kind of Jew: anchored in a national state, they represent a majority and normality at the opposite extreme of the combination German–Jewish—a combination that American Jews in particular tend to regard as incomprehensible or almost indecent.[11] Dischereit is said to be vulnerable and she admits that this is true. She is difficult and cannot change it. She does not like to be compared to other Jewish–German writers, such as Barbara Honigmann, even if they have much in common: they were both socialized into socialism and communism; they each had parents (Dischereit's father) who did not practice any belief; they each decided to be Jewish at a certain point in their lives. "After twenty years of being an Un-Jew I want to become a Jew again" is how Dischereit opens *Joëmis Tisch: Eine jüdische Geschichte* (*Joëmi's Table: A Jewish Story*) (9). Her specific situation as a *feminist* Jewish writer results in many invitations to schools, to read from her books and discuss what happened during the Second World War. She dislikes the kind of preparation pupils get before meeting a Jewish author, as it immediately draws attention away from the literary work and toward her most personal feelings as a human being. She also dislikes a certain kind of philo-Semitism, the kind of over-friendly and cautious behavior she experiences, which she finds worse than overtly hostile anti-Semitism (*Übungen* 206.)[12] Even if such well-intentioned behavior signals good faith and is not meant to hurt, or even if the public has learned to show that they are shocked, the way people behave toward a Jew says a lot about the fact "that it is not normal to be Jewish and alive" (205). Here we find a strong similarity to the problem of being Jewish as presented by Lewinsky and Seligmann.

Dischereit considers herself to be a member of the *Erinnerungsgeneration* ("the remembering generation"). She reflects on her Jewishness and her identity problem in connection with the Shoah as her main experience: a col-

lectively experienced trauma of the past that is still present in her life, causing the destruction of all sense. This feeling might be responsible too for her
lack of a preferred literary genre. She writes essays, poetry, and radio plays.
The narrative *Joëmi's Table* consists of mostly small paragraphs composed in
non-chronological order, following associations, movements, fragments of
memories, discussions, political statements, or historical episodes. There is a
female first-person narrator, Jewish and German, but never quite graspable
by the reader because she is characterized indirectly and is presented as Hannah's daughter. While the mother is seen from the outside, through the eyes
of the daughter or narratives overheard, the narrator comments on political
events in the present and the past; refers to discussions and conversations,
Jewish jokes, fragments of memories; shows letters; and asks questions and
makes comments on statements, sometimes in a sarcastic way.

Dischereit positions herself as a Jewish-feminist writer, using the narrative techniques of the new autobiographical writing that transgresses the
borders between reality and fiction, identity, and constructions of identity
by reference to language and gender. Her writing exposes the problem of
finding a genuine identity. There is the cultural double bind of the German–
Jewish background, where one part is difficult to accept because of the Shoah,
but the other part is essential because of the German language. In addition
to this difficulty, most German–Jewish writers feel disturbed by the continuous confrontation with the modes of identification offered to them by others
and by social interaction burdened by inhibitions. An illustrative example is
provided by the following passage from *Joëmi's Table*,[13] where the narrator is
addressed by an elderly lady:

> I have to confess something to you. I meet you, how should I put it, with
> inhibition. You know, you look like Ruth Deretz. She was in my class in
> those days. And somehow there was something similar about her—she was
> as attractive as you, a big, beautiful girl. You understand, she was then. . . . I
> was born in 1921. . . . Please excuse me. (55)

A person who is met everywhere by this attitude of caution and wariness
will feel uneasy and unable to communicate in an ordinary way. The Jewish woman has a sense of not being seen as the individual she is, but rather
of being reduced to the stereotype of a female Jewish victim by the German
woman who is suffering from a bad conscience about the past. To live as
a Jew in Germany, Dischereit concludes, requires practice, and there is no
guarantee that she will succeed.

Maxim Biller and Rafael Seligmann

Maxim Biller, often compared with Philip Roth and strongly inspired by American writers,[14] has Roth say the following (and clearly endorses his words):

> I am an artist, I am not willing to keep quiet about anything just because Hitler and Goebbels were once up to mischief. I will laugh about me, about the Jews. Every people has a waxworks with heroes, anti-heroes, non-heroes, with good ones and bad ones. I feel responsible for the Jewish panopticon. I am a Jewish writer and I will not allow the Nazis, after all that has happened, to forbid my laughter. I will laugh and feel better afterwards. I know how difficult, how impossible this is. I am not so indifferent as to forget that six million were murdered during the last war. Damn it: I cannot help cracking heretical jokes, I want to get rid of my trauma in exactly the same way, incidentally, as the children of the perpetrators want to get rid of theirs. An irresolvable antagonism. (Hannes Stein, quoted in Braese, *Deutsche Nachkriegsliteratur* 403–4)[15]

Born in Prague in 1960, Biller emigrated with his parents to Germany in 1970. He studied literature in Munich and now lives as journalist in Berlin. He became well known through the scandal caused by his autobiographical novel, *Ezra,* which had to be withdrawn by the publishing company in 2003 following a court judgment.

Up to this point Biller had written stories and novels with quite provocative titles and no less challenging content, for example, *Land der Väter und Verräter* (*Land of the Fathers and Traitors*) (stories 1994); *Wenn ich einmal reich und tot bin* (*When I'm Rich and Dead*) (1990); *Moralische Geschichten* (*Moral Tales*) (2005), a collection of satirical short stories, or *Deutschbuch* (2001), a collection of sharp, always cheeky and funny phrases about politics and public figures, including an essay titled "The Biller Principle." Here is just one example: "I'm happy to talk about Israel. . . . Admittedly, when asked the classic asshole question about what we Jews are doing down there among the Palestinians, I always reply: 'All sorts of things I guarantee the inmates of German concentration camps could only dream about,' and immediately put an end to the conversation" (*Deutschbuch* 298).

Biller is the most extreme of the Jewish writers—he shocks the public by using provocative language, breaking taboos, and writing extensively about sex. It was possible to write about taboos in Germany only by employing black humor and irony, Biller says. He cites all the notorious stereotypes and clichés about Jews, Germans, Arabs, and so forth, which are provocative and tiring at the same time, especially when used in all possible combinations and without scruples of any kind. What may be very witty when referring sarcastically to the media and public figures in a current political context becomes problematic when used in a religious context, in connection with the Holocaust, or generally without any regard to other people's feelings.[16] In his self-portrait, published in 2009 with the title *Der gebrauchte Jude* (*The Jew Everyone Needs*), he extends his role as a non-conforming troublemaker and *enfant terrible* in the direction of melancholy incorrigibility and whipping boy.

Some of Biller's publications can hardly be considered good literature (although there are critics who hold his literary qualities in high regard), but even if we do not apply the criteria of literary quality we have to ask: Why does Biller wish to shock his readers? What does he want to achieve? Is it (self-) hatred, or the conviction that Jewish literature in Germany has to be different from German literature and adopt a non-conciliatory, critical tone? Biller likes to be thought of as a controversial and dangerous Jew; he enjoys his role of *enfant terrible* in Germany. Together with Dischereit and Seligmann, he belongs to that group of intellectuals who characterize the cohabitation of the German Jews with the Germans after the Holocaust as a "negative symbiosis." Since he is convinced that there never will be a symbiosis, he is searching for a radical, anti-assimilatory way of writing in order to accentuate the difference. Karen Remmler, who understands Biller's writing as genealogical in the sense of Foucault, emphasizes the point that the genealogy of Jewish stories is always fractured, and that they reveal not wholeness but the distorted images of a torn existence that bears traces of historical fragmentation ("Maxim Biller" 316). According to this view, Biller is less concerned with a search for identity than he is with making it clear that identity has become an object of consumption, a product of the culture industry bent on producing images of Jewishness to satisfy a German public. Biller's intention is to highlight this "marketing strategy" by polarizing differences beyond the customary limits and by deploying the means of pornography.[17]

Like Biller, Rafael Seligmann has been accused of "dirtying his own nest." He too employs ironic and sarcastic means extensively, but having started in an aggressive mode, he appears to be moving toward a more conciliatory stance. Seligmann likes to spurn political correctness in the positions he takes and to attack openly long-established attitudes that bestow exceptional status on Jews, especially in Germany. He was one of the first Jewish writers to begin writing about everyday life in post-Shoah Germany. His goal is clear: by provoking his readers, he wants them to discuss how the Shoah affects their lives. Nevertheless, he endorses the existence of a hybrid German–Jewish identity (Beegle 83–86).

Seligmann was born in Tel Aviv and followed his parents when they decided to go back to Germany when he was ten years old.[18] He studied in Munich and gained his doctorate with a thesis on Israeli security policy. He then became a journalist and an editor of several well-known German newspapers and magazines, founded the *Jewish Magazine* in 1985, became professor of international relations at the University of Munich, and lives now as a free-lance journalist and chief editor of the *Atlantic Times*.

Seligmann's first novel, *Rubinsteins Versteigerung* (*The Auctioning of Rubinstein*), appeared in 1988 (as a self-funded publication). In 1990 he published *Die jiddische Mamme* and in 1996 *Der Musterjude* (*The Model Jew*). His titles contain pointed references to the Jewish–German double culture, the role in the family of the (strong) Jewish mother, and the phenomenon of overly compensatory social assimilation as an exemplary citizen.

Rubinsteins Versteigerung is about Jewish–German feelings of hatred and weakness and false reactions (born of uncertainty) on the part of German teachers, parents, or friends in everyday situations. The result is confusion on all sides about how to deal with one another, a situation the protagonist Rubinstein exploits to the full in order to take advantage of the German–Jewish victim role and thereby succeed in his personal and academic ambitions.

When we look at the narrative, we see that Seligmann uses a special technique to let the narrator communicate unrestrictedly with the reader, while at the same time pretending that the most awful things remain unsaid. A conversation between the mother and her twenty-one-year-old son Jonathan, who is still attending school and in danger of failing his school-leaving examination, will give an impression of how people interact with each other in this novel, especially when they meet resistance:

> "Donkey, the situation is tough."
>
> "What have you been up to this time?"
>
> "Nothing. It's just that in French my situation is bad. . . . We can still stop me getting a five [the lowest mark], but you have to play along. It is basically very simple. That Schneeberger woman is obsessed with Nazis. She sees Brownshirts where it wouldn't even occur to us Yids to look."
>
> "And why is that good for you?"
>
> "If you'd just shut up you'll find out!"
>
> "Rubinstein, you need to get a grip on yourself! . . . The shouting has helped, as usual." (*Rubinstein* 89–90)

He tells his mother that she must talk to his teacher. If the teacher is not willing to give him a better mark, she has to intervene: "You, my dear donkey,
must make it clear how much our family suffered from the persecutions of
the Nazis and that my failing would ruin us once more. It is of course rotten
of us to exploit her no doubt decent feelings so shamelessly, but we aren't
harming anyone" (91). But his mother refuses to cooperate, accusing her son
of being as cold, calculating, and evil as the Nazis. As he tries to calm her
down before persuading her finally to fight for her child by appealing to her
instincts as a Jewish mother, he simultaneously reveals to the reader his next
steps in overcoming his mother's resistance. Small wonder that no editor
wanted to publish a book that depicted a youngster engaging in such offen-
sive conversations and thoughts. Through these inner monologues, interwoven with the passages of dialogue, Seligmann has his Jewish protagonist
utter quite unbelievable insults about his parents and those he lives among.
Thus the narrator indicates Jonathan's divided mind on the narrative level
through the doubling of his quite contradictory utterances. Jonathan's disrespectful behavior is perhaps not so much the symptom of a rebelling youth
who merely wants to provoke as much as it is a cry for help to get out of an
unbearable identity crisis.

The central issues Seligmann focuses on in the novel are philo-Semitism,
Zionism, the cynical way Jewish Germans profit from the Holocaust, the
widespread reserve toward Jews on the part of the Germans, or simply the
absence of normal behavior toward Jews. Of course, only the means of fictionalization make it possible for Seligmann to write this autobiographically
grounded novel in the way he does without ending up in awkward controversies. The ending of the novel has led some critics to believe that the protagonist finally accepts that it is his fate to live in Germany as a German Jew.
After his girlfriend decides to leave him because she found out that her father
had been a SS soldier, something that would always have been an obstacle
for them and their families, he locks himself in his room in total despair.
When his father finally breaks through the bedroom door and asks what has
happened to him, he answers: *"Ich bin ein deutscher Jude!"* (*"I am a German
Jew!"*) (1991, 199).

Of course, the situation is conveyed through the prism of irony. This
extraordinarily outrageous and impertinent man is now like a helpless child.
I do not believe that we can interpret this sentence as if it were spoken by
a fortunate young man who has achieved his goals in life. Jonathan is stuck
with the insight that he has to live with this double identity that will cause
him trouble in each and every situation, as he just has experienced. Instability is his predominant state of mind and a condition that will also follow him

in all his social contacts. Only if other people were willing to desist from the prejudices that are common in society will German Jews and Germans ever have a chance of living more ordinary lives together.

Charles Lewinsky
Melnitz: *Jews in Switzerland, 1866–1945*

Although he deals with similar topics, Charles Lewinsky (b. 1946) can be seen as the antithesis of the authors discussed above. He is Swiss and lives both in Zürich and in France. He is a writer working for theater, TV, and film, and he established his name as a novelist with his family history, *Melnitz* (2006). Lewinsky's situation is quite different from that of the German Jews who lost their families during the era of National Socialism. Swiss Jews were safe from persecution, but they all had relatives in the occupied countries and they feared for their safety. Thus they too were affected by the fate of the Jews living abroad, and they were therefore confronted with the identity problem: Who are we compared to the others? That is why Lewinsky undertook the project he had had in mind for a long time: to write a family history of Swiss Jews over five generations. In spite of its length (nearly 800 pages), this book enjoyed great success and has already been translated into many languages.

Lewinsky studied the (local) history of Jewish families who had been living in the Swiss countryside for centuries. *Melnitz* is a novel written with the intention of giving these Jews something that those who once lived in Germany no longer have: a family history and the knowledge of a tradition that generates a common feeling of identity and affiliation to the cultural community. Lewinsky portrays the everyday life of the Jewish people who kept to their traditions and thus lived together with the other people in two villages and yet always somehow stood out as different. The story of the Swiss Jews begins in 1866 with the fall of the Second Empire and ends in 1937 with a strong link to Nazi Germany and the increasing persecution of German Jews. There is an epilogue concerning the end of the war in 1945. The narrator reports the various changes in Swiss society over the years; we also read about the gradual adaptation of the Jewish people to the ongoing process of secularization. In the nineteenth century the Jews remained faithful to their religious particularity. The strain of trying to fit into everyday life can easily be felt. The reader is confronted with waves of anti-Semitism as well as solidarity and periods of relatively equal treatment of the Jews.

Lewinsky's principal achievement consists in the connections he makes between contemporary historical events in Europe and the history of the family that unfolds in a backwater, away from the complexities of history. Thereby he imparts a degree of historical representativeness to the life of an extended Jewish family in Europe. From the outset, the none-too-large family has a number of international connections, for at the beginning of the story a distant relative from France marries into the family, later followed by another from Galicia. As they all speak Yiddish, albeit with different accents, they all understand one another.

The narration of the novel is focalized through an authoritative narrator who stands outside the story (heterodiegetic narration), which means that the reader's interest is focused totally on the characters and events. While Lewinsky thus chooses the most traditional way of narrating a family history, giving the prehistory of the Shoah, he starts and ends the novel with an unusual narrative setting: the return of an old ancestor who embodies Lewinsky's response to the Christian legend of Ahasver, the eternal Jew, condemned to wander across the world forever. Old Uncle Melnitz is one of the un-dead who returns to the place after every funeral: "Whenever he had died, he came back." He constantly reminds the Jews of their perennial, inevitable misfortune, thus representing the suffering individual who stands for the suffering of all Jews who know no Christ to bear their pain. The quoted sentence runs as a leitmotif through the novel and dominates the epilogue. Old Melnitz is given the last word to end the narrative with a brief account to the uninformed Swiss Jews of the events between 1937 and 1945, the years that were omitted from the narrative proper:

> He came back and reported. *Narrating made him come alive* [my emphasis]. New stories, he brought many new stories with him, each so fatally alive that the older ones faded away in comparison. . . . Stories that you could not believe, especially not here in Switzerland, where one had lived on an island all those years, on dry ground in the middle of the flood. . . . Melnitz . . . loved this country in which they would complain about hunger simply because there was shortage of chocolate. It was interesting to visit Noah's Ark after her thousand-year journey. (*Melnitz* 761)

Highlighting several well-known myths that the Swiss had lived with during the war years, the narrator represents memory and non-oblivion, tradition, and the connection between the living and the dead. At the end, he has the overview and tells the truth that people do not want to see or hear. Lewinsky uses the means of paradox and irony to express the contradictory fact that an ancient ancestor has to tell the survivors what had happened. At the same time, the realistic representation of the historically verified family history acquires a mythic and an ethical dimension, as Melnitz's narration represents the chances for a renewal of commemoration after the Shoah. The narrative dialogue between the ancestors and the new generation creates a sense of belonging and keeps tradition alive.[19] His narrations represent a kind of guarantee that the chain of generations will not be broken as long as there is someone to tell the others what has happened.[20] Conversely, it makes the loss caused by the Shoah to the other Jews more palpable. *Melnitz* is an important contribution to the history and identity of the Swiss Jews, as well as a significant contribution to the *travail de mémoire* that began in Switzerland at the end of the 1980s.

In connection with his research into the history of the Jews, and in spite of his fear of being marked down as a "professional Jew" and of boring himself by repeating the topic, Lewinsky, a nonbelieving Jew, wrote a text as a film script titled *Ein ganz gewöhnlicher Jude* (*A Quite Ordinary Jew*) (2005) which addresses the problem of how to live as a Jew in post-Shoah Germany.[21] Born after 1945, the protagonist Goldfarb is constantly confronted with the past. He feels he lives a marginalized life as a journalist; he is an outsider and what he dislikes most is demonstrative philo-Semitism. All he wants to do is to live as an ordinary man in Germany. One day he gets an invitation from a headmaster to come to his college and to speak to the students about his identity as a "Jewish citizen." Goldfarb feels it rather as an affront (just as Esther Dischereit dislikes this part of her job as a writer, as it gives her the feeling of being prostituted, exposed as a rarity [*Übungen* 205]). He would like to reject the invitation out of fear of reaching the conclusion that a normal Jew can never again exist in Germany.

The protagonist conducts an inner monologue, discussing the German–Jewish relationship in an attempt to collect all the reasons for his refusal to see the class. He looks at family pictures, remembering his mother's paranoia and the impact it had on him. He gets furious and highly subjective when remembering his adolescence because his whole upbringing consisted of warnings against everything that could result in "Risches" (Jewish for "anti-Semitic reactions") (*Ein ganz* 35). The sight of his wife and child hurts too. The personal relationship founders on Goldfarb's problematic identity, and he simply cannot get over something his wife said to him: "You have become so unbearably Jewish for someone who no longer wants to be one" (57).

Later Goldfarb starts typing. He continues to write during the whole night, finally falling asleep in the early morning. Some hours later he starts his class presentation with the words "Also gut!" (97) ("Now then!"), thus indicating that this night's controversy led him to the conclusion that he must accept it is his fate to live with two identities and always to be reminded of this by the perplexed questions of those whom he lives among. It seems clear that the problem is one with which Lewinsky himself is familiar and that writing about the conflict helped him to answer the question of how to live with his double identity. Goldfarb's fear is that there will never again be normality for such as him, only an everlasting exception: "That we will always be Jews in Germany, and never Jewish Germans" (81). This is Goldfarb's conclusion. It contrasts with Seligmann's position, although it is difficult to know how seriously to take the latter because of the ironic and sarcastic elements in his style. An important feature of Lewinsky's protagonist Goldfarb is the fact that writing serves him as the principal means of finding and creating his Jewish identity. The process will never be completed by the end of the night; rather, it has to be resumed and continued constantly in a debate with the past and a present that confronts German-speaking Jews with a quite unique challenge.

Conclusion

We have seen that all the authors mentioned have to struggle with their identity after having decided to live in Germany as Jewish writers. They share many likes and dislikes, but their literary means are different and so are their convictions. It is difficult to say what kind of impact Biller's and Seligmann's rejection of taboos will have in the long run. It seems that as writers they have to lay claim to the freedom to use precisely the means that they deem necessary, regardless of any objections that they are being indecent or inappropriate. In this respect they are no different from those writers of the first generation who felt compelled to use their artistic freedom to shape their material in accordance with their experiences, often in defiance of conventional expectations.

New generations are open to new perspectives and the prescriptions of the first generation survivors will become less influential. Will it make it easier to "overcome" the Holocaust, do away with prejudices between people when they are articulated openly? Or will the "rifts" be widened by citing the stereotypes and thus perpetuating them?[22] As the Shoah is losing ground in the communicative memory, it will gain more space in collective and cultural memory, but this will depend on *how* the events are passed on. The road passes through cultural storehouses such as literature, art, or museums, and *lieux de mémoire,* where personal memory too gains a more enduring form. The disappearance of the survivors represents a great loss because of the absence of direct personal experience, but on the social level there will be more possibilities of finding ways that are less restricted by existential factors. Like all forms of transmission, the disappearance of personal experience will make it easier to see the world from a different angle than earlier generations did, knowing that memory is a fragile thing. Maurice Halbwachs has made two important observations in this connection: First, "the present determines the past" (20). Second, Halbwachs speaks of the "social framing" of memories, a fact that explains the dissimilar shapes of narrations about the same happenings.[23] Many taboos that constrained the wartime generation will vanish when they are gone. They set a standard for the narratives about the various experiences of ghettos, camps, and other places of misery, narratives that will be questioned by younger historians and writers. What is said about the second generation applies even more clearly to the third: the grandchildren of the Holocaust victims who question the traditional way of remembering the Holocaust and who obviously no longer want their lives to be as deeply affected by the past as those of their parents were. They even feel free to reveal subjective attitudes free from political correctness, and they openly attack habitual attitudes from which the Jews profit because they provide them with an exceptional status (the "Auschwitz-bonus").

On the side of the perpetrators (to use this postwar term) too, the writings of the succeeding generations deal with the same kind of questions—the silence of the parents and the problem of identity after the rupture of civilization. To know that a father or a grandfather was responsible for war crimes in one way or another is a burden that affects a person deeply. To feel guilty for something that happened before one's birth becomes more and more inadequate. And the new generation of writers is willing to look at this problem from a different angle as well.

The fact that a future perspective also will include the civilians on the German side among the victims, what for some people is equal to the perpetrators, shows the ongoing change in the perception of the past. We have to face the fact that it will result in a more holistic view of the entire period. This does not mean that the Holocaust will lose its exceptional character and its importance, but the perspectives will complement each other.[24] The historian Reinhart Koselleck regards shared mourning as more important than the controversies around the question of comparability. He points out that by maintaining the division between victims and perpetrators, one follows the line of the Nazis who divided what once was a unity (205). We have to ask ourselves how long it shall take until this barrier is broken down and the language of memory becomes a common one (Rüsen 58–62).

According to Jörn Rüsen, we should also be aware that, contrary to a commonly held view, there are no grounds to believe that the greater the historical distance, the greater the objectivity. We live at the threshold between contemporary history and history. The loss of direct existential involvement can be compensated by careful critical interpretation of the material from today's perspective, a task in which historians and philosophers mainly are engaged, or by fictional approaches that open new perspectives through new aspects and by asking different questions. But as we all know: thresholds are difficult to cross. While writers have to break new ground, readers will be acquainted with displaced focuses and unfamiliar topics. As many narratives demonstrate, Germany cannot dispose of a common memory because the population has to live with a traumatized memory of the war in general and the Holocaust in particular.[25] Therefore we will find a notable preemphasis on the topic of the search for identity on the part of the German–Jewish writers as well as a relentlessly (self-) critical view of their own mental condition within the self-imposed fate of living in Germany.

Notes

1. See Irmela von der Lühe, 322nn6 and 8.

2. Fred Wander, *The Seventh Well* (*Der siebente Brunnen*), 1971, later edited again 1991, 1997, and 2005.

3. See also Ansgar Nünning, "'Memory's Truth' und 'Memory's Fragile Power': Rahmen und Grenzen der individuellen und kulturellen Erinnerung."

4. "Second generation" is used here, as by Harmut Steinecke and others, as a collective term for the second and the following generations.

5. Charles Lewinsky refers to this reproach, making his protagonist Goldfarb sarcastically use the cliché "There is no business like Shoah-Business" (*Ein ganz*, 56).

6. Many contributions of American critics who deal with German–Jewish writings focus on the status of Jewish–German coexistence as represented in their narratives. They concentrate on finding advances or setbacks for the future of a cultural symbiosis in postwar Germany. Mostly they conclude that there will be nothing more than a *negative symbiosis*. Compare the contributions in Sander L. Gilman and Hartmut Steinecke, eds., *Deutsch-jüdische Literatur der neunziger Jahre,* and Leslie Morris and Jack Zipes, eds., *Unlikely History.* The anthology edited by Hope Herzog et al., *Rebirth of a Culture,* also includes Austria in the survey. Stephan Braese discusses a great variety of cultural aspects in his various contributions. His essay "Writing against Reconciliation" gives a survey of, among others, Dischereit's, Biller's, and Seligmann's writing and this specific issue.

7. See Braese, *Die andere Erinnerung,* 7–24. This survey of relevant research reveals the difficulties experienced by German literary historians when dealing with the relationship between Germans and Jews represented in German literature after 1945.

8. See Seligmann's essay "What Keeps the Jews in Germany Quiet?" in Gilman and Remmler, eds., 173–83, in which he tells about his problems to get his books published.

9. Anat Feinberg, "Die Splitter auf dem Boden," gives a short overview over the characteristic as well as controversial standpoints of these authors.

10. The term is used by Gershom Scholem, Hannah Arendt, Esther Dischereit, Maxim Biller, and Rafael Seligmann. According to Dan Diner, the more adequate description of the relation between Germans and Jews after the Shoah is that of a "negative symbiosis." See Diner, "Negative Symbiosis" and "Über Schulddiskurse"; and Melissa Beegle, *Rafael Seligmann,* who elaborates on both terms.

11. Seligmann's discusses quite different identity problems of Jews living in Israel than Dischereit seems to identify in her texts.

12. In *Mein Judentum,* Jurek Becker answers the question of why he is a Jew simply by stating, "My parents were Jews." In the absence of anti-Semitism, he had not felt Jewish for a second. "I have no affiliation, no feeling of happiness, I do not know any Jewish traditions. I do not feel like a Jew, but I am one, so what?" (15). Becker also objected to being identified as a Jew and finds it unacceptable that a Catholic or a Protestant can leave his church, while a Jew has no such opportunity. He has to bear his identity as a kind of guilt. For Becker, the overt politeness and the pitiful reactions when Auschwitz is mentioned are enervating and enlarge the feeling of foreignness. It deprives Jews of their normality.

13. See Norbert Oellers, "Sie holten mich ein, die Toten der Geschichte," in Gilman and Steinecke, eds., 78–82, in which he discusses Dischereit's enigmatic title and analyzes her elaborate poetic technique that leaves much free space for interpretation to the reader.

14. In an interview with Willing Davidson in *The New Yorker,* Biller mentions the books of Malamud, Heller, Bellow, and Roth as inspirations, and Mordecai Richler as his greatest hero. See http://www.newyorker.com/online/2007/07/02/0707020n_onlineonly_biller. Accessed July 20, 2009.

15. Seligmann likes to parody public figures and to compare himself with American–Jewish authors like Philip Roth. Stein emphasizes the difference between American Jews and German Jews: while the latter are marginal, the former (minorities in the United States, including American Jews) belong to the U.S.–American mainstream even as minorities. Stein finds that Seligmann underestimates the difference between the old American–Jewish and the new German–Jewish literature. For a critical discussion of the relationship see Jefferson Chase on Philip Roth and Rafael Seligmann, 2001.

16. See Rita Bashaw, "Comic Vision and 'Negative Symbiosis,'" for an illuminating analysis that focuses on the conflict of comic vision and negative symbiosis in two of Biller's texts.

17. Characterizing Biller's writing as "counter-memory," Karen Remmler finds that compared to Dischereit, Biller focuses less on identity problems than on exposure, not worrying about political correctness. "Maxim Biller," 311. Biller and Seligmann deconstruct body and sexuality as images for the continuing social and cultural tensions between Germans and Jews, while Dischereit uses the female body per se as the expression of incorporated mourning. See "Maxim Biller," 314–15.

18. The protagonist in *The Auctioning of Rubinstein* does not hesitate to criticize his parents for this decision and to accuse them of weakness and cowardice in an extremely impertinent way.

19. See Bettina Bannasch and Almuth Hammer, "Jüdisches Gedächtnis und Literatur," 277–78, who show the importance of the connection between memory, historiography, and identity within Jewish tradition while secularization and acculturation exerted a negative influence on the culture of commemoration.

20. Hendrik Werner, in "Und da kam Onkel Melnitz," draws attention to the fact that Melnitz seems to occupy an intermediate position between Benjamin (death living on through memory) and Horkheimer (death is dead). Cf. also Fred Wander's belief in narration.

21. In the TV movie directed by Oliver Hirschbiegel, known from the film *Der Untergang* (*Downfall,* 2005), the well-known young actor Ben Becker plays the main character, Emanuel Goldfarb.

22. Katja Behrens used this expression in her speech "The Rift and Not the Symbiosis," given at the Weisman Art Museum, Minneapolis, in 2000. A printed version of the speech is included in Morris and Zipes, eds., 31–48.

23. See the discussions by Aleida Assmann, *Erinnerungsräume,* and Ansgar Nünning, "'Memory's Truth,'" of Halbwachs's topic in connection with Rushdie's term.

24. See articles about the controversies: Jörn Rüsen, "Die Logik der Historisierung," 19–60, and Diner, "Über Schulddiskurse und andere Narrative" (both in Gertrud Koch, ed., *Bruchlinien,* 61–84).

25. Looming large in Holocaust studies, the issue of traumatized memory offers rich and varied illustrations of the reciprocal relationship between memory and narrative. One indication of the complexity of traumatized memory of the Holocaust is that for the individual concerned it can be linked to as well as prompted by memories of all those involved in the event, including perpetrator, victim, and bystander. See Raul Hilberg, *The Destruction of the European Jews,* 3rd ed., who makes systematic use of this tripartite distinction; Arne Johan Vetlesen, *Evil and Human Agency,* especially 1–13 and 235–57; and the studies of Holocaust memory referred to above.

Works Cited

Assmann, Aleida. *Erinnerungsräume: Formen und Wandlungen des kulturellen Gedächtnisses.* Munich: C. H. Beck, 2003.

Bannasch, Bettina and Almuth Hammer. "Jüdisches Gedächtnis und Literatur." In Astrid Erll and Ansgar Nünning, eds., *Gedächtniskonzepte der Literaturwissenschaft: Theoretische Grundlegung und Anwendungsperspektiven,* 277–95. (Media and Cultural Memory 2). Berlin and New York: Walter de Gruyter, 2004.

Bashaw, Rita. "Comic Vision and 'Negative Symbiosis' in Maxim Biller's *Harlem Holocaust* and Rafael Seligmann's *Der Musterjude.*" In *Unlikely History: The Changing German–Jewish Symbiosis 1945–2000,* 263–76, edited by Leslie Morris and Jack Zipes, 265–76. New York: Palgrave, 2002.

Becker, Jurek. "Mein Judentum." In *Jurek Becker,* edited by Irene Heidelberger-Leonard, 15–24. Frankfurt am Main: Suhrkamp, 1992.

Beegle, Melissa. "Rafael Seligmann and the German–Jewish Negative Symbiosis in Post-Shoah Germany: Breaking the Silence." PhD thesis 2007. Bowling Green University. http://www.ohiolink.edu/etd/send-pdf.cgi/Beegle%20Melissa.pdf?bgsu1181192526. Accessed August 8, 2009.

Biller, Maxim. "Harlem Holocaust." In *Wenn ich einmal reich und tot bin: Erzählungen,* 76–122. Munich: Deutscher Taschenbuch Verlag, 1993.

———. *Deutschbuch.* Munich: Deutscher Taschenbuch Verlag, 2001.

———. *Der gebrauchte Jude: Selbstportrait.* Köln: Kiepenheuer & Witsch, 2009.

Braese, Stephan. *Die andere Erinnerung: Jüdische Autoren in der deutschen Nachkriegsliteratur*. Berlin and Wien: Philo, 2001.

——— et al., eds. *Deutsche Nachkriegsliteratur und der Holocaust*. Frankfurt am Main and New York: Campus, 1998.

———."Writing against Reconciliation: Contemporary Jewish Writing in Germany." In *Contemporary Jewish Writing in Europe: A Guide,* edited by Vivian Liska and Thomas Nolden, 23–42. Bloomington: Indiana University Press, 2007.

Chase, Jefferson. "Two Sons of 'Jewish Wit': Philip Roth and Rafael Seligmann." *Comparative Literature* 53: 1 (Winter 2001): 42–57. Published by Duke University Press on behalf of the University of Oregon. Article Stable URL: http://www.jstor.org/stable/3593477.

Diner, Dan. "Negative Symbiose: Deutsche und Juden nach Auschwitz." *Babylon* 1 (1986): 9–20.

———. "Über Schulddiskurse und andere Narrative." In *Bruchlinien: Tendenzen der Holocaustforschung,* edited by Gertrud Koch, 61–84. Köln, Weimar, and Wien: Böhlau, 1999.

Dischereit, Esther. *Joëmis Tisch: Eine jüdische Geschichte* [*Joëmi's Table: A Jewish Story*]. Frankfurt am Main: Suhrkamp, 1988.

———. *Übungen jüdisch zu sein: Aufsätze* [*Exercises on Being Jewish*]. Frankfurt am Main: Suhrkamp, 1998.

Dunker, Axel. *Die anwesende Abwesenheit: Literatur im Schatten von Auschwitz*. Munich: Fink, 2003.

Erll, Astrid and Ansgar Nünning. *Gedächtniskonzepte der Literaturwissenschaf: Theoretische Grundlegung und Anwendungsperspektiven*. Berlin and New York: Walter de Gruyter, 2005.

Feinberg, Anat. "Die Splitter auf dem Boden: Deutschsprachige jüdische Autoren und der Holocaust." In *Literatur und Holocaust, Literatur + Kritik* 144 (1999): 48–58.

Gilman, Sander L. and Karen Remmler, eds. *Reemerging Jewish Culture in Germany: Life and Literature since 1989*. New York and London: New York University Press, 1994.

Gilman, Sander L. and Hartmut Steinecke, eds. *Deutsch-jüdische Literatur der neunziger Jahre: Die Generation nach der Shoah* (Beihefte zur Zeitschrift für deutsche Philologie 11). Berlin: Erich Schmidt, 2002.

Halbwachs, Maurice. *Das Gedächtnis und seine sozialen Bedingungen*. Frankfurt am Main: Suhrkamp, 1985. Originally published as *Les cadres sociaux de la mémoire*. Paris: Alcan, 1925.

Heidelberger-Leonard, Irene, ed. *Jurek Becker*. Frankfurt am Main: Suhrkamp, 1997.

Hillberg, Raul. *The Destruction of the European Jews,* vols. 1–3. 3rd ed. 1992; New Haven: Yale University Press, 2003.

Hofmann, Michael. "Provokation durch Farce und Groteske." In *Literatur und Geschichte* (Beihefte zur Zeitschrift für deutsche Philologie 122), 232–45. Berlin: Erich Schmidt, 2003.

Hope Herzog, Hilary, Todd Herzog, and Benjamin Lapp, eds. *Rebirth of a Culture*. New York and Oxford: Berghahn Books, 2008.

Koch Gertrud, ed. *Bruchlinien: Tendenzen der Holocaustforschung*. Köln, Weimar, and Wien: Böhlau, 1999.

Koselleck, Reinhart. "Differenzen aushalten und die Toten betrauern: Der Mai 1945 zwischen Erinnerung und Geschichte." In *NZZ online* May 14, 2005. http://www.nzz.ch/2005/05/14/li/articleCSW54.html. Accessed July 24, 2008.

Lewinsky, Charles. *Ein ganz gewöhnlicher Jude* [*A Quite Ordinary Jew*]. Hamburg: Europäische Verlagsanstalt, 2005.

———. *Melnitz. Roman.* Munich: Nagel & Kimche, 2006.

Löffler, Sigrid. "Holocaust Literature Shifts Paradigms." www.dw-world.de. January 25, 2005. Accessed June 6, 2007.

Lühe, von der, Irmela. "'Osten, das ist das Nichts.' Grete Weils Roman *Tramhaltestelle Beethovenstraat* (1963)." In *Wechsel der Orte: Studien zum Wandel des literarischen Geschichtsbewusstseins. Festschrift für Anke Bennholdt–Thomsen,* edited by Irmela von der Lühe and Anita Runge, 322–33. Göttingen: Wallstein, 1997.

Morris, Leslie and Jack Zipes, eds. *Unlikely History: The Changing German–Jewish Symbiosis, 1945–2000.* New York: Palgrave, 2002.

Nünning, Ansgar. "'Memory's Truth' und 'Memory's Fragile Power': Rahmen und Grenzen der individuellen und kulturellen Erinnerung." In *Grenzen der Fiktionalität und der Erinnerung: Autobiographisches Schreiben in der deutschsprachigen Gegenwartsliteratur,* vol. 2, edited by Christoph Parry and Edgar Platen, 39–60. Munich: Iudicium, 2007.

Oellers, Norbert. "Sie holten mich ein, die Toten der Geschichte." In *Deutsch-jüdische Literatur der neunziger Jahre: Die Generation nach der Shoah* (Beihefte zur Zeitschrift für deutsche Philologie 11), edited by Sander S. Gilman and Hartmut Steinecke, 75–88. Erich Schmidt: Berlin 2002.

Oesterle, Günter, ed. *Erinnerung, Gedächtnis, Wissen: Studien zur kulturwissenschaftlichen Gedächtnisforschung.* (Formen der Erinnerung, vol. 26). Göttingen: Vandenhoeck & Ruprecht, 2005.

Remmler, Karen. "Maxim Biller: Das Schreiben als Counter-Memory." In *Shoah in der deutschsprachigen Literatur,* edited by Norbert Otto Eke and Hartmut Steinecke, 311–20. Berlin: Erich Schmidt, 2006.

Rüsen, Jörn. "Die Logik der Historisierung." In *Bruchlinien: Tendenzen der Holocaustforschung,* edited by Gertrud Koch, 19–60. Köln, Weimar, and Wien: Böhlau, 1999.

Seligmann, Rafael. "What Keeps the Jews in Germany Quiet?" In *Reemerging Jewish Culture in Germany: Life and Literature since 1989,* edited by Sander L. Gilman and Karen Remmler, 173–83. New York and London: New York University Press, 1994.

———. *Rubinsteins Versteigerung* [*The Auctioning of Rubinstein*]. 1991. Munich: Deutscher Taschenbuch Verlag, 2003.

Stein, Hannes. "Schm'a Jisruel, kalt is ma in die Fiß: Die neue deutschsprachige jüdische Literatur." In *Deutsche Nachkriegsliteratur und der Holocaust,* edited by Stephan Braese et al., 401–11. Frankfurt am Main and New York: Campus, 1998.

Steinecke, Hartmut. "Schreiben von der Shoah in der deutsch-jüdischen Literatur der 'zweiten Generation.'" *ZfdPh,* Sonderheft 123 (2004): 246–59.

Vetlesen, Arne Johan. *Evil and Human Agency: Understanding Collective Evildoing.* Cambridge: Cambridge University Press, 2005.

Wander, Fred. *Das gute Leben oder Von der Fröhlichkeit im Schrecken: Erinnerungen.* 1996. Göttingen: Wallstein, 2006.

———. *Der siebente Brunnen: Erzählung* [*The Seventh Well*]. Göttingen: Wallstein, 2005. (First published 1971, Berlin and Weimar: Aufbau. New York: International Publishers, 1976).

Werner, Hendrik. "Und da kam Onkel Melnitz." In *Welt Online,* February 4, 2006. http://www.welt.de/print-welt/article195527/Und_da_kam_Onkel_Melnitz.html. Accessed June 3, 2009.

Witte, Bernd. "Kulturelles Gedächtnis und Geschichtsschreibung im Judentum." In *Literatur und Geschichte: Neue Perspektiven*. (Sonderheft zur Zeitschrift für deutsche Philologie 11), edited by Michael Hofmann and Hartmut Steinecke, 195–208. Berlin: Erich Schmidt, 2004.

Young, James E. *Writing and Rewriting the Holocaust: Narrative and the Consequences of Interpretation*. Bloomington: Indiana University Press, 1988.

CHAPTER 3

Recent Literature Confronting the Past

France and Beyond

PHILIPPE MESNARD

Translated by TERENCE CAVE

First, a few words about my title. I have chosen to speak of "recent" literature in order to avoid the word "contemporary." The notion of the contemporary, of sharing the same time (whether the present time or the time of the event), remains open to question, and we shall in fact question it later via the opposition between the "news value" (*actualité*) of memory and "memorial renewal" (*actualisation*).[1] It is also important to point out that the word "recent" does not necessarily imply that we are concerned here with young writers: certain of them may be in their fifties or older. Joseph Bialot, who is well known for the score of detective novels he has written, had published nothing on his experience of the concentration camps until he produced *C'est en hiver que les jours rallongent* (*Days Seem Longer in Winter*).[2] Given that libraries assign this work to the shelf marked "eyewitness accounts," and that the detective novels may be regarded as one of the detours that the author, born in Warsaw in 1923, needed to make in order to come to terms with his private memory and a whole painful span of his existence, there is no doubt that since the end of the 1980s, his project as a writer has been overdetermined by a memorial context. It will be apparent here that the very notion of "generation" needs to be reviewed and relativized, at least as regards an emergence into language that brings together at the same moment a number of authors who, as we shall see, were in some cases born forty years apart. As for the expression "confronting the past," I have chosen it because it is sufficiently vast and vague to allow one subsequently to differentiate between history and memory as specific modes of relationship to the past, both being determined by violence and its consequences. Obviously, it does not mean that memory and history are anthropologically determined by violence whatever the context in which we think of them, but, in our *époque* and culture, the main meaning and custom of memory and history—that is, the hegemonic sense of memory and history, our *episteme,* as Foucault might say—is determined in that way.

In this respect, the 1970s mark a gradual shift in the meanings attached to many of the figures through which collective violence is represented—the cultural family, mapped closely onto history, that consists in particular of heroes, saviors, victims, traitors, political criminals, collaborators, and so on. Following the Second World War and decolonization, the economy of these representations in relation to one another can be seen to undergo a striking modification. The shift was crystallized and made permanent at the turning point of the decade 1980–90 with the breakup of the Communist bloc, but it had been set in motion long before. One of the dominant directions of the shift was explicitly determined by the memorial questions at the center of which the genocide of the Jews casts its somber light. The unique character of that event was now explicitly acknowledged, which previously had not been the case; from that point on, it has functioned as a horizon of reference, and even, in some people's view, as a paradigm.

A rereading of collective history then begins to take shape that focuses on civilian victims and those forgotten by official history. In the process, these become the subject of an increasing number of literary works and films, most of which grow out of family scenarios and finally become fully developed narrative schemas. Many theoretical and critical studies have been devoted to such questions, too, basing themselves primarily on textual corpuses. For example, Marianne Hirsch has proposed the concept of "postmemory," Susan Suleiman the expression "the 1.5 generation," while Dominique Viart, with his phrase "the family relation story (*récit de filiation*)" draws on a vast corpus that goes well beyond the Jewish genocide as such. The notion of "autofiction"—that is, a work labeled "novel" which nevertheless features the actual writer as its main character—constitutes another of these new theoretical tools.[3]

While situating myself in close proximity to these various reflections, I would like to approach the corpus by bringing to light certain of the conditions that, in parallel with the historical events the works in question refer to, have helped to make possible the writing of this recent literature. Subsequently, I shall discuss the principal tendencies and themes that have become prominent over the last fifteen years.

1. Narrative Conditions and Sequences

Within the framework of the approach adopted here, I shall limit myself to two questions. The first is the epistemic question of the family, which represents a central point of departure for each of the texts I shall examine. The second, operating at an epistemological level, strives to grasp the 1980s return to autobiography in particular, and to memory in general.

The Model Family and Its Histories

Why is the family located at the center of this memorial configuration? The political terrors of the twentieth century were determined by impulses of annihilation that impinged not only on individuals but also on their whole family, their genealogy, and their group culture. The realization by descendants of what their ancestors lived through has become an integral part of the way the very conception of the family is structured. Thus, many of the imaginary conceptions by which families define themselves have been reconstituted by default around the black hole of terror. Even the groups who are least affected are still burdened with suspicions about what their relatives may have done, or not done, during the war or the occupation period in order to save themselves. In this way, a whole series of possibilities opens up according to whether the family is Jewish, whether the father was in the Resistance, whether he was a passive civilian or a collaborator. Or even worse. In the specific German context, evidently the question of collaboration is not relevant. There are degrees and differentiations, ranging from those who were simple Nazis to those who were more involved in the terror system, all the way up to the Nazi, or worse, the SS staff. At the opposite end, we encounter those who helped Jews or those who participated actively in one of the Resistance movements (Catholic or Protestant or Communist). Would the filiation and its imaginary be sufficient to justify memorial writers when they choose to enter via the family door? In order to clarify the terms of that question, we need to take a brief look backward.

From the nineteenth century onwards, the family became an object, a site, and an agent of social regulation;[4] it remains today a primary site of subject formation and, as a corollary, one of the most powerful normative investments of our culture. In the process, it functions as a relevant indicator, as a sociologist would say, of the state of society, and in this context, of the type of relationship that society maintains with its past. This relationship has evolved in a manner similar to the shift of representations referred to above. In the 1960s and 1970s, the family was decried as harmful: it was considered responsible for the long-term survival of bourgeois values. Pasolini's *Theorem* (1968) or Ettore Scola's *Ugly, Dirty and Bad* (1976) identify the family as a focus of perversions and alienation. In 1971, the family becomes a pathogenic, ultraconservative milieu, both as seen through the lens of Ken Loach's camera and in the language of the anti-psychiatry movement: this is the moment when David Cooper writes *The Death of the Family*. Barthes denounces "The Father—that Talker" ("Au séminaire") in the very same year that he announces the "death of the author." Bourgeois norms become the object of a widely shared hatred.

With its cheap realism, the "mode rétro"[5] that began in the 1970s may have been a harbinger of the reversal that was to take place at the end of the 1980s, when the family became a positive focus of interest and people turned back to it, just as the authors who had previously flaunted the most neutral or "blank" mode of writing (*écriture blanche*) turned to autobiography. If it is with this past that present-day writers construct their family narratives, one may ask oneself whether that signifies a reinforcement of the family as an institution or whether it is not rather a different, non-"revolutionary" way of calling it into question, one that uses the past as a form of mediation.

The Rehabilitation of Autobiography

In 1968, Roland Barthes wrote his groundbreaking article with its categorical title "The Death of the Author." It ends on an irrevocable judgment, pronounced in a prophetic tone: "the birth of the reader must be paid for with the death of the Author." Barthes's disqualification of the author is formulated in the wake of a series of position-taking statements and essays produced by the *nouveau roman* school (of which Nathalie Sarraute's *L'Ère du soupçon* (*The Age of Suspicion,* 1956) was a precursor, followed by, among others, the essays of Alain Robbe-Grillet (written in a highly polemical tone), as well as by Barthes himself (*Le Degré zéro de l'écriture* [*Writing Degree Zero*], for example), by Julia Kristeva, and, more generally, by intellectuals and academics affiliated with non-Althusserian structuralism; to these one may also add Maurice Blanchot. In the 1980s, however, directly countering this erasure of the subject, there comes about a return to autobiography, coinciding with the increasingly persistent presence of memorial questions. Many narrative works bear witness to a shift in which one can perceive the convergence and partial overlapping of the story-telling frameworks of memory, the family, and biography. This trinity gives rise to a new direction that is loaded with significance.

Yet must we therefore conclude that the importance acquired by autobiographical issues and the renewed theoretical interest they elicited represent a genuine reversal of the previous situation? If it is true that from the 1950s to the 2000s, there is a shift from an uncompromising erasure of the subject to self-exhibition, this must rather be understood as the elaboration of new authorial configurations that draw their nourishment from the materials of memory, and vice versa—configurations arising from the dialectic between, on the one hand, the author and what he or she is the focus of (in particular at the level of subjectivity) and, on the other, his or her relationship to the world and to history. The very writers who were emblematic of self-erasure and intransitivity retune their literary awareness to the wavelength of autobiography, and thence (since we must avoid harboring the illusion that autobiography can ever be the shortest and only authentic route leading from the self back to the self) to the question of the subject. Nathalie Sarraute writes *Enfance* (*Childhood*) in 1983, Marguerite Duras *L'Amant* (*The Lover*) in 1984 and *La Douleur* (*War: A Memoir*) in 1985, and Robbe-Grillet *Le Miroir qui revient* (*Ghosts in the Mirror*) in 1984. And Barthes himself, having already published *Roland Barthes par Roland Barthes* (1975), takes the view in 1980 that one must henceforth "observe" a possible "return to the author" (*La Préparation* 276). This return to self, which is also an interplay between self and autobiography, leaves a margin broad enough to accommodate a powerful recharging of the question of genealogy, since autobiography as a genre does not fully account for the majority of the texts I have cited that bring together the family constellation in all its forms: the father figure, whether as a presence in Robbe-Grillet's *Le miroir qui revient* or as a painful absence in Claude Simon's *L'Acacia* (*The Acacia*) of 1989; the close, affectionate relationship between father and daughter in Sarraute's *Enfance,* where the mother figure, distant and clumsily egocentric, is desacralized; the mother again in Duras's *L'Amant,* or as a central structuring presence in Perec's *W ou le souvenir d'enfance* (*W, or the Memory of Childhood*), where the father rarely appears, or in *Roland Barthes,* and then again in Roland Barthes's *La Chambre claire* (*Camera Lucida*) (1980). Another way of putting it, however, would be that the literary program of self-effacement was incapable of resisting the attraction of the force field of memorial questions as they emerged in the 1980s. In that perspective, what occupies the foreground is the writer's whole relationship to society, his or her way of listening to it, being sensitive to it, permeable to it.

The Lure of the Memorial

The return to autobiography is present in works where memorial expression leads the subject to revisit the history of his or her family in the context of history in general, thus anticipating quite specifically the tendencies of recent literature. Let us consider an example from outside the corpus of writing in the French language. In 1976, Christa Wolf's novel *Kindheitsmuster* (*A Model Childhood*) already carries traces of this movement and, one might say, anticipates it. Her project in *Kindheitsmuster* is characterized by the "crabwalk" (*Krebsgang*)[6] long before Günter Grass made the word famous by using it in the title of one of his novels (*Im Krebsgang* 2002):

> The closer someone is to us, the more difficult it seems to be to say something conclusive about them: that's well known. The child who had crept away to hide inside me—has she come out? Or was she so startled that she looked for a deeper, more inaccessible hiding place? Has memory done its duty? Or has it allowed itself to be used to prove by its fallibility that it is impossible to avoid the deadly sin of our times, which is: not to be willing to discover one's own identity?
>
> And the past, which still had the power to impose its own linguistic rules and split the first person into a second and a third—is its authority shattered? Will the voices grow quiet?
>
> I don't know. (Wolf 530)

Christa Wolf here transmits the uncertainty that ties the past to the present via the figures of the parents and the self. In the course of a visit to the town, now in Poland, where she spent the first sixteen years of her life before fleeing the Soviet troops in 1945, Christa Wolf explores the past of her childhood through the mediation of the character little Nelly. The narrative unfolds at three levels: 1) the act of remembrance of that period, during which the child witnessed events and signs that are retrospectively clarified by meanings she was not able fully to grasp, but that seemed nonetheless evident; 2) a visit to the town in the summer of 1971; and 3) a self-conscious reflection on memory and the work that writing allows her to carry out to that end. The narrative construction thus consists in a to-and-fro movement between the present moment of narration and a narrated past interspaced with a critical reflexivity that preserves the distance between what took place and the *a posteriori* consciousness of an irremediable disaster. Although Perec was situated on the symmetrically opposite side (since his parents did not belong to a German "minority" [*deutsche Minderheit*] who had settled in Poland, but were Polish Jewish immigrants who had come to France to live their modest lives and were then persecuted by Vichy and the Nazis), the writing of *W ou le souvenir d'enfance* deploys a closely related approach: it aims at a reconstitution that, articulated on the two complementary levels of autobiography and fiction, carries within itself the knowledge that it will be impossible to fill the gap in an existence fractured by "l'Histoire avec sa grande hache" ("History with a capital H," where "capital" is also to be understood as in "capital punishment") (13).[7] The two approaches may be seen to move even closer together when one notes that Perec's project for this book had included a third level,[8] as in the three-dimensional structure of Wolf's novel, on the question of writing itself; although it did not appear as such in the final version of the work, its presence is visible throughout the whole text. An intermediate narrative level—this time specifically narrative, however— is likewise to be found in several of the novels of Patrick Modiano, who was born, we should recall, just after the war. There again, the expression of uncertainty, the "shifty" element, to use one of the author's own terms, is present from his earliest works, *La Place de l'Étoile* (1968) and *Les Boulevards de ceinture* (*Ring Roads*) (1971), in connection with his father who, probably by making shabby compromises, had managed to evade anti-Semitic persecution.

2. Memorial Permutations

The family, autobiography, and memorial investigation thus constitute the conditions for, and the limits within which, recent memorial literature was eventually to develop. I should like to present that literature here within the frame of two types of discourse: one a discourse of homage or celebration, the other of suspicion, the latter being the one that achieves by far the widest resonance while at the same time accommodating itself within the perspective opened up by the authors mentioned previously. In every case, the writer becomes the archeologist of his own genealogy; in the process, he selects a parental figure as a mediator between himself and history. This is perhaps also one of the few critical and heuristic resources still available to us today when we seek to confront history. What follows from that is the question of the impact of social discourse, the question of the permeability of certain of these texts to the memorial *doxa* that nowadays occupies the public sphere.

Paying Homage

Speaking of the problematics of the notion of filiation, Dominique Viart cites the dynastic fictions of Sylvie Germain: *Le Livre des nuits* (*The Book of Nights*) (1985); *Nuit d'ambre* (*Night of Amber*) (1987); and *Jours de colère* (*Days of Wrath*) (1989). Viart also demonstrates the importance of the double paternal and maternal line, the place assigned to ancestors, or the succession of generations, in Pierre Bergougnoux's *La Maison rose* (*The Pink House*) (1987), *L'Orphelin* (*The Orphan*) (1992), *La Toussaint* (*All Saints' Day*) (1994), and *Miette* (*Crumb*) (1995). To these examples one should add Jean Rouaud's series of novels, beginning with *Les Champs d'honneur* (*Fields of Glory*) (1990),[9] which are devoted to the maternal grandfather, then the father, then the mother; we shall return to Rouaud's work later. Even Michel Quint's *Effroyables jardins* (*Strange Gardens*) (2000) carries a dedication to the memory of the author's grandfather, "a miner who had fought at Verdun," and of the author's father, who "had fought in the Resistance" and was a teacher. "Contemporary writers take for granted their own fragility: it is this that prevents them, in their capacity as both authors and readers, from turning themselves into figures of authority," comments Dominique Viart (131).

"My father was no hero. For a long time, I would doubtless have preferred him to be one. At least so that I could boast about it" (Pachet 9). Pierre Pachet here brings out the dilemma of a mode of writing that no longer draws on classic models in order to evoke the figure of the father. This does not mean, however, that he liquidates "the Father," as certain writers of the 1970s would have done. Pachet belongs to a current of writing in which the father figure moves closer to the ordinary man he should always have been. He is not an anti-hero. The object is to deconstruct the myth of "my Father the hero" without destroying the paternal image. The writer gambles on being able to describe what remains while quietly taking apart the symbolic apparatus that made the father an inaccessible being, someone to be feared but admired. It is easy to associate what Pachet does in this book with Perec's description, in *W ou le souvenir d'enfance,* of his father as a man struck down by a fatal chance that carried with it neither glory nor cowardice. Alternatively, one might recall what Régine Robin says about her father, whose glimpse of Lenin on his white horse crossing the river Bug she conflates with Fabrice's encounter with Napoleon at Waterloo (Robin 1–108).[10] Similarly, in *La Place* (*A Man's Place*), Annie Ernaux speaks about her father with rigorous dignity and no trappings: during the Occupation, he is "the hero of the supply-lines" (44). Or again, a sober idealization of the father may be constructed around a sense of absence and disappearance.[11] One wonders whether it is not by bringing the Father down from his pedestal that the author is himself or herself able to shift to a different narrative and personal position and thence emerge from the illusion of mastering the world through the text.

The Double Bind of Uncertainty, the Double Release of Writing

Certain authors, however, allow what are clearly false notes to slip in. Art Spiegelman gives us a portrait of his father, an Auschwitz survivor, that is often unappealing. Ruth Klüger, deported with her mother, lets her resentment show: "I don't think I've ever forgiven her. That other person I would have become, if only I had been allowed to say a word, if she had not treated me purely and simply as her property" (Klüger 63).[12] What is one to do with the "primeval soup," she then goes on to ask. The answers are many, but they all carry with them suspicion and ambiguity: a real violence that refers to the family as a focus for neuroses, as a source of secrets—ones that one may perhaps have to spirit away by turning them into enigmas—as an originary scene where the place assigned to the ogre (the father or grandfather, or sometimes the brother) assumes historic dimensions, as we shall now see.

The sense of uncertainty that is in play here is expressed in a direct, critical form along the double axis of the parental past and of literary traditions. This angle of approach, which was already apparent in the French Romantics, is undoubtedly germane to those who feel that they have inherited a past they would not necessarily have wished for, a past through which their parents moved or where they themselves may have been on the scene. The arousal of consciousness that is thus set in motion does not only move outwards (toward family members, literary traditions); it also involves the intimate domain of the subject, inciting it to engage in a self-reflexive dialogue. Marc Weitzmann's *Chaos* (1997), Lorette Nobécourt's *Horsita* (1999), and Catherine Cusset's *La Haine de la famille* (*Family Hatred*) (2001) may be cited here as examples. All three narrators settle their scores with a very close family member who has deceived them or whose behavior carries connotations of falsehood.

Chaos draws on the biblical model of Abel and Cain as reconfigured by modernity and psychoanalysis in order to place on the stage a brother, a Holocaust denier who, as the editor of a "New" historical review, apparently purloined their grandfather's manuscript, written during the Resistance. The personal history of the narrator's principal friend, a historian born in 1947, is itself freighted with his father's past in the notorious Vichy militia. In *Horsita*, it is the father who plays the role of the bad lot as seen by his daughter Hortense, the narrator: she reads the father's personal diary, passed on to her by François (the uncle of her lover Samuel, both of whom are Jewish). She discovers that her father was apparently a collaborator who had taken part in the looting of Jewish property and who had also joined the SS. It turns out, however, that the diary is a fake, invented wholesale by Samuel's uncle. The structure of the text remains relatively complex, with split narratives and flashbacks, the presence of a child as a focalizing character and a female narrator who interpolates an episode recounting a visit to San Salvador. The use of different typefaces increases the "broken" character of the text, thus reflecting the psychological anguish of the narrator who finds she has become a prisoner of the inquiry she is conducting into her father's life:

> A construction site! that's what we are, a site for the erection of some kind of witches' sabbath! And in the end it will be language itself that will bury us all, I wish I could experience everything so I could tell you everything, death included, that bellowing of consciousness as it is burned alive, words are executioners, syntax has drilled its way into our skull! (244)

In *Chaos,* the narrator's brother makes away with the grandfather's manuscript: as a result, "its disappearance blocks all means of access to the family heritage" (101–2). What is more, the narrator finds that he has to lie in order to cover up for his brother. Likewise, in Alain Nadaud's *La Fonte des glaces* (*The Melting of the Ice*) (2000), the grandfather's dossier, "bought at a sky-high price" in a hurry, turns out to be "truncated or composed of dubious documents. The moment the pages are put back in their right order, the fact becomes obvious: none of these archives is an original" (41). In this way, not only is the very notion of a written document heavily invested with inauthenticity, thus indirectly shifting the debate to the question of fiction, but the narrator is deceived and abused. This theme, in its feminine aspect, is also endowed with a sexual sense. Horsita, the imaginary double of the female narrator in the novel of that name, has been raped: the abuse thus spreads from mind to body, driving the subject as a whole to a point where it faces possible destruction. A similar situation occurs in Sylvie Germain's *L'Enfant Méduse* (*The Medusa Child*) (1991), which we shall be considering later. As it happens, what is in the news in the late 1990s suggests a connection with literature here. Thus, for example, many a story, from Christine Angot's to Annie Ernaux's, was inspired by media coverage of incest and violence to minors. With the figure of the brother for Germain, and more generally the figure of the father, the site of authority and power is wholly overthrown and obliterated.

In Catherine Cusset's *La Haine de la famille,* which is less parodic than *Chaos* and less experimental in its writing than *Horsita,* it is the mother who, in chapter V ("1943"), appears in the guise of a cheat. She capitalizes on the fact that she was apparently "semi"-traumatized by the arrest of her own mother—in other words, the grandmother of the female narrator. The grandmother herself is treated as a hero, whereas the mother is thoroughly ridiculed. In contrast to the female family line (and one should recall that the transmission of Jewishness passes through the maternal line), the father is "of French stock." He is derisively presented as "apolitical," even though he worked for the "fascist paper *Gringoire.*"

These novels are very much in harmony, as it happens, with the 1990s, the period following the fall of the Berlin Wall, and they respond more or less explicitly to the reference points of a horizon of expectation dominated by the memorial and by the question of the victims. It is in this broader context that we must now consider this "recent literature."

"Social Discourse" and Its Effects

Family questions and secrets over three generations; the genocide of the Jews as "memorial news" (*actualité mémorielle*), with denial as its corollary; the written text as fake; a critique of the blurring of the boundary between fiction and reality and a calling into question of literary illusion; even incest and crimes within the family—such are the problematic concerns that many recent novels share with the current (*actuel*) horizon of expectation. Satisfying that expectation generally means causing no upsets and no disappointments, conjuring up prospects of consolation and redemption, if only by showing that life is possible "afterwards." The observation that literary texts are tuned in to the horizon of expectation is corroborated by the fact that these writers are highly permeable to what Marc Angenot has called "social discourse."[13] They borrow from it both its memorial lexicon and the historical references that motivate and shape it. One even finds, recurring from one text to another, little standard scenarios, narrative micro-models as it were, that reinforce the process of historical connotation. Among these are the opposition between a "Resistance" and a "collaborationist" past; the looting of Jewish goods, which occupied the front pages in the 1990s in the form of the scandal of Nazi gold reported to be held in Swiss banks; the stereotypes of the bureaucrat or the pallid snooper in the archives who turns out to be a counterfeiter; and so forth.

There is thus an important distinction to be made when it comes to recent works. Texts that are permeable to the mood of the day and the impact of fashions exploit the news value (*actualité*) of memory, whereas those that operate by means of memorial renewal (*actualisation*) translate what took place into terms that are compatible with the present time; the object of such translation is that the process of transmission should have its effect, yet without giving rise to the belief that a permanent, successful act of mourning is possible where crimes have been committed that bordered on the very limit of what is human, attempting to destroy it root and branch. The news value of memory is a vast cultural phenomenon that always seems to stifle the energies of memorial renewal, if only because it is always inclined to chatter, whereas genuine transmission requires silences and intervals for reflection.

Perhaps as a result of the interaction between the public news value (*actualité*) of memory and an ethics of transmission, the conditions under which memorial references are reorganized undergo an evolution. The memorial paradigm is flexible, nourished and energized by the tensions between different memories,[14] which in turn proliferate with the emergence of discourses of recognition, demands for justice, and the bringing to light of stretches of history repressed by the political authorities. Although in France the memory of Algeria is present in a number of novels (e.g., Clémence Boulouque's *Sujets libres* [*Free Subjects*] of 2005), it is the 1914–18 war that has acquired the greatest news value (*actualité*) in the domain of the novel. Published a year before Sébastien Japrisot's *Un long dimanche de fiançailles* (*A Very Long Engagement*) (1991), Jean Rouaud's *Les Champs d'honneur* (1990) was certainly a text that anticipated the relaunch of this theme; a considerable number of historical studies on the subject were also published in the 1990s, writing the First World War into the archive of the twentieth century as one of the greatest crimes of the modern world.

At times, the exercise of writing attempts to expose a genealogy of crime. For example, in *Les Champs d'honneur,* the horror of the scene where soldiers are gassed on the front, north of Ypres, provides a premonition of "the future death-camps" (146). Other examples include references to Buchenwald (157) or the firebombing of Dresden (173) in the closing pages of the same author's *Des Hommes illustres* (*Of Illustrious Men*). François Bon, in *Buzon's Crime,* also interpolates the following reference, although it is foreign to the plot: "The gas was a can thrown at human height, the corpses had been burnt by human hands . . ." (46). At other times, the writer's personality gives way to the narcissistic attractions of an easy audience response. "Tomorrow, on

Tuesday, she will be eight months old. I know: when she came out, it was from me. It was horrifying. A thousand times worse than Auschwitz," writes Christine Angot at the beginning of *Léonore, toujours* (*Leonora, Forever*) (12). And two-thirds of the way through, one finds this: "Last night I dreamt of a German called Angst who had been raped. The Jews had taken him prisoner, then tortured him. Since my father, my dreams have become perverted. [. . .]" (103), and it continues in the same way, following a script that is half sadomasochistic, half incestuous. As a more recent example of these effects of fashion, one may cite Amélie Nothomb's *Acide sulfurique* (*Sulphuric Acid*) (2005), where the system of the concentration camps, with its matriculation numbers and its kapos, constitutes the semantic universe of the novel. One may well ask whether history at large, the history of the "great" crimes and wars, is not in some sense conscripted here as a decor within which to approach the central anthropological question of the suffering body.

Philippe Claudel, with his *Les Âmes grises* (*Grey Souls*) (2003), which won the Renaudot Prize, is one of the latest authors so far to have been inspired by the Great War. Situated behind the front lines, his novel features the sordid murder of a little girl and a police investigation. The author thus displays his ability to listen with particular attention to the "sensitive" themes that are carried by the media and on which, in the process, the pathos of the moment is focused. Sylvie Germain draws on the Christological theme *par excellence* of the suffering that is written on the body, at the interface between individual and collective crime, and situates it in the perspective of the disappearance of the body. In her novel *L'Enfant méduse* (*The Medusa Child*) (1991), the 1939–45 war is present only in the background, but it determines the reflection on violence and its transmission that is carried by the story as a whole. Lucie Daubigné is a quiet, innocent child up to the day when her elder half-brother Ferdinand begins to crucify her. He subjects her to ritual rape and reduces her to such a state of moral and physical degradation (she turns into a thin, ugly creature, filled with hate) that she shuts herself away in her secret shame. It turns out not only that the father of the (half-) brother was killed at the front but also that his body was smashed to pieces by a shell. "Lieutenant Morrogues's death could not be doubted, yet his corpse did not exist" (85). Brought up by his mother to believe in the sacredness of his striking resemblance to his father, Ferdinand becomes a "living tomb" (78) to his father's memory and thereby a monster. The irreversible disappearance of bodies was given a new meaning by the genocide of the Jews, which from then on became established as the cultural prism through which it was possible to interpret, or reinterpret, every disappearance of a body.

Sylvie Germain's many books include a biographical essay on Etty

Hillesum[15] and, more recently, a story with a Nazi background, *Magnus* (2005). Since the beginning of her career, she has thus been asking the same question: can an inheritance that comes out of the void be anything other than pathogenic? Can it produce anything other than monsters? It becomes clear, then, that one strand (but not all) of the literature of our day is capable of taking responsibility for transmission by giving currency to the questions that haunt our civilization—or by giving its ghosts the form of a question, thus opening up the possibility of comprehension. The issues of radical violence that are peculiar to the modern world have been so powerfully brought into focus in our day by the genocide of the Jews that authors seem irresistibly drawn to integrating it into their narrative or even using it as their subject matter. This is the case with Philippe Claudel's *Rapport de Brodeck* (*Brodeck's Report*) (2007) and in particular Clémence Boulouque's *Nuit ouverte* (*Open Night*) (2007). Among the other factors (both events and discourse) that have undoubtedly set in motion these memorial associations, there can be no doubt that the Rwanda genocide of 1994 and the ethnic cleansing in the former Yugoslavia (1992–95), the Srebrenica massacre, for example, have played an important part. The "disappeared" of the Argentinean dictatorship should also be taken into account. But they too are often interpreted with a reference to the Shoah somewhere in the background.

3. Was My Grandfather a Nazi?

The narrative schema we have been considering and the approach that underpins it become unavoidable for a considerable number of sons and grandsons from the country where it all began, Germany. In that sense, the title of the book by Harald Welzer, Sabine Moller, and Karoline Tschuggnall, *"Opa war kein Nazi"* (*"Grandpa Wasn't a Nazi"*), exemplifies the impulse that one might describe as an awakening of consciousness leading to a desire to investigate the past. In this instance, instead of a fictional inquiry conceived by a French writer, as with Denis Lachaud's *J'apprends l'allemand* (*German Lessons*) of 1998, one encounters an approach in which a tension is established between fictional projection and autobiography, as, for example, in *In den Augen meines Großvaters* (*In My Grandfather's Eyes*) by Thomas Medicus, a German born in 1953. The author came of age just after the consciousness-raising movement that, in Germany after 1968, incited children violently to denounce their fathers' Nazi past. His grandfather had been the only Wehrmacht general to be killed in Italy: "A German Wehrmacht general who was fatally wounded in 1944 in a partisan ambush in Tuscany and who bears the Italian family name Crisolli—that configuration, as complex as it was accidental, appeared to me, with all of its factual character, as the subject for a novel, as a literary challenge" ("'Comprendre'" 93).

Various factors were responsible for Thomas Medicus's decision to embark on this adventure, mingling the biographical, autobiographical, and fictional genres. In the first place, in 1989, after the fall of the Wall, it became easy to travel to Eastern Europe and visit Poland, where his family had settled. Second, the 1990s were of course a period of intense commemorative activity. There was the long debate on the Holocaust Monument in Berlin, and in particular, the great "Crimes of the Wehrmacht" exhibition that began in 1995 and was shown throughout Germany and Austria. This photographic exhibition might well be considered as comparable, *mutatis mutandis,* to the broadcasting of the television serial *Holocaust* in 1978. It sensitized Medicus, and many other Germans, to questions that had not been raised until then, from that point of view, about the massacres in which the Wehrmacht had taken part or which they had supported logistically on the Eastern Front. Another biographical factor is the death of Medicus's father at age forty-nine, the same age that his grandfather died: as he reaches this critical year, Medicus is himself gripped by the fear of death. It is against this background that, in 2001, his inquiry begins.

Inquiries flourish on clues and documentary sources. "I decided to do some research on Wilhelm Crisolli and solve the enigma of his death. I had some papers in my possession" (*In den Augen* 54). In 1986, when his grandmother died, he received an envelope containing fifty-one photographs of his grandfather taken in Italy and Denmark. It is not until fifteen years later, encouraged by the events we have mentioned above, that Medicus exploits the potential of this material. He now begins to ask questions about the photographs. Ever since the opening sentences of Modiano's *Boulevards de ceinture* (1971) or Perec's *W ou le souvenir d'enfance* (1975), the photograph is recognized as one of the major topoi of memorial investigation, whether mediated by the literary text, by cinema, or by other art forms. It endorses an external narrative point of view that makes it clear that the author knows a good deal less than is hidden beneath the surface of reality, thus setting in motion—and in that sense justifying—the logic of the inquiry as a whole and of its referential grounding.

The first phase takes Medicus to Poland, where he attempts to capture the local atmosphere. Moved by a romantic impulse, he dwells more on the landscapes than on the people. In any case, claiming that his book belongs to the genre of "travel narrative," he tells us that he sees himself as belonging to "a rich literary tradition" in which the human figure and the landscape form "a kind of mythical unity" ("'Comprendre'" 88). Then the tone changes, and so does the approach. He now conducts his inquiry in Italy. He consults the military archives and meets Carlo Gentile, a historian who really exists. Where the facts are not sufficient, he entrusts himself to the powers of literary imagination (*literarische Einbildungskraft*) (*In den Augen* 235). On the technical level, he uses shifts of point of view in order to construct a plurality of perspectives. Thus he imaginatively inhabits the mind of his grandfather and proceeds to elaborate a fictional version of Crisolli's family life. The photographs take their place here to mark the phases of the narrative and provide support for the quest, while at the same time setting aside within the realm of what can be said the unknown quotient of what can be seen. What, then, is the project around which this set of procedures is articulated?

The grandfather is present in the narrator's life only under the auspices of death: this principle is maintained throughout, from his family's evocations of him up to the scene where his body is transferred to a military cemetery. The object, in other words, is to elucidate the grandfather's death, not his life. This is the reason why Medicus is not interested in the Eastern Front—at least, that is how he justifies it. The only episode included from that period is the description by a female cousin of Crisolli's refusal to obey an order given by one of his superiors, an act of resistance that had acquired an almost mythical status (213–14, 222). One is not dealing here, then, with an attempt at biographical reconstitution, and still less with a hagiography. Medicus insists on his grandfather's responsibility for a crime (the murder of a priest and two women) committed in Italy (193), giving him the benefit of no attenuating circumstances. He affirms unequivocally (perhaps a shade too unequivocally) that he was a criminal (*Täter*), citing in support the files of the twentieth Luftwaffen-Felddivision.

This parental figure whom Medicus experienced only via his disappearance provides him with traces, minimal footholds, in the backward, upstream journey of his identity as he brings it face-to-face with his genealogy, or rather his hypothetical genealogy. In that sense, the fact that his grandfather died before he was born frees him from one of the constantly recurring stereotypes of such literature and, as it were, of culture itself: the memory of the "kind old grand-dad" who bounces his grandson on his knee and then, on further inquiry, turns out to be a wicked ogre (a stereotype of which Lachaud has availed himself abundantly). If Medicus does not formulate his relation to his grandfather by way of the topos of disclaimed affection, he nonetheless recognizes a kind of idealization thwarted by fascination/repulsion (62).

The real element of the unknown concerns the subject "Medicus" (or what he will become after the age of forty-nine). "My grandfather appeared to me as the vanishing point of my biography, towards which ran the converging lines of what I had done and what I had not done, what I have become and what I have not become" (54). Elsewhere, the technical advantage of the shifts in point of view also licenses the more ambiguous game—which Medicus plays in the mode of fictional projection, making claims to empathy—of taking the place of a murderer.

> If I wanted to know as much as possible about Wilhelm Crisolli, there was only one approach I would adopt which could not be limited to the collection of mere facts. As the title of my book indicates, I risked making the experiment of discovering how the career officer who was my grandfather had observed his world, and what experiences I could read in that gaze of his which I found captured in different photographic portraits. ("'Comprendre'" 84)

One may then wonder whether one is not dealing here with a literature that achieves expression through the tension between the memorial approach and the emergence of a new autobiographical approach that handles life through the mediation of the figure of a dead person who disappeared from the scene at the age the author has reached at the moment he begins to write. That would invite one to reflect on the place of the dead person—an impossible place—as a focus for the story, as a *position* to occupy in order to open up the possibility of narrative and narrative as possibility. Thus the act of narration conjures into reality the possibility of an impossibility in order to give itself enough distance—for mediation always means taking one's distance—for its own operations without wanting to turn the text into a scene of judgment. Medicus makes it quite clear that he wishes to be neither the plaintiff, nor the defendant, nor the judge. "The only role that I dared to take on was that of the investigator (*Ermittler*)" (*In den Augen* 239). To avoid making a judgment in order to understand the criminal, yet without pardoning him, is something like the approach Primo Levi proposes in order to handle the grey zone of collaboration (24–52). For Medicus, the object is to weigh up the probable and the improbable (*In den Augen* 245).

At the end of the book, the narrator hears that an Italian is writing a novel about a Wehrmacht general. His immediate response is to carry on with his enquiry, but then he stops and offers us instead a conclusion that enjoins reconciliation with oneself:

> To see oneself reflected every day, from one year to the next, perhaps for ever, in the eyes of one's grandfather, appeared to me not to be the most

helpful means of finding one's way out of the labyrinth of *damnatio memo-riae,* the erasure of memory. It was important to remember, but also to forget. (248)

The questioning and the inquiry are not directed primarily toward the discovery of identity; their purpose is to allay the pain of mourning. Such mourning would be not so much for the loss of a family member to whom the subject was presumably closely attached as for the historical event itself, once the subject has taken responsibility for facing up to what took place. In that sense, Crisolli could be said to have been a figure of mediation, making it possible to assume a position not in history itself, which is no longer possible, but face-to-face with the history that the inheritors never wanted.

4. A Brief, General Synthesis

Taken as a whole, these works are characterized, on the one hand, by a writing protocol that combines a complex schema with a narrative logic and, on the other, by the interaction of two kinds of temporal relation, which may also be described as questions.

Let us begin with the writing protocol. The schema in question proves in fact to be mixed, blending a narrative schema with a family schema. This composite structure enables it to serve as a prism through which the narrator, embarking on a quest for his or her own identity, may revisit his family history from the perspective of history at large, and vice versa. The writer then seeks to elucidate the identity of one of his relations; the father is often here a referential construction, one enigmatic aspect of which is linked to an experience that took place, in particular, between 1939 and 1945 and, more generally, in the course of some major historical event. The narrative logic, for its part, gives the schema its dynamic movement and its temporality: it is a logic of enquiry. Combining as it does the detective scenario with the hermeneutic quest, the enquiry focuses on the question of the crimes committed and of guilt. In the process, it brings out the influence of the narrative structures of the *roman noir* on literature in general, which in turn makes sense of these political crimes by establishing their close connection with other crimes, especially those that take place within the framework of the family (incest, the massacre of a whole family by one of its members, etc.).

The interaction of the two temporal questions is situated on an entirely different level. It allows an approach that takes as its starting point the tension between the notions of *actualité* and *actualisation,* which are two specific modes of relation to the time of the event as referential object. The news value (*actualité*) of memory is a product of operative media-related and institutional factors that make memory present in an extreme degree, indeed omnipresent, in the total set of discourses that traverse the domain of the social and establish themselves as the *doxa,* to the point where memory becomes a recurrent frame for our vision of the world (Marc Angenot's notion of "social discourse" is particularly appropriate here). There is a real danger that this "presentification" of memory, a specifically cultural phenomenon of which entry into the economic sphere is only one derivative form, will reify what happened or turn it into a mere cliché. More precisely, the complexity of the event itself is constantly exposed to the risk of being sacrificed to facilitate communication or indeed consumption, where "communication" means overdetermination by the constraints of reception. As we have seen, there are a considerable number of authors who rehearse these effects within their works with a greater or lesser degree of critical distance. As for *actualisation,* it draws on a virtually contrary logic. It consists in the labor of translating an experience with the aim of transmitting it. For even if the historical character of translations shows that the same text is translated differently from one period to another, it remains true that the criterion against which the translation is judged must always be the source text and not, as is often feared, the context of reception, which is in any case not necessarily the same as the target context. It is on the basis of this set of narrative procedures and this tension between two kinds of temporal relation that the corpus of memorial literature offers itself for interpretation.

Yet if one can establish a proximity of this kind between literature and the norms of the moment, the *actualité* of memory, can literature be said to retain its critical power? The reply to this question surely holds no surprises, since between doubt and certainty, the fictional and the factual, autofiction and autobiography, but also between love and hate, mourning and melancholy, this memorial literature, which is also a literature of destabilized identities, can find no definitive answers to the questions it asks. The quest does not end in the discovery of an identity, but rather serves to demonstrate, and sometimes to harness, the fragility of identity. At the same time, to come closer to one's own identity by revisiting one's family via history writ large is also to gain a footing in the history that is staking its claim in our day through a permanent act of remembrance. What really matters for these authors, I would argue, is to take up their position in that memory—not having participated in the events themselves—and strive to use it as a way of gaining some measure of the detachment that emotion will not allow. Perhaps it is in this tension that one may locate the resistance point of literature to the pressure of memorial *actualité*. Perhaps it is at that exact point that literature in particular and the arts in general insert dialectic into the cultural sphere.

Notes

1. [Translator's note:] The opposition between *actualité* and *actualisation,* which plays a key role in the argument of this article, cannot be translated into English as it stands while preserving the same connotations. The adjectival form *actuel* means "belonging to the present moment," "current," "topical"; the noun *actualité* means "current events," and in the plural, "news" (as in "the television news"). I have attempted to preserve something of the opposition here by using the expressions "news value" and "memorial renewal"; elsewhere, I have sometimes varied these expressions to suit the context. Wherever *actualité, actualisation,* or (occasionally) a related word is used, I have added the French word in parentheses after the translation so that the reader can track the argument through. The opposition is lucidly redefined toward the end of the essay, so there should be no doubt about its sense and import.

2. [Translator's note:] Translations of titles (provided only for primary sources, not for critical works and the like) are in most cases those of published versions. Where I have not been able to find a published English translation, I have translated the title myself or (as here) used a plausible version from an Internet site. No translation is given for titles consisting only of names or of words having the same meaning in English. Translations of titles are provided only at the first mention of the work. Where a text is quoted, I have provided the page reference for the original version, not the translation. All translations of quoted passages are my own.

3. See Doubrovsky.

4. See Donzelot; de Singly; Attias-Donfut, Lapierre, and Segalen.

5. On the "mode rétro" and its relation to memories of the Occupation in France, see Rousso, 149–56.

6. "Earlier drafts began differently: with flight—when the child was almost sixteen—or with the attempt to describe the work of memory as a crabwalk, as a laborious backwards movement" (Wolf 11).

7. [Translator's note:] Perec is punning here on the name of the letter "h" in French, which is a homonym of the French word for "axe": thus literally, "History with its capital 'H' / with its great axe."

8. See Lejeune 89ff.

9. Followed by *Des Hommes illustres* (*Of Illustrious Men*) (1993), *Le Monde à peu près* (*The World, More or Less*) (1996), *Sur la scène comme au ciel* (*On Stage as in Heaven*) (1999).

10. [Translator's note:] The reference here is to a scene at the beginning of Stendhal's novel *La Chartreuse de Parme* (*The Charterhouse of Parma*).

11. See Hirsch.

12. This sentence does not appear in the English edition, which was written (and revised in places) by Klüger herself.

13. See Angenot 13ff. In defining "social discourse," Marc Angenot explains that it is

a question of the "generic systems," the "repertoires of topics," the "sequence rules for utterances that, in a given society, organise the *sayable*—what can be narrated and asserted [the narratable and assertable]—and guarantee the discursive division of labour" (13ff.). In the pages that follow, he insists in particular on the "generalized and hegemonic interactive features of [social discourse]." If social discourse may easily be seen as analogous to ideology, there is nonetheless a difference: the meanings that it carries outstrip both in quantity and in organization those circulated by ideology and introduce cultural elements that are not subject to ideology's surveillance.

14. It is therefore necessary here to make a critical reassessment of what some call "competition between victims" (*concurrence de victimes*), with particular reference to Jean-Michel Chaumont's book (Paris: La Découverte, 1997), which uses the phrase as its title. If there may sometimes be rivalry and conflict (terms that do not connote the market as "competition" does), these are only epiphenomena of memorial historicity itself, which functions by a differentiation of memories one from the other and, in the process, by creating an effect of stimulation, promotes mourning and rationalization in a society historically marked by violence.

15. Hillesum was a young Dutch Jew, an intellectual, who was deported to Auschwitz in 1943 and subsequently died there. She is well known for her diary, *Het verstoorde leven* (*An Interrupted Life*).

Works Cited

Angenot, Marc. 1889. *Un état du discours social.* Quebec: Le Préambule, 1889.

Angot, Christin. *Léonore, toujours.* Paris: Stock, 1994.

Attias-Donfut, Claudine, Nicole Lapierre, and Martine Segalen. *Le Nouvel Esprit de la famille.* Paris: Odile Jacob, 2002.

Barthes, Roland. "Au séminaire." *L'Arc* 56 (1974): 54.

———. "La mort de l'auteur." (1968). *Essais critiques IV, Le Bruissement de la langue.* Paris: Seuil, 1984. 61–67.

———. *La Préparation du roman I et II, Notes de cours et de séminaires au Collège de France, 1978–1979, Séance du 19 janvier 1980.* Paris: Seuil, 2003.

Bon, François. *Le Crime de Buzon.* Paris: Minuit, 1986.

de Singly, F., ed. *La Famille: l'etat des savoirs.* Paris: La Découverte, 1991.

Donzelot, Jacques. *La Police des familles.* Paris: Minuit, 1977.

Doubrovsky, Serge. "Autobiographie/vérité/psychanalyse." *L'Esprit Créateur* 20.3 (1980): 87–97.

Ernaux, Annie. *La Place.* (1983). Paris: Gallimard [Folio], 1997.

Germain, Sylvie. *Etty Hillesum.* Paris: Pygmalion Gérard Watelet, 1999.

———. *L'Enfant Méduse.* Paris: Gallimard [Folio], 1991.

Hillesum, Etty. *Het verstoorde leven* [*An Interrupted Life*]. Haarlem: De Haan, 1981.

Hirsch, Marianne. *Family Frames: Photography, Narrative and Postmemory.* Cambridge: Harvard University Press, 1997.

Klüger, Ruth. *Weiter leben* [*Still Alive*]. Göttingen: Wallstein Verlag, 1992.

Lachaud, Denis. *J'apprends l'allemand.* Arles: Actes sud, 1998.

Lejeune, Philippe. *La Mémoire et l'oblique: Georges Perec autobiographe.* Paris: P.O.L., 1991.

Levi, Primo. *I sommersi e i salvati* [*The Drowned and the Saved*]. Turin: Einaudi, 1986.

Medicus, Thomas. "'Comprendre et non pas accuser, sans pardonner.' Retour sur le passé à l'époque de la post-mémoire." Conversation with Carola Hähnel Mesnard, in Carola Hähnel Mesnard, ed., dossier "Secrets de famille, non-dits ou tabous? Présence du passé national-socialiste dans la littérature allemande contemporaine." *Allemagne d'aujourd'hui*. Lille: Presse universitaire du Septentrion, no. 178 (October–December 2006): 83–97.

———. *In den Augen meines Großvaters*. Munich: Deutsche Verlags-Anstalt, 2004.

Nadaud, Alain. *La Fonte des glaces*. Paris: Grasset, 2000.

Nobécourt, Lorette. *Horsita*. Paris: Grasset, 1999.

Pachet, Pierre. *Autobiographie de mon père* [*Autobiography of My Father*]. Paris: Autrement, 1994.

Perec, Georges. *W ou le souvenir d'enfance*. Paris: Gallimard [L'Imaginaire], 1975.

Robin, Régine. *Le Cheval blanc de Lénine ou l'histoire autre* [*Lenin's White Horse or History Otherwise*] (1979). In *Le Naufrage du siècle*. Montreal: XYZ, 1995.

Rouaud, Jean. *Des Hommes illustres*. Paris: Minuit, 1993.

———. *Le Monde à peu près* [*The World, More or Less*]. Paris: Minuit, 1996.

———. *Les Champs d'honneur*. Paris: Minuit, 1990.

———. *Sur la scène comme au ciel* [*On Stage as in Heaven*]. Paris: Minuit, 1999.

Rousso, Henry. *Le Syndrome de Vichy de 1944 à nos jours*. Paris: Seuil [Points], 1987.

Spiegelman, Art. *Maus*. New York: Pantheon Books, 1986.

Suleiman, Susan. "The 1.5 Generation: Thinking about Child Survivors and the Holocaust." *American Imago* 59.3 (Fall 2002): 277–95.

———. *Crises of Memory and the Second World War*. Cambridge: Harvard University Press, 2006.

Viart, Dominique. "Filiations littéraires." In *Écritures contemporaines* 2, *États du roman contemporain*, edited by Jan Baetens and Dominique Viart. Paris: Minard, 1999. 115–19.

Weitzmann, Marc. *Chaos*. Paris: Stock, 1997.

Welzer, Harald, Sabine Moller, and Karoline Tschuggnall. *"Opa war kein Nazi." Nationalsozialismus und Holocaust im Familiengedächtnis*. Frankfurt am Main: Fischer, 2002.

Wolf, Christa. *Kindheitsmuster*. Berlin and Weimar: Aufbau-Verlag, 1976.

CHAPTER 4

Performing a Perpetrator as Witness

Jonathan Littell's Les Bienveillantes

SUSAN RUBIN SULEIMAN

> How convenient it would be if the Third Reich's citizens had been some-
> how evil *by nature,* demons in somebody's album of the damned—in other
> words, unlike us. The actual case, of course, is far more terrible.
>
> —William T. Vollman, "Seeing Eye to Eye" 9

In an essay published two decades ago, before he had embarked on his authoritative two-volume study *Nazi Germany and the Jews,* the historian Saul Friedländer reflected on the "unease in historical interpretation" regarding the Holocaust and the Final Solution. Despite the enormous amount of work that historians had devoted to the subject, he noted, "an opaqueness remains at the very core of the historical understanding and interpretation of what happened" ("Unease" 103). This opaqueness, this stubborn resistance to meaning, manifests itself, Friedländer explained, in two areas in particular: the psychology of the perpetrators and the possibility of "integrating the Holocaust into a global historical interpretation" (104)—that is, of making the Holocaust somehow "usable" for an understanding of the present and the future.[1]

Today, even after Friedländer's own considerable work, we are no closer to a full understanding of the Holocaust—and in particular of the "psychology of the perpetrator," which I take to refer to the tangle of motivations, justifications, and self-understandings that allowed thousands of individual Germans, either by administrative decision or by action on the ground, to engage over several years in genocidal mass murder and industrial extermination of those whom their government considered "not worthy of life"—

than we were twenty years ago. That fact may at least in part account for why, in recent years, novelists and filmmakers have turned their attention to a serious consideration of the "everyday life" of Nazi killers—not Nazis portrayed as caricatures (as in Martin Amis's *Time's Arrow,* which James Phelan discusses in this volume), nor Nazis as secondary characters in stories focused on victims (Amon Goeth in *Schindler's List*), but Nazis as the heroes of their own stories, the way every human being can be said to be the hero of his or her own story. In the case of such figures, whether they are historical (like Hitler or Goebbels in Oliver Hirschbiegel's 2004 film *Der Untergang,* or one of the several Nazi figures whom William T. Vollman focuses on in his 2005 novel *Europe Central*) or else invented, like the main character in Jonathan Littell's *Les Bienveillantes* (*The Kindly Ones*), their personal story is embedded in the larger, collective history of Germany and Europe in the twentieth century. Any insight we may seek about them as individuals is thus indissociable from that larger history—from how they themselves viewed their role in it and how we view both that history and their role.

The phenomenal publishing success of Littell's novel (which the author claims totally surprised him) is by now well known. Published in the fall of 2006 in Paris, this 900-page work by a previously unknown writer who was not even French (Littell, born in 1967 in New York, grew up in France, was educated at Yale, and spent several years working for NGOs in Chechnya and Bosnia before writing the book) won France's most prestigious literary prize, the Prix Goncourt, as well as the Grand Prix of the French Academy, and sold more than half a million copies in its first year. It was reviewed everywhere, eliciting wildly divergent opinions from critics and the public: to some, it was a masterpiece worthy of Tolstoy or Dostoevsky, while to others it was nothing more than voyeuristic, pornographic kitsch that desecrated the memory of the Holocaust. Nor could the reviewers be divided into "elite" versus "lowbrow" or other clear-cut categories: eminent intellectuals, including the historian Pierre Nora, the novelist Jorge Semprun, the psychoanalyst and cultural critic Julia Kristeva, expressed admiration for the book; others, equally eminent (the filmmaker Claude Lanzmann, the Academician Marc Fumaroli, and historians Friedländer and Raoul Hilberg) dismissed it.[2] Its reception in Germany and Israel was equally stormy, although it appears that the negatives were more numerous there than the positives—the book was, however, a bestseller in Germany, and an international conference was devoted to it alone in Jerusalem in June 2009. In the United States, where it did not appear until 2009 due to a delay with the translation, the reception was mixed (I discuss some of the positive and negative reviews below). The *New York Times* noted, in a separate article, that it seemed unlikely the book would earn back the huge advance paid by its publisher (Rich). Independently of the critics and the media, however, *Les Bienveillantes* is certain to continue being discussed in conferences and learned journals, at least for a while. Like it or not, it is a "case," and as such it must elicit serious commentary.

What makes it a case is also well known: this novel, which gives us a comprehensive and historically accurate account of the Nazi genocide of the Jews, starting in June 1941 on the Eastern front and ending with the January 1945 death marches from Auschwitz, is narrated exclusively from the point of view, and in the voice, of a former SS officer who witnessed it all. Critics have pointed out that this ubiquity makes the narrator a kind of Zelig, or Forrest Gump, highly implausible by realist criteria. The important question, I believe, is not that of verisimilitude but rather: What kind of point of view and what kind of voice does Littell's narrator Maximilien Aue represent, and how are we to respond to him as readers? I would like to answer this question in a way that will allow me to engage with some of the novel's most negative critics. This approach is through the concept of performance.

Performance studies has become, over the past two decades, an institutionalized, interdisciplinary field that studies an immense range of phenomena, from theatrical performances of all kinds to sports, cultural rituals, and the routines of everyday life. My own use of the concept of performance is practical rather than theoretical; my purpose is not to engage with the field of performance studies as such, but to think about performance in order to illuminate a particular text.[3]

Performance and the Reader's Judgment

The meaning of "performance" ranges widely, both in actions and in words. The analytic philosopher J. L. Austin, in his foundational work *How To Do Things with Words,* coined the term "performatives" to designate verbal utterances that function as concrete acts in the world, and that can be pronounced with their full force only by certain qualified persons: the justice of the peace who proclaims "I now pronounce you man and wife," or the political leader who declares war on an enemy country in the name of his own. An ordinary individual may also utter performatives—for example, by promising to do something that the speaker is actually capable of doing. Austin noted that performative utterances can be spoken "infelicitously" or "non-seriously," either because the person uttering them carries no actual authority or capacity (a simple citizen cannot truly declare war, and a five-year-old cannot truly promise to help you move your piano) or because he or she is uttering them in a fictional situation, such as a performance onstage; in such cases, the effect of the uttered words on the actual world is imitative, metaphorical, or otherwise indirect. Most verbal performances, like most other actions, fall somewhere between the two extremes: lacking the full force of a declaration of war or marriage, but still engaging the performer in some sort of consequential activity in the world. I can perform, by means of verbal and other actions, my job in its multiple aspects, or a specific task on a given day, or my role as a wife or daughter or mother, with more or less success, more or less pleasure (to myself and others), more or less effectiveness. I can also perform it with more or less reflection about what I am doing, and why, and what its consequences might be. I can even perform it ironically, or parodically, as if I were on a stage, watching myself perform for the benefit of others, who may or may not be aware of, and may or may not share, my ironic self-awareness. If I happen to be an actor, I can perform any one of those actions or roles on a theatrical stage, reverting to my "real self" after the play is over. And I can even perform ironically when I *am* onstage—in that case, I as actor and I as character will not totally cohere, and the effect will be what Brecht called the alienation effect: I and the audience will communicate above the head of the character I am playing, both of us acknowledging the virtuosity of my performance and its distance from verisimilitude as well as from "reality."

What does all this have to do with *Les Bienveillantes*? Since this is a novel with what is generally called a first-person narrator (a character narrator in James Phelan's terminology, or an autodiegetic narrator in Gérard Genette's classification[4]), we can think of this fictional character, Max Aue, as performing the task of telling his own story, which consists not only of salient actions he has accomplished (successfully or not, pleasurably or not, etc.), but also of the thoughts, dreams, or fantasies that may have accompanied those actions. To the extent that Aue also tells what he has seen others do and say, he performs the task of testifying to events in which he participated as an observer rather than as an active agent; and since, in his case, most of the events he refers to concern Germany's role in World War II, with particular focus on the planning and execution of the genocide of the Jews, Aue's testimony becomes—despite his own fictional status—a *historical* testimony. Even unsympathetic critics have acknowledged that Littell did a tremendous amount of historical research in writing this novel and that all of the historical reporting he puts into Aue's mouth is accurate. This kind of documentary exactitude seems necessary if a novelist is to write responsibly about an event that carries as much collective significance as the Holocaust. Indeed, it may be the best criterion for judging the ethical quality of a novel or a fiction film that purports to deal with that (or any other) historical atrocity. If a work evokes the horrors of the Holocaust arbitrarily, as mere background for a story or only for their shock effect, or else commits gross errors in historical representation, it disqualifies itself at the start.[5]

In terms of narrative performance, *Les Bienveillantes* presents a complicated structure of levels of speech and communication. Like all autobiographers, be they real or fictional, Max Aue functions as both narrator in the present (which in the novel occurs some time in the 1970s), addressing himself to "o my human brothers," his assumed readers; and as a character in the past, with most of the past action occurring between 1941 and 1945 but with frequent flashbacks to his childhood and youth in the 1920s and 1930s. Aue thus performs an intricate autobiographical speech act; but he also performs, as I have said, an act of historical testimony when he reports on events of the war that he witnessed or in which he participated. (I will return to this unusual combination of fictional status and historical reliability.) Of course, behind Aue the narrator there is Littell the author, who communicates with what Phelan and other theorists call the authorial audience, or with what Wayne Booth and others called the implied reader, the reader as positioned by the text—and there is the crux, for the responses of an actual reader may not at all correspond to those attributed to this interpretive construct. Leaving that complication aside for the moment, we can think of the author, Littell, as "performing" the role of Max Aue, casting himself into the character's persona and voice. This becomes especially relevant when we consider Aue's role as historical witness, for obviously it is to the author that we must attribute the historical accuracy of the fictional character's reporting.

J. M. Coetzee, in his novel *Elizabeth Costello,* which is a series of reflections about authorship and creativity cast in the thoughts and occasionally in the voice of a fictional, elderly Australian woman author, has his heroine state as she waits "at the gate" after her death (clearly an allusion to Kafka's parable "Before the Law") that her job in life was to "do imitations, as Aristotle would have said" (194). Every author of a fictional narrative can be said to "do imitations," taking on the voice and performance of his characters; and this is especially clear in works narrated by a character protagonist.[6] But the author's performance is more comprehensive than that, for she not only invents—or, in the case of historical figures, evokes—and "impersonates" characters in their words, thoughts, and actions; she also makes decisions about the plot, organization, language, style, and length of the novel, as well as about the ideas expressed there—in short, about everything that constitutes the finished work. The author's performance, both in the narrow sense involving characters and in the more general sense involving the whole work, is directed at the reader (the real reader this time), who is summoned to respond to that performance.

Both author and reader are concerned with ethical as well as aesthetic questions, and this is especially true, or urgent, in the case of works that deal with issues of collective historical significance. The reader is constantly, albeit not necessarily consciously, asking herself as she reads: What does this author's performance overall (including both ethical and aesthetic choices) "say" or "do" about issues that matter to me? The author here is less the actual person than what Wayne Booth called the "implied author" but what might more precisely be called the "constructed or deduced author," since the reader's response is based first of all on the author she has deduced from the work, not on what the actual author-person might say about the work in interviews or other external commentary. The reader's answer to that question—and we must recognize that readers may have astonishingly divergent answers—will determine the emotional coloration as well as the intellectual tenor of his or her response to, and evaluation of, the work.

Obviously, or tautologically, those readers who express admiration for *Les Bienveillantes* judge Littell's performance as author to be highly successful; that means, among other things, that they consider his fictional creature Max Aue complex, original, compelling—even if, in many respects, he repels them or shows himself to be reprehensible, even horrifying. Such readers never lose sight of the fact that Aue is a fictional being, a construction of the author; and they judge Aue precisely in those terms—not as a "person," but as a character created for this particular literary performance. If I may be allowed to quote myself, this is how I put it in an earlier essay:

> We have never yet seen a comprehensive account of Nazi atrocities during the Second World War that is told entirely from the perspective, and in the voice of, a perpetrator. Littell's Maximilien Aue has qualities that only a fictional character can have: he is present, as an observing participant, in just about every place where the worst crimes against humanity were committed; he has access to privileged information available only to the inner circle around the SS leader Heinrich Himmler; and most importantly, he possesses the intelligence and analytical ability, the emotional detachment and temporal distance, as well as a certain moral sensibility, which allow him to act as a reliable historical witness. The combination of participant status as a perpetrator with historical reliability, and with what I will call moral witnessing, which Aue possesses, is a totally new phenomenon in fiction.[7]

The main focus of my interpretation, and I think of all positive appreciations of this novel, concerns Aue's paradoxical function as a reliable historical witness—and even, on occasion, a reliable moral witness, when he reflects on his actions in a way the reader can adhere to. His role as historical witness is paradoxical given his fictional status, but logical if one thinks of the author behind the character, who gets the credit for having invented such a figure. In fact, *as a character,* Aue displays a complex combination of traits, for he is part of the Nazi system, yet he offers an often devastatingly critical analysis of it. I have called this particular combination the "insider/outsider" model of witnessing, since Aue is both within the system—indeed, he rises steadily in its ranks during the war—yet feels sufficiently distanced from it, ideologically and emotionally, to see it clearly (Suleiman, "Raising Hell"). This insider/outsider status becomes even more evident if one compares Aue to another important character in the novel, his good friend and quasi-double, Thomas, who has no distance whatsoever from the system or its values, even though he is sufficiently savvy to exploit the system for his own advancement, like any ambitious climber. Had Littell chosen to make Thomas or a character like him the narrator, we would have a very different novel.

Daniel Mendelsohn, writing in the *New York Review of Books,* also sees Aue as a complex figure:

> [Aue] is a well-educated and indeed sensitive person, musical, literate, cultured, who far from being monstrously indifferent to the crimes he sees perpetrated and which he is called on to commit himself, spends a good deal of time reflecting on the questions of guilt and responsibility that a self-aware person could be expected to entertain.

But Michiko Kakutani, in her review in the *New York Times* (which, given Kakutani's symbolic capital as a critic, is surely partly responsible for the book's cool reception in the United States), sees Aue—and by extension, Littell's performance as author—in a far harsher light:

> Although Aue contends that he is "a man like other men," "a man like you" and depicts himself as a cultivated intellectual who reads Flaubert and Kant, his story is hardly a case study in the banality of evil. [. . .] Aue is clearly a deranged creature, and his madness turns his story into a voyeuristic spectacle—like watching a slasher film with lots of close-ups of blood and guts.
>
> Unable to understand Aue, much less sympathize with him, the reader is not goaded . . . to question his or her own capacity for moral compro-

mise. Instead Mr. Littell simply gives us a monster talking at monstrous length about his monstrous deeds . . .

For Michiko Kakutani, Aue cannot act as a reliable historical witness, let alone as a moral witness to the Holocaust, since he is a monster—not human. And Aue's monstrous performance (but one should say performances, for Kakutani refers to his narration as well as his actions) signals the failure of Littell's performance. Kakutani's review shows beautifully how the evaluation of the character very quickly morphs into an evaluation of the author. In a way, it is Littell himself who here stands accused of voyeurism, perhaps even of monstrosity (in his imagination, to be sure).

This accusation, developed more fully, is also found in the book-length indictment of *Les Bienveillantes* that was published in France six months after the novel's appearance. Titled, parodically, *Les Complaisantes* (*The Complacent Ones*) and co-signed by the historian Edouard Husson and the philosopher Michel Terestchenko, this work—whose seriousness and intellectual passion cannot be doubted, even if one finds it wrongheaded, as I do—presents a long list of accusations that boil down to one essential point: in Max Aue, Littell has created a character who is *inhuman,* and he has thereby led the reader into an ethical trap, for the reader might find herself identifying with Aue despite his inhumanity. Why is Aue inhuman? "Not only because he is incestuous and a parricide, but because, through words, he desecrates the bodies of the victims."[8] This desecration is achieved, Husson and Terestchenko maintain, by Aue's insistent, voyeuristic fascination with the victims' dead bodies and with scenes of horror. Nor is it only Aue who is fascinated by horror. The real problem, according to the authors, is that Littell himself manifests that fascination: he does not take sufficient distance from Aue, does not "warn" the reader against sharing Aue's perverse fascination. Here they evoke Plato's allegory of Leontius, in *The Republic,* which is cited by Aue himself after he sees mounds of dead, rotting bodies in the early days of the German invasion of the Soviet Union. (As it happens, and against Husson and Terestchenko's insistence that the victims "desecrated" by Aue's voyeuristic gaze are the Jews murdered by Nazis, these are bodies not of Jews but rather of Polish prisoners who were presumably shot by the Soviets during their retreat.[9]) In Plato, Husson and Terestchenko tell us, the story of Leontius—who cannot stop himself from looking at a mound of dead bodies after their execution, and who curses his eyes for that weakness—was meant to warn us "not to succumb to that perversion of the gaze" (137). But Aue, they maintain, and by extension Littell himself, feels no Platonic shame at being fascinated by horror.[10] As a result, the reader is also led into such fascination:

"What is particularly pernicious in Littell's novel is that, through a Sadean atmosphere, it leads the reader to be fascinated by Nazi violence" (76).

Husson and Terestchenko support their accusations by selective quotes from the novel; they never analyze a whole sequence, quoting only "shocking" passages in the text wherever they find them. But the aesthetic particularity of this novel, especially where scenes that describe Nazi violence against the Jews are concerned, is that Aue never merely narrates or observes atrocity, with whatever degree of fascination or horror he manifests. He almost always follows observation with reflection, either in his present voice as narrator or as thoughts attributed to his earlier self at the time of the events (which is quite unrealistic, though effective); one must therefore read a whole sequence in order to get the full impact of his account. To cite just one example: in Aue's detailed account of the horrendous killings at Babi Yar—where more than 30,000 Jewish men, women, and children were murdered by shooting in the space of two days—Husson and Terestchenko pick out a particularly awful moment when Aue himself is sent into the ditch to finish off prisoners who were shot but did not die. (This is the only time in the novel we actually see him murdering Jews—I think it is significant that Littell chose to have him perform mercy killings, rather than placing him among the shooters at the edge of the ditch.) At one point, Aue describes seeing a beautiful and dignified-looking young woman who is among the naked prisoners at the edge of the ditch, and whom he finds among the corpses at the bottom a few minutes later, still breathing despite the bullets she received. She looks at him with "large surprised incredulous eyes, the eyes of a wounded bird" [ses grands yeux surpris, incrédules, des yeux d'oiseau blessé], an observation that Husson and Terestchenko don't quote; instead, they quote what comes next, and even that only partially:

Ce regard [the text says "et ce regard" ("and that look") separated by a comma from "oiseau blessé,"] se planta en moi, me fendit le ventre, et laissa s'écouler un flot de sciure de bois, j'étais une vulgaire poupée et ne ressentais rien, et en même temps je voulais de tout mon coeur me pencher et lui essuyer la terre et la sueur mêlée sur son front, lui caresser la joue et lui dire que ça allait, que tout était pour le mieux, mais à la place je lui tirai convulsivement une balle dans la tête, ce qui après tout revenait au même, pour elle en tout cas . . . (*Les Complaisantes* 94; original text with different punctuation: *B* 126)

[That look stuck into me, split open my stomach and let a flood of sawdust pour out, I was a rag doll and didn't feel anything, and at the same time

I wanted with all my heart to bend over and brush the dirt and sweat off
her forehead, caress her cheek and tell her it was going to be all right, that
everything would be fine, but instead I convulsively shot a bullet into her
head, which after all came down to the same thing, for her in any case if
not for me . . .] (*K* 130)

Husson and Terestchenko cut off their quotation here, in mid-sentence, with
the following comment: "Definitely, there would have been every reason to
return the manuscript to its author as unpublishable." But, they go on, Pari-
sian intellectual "chic" likes to "continue to proclaim that we are 'beyond
good and evil' despite the genocides of the twentieth century and those that
threaten our world [today]" (94). In their righteous (if perhaps somewhat
facile) indignation at modern genocides and moral relativism, the authors
fail to note what happens in the rest of Littell's sentence and paragraph,
which continues as follows:

> . . . pour elle en tout cas si ce n'était pour moi, car moi à la pensée de ce
> gâchis humain insensé j'étais envahi d'une rage immense, démesurée, je
> continuais à lui tirer dessus, et sa tête avait éclaté comme un fruit, alors
> mon bras se détacha de moi et partit tout seul dans le ravin, tirant de
> part et d'autre, je lui courais après, lui faisant signe de m'attendre de mon
> autre bras, mais il ne voulait pas, il me narguait et tirait sur les blessés
> tout seul, sans moi, enfin, à bout de souffle je m'arrêtai et me mis à pleu-
> rer. (*B* 126)

> [. . . for her in any case if not for me, since at the thought of this senseless
> human waste I was filled with an immense, boundless rage, I kept shoot-
> ing at her and her head exploded like a fruit, then my arm detached itself
> from me and went off all by itself down the ravine, shooting left and right,
> I ran after it, waving at it to wait with my other arm, but it didn't want to,
> it mocked me and shot at the wounded all by itself, without me; finally, out
> of breath, I stopped and started to cry.] (*K* 130)

The shape and meaning of this very long sentence, with its jerky rhythm
and its hallucinatory description of Aue's own traumatic dissociation as he
meets the face and look of his wounded victim (his arm detaching itself and
running amok independently of his control) are entirely overlooked by Husson and Terestchenko in their drive to condemn Aue's "inhumanity." If one
takes the trouble to read this passage without prejudgment, one sees that Aue
appears here most definitely human: it is one instance in the novel where he

significantly *fails* in his performance as an SS officer, since he breaks down and starts to cry. Aue's failed performance here can be contrasted with the actions of his friend Thomas, who never fails to do what is expected of him, with no scruples whatsoever. Thomas is the "perfect" SS officer, and the divergence between him and Aue underlines the latter's status as an insider/ outsider who is never fully at home in the system.

In fact, the paragraph ends with Aue being relieved of his duty in the ditch by another officer, who tells him, "C'est bon, Obersturmführer, je vous remplace" (*B* 126) ("That's enough, Obersturmführer. I'll take over for you" [*K* 130]). Husson and Terestchenko overlook this ending. And they also overlook the fact that in the very next paragraph, Aue reflects on what has just happened, in a way that places him squarely in the position of an "outsider" analyst even as he continues to say "we":

Même les boucheries démentielles de la Grande Guerre . . . paraissaient presque propres et justes à côté de ce que nous avions amené au monde. Je trouvais cela extraordinaire. . . . Notre système, notre Etat, se moquait profondément des pensées de ses serviteurs. Cela lui était indifférent que l'on tue les Juifs parce qu'on les haïssait ou parce qu'on voulait faire avancer sa carrière ou même, dans certaines limites, parce qu'on y prenait du plaisir . . . Cela lui était même indifférent, au fond, que l'on refuse de les tuer, aucune sanction ne serait prise, car il savait bien que le réservoir des tueurs disponibles était sans fond . . . (*B* 127)

[Even the insane butcheries of the Great War . . . seemed almost clean and righteous compared to what we had brought into the world. I found this extraordinary. . . . Our system, our State couldn't care less about the thoughts of its servants. It was all the same to the State whether you killed Jews because you hated them or because you wanted to advance your career or even, in some cases, because you took pleasure in it. . . . It did not even mind, in the end, if you refused to kill, no disciplinary action would be taken, since it was well aware that the pool of available killers was bottomless . . .] (*K* 130–31)

This is a clear instance where the reader can appreciate Littell's performance as author behind the character, since it is obvious that these reflections are being put into the mouth of the narrator-character by an author who has read real-life analysts of the Holocaust whose work came many years after the time when Aue claims to have thought these thoughts. The authorial audience—or let us just say, the careful reader—understands this, communicating above Aue's head with the author. As I wrote elsewhere, commenting on this very passage:

> This is a reality observed through the later analyses of Hannah Arendt on totalitarian systems, or Christopher Browning on the role of "ordinary men" in mass murder. And it is made, fictively, by an SS officer who was in the ravine shooting people a few hours earlier. Unrealistic, no doubt, but very powerful; and pointing not only to historical facts, but to their ethical and moral implications. ("When the Perpetrator" 10–11)

One could say, then, with all due respect, that in their way of handling quotations, as exemplified in the passage I have been discussing, the authors of *Les Complaisantes* engage in some unseemly "complacency" themselves. They are so intent on indicting Littell (behind his character) for his unethical performance that they lose sight of their own responsibility as readers. Husson and Terestchenko constantly hammer the theme of the writer's ethical responsibility, and Littell's failure to live up to it (in their opinion). But surely there is a case to be made for ethical reading as well. As J. Hillis Miller noted in his *Ethics of Reading,* reading too is a performance. It must therefore be done responsibly: not cutting off an author in mid-sentence, when the end of the sentence radically changes the meaning suggested in the beginning; not rushing to judgment before taking account of a whole sequence, if not the whole work.[11]

This may all be very true. But considering the sharply divergent readers' judgments that have been voiced about *Les Bienveillantes* makes me wonder whether it is ever possible to persuade a reader to change his or her mind about a novel once that mind is made up. Even if one demonstrates, as I have tried to do, that a critic—who is a particular kind of reader, having to defend his or her responses by reasoned argument—has failed to read a certain passage responsibly or failed to make a convincing case, and even if one were to succeed in persuading that very critic to recognize his or her error concerning a particular passage in the novel, that would in no way guarantee that the latter's overall judgment of the work would change. All the more so when "ordinary," nonprofessional readers are concerned: to the extent that reading is subjective and that a reader's response to a text is immediate, one might even say visceral, before any critical reasoning occurs, there is probably not much one can do to persuade a reader that he or she is "wrong" to love or hate a work. At best, one can try to make the strongest case for one's own reading, addressing it implicitly to a virtual third party or "bystander" in the debate.[12] In that process, one can cite other readers whom one agrees with, as allies in interpretation. For example, I can cite Daniel Mendelsohn once again:

> While some will denounce Littell's cool-eyed authorial sympathy for Aue as "obscene"—and by "sympathy" I mean simply his attempt to comprehend the character—his project seems infinitely more valuable than the reflexive gesture of writing off all those millions of killers as "monsters" or "inhuman," which allows us too easily to draw a solid line between "them" and "us." The first line of the novel takes the form of Aue's unsettling salutation to his "human brothers": the purpose of the book, one in which it largely succeeds, is to keep alive, however improbably, that troubling sense of kinship.

Thus are interpretive communities formed, consisting of like-minded readers of a text. But there will always be other communities, with equally strong views, to make the opposite case where certain controversial works are concerned. I would suggest, furthermore, that the kind of performance engaged in by Littell in this novel, consisting of an "act of impersonation" (to use Sidra DeKoven Ezrahi's phrase) of a Nazi, carries with it a particular danger. Quite possibly, a writer or artist cannot imaginatively project himself, even with distantiating devices such as irony or paradox, into the mind and words of a participant in genocide without running the risk of being identified—or even, at times, genuinely identifying—with such a character. Sidra DeKoven Ezrahi, commenting on similar "acts of impersonation" undertaken by the artists who participated in the controversial exhibit *Mirroring Evil: Nazi Imagery/Recent Art* organized by the Jewish Museum of New York in 2002, noted, "What is common to most of this art is a form of appropriation that is always in danger of becoming, or being confused with, collaboration" (19). Although my own reading of *Les Bienveillantes* credits Littell with major critical intentions—if not always toward his character, certainly toward the system whose description he puts into the character's mouth—I must recognize that far less sympathetic readings of Littell's achievement and intentions are also possible.

Transgression and Witnessing
An Uneasy Union

My admiration for Littell's performance in *Les Bienveillantes* does not come without reservations. Like a number of other critics, I am troubled by a jarring discrepancy that the novel does not satisfactorily resolve: on one side, there is Aue's paradoxical and artistically highly successful role as an insider/outsider who functions as a historical and moral witness to the Holocaust; on the other side, there is Aue's personal story, featuring incest (with his twin sister Una, whose name is borrowed from Poe's "Colloquy of Monos and Una" and whose status as an incestuous twin is borrowed from Musil's *The Man without Qualities*), matricide, homosexuality, and increasingly delirious sexual fantasizing. The relation of the personal story to the historical account is never made clear, or even hinted at, by Littell. The personal story is the one pointed to in the novel's title, which evokes the Greek trilogy of the Oresteia. In Aeschylus, the Furies who pursue Orestes after his double murder (of his mother and his stepfather) are placated at the end and are renamed the "Eumenides," "The Kindly Ones," even as Orestes goes scot-free. In Littell's novel too, Aue goes unpunished (he escapes from Berlin at the end of the war and ends his days as the director of a lace factory in northern France), but that is not the part I find most troubling. Rather, it is the "disconnect" between Aue's private excesses and his function as historical witness: if Aue is meant to appear as a reliable historical witness who gives detailed accounts of the massacres in Ukraine, the rout of the German army at Stalingrad, the machinery of the extermination camps in Poland, and the last days of the war in a bombed-out Berlin, how does that role square with the fact that he has no memory of the family murders he committed in the middle of all that? And if he is to appear as a "human brother" to the reader, situated both inside and outside the system he describes and analyzes, how can we reconcile that representative status with his excessive sexual tastes and desires, which are quite far from those of most "normal" people? Michiko Kakutani was not wrong to say that he is not a "banal" Nazi—but oddly, his "non-banality" *as a Nazi,* that is, his inability to perform his role as perpetrator as evidenced by his breakdown at Babi Yar, for example, allows the reader to feel a certain shared humanity with Aue. The excesses of his personal history, however, which constitute the other aspect of his "non-banality," emphasize the difficulty that most readers will have in considering him as a "human brother."

In terms of narrative theory, we could formulate the problem as one of conflicting reliabilities: whereas Aue is a reliable narrator where the historical narrative is concerned—not only in the accuracy of his reporting but even in many of his judgments, to which the reader adheres—he is stunningly unreliable in recounting some major events of his personal story. Thus he never relates his murder of his mother and stepfather, and the reader must deduce it from an ellipsis in the narrative.[13] Nor does he remember his action later, and he fails in other ways as well—for example, in understanding (as the reader certainly does) that the twin children he meets at his mother's house are most likely his own offspring from his incestuous relationship with his sister.

I have suggested elsewhere that the Oresteia plot may have to be read alongside the historical account (rather than implicated with it), as a parallel reflection on the question of guilt and justice that Aue struggles with throughout most of the novel ("When the Perpetrator" 18–19). In fact, in a striking *mise en abyme,* Aue himself evokes Greek tragedy and its notions of justice, right after a long reflection on the humanity of the "ordinary" Germans who were enrolled in the machinery of extermination. Having just had a conversation, in Sobibor, with one such man, a family man named Döll who has been gassing people ever since he was assigned to the euthanasia program in Germany in the late 1930s, Aue affirms that, contrary to what some commentators have said, the actions of that individual were not inhuman but were part of "l'humain et encore de l'humain" ("humanity and more humanity"; *B* 542, *K* 589). He then goes on to ask whether Döll should be held responsible for his actions, for after all, it was by chance that he and not some other German was sent to Sobibor. Perhaps it is all of Germany that should be called to account for his crimes—unless, Aue muses, one considers the question not in terms of Judeo-Christian ideas of justice, which take into account the intention of one who commits a crime, but rather in terms of Greek notions of guilt and punishment, where the action alone matters, independently of intention:

> Le lien entre volonté et crime est une notion chrétienne. . . . Pour les Grecs, peu importe si Héraclès abat ses enfants dans un accès de folie, ou si Oedipe tue son père par accident: cele ne change rien, c'est un crime, ils sont coupable; on peut les plaindre, mais on ne peut les absoudre—et cela même si souvent leur punition revient aux dieux, et non pas aux hommes. (*B* 546)

> [The link between intention and crime is a Christian notion. For the Greeks, it makes no difference that Heracles murders his children in a fit of madness, or that Oedipus kills his father by accident. It doesn't change anything, it's a crime, they're guilty. We can pity them, but not absolve them—even if often their punishment is done by the gods, not by men.] (*K* 589)[14]

If we recall that Aue kills his mother and stepfather without having any memory of the crime and without ever acknowledging it as his own, then this commentary (which occurs in the novel after the double murder) can be considered as an oblique reference to his own guilt in Greek terms. The burlesque detectives, Weser and Clemens, who pursue Aue with increasing circumstantial evidence of his guilt (his bloodstained clothes were found in the bathtub, for example) and whom he manages to elude until the very end, would then function as the human attempt at punishment, which fails.[15] But the somewhat ambiguous last line of the novel, "Les Bienveillantes avaient retrouvé ma trace" ("The Kindly Ones had picked up my scent"— *B* 894, *K* 975; translation modified) could be read as an indication that the "Kindly Ones"—who despite their euphemistic new name are representatives of divine retribution—have never actually left him. In Greek terms, Aue is guilty—not only of the matricide he does not remember committing, but also of the murders he does recall, such as the killing of the beautiful girl in Babi Yar. It was a mercy killing, and he accomplished it in a sense despite himself; but it was a killing nevertheless.

In one way, then, we can think of the "excessive" personal story as a displaced (in the psychoanalytic sense) commentary on the question of guilt and responsibility—a question that concerns *above all* the historical narrative of Nazi atrocities, but that is displaced into the realm of individual family history, away from the more horrific realm of collective murder. Displacement, as Freud showed about dreams and other psychic phenomena such as screen memories, is a defense mechanism to protect the subject against truths that would be unbearable if stated directly. Aue, who tells us at the start that he does "not regret anything" ("ne regrette rien"— *B* 12, *K* 5) about his wartime actions, is clearly unable to face his guilt about the Nazi genocide directly. His body responds to the killings he witnesses (witnessing, as he himself admits, is a form of participation) with symptoms of rejection— vomiting, diarrhea, which later turns into constipation—and with insomnia, but he never explicitly acknowledges either his guilt or his disgust at the killings. I am suggesting that on the *authorial* level, Aue's whole personal story can be seen as a displacement—and here its function is not to evade, but rather to reinforce the questions about guilt and responsibility by creating a parallel story that transposes the historical crimes into a personal register. The intertextual weight of the Oresteia myth would then function as additional reinforcement.

Another explanation for the problematic relation between the wartime story ("the genre of testimony") and the private story ("the genre of excess")— has been offered by the Israeli scholar Liran Razinsky. Razinsky argues, in an unpublished paper, that the "literature of excess," epitomized in the chapter titled "Air" toward the end of the novel—when Aue spends a week alone in a Pomeranian castle belonging to his sister and her husband, masturbating in every room and engaging in increasingly scatological fantasies—is necessary to the novel's testimonial project, because it is through his transgressive sexuality that Aue reaches an ethical awareness of "the other."[16] Thus, while fantasizing about his sister, he remembers a young woman he saw hanged in the Ukraine, fantasizes about her too, and then sobs in helpless rage: "nous l'avions pendue comme un boucher égorge un boeuf, sans passion, parce qu'il fallait le faire . . . et une telle cruauté n'avait pas de nom, quelle que soit sa nécessité, elle ruinait tout, si l'on pouvait faire ça,. . alors on pouvait tout faire" ("We had hanged her the way a butcher slaughters an animal, without passion, because it had to be done . . . and such a cruelty had no name, even though it was necessary, it ruined everything, if one could do that . . . then one could do anything"; *B* 835–36, *K* 912). Razinsky argues that through an excessive *jouissance* (his own and the ones he fantasizes in his sister and in the young woman victim), Aue arrives at an ethical awareness he would not have reached otherwise.

This elegant argument resonates with Susan Sontag's well-known observations about the "pornographic imagination" as a conduit to the experience of limits that has fascinated avant-garde European literature for over a century. Indeed, Littell's debt to Georges Bataille and other avant-garde theorists of transgression has often been noted. Still, this argument does not explain the many places in the novel—notably before the "Air" chapter, which occurs very late—when Aue acts as a clearheaded analyst of the Nazi system *sans* erotic fantasies; nor does it explain his murderous actions *after* his supposed epiphany in the castle. The only murders he commits before this episode are the matricide, of which he has no memory, and the mercy killings in the pit at Babi Yar, which make him sick and soon get him transferred out of Ukraine. (Later, he also orders the execution of an old Jewish man in the Caucasus, but only after the man himself has demanded that he do so—this is one of the stranger episodes in the novel.) After the "Air" chapter, however, in quick succession, he shoots an old man playing Bach's *Art of the Fugue* in a village church; kills a homosexual acquaintance with whom he had had casual sex and who makes another pass at him in public; and kills a policeman with a stone, after tweaking Hitler's nose in a burlesque incident staged in Hitler's bunker! Finally, in a real shock to the reader, he kills his friend Thomas, allowing for an exchange of identities and his eventual escape to France. Thus his most cold-blooded and amoral actions occur after the great sobbing scene in the castle, which suggests that if he gained ethical insight and an awareness of "the other" in that chapter, it didn't last very long. Significantly, in these final pages of the novel, we have no philosophical reflections or other internal monologues by Aue: he performs his bizarre or criminal deeds with no warning, and he reports them with brutal directness, unaccompanied by any explanation or commentary.

In fact, as Leland Deladurantaye has noted, the last hundred or so pages of the novel, after the "Air" chapter, read quite differently from the rest: in contrast to the "meticulously realistic main plot . . . , brilliantly organized and written," these pages "show signs, if not of fatigue, then of something approaching fever." Deladurantaye sees this as a serious flaw in the novel, a weakening in Littell's authorial performance; but this "feverishness" could be interpreted as Aue's rather than the author's (as such, it would be part of the author's design), serving to indicate the increasingly nightmarish and unreal quality of the last days of the war in Germany. In that case, we could see the growing loss of control in the narration as textually mirroring the disintegration of Berlin, bombed to smithereens, of the German army and bureaucracy, of Aue himself as he becomes another man—and also the disintegration of realist narrative, as Aue's narration becomes more and more hallucinatory and grotesque.

Notes

1. Eight years later, in his introduction to the first volume of *Nazi Germany and the Jews,* Friedländer appeared to have revised his views at least on the second of these areas: a study of Nazi Germany, he maintained, could in fact yield some enlightenment about the present; for together with its "peculiar frenzy of . . . apocalyptic drive against . . . the Jew," Nazi Germany shared in the "murderous potentialities of the world that is also ours." Whence the universal significance of "The Final Solution of the Jewish Question" (Introduction, 6).

2. For a brief account of the critical reception of the novel in France, see Suleiman, "When the Perpetrator Becomes a Reliable Witness of the Holocaust," 3–4. Saul Friedländer and Raoul Hilberg did not write reviews, but spoke dismissively about the book in public and private conversations.

3. For a wide-ranging panorama of the possibilities of performance studies around the time it was stabilizing as an academic field, see the 1998 collective volume edited by Peggy Phelan and Jill Lane, *The Ends of Performance.* Many other works seeking to define this enormously varied interdisciplinary field, whose borders are not at all clear, have been published since then.

4. See Phelan, *Living to Tell about It,* and Genette, *Narrative Discourse.*

5. As always, such self-confident generalizations can be contested by reality—in this case, by the reality of Quentin Tarantino's 2009 film *Inglourious Basterds,* which I found to be a highly successful work of art and not ethically irresponsible, even though it ignores some of the most basic historical facts about the Holocaust—for example, by having Hitler and all his top lieutenants burned to death in a movie theater in Paris circa 1944! Many critics do not share my positive view of the film, however, for various reasons, including that of historical accuracy.

6. Phelan, in his book *Living to Tell about It,* proposes a detailed terminology for analyzing the complex relations between author and character, and between author, char-

acter, and authorial audience. I will not attempt to duplicate his terminology here, which he summarizes very usefully in his own essay in this volume. He situates his model not in the field of performance but in that of rhetoric (following the precedent of Wayne Booth's classic work *The Rhetoric of Fiction*).

7. Suleiman, "When the Perpetrator Becomes a Reliable Witness of the Holocaust," 5. In that essay, I focus specifically on the fictional Aue's paradoxical role as a reliable historical witness, without evoking the concept of performance. I have not changed my overall interpretation of the novel since that first analysis, but in the present essay I attempt to take into account more of Aue's problematic aspects, as well as engaging with his negative critics.

8. Husson and Terestchenko, *Les Complaisantes,* 131. Here and throughout, translations from the French are my own, unless otherwise indicated.

9. See Littell, *Les Bienveillantes,* 97, and *The Kindly Ones,* 98; hereafter, page numbers will be cited in the text, with *B* for the French version and *K* for the English translation by Charlotte Mandel.

10. In my reading of Plato's text, the "moral" of the story of Leontius is not as clear as Husson and Terestchenko suggest. The story, told by Socrates to illustrate the three parts of the soul, does not necessarily carry the heavy didacticism (about the "perversion of the gaze") attributed to it in *Les Complaisantes.* It's true, however, that Plato insists on the need to subdue the baser passions, bringing them under the control of reason. Whether Littell takes no distance from Aue, and whether Aue is an exclusively "base" character, as Husson and Terestchenko assert, are precisely the questions up for discussion. Relevant to that discussion is the fact that Littell has Aue himself quoting the Leontius parable from *The Republic* and then commenting, "To tell the truth, the soldiers rarely seemed to feel Leontius's anguish, only his desire [to look], and it was this that was disturbing the hierarchy, the idea that the men could take pleasure in these actions" (*K* 98). Husson and Terestchenko ignore the complications—and the distancing—introduced by this and similar reflections throughout the novel.

11. Husson and Terestchenko refer to Coetzee's *Elizabeth Costello* (though not to the episode I mentioned earlier) to support their contention about the writer's duty to write responsibly. They cite with approval a chapter wherein the heroine expresses strong doubts about whether writers should engage with certain painful or horrifying subjects, but they don't seem to recall that some of Coetzee's own works (e.g., *Disgrace* or *Waiting for the Barbarians*) are strong examples of that very kind of engagement. Not every opinion expressed by the heroine of *Elizabeth Costello* is to be taken at face value, or as representing Coetzee's own philosophy.

12. It can be asked whether this view does not put into question the value of teaching literature, since after all, teachers try to persuade their students to share their view of a work. I would say that it is easier to persuade students (or any reader) who have not yet made up their minds than to change the minds of those who have already formed a strong reaction, especially to a work that is perceived as controversial. For a recent, hostile discussion of *Les Bienveillantes,* see Charlotte Lacoste's book, based on her doctoral dissertation: *Séductions du bourreau* (Paris: Presses Universitaires de France, 2010). The author and I participated in a 2009 conference in Paris where we both spoke about Littell's novel and where I was able to note first-hand that mutual persuasion was impossible: neither she nor I changed our minds after hearing the other.

13. The murder occurs between two sentences: "I went upstairs and fell asleep. When I woke up the light had changed, it was quite dark" (*K* 529).

14. Littell has expressed the same idea in his own name in interviews; see, for example, Georgesco, "Jonathan Littell."

15. The names of these grotesque detectives are actually borrowed from volume two of Victor Klemperer's diary, *I Will Bear Witness,* where they figure as real-life anti-Semitic policemen whom Klemperer fears and loathes. This may be a wink to the reader on Littell's part, one of the many intertextual allusions that permeate the novel.

16. Razinsky, "History, Excess and Testimony in Jonathan Littell's *Les Bienveillantes* (*The Kindly Ones*)," unpublished paper, 2008. I understand from Razinsky that he has modified his views somewhat subsequently; but I find his argument in this paper interesting, even if I don't fully agree with it.

Works Cited

Booth, Wayne. *The Rhetoric of Fiction.* Chicago: University of Chicago Press, 1961.

Deladurantaye, Leland. "The Sound of the Furies." Review of *The Kindly Ones. Bookforum* (February/March 2009): 20.

Ezrahi, Sidra DeKoven. "Acts of Impersonation: Barbaric Space as Theatre." In Catalogue of the Jewish Museum (NY) exhibition *Mirroring Evil: Nazi Imagery/Recent Art,* edited by Norman Kleeblatt, 17–38. New Brunswick, NJ: Rutgers University Press and The Jewish Museum, Fall, 2001.

Friedländer, Saul. *Nazi Germany and the Jews.* Vol. I: *The Years of Persecution, 1933–1939.* New York: HarperCollins, 1997.

———. "The 'Final Solution': On the Unease in Historical Interpretation." In *Memory, History, and the Extermination of the Jews of Europe.* Bloomington: Indiana University Press, 1993. 102–16.

Genette, Gérard. *Narrative Discourse. An Essay in Method.* Translated by Jane E. Lewin. Ithaca: Cornell University Press, 1980.

Georgesco. "Jonathan Littell: 'Maximilien Aue, je pourrais dire que c'est moi.'" *Le Figaro* (December 30, 2006): 48–52.

Husson, Edouard and Michel Terestchenko. *Les Complaisantes. Jonathan Littell et l'écriture du mal.* Paris: François Xavier de Guibert, 2007.

Kakutani, Michiko. "Unrepentant and Telling of Horrors Untellable." Review of *The Kindly Ones. The New York Times,* February 24, 2009. Consulted online, June 5, 2009.

Klemperer, Victor. *I Will Bear Witness: A Diary of the Nazi Years.* Vol. 2: 1942–1945. Translated by Martin Chalmers. New York: Random House, 1999.

Littell, Jonathan. *Les Bienveillantes.* Paris: Gallimard, 2006.

———. *The Kindly Ones.* Translated by Charlotte Mandel. New York: Harper, 2009.

Mendelsohn, Daniel. "Transgression." Review of *The Kindly Ones. The New York Review of Books* 56, no. 5 (March 26, 2009). http://www.nybooks.com/articles/archives/2009/mar/26/transgression/.

Miller, J. Hillis. *The Ethics of Reading: Kant, De Man, Eliot, Trollope, James, and Benjamin.* New York: Columbia University Press, 1987.

Musil, Robert. *The Man without Qualities.* Translated by Sophie Wilkins. New York: Alfred A. Knopf, 1995.

Phelan, James. *Living to Tell about It: A Rhetoric and Ethics of Character Narration.* Ithaca: Cornell University Press, 2005.

Phelan, Peggy and Jill Lane, eds. *The Ends of Performance.* New York: New York University Press, 1998.

Plato. *The Republic.* Translated by Francis M. Cornford. New York: Oxford University Press, 1945.

Poe, Edgar Allan. "Colloquy of Monos and Una." Consulted on Internet, e-book from University of Virginia Library.

Rich, Motoko. "Publisher's Big Gamble on Divisive French Novel." *The New York Times,* March 4, 2009. Consulted online, July 17, 2009.

Sontag, Susan. "The Pornographic Imagination." In Sontag, *Styles of Radical Will.* New York: Farrar, Straus and Giroux, 1969.

Suleiman, Susan Rubin. "Raising Hell." Review of *The Kindly Ones. The Boston Globe,* March 15, 2009, "Ideas" Section.

———. "When the Perpetrator Becomes a Reliable Witness of the Holocaust: On Jonathan Littell's *Les Bienveillantes.*" *New German Critique* 106 (Winter 2009): 1–20.

Vollmann, William T. "Seeing Eye to Eye." *Bookforum* (February/March 200): 8–11.

———. *Europe Central.* New York: Viking Press, 2005.

CHAPTER 5

The Ethics and Aesthetics of Backward Narration in Martin Amis's *Time's Arrow*

JAMES PHELAN

As Susan Rubin Suleiman notes in her essay in this volume, historians and artists working on the Holocaust have recently been giving more attention to the difficult task of comprehending the psychology of the perpetrators. When undertaken by novelists, as Suleiman shows in her insightful analysis of Jonathan Littell's *Les Bienveillantes,* this effort inevitably raises significant ethical and aesthetic issues. How can the novelist plausibly render the psychology of the perpetrator? How does history constrain the fictional representation of perpetrators, and how does fiction provide some freedom from the constraints of history? What are the ethical and aesthetic consequences of narrative techniques that put the reader in the position of sharing the perpetrator's perspective, even if the novelist marks that perspective as unreliable? These challenging questions are for now best addressed not at the level of general theory but rather at the level of theoretically informed interpretation of individual cases such as we find in Suleiman's analysis of Littell's novel through the lens of performance. Once scholars have examined a wide range of representations from a variety of theoretical perspectives, we will be in a better position to draw broader conclusions. Consequently, in this essay, I propose to contribute to the same general project as Suleiman's by using principles and concepts of a rhetorical approach to narrative to analyze the ethics and aesthetics of one of the earlier attempts to capture the psychology of the perpetrator: Martin Amis's representation of a Nazi doctor in his 1991 novel *Time's Arrow.*

Time's Arrow is an especially intriguing case because Amis foregrounds the psychological state of Odilo Unverdorben (the last name is German for "uncorrupted" or "innocent") by emphasizing his dissociation of personality and using one side of that personality, a figure I shall, following Seymour Chatman, call Soul, to narrate the action.[1] What's more, Soul experiences time backwards, and thus he recounts Unverdorben's life from the moment just before his death to the moments of his earliest consciousness. In my analysis, I will begin with a sketch of my rhetorical approach to narrative, then move to consider some general reasons for—and consequences of—Amis's technique, and then, for the bulk of the essay, undertake a more specific examination of its workings. This examination will include a detailed account of how Amis manages the relation between reliability and unreliability and how he treats Unverdorben's behavior at Auschwitz. My goal is to demonstrate that Amis's technique is not just a clever conceit but part and parcel of an artistic response to the Holocaust that is at once aesthetically innovative and ethically valuable.

A Rhetorical Approach to Narrative
Some Key Concepts

This approach conceives of narrative as a multi-leveled purposeful communication from an implied author to an authorial and ultimately an actual audience. This conception leads to my interest in the cognitive, affective, ethical, and aesthetic dimensions of reading (the main levels in the multi-leveled communication), dimensions that I analyze through attention to narrative judgments and narrative progressions.[2] Judgments open up the different levels of communication, and progression governs the arc of the authorial audience's experience of these various dimensions from a narrative's beginning through its ending. More specifically, I define narrative as somebody telling somebody else on some occasion and for some purposes that something happened, and I define narrative progression as the synthesis of textual dynamics and readerly dynamics.

Textual dynamics are the workings of the mechanisms in the story (instabilities between, among, or within characters) or in the discourse (tensions of belief, value, or knowledge among authors, narrators, and audiences) that generate, sustain, and bring to resolution (however partial) a narrative's movement. Readerly dynamics are (1) the audience's experiences of different kinds of narrative interest and of the different levels of communication (cognitive, affective, ethical, and aesthetic) and (2) the trajectory of those experiences over the course of the narrative. I identify three main kinds of narrative interest: mimetic, thematic, and synthetic. The mimetic involves our interest in the characters and events as what Aristotle called imitations. The thematic involves our interest in the characters and events as a means to explore ideas or beliefs about the world. The synthetic involves our interest in characters and events as artificial constructions of an authorial design. The rhetorical approach does not posit any particular relation among these interests as optimal but instead emphasizes that different successful narratives can establish different relations among these three components as they pursue their different purposes.

Narratives with surprise endings provide a good illustration of the mutual influence of textual and readerly dynamics and of the reason that I regard progression as the synthesis of these two sets of dynamics. In these narratives, authors manage the movement of instabilities and tensions so that readers will experience the surprise, and readers who follow that movement are surprised or not according to the effectiveness of that management.

Narrative judgments are the bridge between textual dynamics and readerly dynamics because they are encoded into narrative texts and decoded by readers; in addition, the anticipation of readerly judgments and their consequences influences authorial choices about the textual dynamics. Three types of readerly judgment are central to the rhetorical experience of narrative:

A. Interpretive judgments about the nature of events and other elements of the narrative.
B. Ethical judgments about the moral value of characters and actions.
C. Aesthetic judgments about the artistic quality of the narrative and of its parts.

Rhetorical theory seeks to identify the judgments that readers are guided to make, the consequences of those judgments for the ongoing interaction of the textual and readerly dynamics, and the ways in which those judgments and their interactions point toward the larger purposes of the narrative.

The What and (Some of) the Why of Amis's Technique

Apart from its detailed workings, Amis's technique of backward narration has two significant and interrelated general effects: (1) It implicitly comments on the backward logic of National Socialism, the reversal of values that

led to the systematic extermination of millions of people. This massive genocide is such a crime against nature, Amis suggests, that it leads to the reversal
of a fundamental natural process, the forward movement of time. To enter
the orbit of National Socialism is to enter a world of inverted logic, or in the
words of Primo Levi, which Amis uses as the title for chapter 5 detailing the
experience of Auschwitz, a world in which one can say with justice "here
there is no why" (hier ist kein warum).[3] (2) The technique defamiliarizes
our perceptions and our understandings of every event it describes, from the
most mundane (shopping in a grocery store, hailing a taxicab) to the most
horrific (the killings at Auschwitz). It requires us to correct all the reversals of
order and the concomitant misunderstandings of cause and effect, and as we
make these corrections, we see things afresh. In this respect, Amis's project
entails not only rendering the psychology of the perpetrator but also refresh-
ing his audience's perceptions of the Holocaust. To be sure, Amis's technique
does yield some diminishing returns—once readers get used to inverting
temporal order, the defamiliarization becomes less pronounced. But such a
decline also helps to shift our attention from the technique itself to what it is
representing. In addition, Amis retains the ability to tap into the defamiliarizing effects of the technique by varying other elements of it—including the
situations in which Soul finds himself and his perspective on Odilo (sometimes Soul says "he" and "I," and sometimes "we" and "us."). I will return to
this point when I consider the narration of the events at Auschwitz.

Even as the narration performs these general functions, Amis specifically
motivates it through Unverdorben's experience as a doctor in Auschwitz. As
Amis explains in the novel's afterword, he had been "considering the idea of
telling the story of a man's life backward in time" (167), but it was only after
reading Robert Jay Lifton's study *The Nazi Doctors* that he was able to execute
the idea. Indeed, Amis notes that "my novel would not and could not have
been written without" Lifton's book (167). Lifton argues that the Nazi doctors managed to function in the camps only through a psychological doubling that allowed them to compartmentalize their behavior in such a way
that they could both maintain some level of humanity and participate in systematic genocide. One compartment contained their technical skill and task
orientation, while another contained the emotional and ethical dimensions
of their being. The strong compartmentalization allowed them to function,
but it also induced a significant dissociation of personality.

Amis's innovation is to take Lifton's findings and give them another
turn of the screw by creating a protagonist with such an extremely dissociated personality that the side of himself tuned in to emotions and ethics

experiences time backwards. More specifically, this narrator is aware that he is connected to Unverdorben because he is physically bound to him and because he has access to Unverdorben's feelings and dreams. But he also feels separate from Unverdorben because he does not have access to his host's conscious thoughts and does not have any control over his actions. Furthermore, Unverdorben, who is initially called Tod Friendly (friendly death), and then John Young and Hamilton de Souza before we discover his given name, remains wholly unaware of the narrator's presence.

These features of the technique give rise to a progression that moves simultaneously along two different but interrelated tracks: the first involves the instabilities and tensions surrounding Soul's quest to make sense of the life he is suddenly thrown into, a quest that includes his interest in discovering the ethical nature of his host and such things as the closely guarded secret of his host's life. This first track includes the tensions resulting from the global and local unreliability of the backward narration. With respect to readerly dynamics, this track orients Amis's audience in one temporal direction, that of the reverse chronology. The second track of the progression involves the set of instabilities in Unverdorben's life as it follows the usual direction of time's arrow. With respect to readerly dynamics, following this track means not only re-orienting our temporal direction but also properly configuring the events of Odilo's life as he lives it forward. Thus, what functions for Soul as forward movement in time and an advancing understanding of Unverdorben's developing life simultaneously functions for Amis's audience as backward movement and backstory. Furthermore, as Soul moves in his forward direction, we continually seek to configure the unfolding elements of backstory into a larger coherent narrative of Unverdorben's life. Following the two tracks simultaneously puts a heavy cognitive load on us, one that requires extensive and often complex interpretive judgments, and, as we shall see, similarly extensive and complex ethical judgments. Our aesthetic judgments will depend to a great extent on whether we find the intense cognitive labor of following the progression to be appropriately rewarded.

Because Soul has access to Unverdorben's feelings, he is not exactly on the outside looking in. Instead it would be more accurate to say that he is on the inside looking in, but doing so by looking from the wrong temporal direction. Furthermore, as I noted above, within this basic setup, Amis varies the relationship between Soul and Unverdorben. Sometimes Soul treats Unverdorben as a wholly other being, but at other times as the larger part of himself, and on a few occasions as someone with whom he has just about fully merged. In addition, as the discussion so far suggests, Amis constructs a doubled experiencing-I: first, Soul as the experiencer who seeks to make sense of Unverdorben and his actions, and, second, Unverdorben as an experiencer containing but also distinct from Soul.

Describing the what and the why of the technique also entails analyzing the relation between the mimetic and the synthetic components of the narrative. At first glance, Amis's technique, which Brian Richardson would regard as an example of "unnatural narration," suggests that Amis wants to plant his stake firmly in the territory of the synthetic. But a closer look reveals that in all other respects, Amis follows the conventions of standard mimesis. The characters in the storyworld, including Odilo, are bound by all the other rules and restrictions on human powers of action, and they all have recognizable human psychologies. In addition, the novel's storyworld has a familiar and documentable history and geography that includes the Nazi death camp at Auschwitz, and such historical figures as Josef Mengele and Eduard Wirths.[4] Consequently, our readerly interest in the synthetic becomes subordinated to our interest in the mimetic and the thematic. We can better understand what Amis does with those interests after a look at the detailed workings of Amis's narration.

The How and (More of) the Why of the Technique

Addressing the how of the technique entails (1) identifying the logic underlying Amis's decision to divide the narration into eight chapters that coincide with the eight different temporal points from which Soul offers his retrospective narration;[5] and (2) unpacking the relation between reliable and unreliable narration. It's worth noting that Amis further divides his eight installments of Soul's narration into the three distinct parts of his novel. Part I, which consists of chapters 1–3, follows Unverdorben's life in the eastern United States after World War II. The first chapter starts at the moment of his death and goes backward approximately six years to recount his time in Wellport, a suburb of Boston. The second focuses on his work as a doctor in Wellport and his series of unsatisfying love affairs. The third gives Soul's account of Unverdorben's time in New York, where he is a successful doctor and an active womanizer. Part II consists of Unverdorben's experiences in Europe as an adult. Chapter 4 traces his movements (backward) from the journey by boat across the Atlantic to various stops that bring him to the edge of the experience of Auschwitz. Chapter 5 focuses on Auschwitz. Chapters 6 and 7 focus on the highlights of Unverdorben's pre-Auschwitz life, especially his training as a doctor at Schloss Hartheim, the place where the Nazis first experimented with different modes of mass extermination, and his marriage to a woman named Herta. Part III consists only of the short, final chapter 8, which is split between Unverdorben's visit to Auschwitz at age thirteen and his early experiences at age three.

We can understand the logic of Amis's choice to have Soul narrate from discrete temporal moments by considering its effect on the first track of the progression. As Soul observes Unverdorben early in the narration, he notes that Unverdorben frequently feels shame and fear, that he is unable to have a relationship with a woman that is both durable and satisfying, and that he gets annual letters from "some guy in New York" (16) that report only on the weather. In short, the narration by installment allows Amis to introduce significant tensions about Unverdorben's past and to resolve those tensions very slowly, even as the resolutions of the tensions—as, for example, when we find out that Unverdorben has indeed been a Nazi doctor—increase our understanding of the instabilities along the second track of the progression, the one concerned with Unverdorben's life as lived forward. If Amis were to adopt the alternative approach of having Soul narrate retrospectively from a single point in time, he would need to choose a point near the beginning of Unverdorben's life—perhaps in his adolescence—so that he could give a full account of his experiences from the moment of death back to that temporal point. But then Soul's narration would necessarily be informed by the knowledge he had acquired throughout his adult years, including from his experiences in Auschwitz, and that would effectively eliminate the first track of the progression and its resulting readerly dynamics. Amis's choice of narration by installment allows him to combine Soul's retrospection and his gradual discoveries, which he nevertheless often misinterprets, in an especially compelling way.

As I turn to analyze the unreliability of the narration itself, I draw on my previous work on the rhetoric and ethics of unreliable narration (see *Living to Tell about It* and "Estranging Unreliability"). In fictional narrative, there are at least two tellers: the narrator who communicates to an explicit or implied narratee and the author who communicates to his or her authorial and actual audience by means of the narrator's communication to the narratee. Furthermore, narrators perform three main tasks, and these tasks can be located along three distinct axes of communication. (1) Narrators **report** on settings, characters, and events (who did what where when) along the axis of events and existents. (2) Narrators **read or interpret** what they report (this action had this meaning) along the axis of perception and interpretation. (3) They **ethically evaluate (or regard)** characters and their actions (e.g., Huck Finn judging himself as condemned to hell for deciding not to tell Miss Watson where Jim is) along the axis of ethical values. Consequently, narrators can be unreliable in three main ways: they can **misreport** (by, for example, distorting what happened, getting the order of events wrong, or even outright lying); they can **misread or misinterpret** (naïve narrators demonstrate their naïveté by misreading); and they can **misregard or misevaluate** (judging evil characters to be good, and vice versa). We can add another layer of precision to this taxonomy by noting that sometimes a narrator's report, reading, or regarding is reliable as far as it goes, though it clearly does not go far enough. This observation yields three other kinds of unreliability: underreporting, underreading, and underregarding.

By reversing time's arrow, Amis makes unreliability the default condition of the narration, because Soul is reporting events in the wrong order and compounding that misreporting with a misreading of the relations between cause and effect. Soul of course believes that his reports and readings are on target—the unreliability is unintentional on his part—and Amis relies on his audience to recognize that Soul has things backwards. Our interpretive judgments are further complicated because within this dominant fabric of unreliability, Amis inserts what I will call pockets of reliability, and so we must frequently negotiate the shifts between the two modes.

A passage from early in the novel allows us to see the weave of the fabric of unreliability: "A child's breathless wailing calmed by the firm slap of the father's hand, a dead ant revived by the careless press of a passing sole, a wounded finger healed and sealed by the knife's blade: anything like that made me flinch and veer" (26). The passage has an initially—and deliberately—disorienting effect as Soul attributes positive outcomes to small acts of violence. And although we can readily invert the order of events and reassign cause and effect (the slap causes rather than calms the wailing), Amis also gives us pause by concluding the passage with Soul's response to the violence, a response that is more in line with the one we have to our revised understanding of his report. Indeed, the last phrase of the passage helps illustrate the point that misreporting and misreading may or may not be closely linked with misregarding. In this passage, Soul's flinching at violence is a sign of his reliable regarding.

But now consider Soul's description of Tod Friendly's motivation for going to church on Sunday, where his backward experience of time leads him simultaneously to misreport, misread, and misregard.

> The forgiving look you get from everybody on the way in—Tod seems to need it, the social reassurance. We sit in lines and worship a corpse. But it's clear what Tod's really after. Christ, he's so shameless. He always takes a really big bill from the bowl. (15)

The difference between the two passages is instructive: in the first, Soul is directly reporting his own response, and it is not at all surprising that his narration is reliable on the axis of values. In the second, Soul is judging the experiencing-Unverdorben after having misreported and misread his behavior, and, again, it is not surprising that he misregards Tod as selfish rather than generous.

In addition to distinguishing among kinds of unreliability, we also need to distinguish among their affective and ethical effects. While most work on unreliability, since Wayne C. Booth coined the term in *The Rhetoric of Fiction* in 1961, has assumed that unreliability creates affective and ethical distance between the narrator and the authorial audience, some unreliable narration actually closes such distance. To capture these different effects, I have proposed a distinction between "estranging unreliability," which increases or reinforces distance and "bonding unreliability," which closes distance. The six types of unreliability—misreporting, misreading, and misregarding; underreporting, underreading, and underregarding—can each have either estranging or bonding effects. Furthermore, I suggest that we think not of an either/or binary between estranging and bonding unreliability but rather of a spectrum going from extreme estrangement at one end to up close and personal bonding at the other end.

Not surprisingly, Amis often uses Soul's unreliability for bonding effects on the ethical axis. That is, even when he is misregarding, as in his judgments of Tod's motives for going to church, he employs a set of values that the authorial audience shares. Or to take another example, consider this passage about Soul's experience in New York City:

> This business with the yellow cabs, it surely looks like an unimprovable deal. They're always there when you need one, even in the rain or when the theaters are closing. They pay you up front, no questions asked. They always know where you're going. They're great. No wonder we stand there, for hours on end, waving goodbye, or saluting—saluting this fine service. The streets are full of people with their arms raised, drenched and weary, thanking the yellow cabs. Just one hitch: they're always taking me places where I don't want to go. (65–66)

Here too Soul misreports and misreads: his inability to recognize the actual order of events leads to his misattributing the relations between cause and effect. His generous praise for the enterprise indicates that he is also misregarding. But all this unreliability makes the passage—and the self who narrates it—endearingly funny. Amis uses Soul's reversal of time as the basis for what we regard as essentially naïve narration: the narration captures the events but is clueless about interpreting them. Soul's naïveté defamiliarizes the whole business of using taxicabs in New York, highlighting its difficulties and annoyances ("we stand for hours on end," trying to flag one down) as well as its compensations (the cabs do take their users where they want to go). But most significantly, Soul's enthusiastic misregarding demonstrates a generosity of spirit that is ethically appealing. Consequently, the passage as a whole has a bonding effect, one that increases our sympathy for him and his quest to have his life make sense.

Just as important as these passages that are dominated by unreliability are those containing what I call pockets of reliability. I use the term "pockets" in order to emphasize the point that these instances of reliability are almost always surrounded by the larger fabric of unreliability. Examining these pockets along the three axes of communication will take us deeper into the how of Amis's technique.

A. The Axis of Ethics

Along this axis, we find numerous such pockets, often occurring when Soul offers ethical judgments that distinguish him from what he understands as the ethically deficient Unverdorben. The following passage from chapter 1 provides the larger context for the one in which Soul comments on his responses to small acts of violence.

> Surprisingly, Tod is known and mocked and otherwise celebrated for his squeamishness. I say surprisingly because I happen to know that Tod *isn't* squeamish. *I'm* squeamish. I'm the squeamish one. Oh, Tod can hack it. His feeling tone—aweless, distant—is quite secure against the daily round in here, the stares of vigil, the smell of altered human flesh. Tod can take all this—whereas I'm harrowed by it. From my point of view, work is an eight-hour panic attack. You can imagine me curled up within, feebly gagging, and trying to avert my eyes. . . . I'm taking on the question of violence, this most difficult question. Intellectually, I can just about accept that violence is salutary, violence is good. But I can find nothing in me that assents to its ugliness. (26)

The pocket of reliable regarding can be found in Soul's underlying ethical and *aesthetic* judgment that there's something wrong with the pain and corresponding ugliness of violence. Not surprisingly, that reliable regarding creates a bonding effect: Amis, his audience, and the narrating self all share the same values. But Amis complicates this bonding by juxtaposing this reliability with the unreliable report that Tod is not squeamish. If the report were reliable, then Tod would not be celebrated among his coworkers for his squeamishness. The consequence of this unreliability reverberates throughout the whole narrative because it complicates our view of the relations between Soul and Tod/Unverdorben. We realize that the neatness of Soul's frequent dichotomy between those two selves cannot be sustained, since the "other" narrated self actually shares traits and responses that Soul does not acknowledge, either because he cannot recognize them or because doing so would mean that he cannot claim ethical superiority over Tod/Unverdorben. But the larger effect is that we come to see that Unverdorben, the larger being who contains both the narrating self and the narrated self, is neither simply an unfeeling monster nor a sensitive soul who has been corrupted against his will. Instead, we come to see him as someone capable of both an ethical and an aesthetic objection to violence and pain and of being wholly indifferent to them.

The ending of the passage reinforces this point. Soul's view of violence as salutary stems immediately—and forgivably—from the reversal of time's arrow, since from that perspective, violent acts seem to heal people. In addition, his view of violence as ugly stems from an apparently inherent sense of the aesthetic. But having now seen that Soul and Tod are not as distinct as Soul believes, we can also see that Tod shares these attitudes. The underlying ethic of the Holocaust, according to Nazi doctrine, was that violence against the Jews was salutary and good, and we eventually learn that Tod/Unverdorben acted in accord with that belief even though he is someone who has an aversion to the ugliness of violence. The larger effect is to humanize Tod/Unverdorben and, in that way, to make his behavior more horrific.

B. The Axis of Facts and Events

Along this axis, there are two recurring pockets of reliability. (1) While the narrating self consistently misreports *the order* of events, he reliably reports the *events themselves*. Indeed, our ability to recognize his misreporting and misreading and our ability to reconstruct the chronological sequence of events in Unverdorben's life depend on this substrate of reliable reporting. In addition, this reliable reporting allows Amis to establish brief pockets of reliability even within passages of strong misreading and misregarding. (2) Soul reliably reports on his own inner life as well as on the dreams and feelings of Unverdorben. Consider this passage from the end of chapter 3, a point in the story during which Unverdorben, then known as John Young, is working as a doctor in New York:

> Is it a war we are fighting, a war against health, against life and love? My condition is a torn condition. Every day, the dispensing of existence. I see the face of suffering. Its face is fierce and distant and ancient.
>
> There's probably a straightforward explanation for the improbable weariness I feel. A perfectly straightforward explanation. It is a mortal weariness. Maybe I'm tired of being human, if human is what I am. I'm tired of being human. (93)

The immediate impetus for Soul's initial question is his misreading of a doctor's work: with time's arrow reversed, he sees that medical treatment almost always makes people worse—patients who are initially healthy become sick or injured. But his report of his incredible weariness is totally reliable, and that, in turn, leads us to take seriously his hypothesis that he is tired of being human. Since that hypothesis goes beyond the specific condition of being a doctor, our taking it seriously also means generalizing that condition. And here Amis's use of the first-person plural pronoun before switching to the singular becomes especially significant. The pronoun usage, combined with the absence of any "I–he" comparison such as we have seen in the passage about squeamishness, signals that Soul's weariness is shared by Unverdorben, even if Soul does not understand why. And when we ask why Unverdorben should feel this weariness, we can infer that the answer is to be found in something beyond these experiences in New York, that is, experiences from Unverdorben's yet-to-be-narrated past. He has likely seen the face of worse suffering and perhaps been more responsible for it. That Soul can now register the suffering of others in Unverdorben's apparent campaign against life and love also suggests that at some level Unverdorben registered such suffering in the past. But we also infer that his registering the suffering had no consequences for his behavior. The interaction between reliable and unreliable narration here aids Amis in his larger nuanced treatment of the ethical being of the perpetrator: he portrays Unverdorben as a fellow human, highlights the cost of his actions in his dissociation of self, and simultaneously suggests that his weariness now pales beside the actual destruction that he participated in.

C. The Axis of Perception and Interpretation

The reversal of time's arrow means that Soul's unreliability is greatest on this axis, but even here there are two recurring pockets of reliability. The first involves Soul's ability to analyze reliably once he steps backs from his assumptions about the direction of time's arrow. Consider this passage from the end of chapter 2. Unverdorben is riding on a train away from one city and toward another, and Soul in his usual fashion gets the direction wrong. But within that framework of misreading, Amis creates a remarkable pocket of reliable reading:

> It must be New York. That's where we're going: to New York and its stormy weather.
>   He is traveling toward his secret. Parasite or passenger, I am traveling with him. It will be bad. It will be bad, and not intelligible. But I will know one thing about it (and at least the certainty brings comfort): I *will* know *how* bad the secret is. I will know the nature of the offense. Already I know this. I know that it is to do with trash and shit, and that it is wrong in time. (63)

Because, as we learn on the very next page, his inference about New York is correct, the passage initially establishes his reliability as a reader of the situation. This reliability leads us in turn to take the other interpretations—that the secret has to do with trash and shit and that it is wrong in time—as equally reliable. But this reliability exists alongside the standard misreporting of the distinct separation between the two narrated selves, between the experiencing Soul and the experiencing Unverdorben, a separation that seems even less warranted here where the narration has shifted to the present tense. Once we focus on that unreliability, we realize that Unverdorben is aware of how bad the secret is—and that in *traveling away from* New York he is vainly trying to escape it. Indeed, once we reset time's arrow this way, we can see that the passage is informing us that Unverdorben lives with the consciousness of what Primo Levi referred to as "the nature of the offense" (quoted by Amis 168). This passage has even more weight because Amis uses that phrase as the alternate title for the book (the title page reads *Time's Arrow or The Nature of the Offense*).

The realization that Unverdorben lives with this consciousness, in turn, sheds a retrospective light on the second track of the progression to this point, that is, the part of Unverdorben's life that has already been narrated—his postwar life in America—because it shows that he does not deal with that consciousness very well at all. Although the outer trappings of his life are fine, his inner life is ruled by fear and shame and by various unsuccessful efforts to forget, deny, or overcome these emotions, including his endless pursuit of sexual conquest and his inability to sustain a serious relationship with a woman.

Once again, then, the overall effect of the passage is to lead us to a series of complex ethical judgments that initially have both bonding and estranging effects. On the one hand, we can endorse not only Soul's reliable reading but also his willingness to face the secret and learn how bad it is. But on the other hand, we infer both that Unverdorben is himself an active agent in what is terrible about the secret (indeed, his agency is connected to its being terrible) and that he has not managed to deal with his behavior in an ethically productive way. The best he can do, it seems, is to dissociate.

The second pocket of reliable narration along the axis of perception and interpretation involves Amis giving Soul the intermittent recognition that his temporal orientation is backward. For example, during a passage when Soul is employing the first-person singular as he describes his doctoring in America, he suddenly remarks:

> But wait a minute. The baby is crawling, only one or two panting inches at a time—but crawling *forward*. And the mother with the magazine, the glossy pages ticking past her face: she's reading *forward*. Hey! Christ, how long has it been since I. . . . ? Anyhow, it's soon over, this lucid interval. (82)

This intermittent recognition functions as a strong reminder that the split between the two narrated selves requires a huge effort to maintain and is therefore subject to breaking down at just about any point. That Unverdorben is nevertheless able to maintain the split self points, first, to the depth of his guilt and shame and, second and more powerfully, to the horrible actions that are the source of those feelings.

The Narration of Unverdorben's Experience at Auschwitz

Amis's use of Soul's consistent misreading of the relation of cause and effect for bonding effects complicates his task in chapter 5, the central chapter of the novel, because it deals with Unverdorben's experience at Auschwitz. Because Soul experiences time backwards, he must (mis)interpret Unverdorben's diligent participation in the extermination of the Jews as his heroic efforts toward what Soul calls the "preternatural purpose" of creating a race.

Indeed, because of these views, Soul feels that in Auschwitz, life suddenly makes more sense than it has before.[6] If Amis were to narrate the chapter using primarily unreliable narration with bonding effects, he would run the risk of undermining his own ethical authority, and, in so doing, seriously mar the quality of the novel. But he varies the narration in significant ways: sometimes he uses the unreliability for estranging effects, and sometimes he employs pockets of reliability to convey his own strongly negative ethical judgments. A closer look at both variations shows how his handling of Soul's narration both defamiliarizes our perceptions of the Holocaust and effectively uses aesthetics in the service of ethics.

Consider how Soul's naïveté works in this passage:

> . . . to prevent needless suffering, the dental work was usually completed while the patients were not yet alive. The *Kapos* would go at it, crudely but effectively, with knives and chisels or any tool that came to hand. Most of the gold we used, of course, came direct from the Reichsbank. But every German present, even the humblest, gave willingly of his own store—I more than any other officer save "Uncle Pepi" himself. I knew my gold had a sacred efficacy. All those years I amassed it, and polished it with my mind for the Jews' teeth. (121)

Once again we have misreporting, misreading, and misregarding for defamiliarizing effects. As Soul praises the generosity of the German executioners, Amis underlines their greed and their brutality, especially Unverdorben's. Soul's host, we recognize, has distinguished himself among the group by hoarding more of the victims' gold fillings than anyone else. Furthermore, Amis uses the first-person singular here, thus eliminating much of the distance between the narrating-Soul and both narrated selves (experiencing-Soul and experiencing-Unverdorben). Consequently, Amis matches Soul's enthusiasm for this work with Unverdorben's even as he underlines the sharp ethical contrast between their respective reasons for their enthusiasm. In addition, the technique reminds us that Soul and Unverdorben are ultimately part of the same person. The larger result is to estrange the authorial audience from Unverdorben by deepening the horror of his actions and underlining the depth of his dissociation of personality. This estranging effect is frequently repeated throughout chapter 5, where Amis frequently conflates Soul and Unverdorben by means of the first-person singular pronoun.

Amis also uses pockets of reliable reporting to influence our ethical judgments of Unverdorben and of Auschwitz. Consider the second sentence in the passage about the extraction of gold fillings from the victims' teeth: "the

Kapos would go at it, crudely but effectively, with knives and chisel or any tool that came to hand." Divorced from Soul's understanding of sequence, and thus, his mistaken understanding that the knives and chisels are tools for filling cavities, the sentence is a very reliable report of the perpetrators' behavior, and it functions to enhance the estranging effects of the surrounding unreliability.

Within chapter 5, Amis also uses the pockets of reliability to make a remarkable link between ethics and aesthetics, one that extends the link in the earlier passage about squeamishness. Consider these two passages that occur within just a few pages of each other in the beginning of chapter 5.

> Ordure, ordure everywhere. Even on my return through the ward, past ulcer and edema, past sleepwalker and sleeptalker, I could feel the hungry suck of it on the soles of my black boots. Outside: everywhere. This stuff, this human stuff, at normal times (and in civilized locales) tastefully confined to the tubes and tunnels, subterranean, unseen—this stuff had burst its banks, surging outward and upward onto the floor, the walls, the very ceiling of life. Naturally, I didn't immediately see the natural logic and justice of it. (117)

> What tells me that this is right? What tells me that all the rest was wrong? Certainly not my aesthetic sense. I would never claim that Auschwitz-Birkenau-Monowitz was good to look at. Or to listen to, or to smell, or to taste, or to touch. There was, among my colleagues there, a general though desultory quest for greater elegance. I can understand that word, and all its yearning: *elegant*. Not for its elegance did I come to love the evening sky above the Vistula, hellish red with the gathering souls. Creation is easy. Also ugly. (119–20)

In the first passage, Amis gives us reliable reporting and juxtaposes it with underreading and underregarding. Auschwitz in its last days—albeit the first days from Soul's perspective—has become overtaken with human excrement, a development that we interpret as having a logic and justice entirely different from anything that Soul is able to assign. Indeed, in Amis's audience, we interpret the aesthetic horror and ugliness of the camp as a sign of its ethical horror and ugliness, something that Soul is wholly unable to grasp and that Unverdorben is, at this point in his forward experience of time, still able to deny. In the second passage, the effects depend on Amis's juxtaposition of reliable reading with misreading and misregarding. Soul reliably represents the aesthetic ugliness of Auschwitz, its assault on all five senses, and the hellish quality of the sky above the crematorium, but his misplaced love of that sky underlines for us the horror of the destruction that Unverdorben, in his dissociated state, cannot face. Indeed, Soul's description of the sky underlines not only that dissociation but also Amis's close juxtaposition of reliability and unreliability for defamiliarizing effects. We readily endorse Soul's reading of the sky as "hellish red," but then suddenly must reject his phrase "with gathering souls" and replace it with its opposite: "with people literally going up in smoke."

Two Final Pockets of Reliability

Some significant additional effects of our ethical judgments in chapter 5 result from their influence on the readerly dynamics of two final pockets of reliability, one at the very end of chapter 7 and the other in the very last lines of the novel. The first pocket provides a partial resolution to one of the global tensions of the first track of the progression: Soul's question about Unverdorben's ethical being. After reflecting on whether Unverdorben could use violence (which from Soul's perspective "mends and heals") in his developing relationship with Herta, Soul says,

> I have come to the conclusion that Odilo Unverdorben, as a moral being, is absolutely unexceptional, liable to do what everybody else does, good or bad, with no limit, once under the cover of numbers. He could never be an exception; he is dependent on the health of his society, needing the sandy smiles of Rolf and Rudolph, of Rüdiger, of Reinhard. (157)

Amis has ensured the reliability of Soul's conclusion not only by making it a culminating point of the progression but also by giving us evidence of how well Unverdorben has fit in at Auschwitz. This reliable conclusion in turn functions as Amis's thematic generalization about the perpetrator. Amis has clearly been influenced by Lifton's contention that the Nazi doctors were neither beasts nor demons but human beings who were "neither brilliant nor stupid, neither inherently evil nor particularly ethically sensitive" (4) and who had to engage in some kind of doubling to participate as they did in the genocide. But by using the resources of fictional narrative, and especially those of reliable and unreliable narration, Amis's exploration gives us a perspective on the perpetrator that substantially complements Lifton's. Amis defamiliarizes the horror of Auschwitz, enables us to view it, albeit indirectly (via Soul rather than Odilo), from the perpetrator's perspective, and ably guides our judgments so that we recognize the links among Unverdorben's conformity, his dissociation, and his participation in the genocide. In this way, Amis also paves the way for us to move from our immersion in his fictional world back to our own with a deeper understanding of how the Holocaust could have happened—and, indeed, how such an event could happen again.

With the final pocket of reliability in the last lines of Soul's narration, Amis gives the narrative one final, defamiliarizing twist. He has shifted to the present tense in order to capture the process of Odilo's becoming ever younger.

> Look! Beyond, before the slope of pine, the lady archers are gathering with their targets and bows. Above, a failing-vision kind of light, with the sky fighting down its nausea. When Odilo closes his eyes, I see an arrow fly—but wrongly. Point first. Oh no, then. . . . We're away once more, over the field. Odilo Unverdorben and his eager heart. And I within, who came at the wrong time—either too soon, or after it was all too late. (165, ellipsis in original)

Soul reliably reports that the archers shoot their arrows, but he has a moment of unreliable reading, when he interprets their first direction as the wrong one. He soon recovers, though, and reliably notes that time's arrow has now reversed direction, propelling him not toward the oblivion of nonexistence but toward experiencing everything he has just told us about in the opposite order.[7] Unverdorben is not made whole by the reversal of time's arrow, and that fact renders the ending both poignant and horrific. It is poignant because, as Soul says, he will remain within Unverdorben unable to do anything but observe and report as he has done throughout this narrative. He is too soon or too late, depending on where one stands in time, but in either case, he is powerless. This new reversal of time's arrow is horrific, because Soul will no longer be able systematically to misread the relation between cause and effect in the events of Unverdorben's life—and because Unverdorben will repeat his participation in the atrocity of the Holocaust. Furthermore, by reversing time's arrow once more at the end of the narrative and implying an eventual return to Auschwitz, Amis suggests something about the continuing effects of the Holocaust as history marches on, about its living on in historical memory, and its lingering effects on all of us who are still trying to come to terms with it.

Looking back on the whole narrative, we can see that Amis, inspired by Lifton's book on Nazi doctors, has found an effective way to confront the ethical and aesthetic challenges of representing the perpetrator. To be sure, his approach is oblique—through Soul, not Odilo himself—and that approach involves significant trade-offs. We can bond with Soul in a way that we could not with Odilo, but that very bonding reinforces a certain distance from Odilo. That distance, in turn, heightens our negative ethical judgments of Odilo, but it also means that Amis will only partially get inside the psychology of the perpetrator. Consequently, as I hope this rhetorical analysis has shown, Amis is able to use what appears as a gimmick—the backwards narration—as a key building block in what becomes for his audience a rich ethical and aesthetic experience, even as we remain aware that this experience is ultimately just one partial glimpse into the complexity of the perpetrators.

Notes

1. Chatman's essay does an excellent job of analyzing the basic mechanism of the backwards narration and discussing its relation to similar techniques. Vice offers another impressive analysis of Amis's technique, one that effectively responds to the charge that Amis is more interested in his narrative technique than in the subject matter of the Holocaust. McGlothlin ("Theorizing the Perpetrator") develops an instructive comparison between *Time's Arrow* and another representation of a perpetrator, Bernhard Schlink's *Der Leser*. Other insightful work on Amis's novel has been done by Diedrick, Harris, Finney, Easterbrook, and McCarthy, but none of these critics focuses on the ethics and aesthetics of its technique to the extent that I do here.

2. For a fuller exposition and demonstration of this rhetorical approach, see my *Living to Tell about It* and *Experiencing Fiction*.

3. Levi's phrase has become a useful shorthand for referring to the inverted logic of the camps, but here is the context in which it occurs:

> Driven by thirst, I eyed a fine icicle outside the window, within hand's reach. I opened the window and broke off the icicle but at once a large, heavy guard prowling outside brutally snatched it away from me. 'Warum?' I asked in my poor German. 'Hier ist kein warum' (there is no why here), he replied, pushing me inside with a shove.
>
> The explanation is repugnant but simple: in this place everything is forbidden, not for hidden reasons, but because the camp has been created for that purpose. (35)

4. Like Mengele, Wirths was a Nazi doctor at Auschwitz. Lifton, who devotes a chapter to Wirths in *The Nazi Doctors*, succinctly summarizes his role: he "established the camp's system of selections and medicalized killing and supervised the overall process during the two years in which most of the mass murder was accomplished" (384).

5. The retrospection is intermingled with narration from the time of the telling and occasionally with simultaneous present-tense narration such as at the end of section 2, when acting and telling coincide: "I am on a train now, heading south at evening" (62).

6. See Vice for an excellent discussion of Amis's re-appropriation of parts of Lifton's study in his representation of Auschwitz.

7 . I am indebted to Brian Finney for calling my attention to Amis's move here. Finney describes its effect this way: "the narrative condemns [its readers] to share with the narrator an endless oscillation between past and present, incorporating the past into our sense of modernity" (111).

Works Cited

Amis, Martin. *Time's Arrow: Or the Nature of the Offense.* New York: Harmony Books, 1991.

Chatman, Seymour. "Backwards." *Narrative* 17, no. 1 (January 2009): 31–55.

Diedrick, James. *Understanding Martin Amis.* 2nd ed. Columbia: University of South Carolina Press, 2004.

Easterbrook, Neil. "'I know that it is to do with trash and shit, and that it is wrong in time': Narrative Reversal in Martin Amis' *Time's Arrow.*" *CCTE Studies* 55 (1995): 56–57.

Finney, Brian. "Martin Amis's *Time's Arrow* and the Postmodern Sublime." In *Martin Amis: Postmodernism and Beyond,* edited by Gavin Keulks, 101–16. New York: Palgrave, 2006.

Harris, Greg. "Men Giving Birth to New World Orders: Martin Amis's *Time's Arrow.*" *Studies in the Novel* 31, no. 4 (Winter 1999): 489–505.

Levi, Primo. *If This Is a Man* and *The Truce.* London: Abacus, 2003.

Lifton, Robert Jay. *The Nazi Doctors: Medical Killing and the Psychology of Genocide.* New York: Basic Books, 1986.

McCarthy, Dermot. "The Limits of Irony: The Chronillogical World of Martin Amis' *Time's Arrow.*" *War, Literature, and the Arts* 11, no. 1 (Spring/Summer 1999): 294–320.

McGlothlin, Erin. "Theorizing the Perpetrator in Bernhard Schlink's *The Reader* and Martin Amis's *Time's Arrow.*" In *After Representation? The Holocaust, Literature, and Culture,* edited by R. Clifton Spargo and Robert M. Ehrenreich, 210–30. New Brunswick: Rutgers University Press, 2010.

Phelan, James. "Estranging Unreliability, Bonding Unreliability, and the Ethics of *Lolita.*" *Narrative* 15, no. 2 (May 2007): 222–38. Rptd. in *Narrative Unreliability in the Twentieth-Century First-Person Novel,* edited by Elke D'hoker and Gunther Martens, 7–28. Berlin: Walter de Gruyter, 2008.

———. *Experiencing Fiction: Judgments, Progressions, and the Rhetorical Theory of Narrative.* Columbus: The Ohio State University Press, 2007.

———. *Living to Tell about It: A Rhetoric and Ethics of Character Narration.* Ithaca: Cornell University Press, 2005.

Richardson, Brian. *Unnatural Voices: Extreme Narration in Modern and Contemporary Fiction.* Columbus: The Ohio State University Press, 2006.

Vice, Sue. *Holocaust Fiction.* London: Routledge, 2000.

PART II

Intersections/Border Crossings

CHAPTER 6

The Face-to-Face Encounter in Holocaust Narrative

JEREMY HAWTHORN

In Tolstoy's novel *War and Peace* the captured Pierre is brought in to be interrogated by the French General Davoust. The General is aggressive, accuses his captive of being a spy, and when Pierre gives his name asks: "What proof have I that you are not lying?"

> "*Monseigneur!*" exclaimed Pierre in a tone that betrayed not offence but entreaty.
>
> Davoust lifted his eyes and gazed searchingly at him. For some seconds they looked at one another, and that look saved Pierre. It went beyond the circumstances of war and the court-room, and established human relations between the two men. Both of them in that one instant were dimly aware of an infinite number of things, and they realized that they were both children of humanity, that they were brothers.
>
> When Davoust had first half raised his head from his memorandum, where men's lives and doings were indicated by numbers, Pierre had been only a case, and Davoust could have had him shot without burdening his conscience with an evil deed; but now he saw in him a human being. (1140–41)

For anyone familiar with accounts of the terrible events of the Nazi Holocaust this passage is likely to inspire conflicting responses. The sentiment that the pen is mightier than the sword is an ancient one, yet Tolstoy's perception that modernity vastly increases its purchase is prophetic. His vision of a murderer whose countless victims are never confronted in person but whose "lives and doings" are indicated only by numbers points straight towards the genocidal acts of Eichmann and his fellow bureaucrats, who killed millions who were literally "just numbers" to them. At the same time, Tolstoy's confidence that face-to-face contact between individuals will render killing difficult or impossible may well seem misplaced to a modern reader. Emmanuel Lévinas—who had firsthand experience of the horrors of Nazism—was able to maintain a Tolstoyan belief in his 1953 essay "Freedom and Command" that the

> absolute nakedness of a face, the absolutely defenseless face, without covering, clothing or mask, is what opposes my power over it, my violence, and opposes it in an absolute way, with an opposition which is opposition in itself. The being that expresses itself, that faces me, says *no* to me by his very expression. This *no* is not merely formal, but it is not the *no* of a hostile force or a threat; it is the impossibility of killing him who presents that face . . . (21)

Most of us, however, are more likely to believe that if there is one lesson that can be learned from the Holocaust, it is that, as a line from Geoffrey Hill's poem "Ovid in the Third Reich" expresses it, "Innocence is no earthly weapon."

Testimony is, of its very nature, if not face-to-face then certainly a matter of personal witness, and using accounts by and about single individuals to depict aspects of the Holocaust is very far from uncontentious. Such a focus, it has been argued, risks obscuring the mass, industrialized nature of the murders, and it may also encourage us to attribute utterly inappropriate powers of self-determination and choice to victims. Accounts of individuals risk transforming the exception (survival) into the representative example. More disturbingly, any attempt to make the experience of a single survivor somehow representative of the fate of thousands—or millions—may unintentionally reduce victims to a uniformity that is worryingly reminiscent of the Nazi assertion that all racial *Untermensch* are essentially the same. It is a useful thought-exercise to imagine how we ourselves would feel were we to know that our own life and fate were to be preserved only through the memory of the life and fate of a friend or contemporary who would somehow "represent" us.

Against this it can be argued that a refusal to portray any of the victims of the Nazis as individuals also dehumanizes them: photographs of bodies being bulldozed into mass graves do nothing to display the humanity of the murdered. We cannot dispense with the accounts of the historian for whom most of the millions of victims are inevitably "indicated by numbers." But to convey the humanity of victims and the full extent of the guilt of perpetrators and bystanders, accounts by and about individuals are irreplaceable. To appropriate a distinction made by Roland Barthes, we can say that if the wide sweep of the historian gives us the "studium," the personal account of the individual provides us with the "punctum." In his essay "The Grey Zone" (in *The Drowned and the Saved*), Primo Levi refers to the Holocaust account that has probably been read more than any other, noting that "a single Anne Frank excites more emotion than the myriads who suffered as she did but whose image has remained in the shadows." And he adds: "if we had to and were able to suffer the sufferings of everyone, we could not live" (39).

However, perhaps the strongest ground for insisting on the importance of narratives that focus on encounters between individuals is that survivors themselves repeatedly include such accounts in their own writings. Here, for example, is a brief passage from the memoir of a Norwegian Auschwitz survivor, Herman Sachnowitz, in which he remembers his first meeting with a fellow-inmate named Felix Pavlowsky.

> I had noticed him as we were singing—he was lying on his stomach in one of the upper bunks, relaxing. He was a good-looking man with a strong, firm-looking face. When he got up and jumped down to the floor I noticed he was a little bent over. His eyes were blue and friendly. His age was difficult to determine, since his head was shaved. The chevron on his chest was red. But what distinguished him *most* from the rest of the inmates—and what riveted my attention in a special way—was his *smile*. It was a wry and sad little smile that had so much in it, I was not sure how to interpret it right. Was it pity, or compassion? Was it cordiality, or deep wisdom? It seemed to me that the smile emanated from a person that really understood how we felt. (67)

As I will argue below, the *smile* and a *curiosity* about others are markers of humanity that recur time and time again in survivor accounts. In its miraculous compression this passage tells us volumes about Sachnowitz, Pavlowsky, and what was sometimes preserved in the camps and discovered by victims through personal encounters. But what of encounters that involve perpetrators?

1. Victims and Perpetrators

Charlotte Delbo's extraordinary nonfictional trilogy *Auschwitz and After*—extraordinary both in terms of what it recounts and in terms of Delbo's creative mixing of narrative and poetic genres to convey her multifaceted experiences and musings over them—provides ample proof that in Auschwitz confronting one's persecutor directly guaranteed no such shared moment of perceived humanity. "The Farewell"—a short, self-contained account in the first part of the trilogy—recounts Delbo's observation of a female guard named Drexler who was supervising the loading of women into a truck taking them to the gas chamber.

> The Drexler woman observes the departure. Her fists on her hips, she supervises, like a foreman who oversees a job and is satisfied.
>
> The women in the truck do not shout. Pressed tightly together they try to release their arms from their torsos. It is incomprehensible that one would still try to work an arm free, that one could wish to lean on something.
>
> One of the women thrusts her chest far over the side panel. Straight. Stiff. Her eyes shine. She looks on Drexler with hate, scorn, a scorn that should kill. She did not shout with the others, her face is ravaged only by illness.
>
> The truck starts up. Drexler follows it with her eyes.
>
> As the truck pulls away, she waves a farewell and laughs. She is laughing. And for a long time she keeps on waving good-bye. (51)

The passage confirms what the history of our time has corroborated innumerable times already: human beings observe and even interact with those they are mistreating or murdering without displaying pity or remorse. They may even, as here, appear to enjoy the suffering they are inflicting. Sixty-seven years after Delbo observed Drexler's behavior, a thirty-two-year-old Norwegian named Anders Behring Breivik detonated a massive bomb outside a Norwegian government building, killing eight people. He then traveled to an island outside Oslo named Utøya, where the Labour Party youth organization was holding a summer camp. There he proceeded to shoot participants, killing an additional sixty-nine individuals, most of whom were teenagers or young adults, and the youngest of whom was a girl of fourteen. Many of those who survived reported that as he killed he smiled and laughed. Writing these words in Trondheim a week after this atrocity, I find that the implicit question in Delbo's account has an added force for me. Why is Drexler laughing?

The narrator of Anne Michaels's novel *Fugitive Pieces* suggests one answer.

> If the Nazis required that humiliation precede extermination, then they admitted exactly what they worked so hard to avoid admitting: the humanity of the victim. To humiliate is to accept that your victim feels and thinks, that he not only feels pain, but knows that he's being degraded. And because the torturer knew in an instant of recognition that his victim was not a "figuren" but a man, and knew at that moment he must continue his task, he suddenly understood the Nazi mechanism. Just as the stone-carrier knew his only chance of survival was to fulfil his task as if he didn't know its futility, so the torturer decided to do his job as if he didn't know the lie. The photos capture again and again this chilling moment of choice: the laughter of the damned. When the soldier realized that only death has the power to turn "man" into "figuren," his difficulty was solved. And so the rage and sadism increased: his fury at the victim for suddenly turning human; his desire to destroy that humanness so intense his brutality had no limit. (166)

Michaels's analysis suggests, paradoxically, that the most extreme cruelties of the Nazis were not the result of a failure to recognize the humanity of their victims but, on the contrary, the result of just such a recognition. A Tolstoyan recognition of the humanity of your potential victim may, if Michaels is right, lead to a grotesque frustration that erupts in acts of cruelty designed to remove the victim's humanity in the only way remaining: by killing him or her. The analysis carries with it the paradoxical implication that in certain circumstances it may be safer for the victim to be perceived as not human.

Primo Levi's *If This Is a Man* contains a chapter titled "Chemical Examination" in which Levi describes another person-to-person encounter between perpetrator and victim (himself). A prisoner in Auschwitz, Levi is attempting to prolong and even to save his life by obtaining work in a laboratory. He has reported that he is a chemist and is taken to be interviewed by a Doktor Pannwitz to see if his skills can be used by the Germans. Perhaps because the account (unusually) depicts a confrontation between two individuals alone in a room, the account is uncannily reminiscent of the previously quoted scene in *War and Peace*.

Pannwitz is tall, thin, blond; he has eyes, hair and nose as all Germans ought to have them, and sits formidably behind a complicated writing-table. I, Häftling 174517, stand in his office, which is a real office, shining, clean and ordered, and I feel that I would leave a dirty stain on whatever I touched.

When he finished writing, he raised his eyes and looked at me.

From that day I have thought about Doktor Pannwitz many times and in many ways. I have asked myself how he really functioned as a man; how he filled his time, outside of the Polymerization and the Indo-Germanic conscience; above all when I was once more a free man, I wanted to meet him again, not from a spirit of revenge, but merely from a personal curiosity about the human soul.

Because that look was not one between two men; and if I had known how completely to explain the nature of that look, which came as if across the glass window of an aquarium between two beings who live in different worlds, I would also have explained the essence of the great insanity of the third Germany.

One felt in that moment, in an immediate manner, what we all thought and said of the Germans. The brain which governed those blue eyes and those manicured hands said: "This something in front of me belongs to a species which it is obviously opportune to suppress. In this particular case, one has to first make sure that it does not contain some utilizable element." And in my head, like seeds in an empty pumpkin: "Blue eyes and fair hair are essentially wicked. No communication possible. I am a specialist in mine chemistry. I am a specialist in organic syntheses. I am a specialist . . ." (111–12, ellipsis in original)

Here there is no confident reassurance that direct eye contact between two men can penetrate the distorting and corrupting interference of nation, creed, and culture, no mutual perception of each other's humanity. Not only is Pannwitz portrayed as perceiving Levi as a species that is not human (Levi is "it," not "he"), but reading Levi's account we are encouraged to wonder whether Pannwitz can himself be reckoned within the ranks of humanity. In spite of Levi's curiosity about him "as a man" and as a possessor of a "human soul," his failure to perceive Levi's humanity undermines his own claim to be a member of the human race. As Levi has it: "that look was not one between two men." If Anne Michaels is right, this may have saved Levi's life.

The scene as presented constitutes a direct challenge to Tolstoyan optimism and to the confident liberal-humanist meliorism to which it has contributed. The scene implies that we possess no "essential humanity" but instead develop whatever humanity we posses through engagement with the cultural, historical, and political realities into which we are thrust. In other words, there is no extra-social self that can be miraculously exposed by means of an exchanged gaze with another. There is only the self that we develop through action in the world and interaction with others: that self is what we are, even if we may be compelled to conceal it from others on occasions. While *War and Peace* is a work of fiction, *If This Is a Man* is an auto-biographical account of Primo Levi's time in Auschwitz. Tolstoy's narrator is thus able to tell the reader about things of which neither of his characters is more than "dimly aware." When we read that Pierre and Davoust "realized that they were both children of humanity, that they were brothers," the form of the narrative allows for the possibility that this realization is not a fully conscious or verbalized one—there is a sense in which the passage invites the reader to assume that the narrator is providing words for sensations that are indistinctly apprehended rather than understood by the two. (We cannot in a brief moment of time put "an infinite number of things" into words.) A fictional narrator can know things of his or her characters that human beings can never know for sure about their fellows.

Levi's narrative technique is, necessarily, very different from Tolstoy's but it is no less subtle and complex. It plays with the relation between the experiencing-I and the narrating-I, the gap between the Levi who can sign his own death warrant by the wrong word or gesture and the Levi in his secure postwar world looking safely and mockingly back in time at the (now) absurdly limited Pannwitz. Note, for example, how the changes in the form of the verb in the first three paragraphs ("is tall," "he finished," "I have thought") denote and evoke significant shifts of perspective on the events described.

Pannwitz's dehumanizing vision of Häftling-Levi is countered by narrating-Levi's derisive portrayal of the somehow not-fully-human Pannwitz. We thus get a very clear sense of the scene as composed of three participants: Häftling-Levi, Pannwitz, and narrating-Levi. As I read the passage I have a clear visual-spatial sense of the powerful Pannwitz looming large over the terrified prisoner-Levi, while above and behind him looms the unremarked author-Levi, with a cool, mocking, but also appalled smile on his face. I see him smiling because there clearly is a strain of very somber humor in this passage—witness the first quoted paragraph. And if Anne Michaels associates the laughing of the perpetrators with their frustrated recognition of their victims' humanity, so too the humor in this passage can be explained only by narrating-Levi's recognition of some element of twisted human-like qualities in Pannwitz. But if recognizing the humanity of their victims prompts cruelty and murder on the part of the perpetrators, the humor that bespeaks a recognition of something human in Pannwitz leads not to "a spirit of revenge" in Levi but to *curiosity*. In "The Quiet City," one of the essays in *Moments of Reprieve*, Primo Levi makes it clear that his curiosity about Pannwitz was not an isolated experience: "It might be surprising that in the Camps one of the most frequent states of mind was curiosity. And yet, besides being frightened, humiliated and desperate, we were curious: hungry for bread and also to understand" (99). Levi's curiosity about Pannwitz infects the reader so completely that as we follow Levi's account of the meeting between his younger self and the German, we almost forget "Häftling-Levi." If our human sympathies are all with the victim, it is the perpetrator who inspires and then monopolizes our curiosity. Indeed, to a very large extent "understanding the Holocaust" has to be a matter of attempting to understand the perpetrators: the sufferings of victims demand our respect and our witness, but they cannot explain the human actions that have produced these sufferings.

Some sense of the complex narrative orchestration of the passage is necessary to engage with other details in it. "I, Häftling 174517, stand in his office, which is a real office, shining, clean and ordered." What is the force of that "which is a real office"? What else could it be? Does not this communicate to us that sense of the surrealistic in the meeting? The office is "real" in the sense that it is indistinguishable from offices in the normal world outside (and after) Auschwitz, offices in which bosses do not send their employees to the gas chamber. For Levi, too, its "real-ness" strikes him so forcibly doubtless because of its contrast to the horror he has become used to in the camp. For the reader, though, this mixture of the familiar and the quotidian with the unfamiliar and the obscene helps to link the hideous reality of the Holocaust with our day-to-day experiences, just as the familiar furniture of our waking life can exist within our worst nightmares. The hardest challenge to us in this passage is to accept that some of the furniture of Auschwitz was and is just like the furniture of our own familiar world, that Auschwitz was both a world apart and our world.

Levi's alternation between his two historically distinct selves is not without its risks. There is a danger in thus narrating the experiences of the suffering victim from the perspective of the survivor. In another of Charlotte Delbo's short sequences—"Morning"—we can, I think, see an alternative way of negotiating this danger.

I am standing amid my comrades and I think to myself that if I ever return and will want to explain the inexplicable, I shall say: "I was saying to myself: you must stay standing through roll call. You must get through one more day. It is because you got through today that you will return one day, if you ever return." This is not so. Actually I did not say anything to myself. I thought of nothing. The will to resist was doubtlessly buried in some deep, hidden spring which is now broken, I will never know. And if the women who died had required those who returned to account for what had taken place, they would be unable to do so. I thought of nothing. I felt nothing. I was a skeleton of cold, with cold blowing through all the crevices in between a skeleton's ribs. (64)

In technical terms, what we see here is a hypothetical alternative response to her suffering, presented so that it is first read not as hypothetical but as actual. The suffering Delbo is initially characterized as heroic, as one capable of hanging on to hope, not stripped of the capacity to desire survival, not too reduced to have lost the will to resist. Why does Delbo dangle this optimistic—almost sentimental—fiction in front of the reader, only to snatch it away? First, I think, to underscore the danger that her present self will rewrite the past and will inject qualities into her camp-self that were not there; and, second, in order to remind us of the stereotypes and clichés that we must strip away if we are to come close to the unheroic reality of what the Nazis reduced their victims to. However, these two suggestions may make the backtracking in the sequence more considered, more artful, than it is or was. It is tempting to read the first quoted sentence as having been written in good faith, with the qualification that follows it the result of brutally honest self-revision on Delbo's part. And having that possibility in mind serves to alert the reader to the enormous difficulty faced by the survivor who attempts after the event to narrate his or her experience as a victim.

Levi uses a different method to prevent the reader from confusing his victim-self, whose head is like an empty pumpkin containing a few seeds, with his survivor-self, a self that is relaxed, and curious about Pannwitz in ways that had to be unavailable to him at the time. If I suggested earlier that Pannwitz's inability to see Levi as a human being is symmetrically matched by the narrating-Levi's inability to grant full humanity to Pannwitz, there is also a crucial element of asymmetricality. Had Pannwitz sent Levi to the gas chamber, it would doubtless have been, as Tolstoy remarks of Davoust prior to his meeting Pierre's eyes, "without a thought." Levi, however, a free man back in Italy and a witness to the destruction of all that Pannwitz stood and worked for, does not dismiss him from his thought. "From that day I have thought about Doktor Pannwitz many times and in many ways." Levi wants to understand Pannwitz in the way that Tolstoy understands Pierre and Davoust—but he cannot. This seeking for such knowledge, however, this *curiosity* about another person confirms Levi's humanity. In marked contrast, Pannwitz's total lack of interest in anything about Levi beyond his skills as a chemist puts his own incomplete humanity on display. Not only does Levi think about Pannwitz, but he also requires us to think about him too. And by contrasting his own curiosity about Pannwitz with Pannwitz's total lack of interest in himself, Levi manages to exhibit in his narrative what it is that makes him fully human and Pannwitz less than this. Levi's account, in other words, contains instructions to us on how to avoid becoming like Pannwitz. Among them: be curious about others. Indeed, to return briefly to my opening quotation from Herman Sachnowitz's memoir, we can say that Sachnowitz's curiosity about Pavlowsky as they interact depicts their shared humanity as something that is generated and sustained through a process of active mutual exploration.

In his memoir *Hanged at Auschwitz*, French Jew Sim Kessel tells a story that contains a number of quite extraordinary events. At the same time, the very fact that Kessel survived only by virtue of such extraordinary strokes of chance and luck demonstrates the point that survivor memoirs can by their very nature be misleadingly unrepresentative. Kessel was twice rescued from an apparently inevitable death because his past as a professional boxer enabled him to appeal to sympathy from two of his captors who had also been boxers. The first time he is minutes away from death, standing naked in a group of prisoners destined for the gas chamber, waiting for more victims to make up the numbers so that the gassings are economic. A group of SS men ride up on motorcycles, and one of them positions himself near Kessel. Looking at his face, Kessel recognizes "the marks of a boxer: broken nose, ridges over the eyes, cauliflower ears."

> I simply blurted out in German:
> "*Boxer?*"
> "*Boxer? Ja!*"
> He didn't wait for me to explain, he understood. I too had a broken nose. An enormous bond existed between the two of us, despite the poles-apart difference in our positions. A few feet away, naked scarecrows stared at us and forgot for a moment their imminent deaths.
> He questioned me.
> "Where'd you fight?"
> "Pacra, Central, Delbor, Japy, and once at the Vel d'Hiver."
> Focal points of boxing, universally known. Something like a smile flickered briefly over his flattened face, revealing a row of metal-capped

teeth. He hesitated for a moment, looked around, and made a quick decision.

"Get on!" he bellowed.

Apparently he was in charge of the S.S. detachment; I suppose he didn't stand to lose a thing. Anyway, the miracle had happened. (117–18)

Kessel gets, naked, on to the motorcycle and is driven to safety. The fantastic nature of his personal survival does not end here. Condemned to death at a later point in his imprisonment in Auschwitz, he is sentenced to be publically hanged. But during the hanging the rope breaks. Because the Nazis cannot admit publicly that anything has gone wrong, he is taken away and scheduled for execution the next day. But again he has an ex-boxer as a guard, and again the man allows him to escape and assume a new identity.

The passage quoted recounts extraordinary events, but is not the most extraordinary aspect of this brief scene Kessel's report that "[a]n enormous bond existed between the two of us"? There is a minor irony, of course, in the fact that this bond is founded on a common involvement in that most brutal of sports, boxing. This bond is established with hardly any words, primarily on the basis of the physical scars left by a career as a boxer, and it is acknowledged by the German almost without apparent cerebration by (again!) "something like a smile" that flickers "briefly over his flattened face." Kessel is not at all sentimental about this moment. He certainly does not present the reader with a Tolstoyan moment of mutually perceived, common humanity. He goes on to remind his reader that this was a man who had been instrumental in the murder of very large numbers of innocent victims, that he doubtless went on to murder thousands more (including those other naked victims waiting with Kessel), and that his action in saving Kessel was in the nature of a whim, much like a man who decides not to step on a worm. What this man did was almost unimaginably evil, and this one act of cynical and possibly sentimental mercy is but a single drop in an ocean of wickedness. If the other victims waiting with Kessel could write their accounts, they would not be like the account we are able to read. It is only some time later in his account when Kessel reminds us of these victims that we realize that his narrative has carried us along, celebrating his escape and forgetting the murders.

Having said all this, the account still contains, from the perspective of the Nazi perpetrators, an element of Tolstoyan subversiveness. It suggests that some sort of recognition of, if not a shared humanity then a shared something, could break out in the most unlikely situations. The almost-smile betokens again something approaching a recognition of the victim's humanity. For once it is not followed by a renewed attempt to destroy what it has unwillingly witnessed.

2. Victim and Collaborator-Victim

Tadeusz Borowski's chilling short story "This Way for the Gas, Ladies and Gentlemen" was first published in Polish in 1948. Although Borowski's stories, collected in English in a book with the same title, are presented as fiction, they build on Borowski's experiences as a non-Jewish political prisoner in Auschwitz, where he had a number of relatively (but only relatively) privileged jobs. Sidra DeKoven Ezrahi has commented that in some cases "the testimonial imperative so controls the artistic impulse that the boundary between the memoir literature and the fiction (the *histoire* as history and as story) seems hardly distinguishable" (23). Borowski's stories surely represent one such case. Like Primo Levi, Borowski took his own life (ironically by gassing himself) after the war, in 1951. He was not yet thirty. In his introduction to *This Way for the Gas, Ladies and Gentlemen*, Jan Kott comments, "The most terrifying thing in Borowski's stories is the icy detachment of the author" (24). Reading the stories, one can see what Kott means, but his characterization strikes me as not quite right, and I will try to explain why.

The following sequence comes from the title story in *This Way for the Gas, Ladies and Gentlemen*. The story is set at the point of disembarkment for victims arriving at Auschwitz by train. The first-person narrator of the story—like Borowski himself—has a job sorting and storing the possessions stripped from the new arrivals, who are to be sent either straight to the gas chamber or on to slave labor, starvation, and death by maltreatment or gassing. From the mass of those arriving the narrator's attention is suddenly directed to a single individual.

> She descends lightly from the train, hops on to the gravel, looks around inquiringly, as if somewhat surprised. Her soft, blonde hair has fallen on her shoulders in a torrent, she throws it back impatiently. With a natural gesture she runs her hands down her blouse, casually straightens her skirt. She stands like this for an instant, gazing at the crowd, then turns and with a gliding look examines our faces, as though searching for someone. Unknowingly, I continue to stare at her, until our eyes meet.
>
> "Listen, tell me, where are they taking us?"
>
> I look at her without saying a word. Here, standing before me, is a girl, a girl with enchanting blonde hair, with beautiful breasts, wearing a little

cotton blouse, a girl with a wise, mature look in her eyes. Here she stands, gazing straight into my face, waiting. And over there is the gas chamber: communal death, disgusting and ugly. And over in the other direction is the concentration camp: the shaved head, the heavy Soviet trousers in sweltering heat, the sickening, stale odour of dirty, damp female bodies, the animal hunger, the inhuman labour, and later the same gas chamber, only an even more hideous, more terrible death . . .

Why did she bring it? I think to myself, noticing a lovely gold watch on her delicate wrist. They'll take it away from her anyway.

"Listen, tell me," she repeats.

I remain silent. Her lips tighten.

"I know," she says with a shade of proud contempt in her voice, tossing her head. She walks off resolutely in the direction of the trucks. Someone tries to stop her; she boldly pushes him aside and runs up the steps. In the distance I can only catch a glimpse of her blonde hair flying in the breeze. (44, ellipsis in original)

As with the passage describing Primo Levi's encounter with Doktor Pannwitz, this extract is disturbing in ways that are not easy to isolate.

Borowski understands that to portray the obscenity of murder, we must be confronted with what death deletes—life in all its fullness. The passage stuns us not by depicting a person being tormented and killed, but simply by depicting a person—a person who *will* be killed. As Sidra DeKoven Ezrahi puts it, "Borowski's characters are *human*, and even as they collaborate, even as they adopt an attitude of indifference or even cynicism in order to get through the day's work, they cannot banish the images of human suffering that lodge in their memory" (56). And if Pannwitz's inability to perceive Levi's humanity makes him less than human, Borowski's narrator's shamed perception of the young woman's life and humanity reminds him and us of his and of his author's membership of the human race. The portrayal of the fully human woman forces us to confront what will be or has been destroyed by her murder. She is presented as physically attractive, but more important she is presented as fully alive. She is light on her feet, active, enquiring, impatient, natural—and she asserts her quality as a living human being by—again—her curiosity, by seeking contact with other living human beings.

Moreover, as her "gliding look" examines "our faces," the reader is forced into the narrator's subject-position and required to experience as his or her own a refusal to answer her question honestly and fully. The passage prompts the question: in the narrator's position, in Auschwitz, what would we have done? Would we have been heroic enough to provide the answer that might have threatened our own vulnerable security in a "safe" job? In this sense the woman's gaze challenges both the narrator and the reader. She confronts us as a human being and requires us to respond in like manner. Who among us can be sure that, unlike Borowski's narrator, we would have had the courage to grant the woman a full, open, and honest human response?

Like Tolstoy and Levi, Borowski depicts an encounter that focuses on direct eye-to-eye contact between two individuals. And in the life, independence, and bravery of the young woman the narrator perceives the loss of significant parts of his own humanity. She meets him openly and honestly, asks him a question as an equal, and is denied an honest and open answer. His failure to rise to her challenge to be a human being provokes her "shade of proud contempt" for his suppressed humanity, and it stands as a marker for a personhood that the Nazis, as Anne Michaels points out, both denied in and attempted to remove from their victims. As we read the passage, her contempt becomes first the narrator's self-contempt and then, through our identification with the narrator, ours too. In the face of the narrator's inaction and tacit compliance, she "walks off resolutely" and "boldly" pushes aside someone who tries to stop her.

In a passage discussing his curiosity about "the lords of evil," Primo Levi suggests that "the essential inadequacy of documentary evidence" to satisfy this curiosity means that the depths of a human being are more likely to be given to us by the poet or dramatist than by the historian or psychologist (*Moments of Reprieve* 99–100). Not all commentators have felt that imaginative literature can extend our understanding of the Holocaust. In an essay titled "Aharon Appelfeld and the Problem of Holocaust Fiction," for example, Bernard Harrison cites Berel Lang's argument that "certain features essential to imaginative fiction make it incapable of dealing effectively with the historical realities of the Holocaust."

> Lang notes, to begin with, that imaginative fiction lives by the representation and analysis of individual consciousness in all its diversity. It is equally essential to our understanding of the Holocaust, Lang suggests, to see that, by its nature, it denied the diversity of consciousness. That denial is, for Lang, a function of the dispersal of causality. The fate which overtook European Jewry was neither the consequence of, nor capable of being averted by, any act or volition on the part of its victims; equally, it was in the nature of Nazism that it worked to submerge the individual wills and personalities of its adherents and tools in the workings of a vast and impersonal bureaucracy of death. So far, then, as Holocaust fiction follows

the general rule of all fiction in representing to its readers characters whose choices determine events, it falsifies its subject matter. (80)

If we direct such criticisms back toward the passage from Borowski's story, how much force do they have?

The passage does not, it is true, depict an individual able to determine her own destiny. But it does show us an individual attempting so to do. That the narrator knows, and we know, that this attempt must fail does not render this depiction false or misleading. Moreover, while the Nazi project of genocide attempted to deny "the diversity of consciousness" in its chosen victims, this is not to say that it always succeeded. Who are we to deny the right of each individual victim to his or her most personal and private experiences in the face of oppression and murder? We know, it is true, that the Nazis did succeed in denying most of the objects of their murderous plan the ability to make any choice that could determine events, but it would be insulting to the dead to presume to know what choices they attempted or what unique individual sufferings they went through and reflected upon. In the above-quoted passage from Borowski, there is no optimistic attempt to portray the young woman as one who may fall through the Nazi net. There is no SS man on a motorcycle there to save her, and the narrator spells out to us what awaits her—what awaited her nonfictional fellows. Moreover, even in the presentation of the narrator himself we do not quite witness a man who has no will apart from that of obeying the orders of his oppressors. The very fact of his shame, of his ability to register the young woman's contempt, reveals that, in contrast to Doktor Pannwitz, he has not been totally stripped of his personhood. This surely is something quite different from "icy detachment."

3. Survivors and Perpetrators

Eva Schloss's account of her arrest, deportation, and incarceration in Auschwitz ends with an account of a meeting, after liberation, with a man in the striped uniform of a prisoner who tells her and her fellows that he is an escaped prisoner. They are suspicious of him but feed him and send him in the direction of the Russian forces. The next day they witness him with his hands tied behind his back, being roughly treated by his Russian captors. When they protest this treatment, the exasperated Russians reveal his SS tattoo. "Oddly enough we weren't pleased in any way, we were extremely upset. We should have been immune to any kind of suffering but we were not. It sickened us to imagine what was going to happen to him. It was a strange emotional reaction" (157). The reaction is indeed "strange"—to us as much as to the author. Most important: our disquiet is unstable and volatile; it does not settle down into an ordered meaning, but remains to disturb us as we search for a reconciliation between these forces that we cannot find. It is again a reaction that evokes curiosity and requires discussion.

At the risk of a banal pointing out of the obvious, what comes across so strongly in this particular encounter is the fact that the liberated prisoners, who have had their humanity denied and assaulted in the most extreme form, find it immediately at hand when faced by the need of another human being—even if in this case the human being in question must be ranked among the least deserving of humane consideration. Does this account allow us to accord Tolstoy's optimistic belief in the possibility of establishing human contact between the empowered and the disempowered some credence? What about the readers of this account, we who have experienced none of the horrors or cruelties of the Holocaust? Can we share any of Schloss's sympathy for this man? Does the narrative manipulate the reader into a morally uncomfortable or even untenable position?

To feel that the account does Schloss and her fellow victims immense credit does not entail that the SS man is in any way worthy of their sympathy or fellow-feeling. Even so, it offers us no easy solutions: it forces the reader to consider that a human sympathy for the victim cannot necessarily be switched off even when the victim was, a few days earlier, one of the perpetrators. We may feel—as I do—that those who have not been victims have no right even to consider the possibility of pity for those who were perpetrators. But Schloss's account reminds us that to be human is to be unable to switch our pity on and off at the behest of our moral judgments. The passage makes us uncomfortable, but it does not manipulate us. In "The Trip," another short sequence in her memoir, Charlotte Delbo provides an account of a journey from Birkenau to Ravensbrück during which some fellow passengers were SS soldiers. Like Primo Levi, she is again *curious* about her oppressors.

Traveling along the tracks next to ours, a convoy of tanks and cannons passed us, eastward-bound. Our SS rise and explain, "Panzer divisions. On their way to Russia."

I was dying to approach them, start a conversation, find out, as little as it was bound to be, what's an SS. Why and how does one become an SS? The others go along with that. I go. They turn out to be Slovenes, forcibly enrolled in the SS. They say they know nothing about Auschwitz—all those smokestacks . . . Otherwise . . . They offer us cigarettes, light them for us. When we stop they go to the railway canteen, return with ersatz coffee distributed by Red Cross nurses to the soldiers. We had never seen a look of pity or a human expression in the eyes of an SS. Do they strip off the assassin on departing from Auschwitz? (179, ellipses in original)

Delbo ends "The Trip" by reproducing without comment a newspaper account of the American William L. Calley's "deep distress" on learning that a little Vietnamese girl for whom he had cared had escaped. Calley, at that time, was awaiting trial for having killed 109 Vietnamese civilians. The newspaper account sets Delbo's questions in a certain relief, but it does not answer them.

Herman Kahan's memoir *The Fire and the Light* contains a comparable anecdote. Kahan was brought up in a small Orthodox Jewish community in Romania and was a childhood friend of Elie Wiesel. When American troops liberated the Ebensee camp to which Kahan had been forced-marched from Auschwitz, he was naked in a truck loaded with bodies. Only because an American soldier saw some faint movement was he taken for treatment and saved. Having recuperated, he and three other survivors encounter a very frightened German soldier whom they drag into a house, strip, and again discover an SS tattoo. "With his hands folded, he pleaded and cried, '*Mensch, ich habe eine Frau und Kinder.*'" Kahan then takes command of the situation and allows the man to escape.

At first I did not want my friends to know that I had allowed an SS thug to escape. When they realized that this was the case, they were enraged. For a while it looked as though they would kill me instead of the German. They hit me and roughed me up, screaming at the top of their lungs that I was a traitor and a damned coward. In the midst of it all, I kept thinking, "Did I have the right to do this? He was one of the executioners." I tried to defend myself but they would have none of my explanations. I agreed with them: an SS guard deserved death. They finally stopped, but I do not know if they ever forgave me. For some reason, my impulsive act became a turning point in my life. The obsessive thoughts, "Will I ever be a human being again? Will I ever be rid of my hatred?" began to lose their urgency. My depression began to ease, if only slightly, for the first time.

At least I was not party to a murder. The world had had enough murders. (128–29)

If as readers we approve of Kahan's actions and of his much later assessment of them, how do we stand with regard to those survivors who did capture and kill SS guards? (Tadeusz Borowski's chilling three-page story "Silence" depicts such an event, contrasting the naïve innocence of the "young American officer" who appeals to the liberated prisoners not to take the law into their own hands but to deliver SS men to formal justice, with the determination of the men who, once the officer has left them, pull out their gagged and concealed prisoner and trample him to death.) How, we cannot help asking, *could* the SS man appeal to the four Jews as "Mensch" when the Nazis for decades had been insisting that they were not human, not "Mensch" at all? Must one get rid of hatred to regain a humanity that has been stolen from one? Are Kahan's companions right to be outraged by his action? When the SS man addresses Kahan and his companions as "Mensch," he admits that he knows and has always known that the Nazi view of the Jews is a lie. There is, too, a clear sense in Kahan's account that his desire to be rid of his hatred is not one that focuses just on the interests of the SS man, but one that is also concerned with the re-establishment of his own full humanity.

4. Conclusion

The central conceit in Wilfred Owen's poem "Strange Meeting," written in the final year of the Great War, is that of a meeting in Hell between a soldier and the man he killed the day before. The killed man's account, and his smile, assert and confirm their shared humanity, a commonality that renders absurd their murderous confrontation as members of opposing armies. In the passage I quote from Tolstoy, it is the man holding the power of life and death who perceives the humanity of his potential victim and thus allows both individuals to confront their shared humanity. Accounts of the Holocaust written by perpetrators have not, so far as I know, bequeathed us any comparable descriptions by the murderers of moments when, either during or after their genocidal acts, they recognized the humanity of the people they killed. In general, the perpetrators remain as much an enigma to us as they did to Primo Levi, who thought about Doktor Pannwitz "many times and in many ways" but who still wished to meet him again to satisfy his curiosity about him. Such a meeting was not to take place: as Levi reports in a list of answers to questions asked by his readers, when the Red Army was about to reach the Buna factory, Pannwitz "conducted himself like a bully and a coward," "ordered his civilian collaborators to resist to the bitter end, forbade them to climb aboard the train leaving for the zones behind the Front, but jumped on himself at the last moment." His escape won him little time: as Levi reports, he died in 1946 of a brain tumor (*If This Is a Man* 394). But had such a strange meeting ever taken place, it is surely unlikely that Levi's curiosity would have been satisfied. The curiosity remains, however, as a token of that humanity which, against enormous odds, he retained.

Works Cited

Borowski, Tadeusz. *This Way for the Gas, Ladies and Gentlemen*. Selected and translated by Barbara Vedder. Introduction by Jan Kott. First published in Polish, 1948. First published in English translation, 1967. New York and London: Penguin, 1976.

Delbo, Charlotte. *Auschwitz and After*. Translated by Rosette C. Lamont. Introduction by Lawrence L. Langer. New Haven and London: Yale University Press, 1995.

Ezrahi, Sidra DeKoven. *By Words Alone: The Holocaust in Literature*. First published 1980. Chicago: The University of Chicago Press, 1982.

Harrison, Bernard. "Aharon Appelfeld and the Problem of Holocaust Fiction." *Partial Answers* 4, no. 1 (2006): 79–106.

Kahan, Herman. *The Fire and the Light*. As told to Knut M. Hansson. Foreword by Elie Wiesel. Translated by Dahlia Pfeffer. First published in Norwegian, 1988. Jerusalem: Yad Vashem, 2006.

Kessel, Sim. *Hanged at Auschwitz: An Extraordinary Memoir of Survival*. First published in French, 1970, and in English, 1972. Translator not given. New York: Cooper Square Press, 2001.

Levi, Primo. *The Drowned and the Saved*. Translated by Raymond Rosenthal. Introduction by Paul Bailey. First published in Italian, 1986, and in English, 1988. London: Abacus, 1989.

———. *If This Is a Man* and *The Truce*. First published in Italian, 1958 and 1963, and in English, 1965 and 1969. Translated by Stuart Woolf. Introduction by Paul Bailey. London: Penguin. Contains an Afterword, "The Author's Answers to His Readers' Questions," translated by Ruth Feldman.

———. *Moments of Reprieve*. Translated by Ruth Feldman. Introduction by Michael Ignatieff. First published in Great Britain, 1986. London: Penguin, 2002.

Lévinas, Emmanuel. "Freedom and Command." First published 1953. *Collected Philosophical Papers*. Translated by Alphonoso Lingis, 15–23. Dordrecht, Boston, and Lancaster: Martinus Nijhoff Publishers, 1987.

Michaels, Anne. *Fugitive Pieces*. First published in Canada, 1996. London: Bloomsbury, 1998.

Sachnowitz, Herman, as told to Arnold Jacoby. *The Story of "Herman der Norweger" Auschwitz Prisoner #79235*. Translated and with an introduction by Thor Hall. First published in Norwegian, 1976. Lanham, MD: University Press of America, 2002.

Schloss, Eva, with Evelyn Julia Kent. *Eva's Story*. 5th ed. First published in Great Britain, 1988. Edgware: Castle-Kent, 2005.

Tolstoy, Leo. *War and Peace*. Vol. 2. Translated and with an Introduction by Rosemary Edmonds. Harmondsworth: Penguin, 1982.

CHAPTER 7

Knowing Little, Adding Nothing

The Ethics and Aesthetics of Remembering in Espen Søbye's
Kathe, Always Lived in Norway

ANNIKEN GREVE

Speaking by Proxy

Can the story of the victims who perished in the Holocaust be adequately told? Clearly, those who perished cannot tell their own stories. But according to Primo Levi, the question has a particular significance in connection with the *Muselmänner,* those victims of the Holocaust who were destroyed as human beings before they died biologically. "Even if they had paper and pen, the submerged would not have testified because their death had begun before that of their body. Weeks and months before being snuffed out, they had already lost the ability to observe, to remember, compare and express themselves" (*The Drowned and the Saved* 64). The story of the way they ended their lives could only be told by others: "We who were favoured by fate tried, with more or less wisdom, to recount not only our fate, but also that of the others, the submerged; but this was a discourse on 'behalf of third parties,' the story of things seen from close by, not experienced personally" (64); the victims speak "by proxy" (64).

Parameters of Evaluation and the Case of
Kathe, Always Lived in Norway

Responding to this situation, some work on the Holocaust has generated a hierarchy of representations and parameters of evaluation according to which the privileged account is the one closest to the story we cannot have: that of the victim speaking about his or her experience at the time and in the very place of the extermination. In Sidra DeKoven Ezrahi's words: "The voices that have been heard are measured, then, by degrees of access, by the privileged status of the witness or the act of witnessing and by relative claims to authenticity and artistic licence" (53). Thus, accounts that are nearer to the gas chamber, as measured along the three main variables of time, place, and person, are deemed to be more authoritative than those produced further away from it. In turn, this principle of authority by proximity privileges documentary forms of representation over imaginative ones, a point that seems to hit fictional accounts particularly hard: whatever authority they have will not be grasped by applying this principle.

Scholars such as Ezrahi and Geoffrey Hartman, however, have persuasively argued against this principle by rejecting its premise that there is a single standard against which to judge efforts to engage with the experience of the Holocaust.[1] Hartman succinctly expresses the alternative view, which I take as my point of departure. "To 'transmit the dreadful experience' [as Aharon Appelfeld puts it][2] we need *all* our memory institutions: history writing as well as testimony, testimony as well as art" (155).

In this chapter I will analyze a biography of a Holocaust victim that might throw light on the importance of not using testimony by victims or witnesses as the measuring rod for all Holocaust narratives. This biography, Espen Søbye's *Kathe, Always Lived in Norway,* is by no means unique in taking an unknown victim of the Holocaust as its biographee,[3] but thus far it is virtually unknown to the wider international readership of Holocaust literature. Eight years after its publication in Norwegian in 2003, however, it has already established itself as a seminal work on the Norwegian participation in the Holocaust. A source-based biography written approximately sixty years after the deportation and death of Kathe Lasnik by a non-Jewish Norwegian author with no personal connections to the Holocaust, *Kathe, Always Lived in Norway* can make no claims to the nearness to the events similar to that of testimonies. In her criticism of the principle of authority by proximity, Ezrahi emphasizes the way in which distance invites imaginative (and especially fictional) modes of telling into the exploration of the significance of the Holocaust (60–64). However, Søbye's biography quite consciously *does not* venture into imaginative modes of writing, and I shall argue that his decision to not fill in the many gaps in Kathe Lasnik's story is crucial to the ethical and aesthetic power of his narrative.[4] Before I turn to analyze the biography, I need to place it in the broader context of thought on the Holocaust and memory.

War against Memory

In *The Drowned and the Saved,* Primo Levi presents the difficulties of remembering the Holocaust in terms that may help us get a better grasp of what is at stake in our effort to do just that. He suggests that "the entire history of the brief 'millennial Reich' can be reread as a war against memory, an Orwellian falsification of memory, falsification of reality, negation of reality" (18). As I understand Levi, the term "war against memory" points partly to the malicious intention of the Nazi regime to obliterate from human memory what happened in the camps, expressed most directly in the destruction of evidence that could prove what had happened: crematoria that were used to burn dead bodies were also used to burn the files and lists that could prove the facts. Himmler, in a famous statement, explicitly stated that the Holocaust was "a page of glory in our history which has never been written and which will never be written" (quoted in Stark 192).

By juxtaposing the term "war against memory" with the term "negation of reality," Levi highlights another aspect of the Holocaust: the very nature of the event itself seems to make it resistant to being remembered. The event seems to weaken the capacity of most parties involved to relate to this particular part of the past, and this weakness underlies a more general logic of oblivion that has impeded later attempts to come to terms with it. The various aspects of this logic of oblivion are well known to anyone familiar with the huge literature on the Holocaust, but let me just give a reminder of a few of them. First, there is the unwillingness of the perpetrators to face up to their participation in the atrocities: forgetting that it happened may seem the only way to live with the past. Second, there is the "traumatic impact" (Stark 197) of the Holocaust, the survivors finding it hard to articulate in words what happened without being crushed by those very words, and in some cases finding it just as hard to trust their own memories. "Everything that happened was so gigantic, so inconceivable, that the witness even seemed like a fabricator to himself" (Appelfeld, quoted in Hartman 124). And clearly the survivors who did break the silence were not helped by a frequent attitude of their audiences: sheer lack of interest. This attitude was actually anticipated in the prisoners' collective dreams that Levi famously recounts and calls "the ever-repeated scene of the unlistened-to story" (*If This Is a Man* 66). This lack of interest is perhaps best understood as another effect of the enormity of the Holocaust. Both the numbers killed and the harm done to each one as an individual contribute to weaken our capacity to face up to and stand by the facts, even for those of us who have no direct involvement in the events.

One way of taking Levi's remark about the war on memory in *The Drowned and the Saved* is that he invites us to consider efforts to remember what happened in the concentration camps as *acts,* more specifically as acts of resistance or counter-acts in this war against memory, and consequently as ways of protecting both reality and our sense of it. However, this emphasis on protecting (our sense of) reality should not be taken to imply that the sole function of such counter-acts is to make available *information* about the past. Memory and memory institutions are not merely repositories of information; if they were, art would count as a memory institution only insofar as it provided facts, which it may or may not do, but providing facts is seldom all art does. More generally, different acts of remembering may differ in function, one single act may have more than one function, and in many cases the function(s) of a particular act of remembering cannot be determined independently of its context of utterance and its concern(s). The proximity to or distance from the Holocaust—in terms of time, space, and person—is one aspect of its context, and as such it may influence deeply both the form and the purpose of the act of remembering in question, but, again, it is only one aspect.

Seeing Holocaust narratives as acts of resistance in the war against memory helpfully foregrounds the distinction between the *conditions* of remembering the victims of the Holocaust and the *significance* of doing so. The obstacles to remembering the Holocaust may increase as the distance between the act of remembering and the remembered event increases. However, this distance does not necessarily diminish the *significance—especially the ethical significance*—of the act of remembrance. Quite the contrary: one may hold that those of us who have no personal memories of the Holocaust have a *duty* to remember its victims that one hesitates to ascribe to survivors. (What expressions this duty should take will certainly vary with where we stand in relation to the victims.)

If this line of reasoning holds, parameters of evaluation based solely on the principle of authority by proximity turn out to be counterproductive, to put it mildly. Rather than ranking the various accounts in relation to their nearness to the source, we should ask what significance, ethical or otherwise, we may attribute to each one of the acts of remembering that we encounter. I turn now to consider the ethical and aesthetic significance of Søbye's biography of Kathe Lasnik.

A Biography Emerging from Statistics

The most surprising fact about *Kathe, Always Lived in Norway* is perhaps that it came to be written at all, that this ordinary girl has been subject to a biography sixty years after she, on November 26, 1942, was brought to the harbor in Oslo and taken onboard *MS Donau* together with 531 other Jews on a journey that ended in Auschwitz-Birkenau on December 1 that year. Who is the author, and how did this girl who died at fifteen come to his notice?

Espen Søbye is a philosopher by training who for many years worked in *Statistics Norway,* the Norwegian Central Bureau of Statistics. In the late 1990s, while still employed by *Statistics Norway,* he was approached by a colleague on behalf of a historian at Bronx University, William Seltzer. Seltzer was doing research into what role statistics had played when Jews were identified, located, and arrested during World War II, and he wanted Søbye to comment upon the portion of his paper dealing with Norway. Søbye discovered that the Norwegian historiography of the war had little to offer on this issue: it had hardly been dealt with at all, and he decided to do the research himself.

Going through the bundle of forms that all the Norwegian Jews were asked to fill out in 1942, "Questionnaire for Jews in Norway," 1,419 forms altogether, one particular form catches his attention, that of a fifteen-year-old girl, Kathe Rita Lasnik. On the question "How long have you lived in Norway?" she had responded, in her young girl's handwriting: "Always lived in Norway." Looking for more information about her long after his research project was finished, Søbye finds her name on a commemoration relief at her school, Fagerborg, a relief dedicated to those who "gave their life for Norway during the war 1940–1945."[5] Her name is also on the memorial of the altogether 620 Jewish Holocaust victims from the Oslo area in the Jewish cemetery at Helsfyr. Finally, he reads a short notice about her in the Norwegian state's four-volume work, *Our Fallen,* which officially commemorates the Norwegian war victims. He finds few other traces of her.

Søbye decides to ask to see her file in the National Archive in which confiscated assets of the deported Jews were kept. The file, however, turns out to be empty. Nothing whatsoever is kept in the box: not a small collection of books, no toys, no birth certificate, nothing at all. Reflecting on the sadness of a person's being remembered only for the way she died ("I thought it was terrible that she was remembered only as a victim" [6]), Søbye decides to find out everything possible about Kathe Lasnik and to tell her story. The narrative *Kathe, Always Lived in Norway* is the outcome of this decision. Regarded as a counter-act in the war against memory, it is a narrative deeply marked by its point of departure: the author's concern with statistics (picking Kathe out from a vast number of victims of the Holocaust) and the lack of readily available information about her.

Interacting Story Lines

To see how this point of departure matters to the narrative regarded as a counter-act in the war against memory, we need a more detailed picture of its structure. There are three significant story lines in this narrative, the interaction of which is crucial to its overall effect. The core of the narrative is certainly the account of the short life and abrupt death of Kathe Lasnik herself, lodged in quite a bit of family history and a general account of the situation of the Jews in Oslo in the first decades of the twentieth century. This story line, which for convenience I will call the Kathe Lasnik Line, also recounts the growth in anti-Semitism in Norway during the 1930s and is brought to a close with the deportation and death of the whole family except two sisters who managed to escape to Sweden. The closure of this story line marks the opening of the second, the one telling how the Jews were treated by the Norwegian state during and after the war. This story line, which I will call the Norwegian Response Line, starts with an account of the way in which the deportation was prepared for and carried out, with a special emphasis on the deportation of Kathe Lasnik and her family. The high point of this line of action is the treason trial just after the war against Knut Rød, the head of the police in Oslo who was in charge of the police operation that led to the arrest of the Norwegian Jews.

The third line of action focuses not on the biographee and the series of events that led to her death, but rather on the researcher himself and his struggle with his material. It fleshes out the series of events that led to the biography's being written, but above all it revolves around the author's difficulties with finding sources on which to base his story. (This line of action makes *Kathe, Always Lived in Norway* similar to the narratives Irene Kacandes discusses in her essay in this volume.) This third line, which I will call the Research Line, is placed first in the discourse, but in the chronology of the fabula it is temporally removed from the two others, starting almost sixty years after the closure of the Kathe Lasnik Line and the opening of the Norwegian Response Line. What precisely is its function? Is it just another expression of the widespread, epistemologically grounded, skeptical attitude toward the genre of biography? Is its function to give the self-reflexive author room for thoughts about the impossibility of writing the life story of some other person while he is doing just that?

Undermining the Moral High Ground
The Interaction of the Research and the Norwegian Response Story Lines

As we shall see, the Research Line has several functions, and one of them is to interact with the two other story lines so as to establish what I take to be the two main areas of concern in the work. One of these concerns is closely linked to the result of Søbye's historiographic inquiry that led to the biography's being written: Why has the fate of the Jews played such a minor part in Norwegian historians' concern with the war? The answer is suggested in the Norwegian Response Line but requires some contextualization to be grasped. Because Norway was an occupied country, both the historiography and the more popular historical memory of the Norwegian experience in World War II have revolved around the conflict between collaborators and resisters. Who belongs to what group may not always be obvious, but the overall picture has been pretty clear: resistance to the occupants is the moral high ground, collaboration with the Nazis a matter of treason.

By making Knut Rød—the head of the state police force in Oslo and in charge of rounding up the Jews in Norway—the central figure of the Norwegian Response Line, Søbye complicates this picture considerably. Rød was acquitted in the treason trial after the war because he was presumed to have given practical support to the Norwegian Resistance movement. The fact that he had played a major role in the deportation of the Jews was described as a relatively minor offense compared to the actions he had taken to save ethnic Norwegian lives. Men with high positions in the Resistance testified in his favor. After examining the outcome of the treason case, the various arguments which Rød, his defense council, and some witnesses brought to his defense, Søbye more than suggests that both the court and the Resistance revealed an attitude to the Jews that was not as far removed from that which motivated the Holocaust as one would like to think. He quotes the court sociologist Knut Sveri to this effect: "In my view it raises the most uncomfortable thought that the court did not view Norwegian Jews as equal to other Norwegians" (153).

Through his analysis of the acquittal of Knut Rød, Søbye brings to light a feature of the Norwegian postwar consciousness that is both painful and embarrassing. As a nation and as a people, we Norwegians have had our own quite specific motivation for letting the fate of the Norwegian Jews during World War II fade into oblivion. The Norwegian contribution to the Holocaust does not fit the general moral map that has governed our picture of the war and our participation in it. This racist undercurrent in the Norwegian collective consciousness is brought to the foreground in Søbye's work by the interaction between the story lines. The Norwegian Response Line enables the reader to understand the significance of the lack of information about the role of statistics in the deportation of the Norwegian Jews that is central to the Research Line: we recognize the connection between how the Jews were treated during the war, how the people responsible for the deportation were treated immediately after the war, and the popular and historiographic lack of attention to the fate of the Norwegian Jews during the postwar decades.

In other words, Søbye structures the biography so that it brings to the surface not only the Norwegian collective indifference to the fate of the Jews but also a sense of shame and guilt for this indifference. The self-reflexive Research Line, in which the lack of available information, sources, and research is thematized, is crucial to establishing this critical perspective on the historiography and collective memory of World War II in Norway. Being a non-Jewish Norwegian, the biographer is able to give voice to this moral consciousness, and the fact that the biography is written at the distance of many decades from the event itself gives urgency to the telling of the story. It comes across as a belated but necessary confrontation with Norway's particular reasons for ignoring the fate of the Norwegian Jews.

Remembering the Victim as an Individual
The Interaction of the Research and the Kathe Lasnik Story Lines

Being vital for the biography's capacity to reveal the shortcomings of the Norwegian war historiography, the narrative's point of departure in statistics plays a crucial role also in relation to another of its aspects: its ambition to remember Kathe Lasnik not only as a victim but as a person, as an individual. In my view, this is the most important aspect of this particular biography read as a counter-act in the war against memory. Consequently, the Kathe Lasnik Story Line is the central component of the narrative, though, as we shall see, its force depends on its interactions with the Research Line. By singling out one victim from a statistical database containing information about 1,419 Norwegian Jews, and ultimately one victim among six million Jews, the work confronts a general difficulty in our response to the Holocaust victims. On the one hand, the unbelievably high number of victims seems to stand in the way of our taking on board the fact that each one of them is an individual. Each one of the victims, each name on the commemoration reliefs, seems to "drown" among the many. On the other hand, the significance of the high numbers cannot be grasped unless we insist on trying to encompass in our mind that each one of them is a particular human being. Thus, if we wish to hear what the statistics tell us, we have to make an effort to remember each one of the victims as the particular human being he or she is.

I will return to some of the difficulties involved in the idea of remembering the perished victim as this particular human being and the response to these difficulties in *Kathe, Always Lived in Norway.* Let me just note that the importance of grasping the victims as individuals becomes all the more pressing in light of the efforts of the Nazis not only to kill them, but to *obliterate them as individuals,* as human beings who are to be remembered: giving them numbers instead of names, robbing them of all personal belongings, and otherwise dehumanizing them. The testimony of survivors is so valuable in large part because it works against this obliteration of their individuality. This point is eloquently expressed by Hartman who in turn quotes Aharon Appelfeld: "Testimony [. . .] considered not just as a product but also as a humanizing and transactive process, [. . .] works on the past to rescue [in the words of Appelfeld] the 'individual, with his own face and proper name' from the place of terror where that face and name were taken away" (Hartman 155). Hartman has in mind the recorded testimonies at Yale, and he emphasizes the importance of the *voice* in these recordings: "Though speech may stumble, get ahead of itself, temporarily lose its way, it is a *voice* as well as *memory* that is recovered from the moments of silence and powerlessness" (155). Being able to speak in one's own voice is here envisaged as an overcoming of powerlessness, the testimony embodying the victim's capacity to mark his or her own status as an individual.

If the testimonies of the survivors are regarded as a sign of the partial failure of the Nazi regime to obliterate the victims as human beings who can tell their own story, it is important to bear in mind that the perished victims remain human beings who are entitled to being recognized and remembered as such. As noted before, Primo Levi in *The Drowned and the Saved* makes the point that the *Muselmänner* had lost their capacity to express themselves as individuals before they died, and this may make it harder for us to remember them as individuals. But their status as human beings to be remembered is not affected by their loss of capacity for self-expression, and the difficulties of remembering the Holocaust victims as individuals in no way reduce the force of the injunction to do so. On the contrary, insofar as these difficulties spring from the perpetrators' intentions to obliterate the victims as individuals, the ethical importance of the effort to remember them as such may be regarded as all the more pressing.

Kathe, Always Lived in Norway can be understood as emerging directly from this tension between the difficulties of remembering and the injunction to do so: Søbye's urge to explore Kathe Lasnik's life, to find out everything he possibly can about her, is fueled by the empty file. It is as if the subject of the biography withdraws from the author at the outset of his project, and the ensuing book is his response to this withdrawal.

As it turns out, the empty file is emblematic of the obstacles the project will meet. Søbye discovers that hardly any of his oral sources have much to say. Kathe Lasnik's school mates, her friends and nearest neighbors are all incapable of providing much information about her. "Why was it so difficult to remember Kathe Lasnik? The act of remembrance was difficult for her friends too. Had the Holocaust also eliminated other memories? It seemed that way" (12). It was as if "the weight of what happened" (Hartman 27) had worked directly on their capacity to remember. This effect of the event on the ability to remember proves an obstacle also in Søbye's meeting with her two sisters, Jenny Bermann and Elise Bassist, whom he traces to the United States and to Israel, respectively. They turn out to be rather unhelpful as sources, not because of a lack of goodwill, but because talking about her turned out to be too painful. "Kathe Lasnik's two sisters answered my questions, but it was difficult to probe. I could feel the pain of once again having to recall the memory of the little sister and the time they had spent together. I had not been prepared for this—that my efforts to find out as much as possible about Kathe Lasnik would be hindered by the pain of remembrance" (10).

The Effect of Adding Nothing

Thus the hope of being able to obtain the information needed to tell Kathe Lasnik's life story is time and again frustrated by the dynamics of oblivion inherent in the Holocaust. What are the consequences of this lack of sources on which to build a biography for Søbye's project? Does he fail in his attempt to remember Kathe Lasnik as an individual? Is the value of his attempt limited to providing insight into the difficulty of doing so? In my view the answer to both questions is no, and the clue to this answer lies in Søbye's attitude to and handling of the meager sources in this narrative. His general method is to respond to the difficulties of finding informative sources by sticking very closely to those that he finds, to glean as much as he can from them, and to stop there. He knows very little, and he adds virtually nothing. He does hypothesize a little every now and then on the basis of the sources, but in a careful, inconclusive manner, with very little propositional force invested in his words.

One effect of this method is his dependence on official statistics and publicly available data. These sources allow him to give a rather comprehensive account of the wider social and geographical world in which Kathe Lasnik lived. We learn about the wave of immigration that brought Kathe Lasnik's parents to Norway from Vilnius in Russia in 1908, the general living conditions of Jews in Oslo, their struggle to make a living, the quite sharp anti-Semitism they experienced, the legislative and economic conditions of a metal sheet worker rising from apprenticeship to owning his own shop, and the trades Kathe Lasnik's sisters were involved in. We also get a fairly comprehensive picture of the various social milieus Kathe Lasnik experienced during her childhood, as she moved into new neighborhoods and attended new schools. We get a broad and detailed picture of the world she lived in, we get a rich circumstantial backdrop, which in itself is not irrelevant, but what we do not get is an account of her various *responses* to these circumstances. We get to know her social world, but important aspects of how she acted in this world, how she interacted with it, are for the most part missing.

There are, however, exceptions to this pattern. A few episodes, the narration of which depends on oral sources, show her awareness of her "otherness." Most telling, perhaps, is her awkwardness when being placed in the same class as Celia Century, a Jewish girl from a more intellectual and self-conscious family. Celia Century was proud of her Jewishness and able to turn her otherness into a strength. Although the two of them were placed in the same class so that each would have a classmate with the same background, the move turned out to be fundamentally unhelpful for both. Celia Century's self-assertive behavior exposes Kathe Lasnik's otherness in a way she has tried to avoid, whereas Kathe Lasnik's strategy of making as little point about her otherness as possible marks Celia Century out for the other children as particularly difficult and unnecessarily self-assertive. In consequence, Celia Century turns aggressively against Kathe Lasnik in the schoolyard, but a classmate comes to her rescue.

This is an episode that clearly individualizes Kathe Lasnik, and it brings us as readers closer to her as a person by revealing how she in her attitude and actions longed for being one among the many, how she sought inclusion and integration, and how she feared exclusion. This picture is strengthened by other episodes, such as this one: "One winter afternoon in 1939, Kathe Lasnik took off on skis together with Fride Prytz and Ingrid Prytz, the daughters of the priest from the fourth floor. Suddenly Kathe Lasnik stopped and asked: 'Do you want to play with me?' The mere question surprised the sisters. They played with everybody, but understood that the girl from the ground floor was not used to taking this for granted" (70). There are also episodes without the emphasis on her insecurity, simply portraying her as integrated and (we assume) happy: "Turid Ekestrand, who lived at no. 6 Schultz' gate, accompanied Kathe Lasnik home every day from teacher Heyerdahl Larsen's flat to do homework together. Since her father was active in the fight against the Wehrmacht, Turid Ekestrand had gone with her mother and siblings to a house the family owned on Ringerike. She had brought her schoolbooks with her so that she could do her homework, but the house burnt down together with her books. For that reason Turid Ekestrand did not have schoolbooks when she arrived back in the city at the beginning of May, but she followed Kathe Lasnik home anyway. They sat together in the girls' room and Dora Lasnik came with biscuits and even a sugar trifle cake for the diligent students" (76–77). On other occasions, the cultural difference between Kathe Lasnik and her fellow pupils has an impact on their relationship: "While the rest of the children attended classes on instruction in the Lutheran Protestant religion, Kathe Lasnik left class. Karin Swärd always wondered where Kathe Lasnik went and how she spent her time while the class had instruction in the Lutheran Protestant religion. Did she wait around in the hallway or did she walk about in the schoolyard? She had a strong urge to ask [Kathe], but could not force herself to do it" (62). On the whole we learn very little about how her Jewish customs interfered with the routines of her Protestant surroundings. One schoolmate, however, "remembered that Kathe Lasnik had eaten fish pudding every Saturday. This was her way of honouring the Jewish day of rest" (64). In such passages we see both how valuable the oral sources are to give us a sense of Kathe Lasnik as this particular person and how insufficient they are to give us a fuller picture of her. They give important glimpses into her life and responses, but on the whole her schoolmates don't remember enough, or they have not been close enough to her to allow a more comprehensive picture of her to emerge. We never feel familiar with her in the way that we do with the subjects of conventional biographies.

The tempting way to tell the story of a person about whom so little is known, about whom the sources are so few and so silent or nearly silent, is to individualize her by fictionalizing her, by giving her thoughts and feelings, ups and downs, blessings and curses we take to belong to any individual human being. Søbye resists the temptation and, in fact, goes in the opposite direction. He respects the limitations of his sources: the distance between the sources and the biographee is reflected in the narrative. He tells a story with many gaps, and he leaves those gaps open; the gaps are part of what we are invited to see and acknowledge.

The result is a biography with a strangely vacuous central character. What is the point of this strategy? What is an adequate response on the part of the reader? My suggestion is that we take the respect for Kathe Lasnik as an individual to be expressed *in just that distance* that the narrative maps out between us, the readers, and her. The implicit claim seems to be that to equip her with an inner life that has no basis in the sources, to pretend that we can know her intimately, is in fact *to fail* to respect and acknowledge her as an individual, as a person with her own set of thoughts, feelings, and responses. Søbye's respect for Kathe Lasnik as this particular person with a name and a face is expressed in the acknowledgment that she cannot be brought within our reach: in an important sense she remains unknowable to us.

Documentation and Narration

Søbye's attitude to his sources also affects the narrative discourse in a way that brings out more succinctly what is attempted and achieved in this biography. Let me explain what I mean by illuminating another important feature of the way in which the different story lines interact. The opening chapter, "The Empty File," is dedicated to the Research Story Line. In the second chapter the Kathe Lasnik Story Line takes center stage. But because the sources are so meager and lacking in information about her, the telling of her story takes place in a constant dialogue with the sources, a strategy that means that the Research Line and the Kathe Lasnik Line overlap more or less constantly.

This feature of the narrative creates an intense interaction between documentation and narration. This technique comes to a peak in the role that the questionnaire for Jews living in Norway plays in the narrative. It is central to all three of the lines of action: it is crucial to the Research Line in that it sets the whole process of investigating Kathe's life in motion; crucial to the Kathe Lasnik Line in the sense that the filling in of the form was part of the procedure that eventually led to her deportation and death; and crucial to the Norwegian Response Line insofar as it is vital to the rounding up of the Norwegian Jews and as it becomes emblematic of the racism the Norwegian Jews were subject to.

The document holds a special place in the work for other reasons as well. One is that it contains one of the very few utterances in the book that with certainty can be traced back to Kathe Lasnik herself, the phrase "Always lived in Norway." Søbye reflects on why she wrote just this answer. Clearly it was redundant; it gave a piece of information that could be inferred from her answers to questions already answered. "She must have answered 'Always lived in Norway' because she thought this might help protect her. 'Always lived in Norway' was a prayer, 'I am one of you, you are not going to hurt me, are you?'" (5). Indeed, there are other possible interpretations, such as "You take me for an outsider—but I belong here," or something along this line: "There is no other place to which I belong, so don't send me away." However we interpret the utterance, it gets an expressive power we normally do not ascribe to documents, because we know these words are hers, and because of the contrast between her response and the use to which the information in the document was put.

Kathe Lasnik's answer in the questionnaire also features in the title of the book. The full title is not a direct quote from the questionnaire, but Søbye's melding of two of her responses. The comma is the only part of the phrase that belongs solely to Søbye. This authorial sequencing of her words allows us to hear the author's voice containing within itself the voice of Kathe. The title is an example of Bakhtin's concept of double-voiced discourse, one that with reference to Dorrit Cohn's term "psycho-narration" we might call "docu-narration," a kind of narration in which we characteristically hear both the mind of the person filling in the form and the narrator's voice.[6]

Being double-voiced in this way, and pointing to the story told as much as to the document forming the basis of this biography, the title gives us the prime example of the author's attitude to and handling of the sources in this narrative: he uses the interaction of the documentation and the narration to bring us as close to this person as the sources permit. The reproduction of the form itself, showing the crucial sentence "Alltid vært i Norge" [Always lived in Norway] in Kathe Lasnik's own handwriting, strengthens our sense of her being this particular person, but it also reinforces our sense that she is somehow unknowable to us: perhaps we never get closer to her as a person than we do when confronted by this particular document.

This interaction between documentation and narration carries over so as to integrate several of the other paratextual elements directly in the main narrative. The notes appear as part of the Research Line of the narrative and so do The Epilogue (in which the sources are accounted for) and the rest of the documents reproduced in the book.[7] Some of these documents fill out the picture of the general circumstances of Kathe Lasnik's life, while many of them, most significantly the black-and-white photos of her (alone, one of them being on the cover of the book, or together with family, friends, or schoolmates) contribute to the reader's sense of her individuality. Again the interaction between the Research Line and the Kathe Lasnik Line colors how we see these paratextual elements: we see them *both* as contributing to the picture of the life of the young girl *and* as sources for the struggling author, a way for Søbye to integrate the struggle to tell the story into the telling. But Søbye does not make his struggles a focal point of interest: the narrative never turns into a mystery story in which the author becomes the detective trying to solve the puzzle, nor does it turn into a by-now-familiar, postmodern, self-conscious meditation on the general problems of grasping the elusive "other." Rather than diverting the reader's attention from the main story about Kathe Lasnik, the perpetual presence of the Research Line is geared toward making us all the more aware of the nature of Kathe Lasnik's fate and to help us acknowledge, as an important feature of this fate, the unbridgeable gap between us and her.

The Significance of Remembering Kathe Lasnik

It is by handling his sources in this particular way that Søbye shapes his resistance to the oblivion that the Holocaust prescribed for Kathe Lasnik. He develops an aesthetics and an ethics of remembering the individual in which what we cannot know about this person looms almost as large as what we do know. Her remaining in an important sense unknown and unknowable to us is part of how this biography teaches us to see her and acknowledge her existence as an individual. In this way the biography seems to point beyond the initial project: to save this one individual victim from the statistics that threaten to drown her as an individual. Her remaining largely unknown to us by the end of the reading in fact seems to *reinforce* the connection between the biography and the statistical material it emerged from. We are brought to reflect on the distinction between two different forms the acknowledgment of the perished victim as an individual may take: it may take the form of writing a narrative that grasps, or seeks to grasp the life story of this particular individual, or it may take the form of an acknowledgment that there is such a story to be told, whether or not we know it.

One effect of the author's respect for the limits of the possibility of knowing Kathe is that her biography throws light on our relation to all those whose fate she shared, all those who in the statistics remain one among the millions of people who perished in the Holocaust. All of them are human beings with a history that we mostly do not know. In fact, for the vast majority of victims of the Holocaust we have far less to go on than in the case of Kathe Lasnik, and less than we have in the case of the victims named on reliefs and memorials: we cannot even identify an individual whose story we do not know. To acknowledge the reality of these human beings is the only resistance we can muster against the willful obliteration of their memory, and the only way in which we can mark the impossibility of obliterating them as individuals.

We can come at this important ethical point by reflecting further on the material that Søbye had to work with. From the sources available to Søbye and made available to us, both in the text and in the paratexts, we can make the qualified guess that Kathe Lasnik was a completely ordinary person. Not only was she too young to have left many marks on the world around her; she also comes across as someone who had no ambition to do so. There was nothing outstanding about her to that point in her life; she was not particularly talented, beautiful, or striking in any other respect. Most likely she was just a nice, shy girl, neither particularly popular nor strongly disliked. As the confrontation with Celia Century shows: she was different, but unable—at that age, at least—to turn her difference into an asset. In social contexts in which she detected the danger of exposure, she sought invisibility.

Ironically, in view of the legacy of remarkable young Jewish women in the Holocaust literature, Kathe Lasnik almost stands out as *the different one*. She is not Anne Frank. Nor is she Ruth Maier, the young Austrian woman who came to Norway as a refugee before the war, and who was deported to Auschwitz on *MS Donau* on November 26, 1942, together with Kathe Lasnik. When Maier's diaries finally were published in 2007,[8] revealing an astonishing talent for writing and thinking, she was immediately named "the Norwegian Anne Frank," and one wonders what would have become of her had she been allowed to live.

Kathe Lasnik does not belong to this group of promising Jewish women whose early and brutal death represents a great loss also to the wider culture. On the other hand, Søbye's biography reminds us of something that may not stand out so clearly in connection with Anne Frank and Ruth Maier: the importance or significance of her being a person is not in any way connected with her importance or significance *as* a person. There is no horrible loss connected with Kathe Lasnik's death over and beyond the loss of *her*. In other words, what ultimately gives the injunction to remember *her*, this particular person, its force is what she shares with all the other victims of the Holocaust, and indeed with any one of us. In virtue of Kathe Lasnik's character and Espen Søbye's shrewd narrative strategy, *Kathe, Always Lived in Norway* combines a craving for respect for the particularity of this one human being with a strong conception of the common humanity—the term "common" here pointing to both the *ordinary* and the *shared*—of which any racism is a denial, and of which the anti-Semitism that culminated in the Holocaust is a particularly brutal and evil denial.[9]

Notes

1. In addition to being an obstacle to understanding the significance of the broad variety of non-testimonial accounts of the Holocaust, this line of thought leads, as Ezrahi ("Questions of Authenticity") convincingly demonstrates, to absurd conclusions for our judgment of testimonies. A poem written in the concentration camp is *in principle* worth more than the poet's revision of it some time after the war (cf. Ezrahi 54–55). We should be able to acknowledge the special significance it may have for us that a certain text was written in the camps, under the very special circumstances that prevailed there, without turning that proximity to the camps into the only relevant criterion by which we evaluate and compare Holocaust representations.

2. Hartman quotes from Appelfeld's *Beyond Despair: Three Lectures and a Conversation with Philip Roth,* 22

3. Other examples of biographies that reconstruct the life of a victim unknown to the author are Erick Hackl, *Abschied von Sidonie* (*Farewell Sidonia*), and Patrick Modiano, *Dora Bruder.*

4. At this point it is markedly different from, for example, Modiano's *Dora Bruder,* in which the author's imaginative engagement in what might have happened to his biographee, and indeed also his partial identification with her, play a significant role.

5. My translation. A picture of the relief is reproduced in Søbye's book.

6. Or perhaps the term "docu-presentation" is more apt, as the sequence occurs in a presentational paratext rather than in the narration as such. However, given the tendency in this text to let the Research Line of the narrative encompass the paratexts, it may not be so far-fetched after all to regard it as part of the narration.

7. Søbye has in conversation explained that the narrative first was written without the Research Line. He thought it was a shame that Kathe Lasnik's sisters were relegated to the footnotes as sources, and the Research Line grew from this wish to let the sisters play a part in the narrative itself. As the Research Line developed, it produced a narrative that subsumes and transforms those original endnotes.

8. Jan Erik Vold: *Ruth Maiers dagbok: En jødisk flyktning i Norge* (*The Diary of Ruth Maier: A Jewish Fugitive in Norway*), 2007.

9. I am grateful to Rolf Gaasland, James Phelan, and Daphna Erdinast-Vulcan for discussions and comments on an earlier version of this essay. I am particularly grateful to David Cockburn for detailed comments on an earlier version and for discussions over the years on what a human being is.

Works Cited

Appelfeld, Aharon. *Beyond Despair: Three Lectures and a Conversation with Philip Roth.* Ontario, Canada: Fromm International, 1994.

Ezrahi, Sidra DeKoven. "Questions of Authenticity." In *Teaching the Representations of the Holocaust,* edited by Marianne Hirsch and Irene Kacandes. New York: Modern Language Association, 2004.

Hackl, Erich. *Abschied von Sidonie: Erzählung.* Zürich: Diogenes, 1989.

Hartman, Geoffrey. *The Longest Shadow: In the Aftermath of the Holocaust.* New York: Palgrave Macmillan, 2002.

Hirsch, Marianne and Irene Kacandes, eds. *Teaching the Representations of the Holocaust.* New York: Modern Language Association, 2004.

Levi, Primo. *If This Is A Man/The Truce.* London: Sphere Books, 1987.

———. *The Drowned and the Saved.* London: Sphere Books, 1989.

Modiano, Patrick. *Dora Bruder.* Paris: Gallimard, 1997.

Stark, Jared. "Broken Records: Holocaust Diaries, Memoirs and Memorial Books." In *Teaching the Representations of the Holocaust,* edited by Marianne Hirsch and Irene Kacandes. New York: Modern Language Association, 2004.

Søbye, Espen. *Kathe, alltid vært i Norge.* Oslo: Oktober, 2003.

———. *Kathe, Always Lived in Norway: From Oslo to Auschwitz,* translated by Schlomo Liberman (unpublished), 2004.

Vold, Jan Erik. *Ruth Maiers dagbok: En jødisk flyktning i Norge.* Oslo: Gyldendal, 2007.

CHAPTER 8

"When facts are scarce"

Authenticating Strategies in Writing by Children of Survivors

IRENE KACANDES

Basic premises of this volume are that soon there will be no eyewitnesses alive who can testify to the complicated and tragic series of events we group under the single words "Holocaust" or "Shoah" and, further, that something will be different because all eyewitnesses will be gone. A group of individuals who have been concerned about this issue for a long time are the offspring of those survivors. While I do not occupy this identity position, I am fascinated by the appearance, starting in approximately the 1990s, of a small but noteworthy number of personal texts produced by those who count themselves as familially connected to the Shoah. Building on the subtitle from one example of such writing, Lisa Appignanesi's *Losing the Dead*, I propose that we might call these texts "Holocaust family memoir." The phrase aptly describes Appignanesi's book and several others written by children of survivors because, as in *Webster's* definition of "memoir," this writing can be characterized as "narrative composed from personal experience" (def. 2a) and because such books also draw on the personal experiences of family members of their authors.

Holocaust family memoirs may on the surface seem quite different. In addition to Appignanesi's wistful elegy *Losing the Dead*, my corpus includes Art Spiegelman's self-conscious comix treatment of the Holocaust, *Maus,* panels of which started appearing in 1973 and a "complete" version of which was published as a two-volume set in 1991; Anne Karpf's biting critique *The War After;* Helen Epstein's scholarly report *Where She Came From;* Helen

Fremont's pained detective work *After Long Silence;* George Gerzon and Helen Gerzon Goransson's plodding chronicle *The Hand of Fate;* Michael Skakun's gripping adventure story *On Burning Ground;* Barbara Honigmann's understated mystery *Ein Kapitel aus meinem Leben* (*A Chapter from My Life*); and Bernice Eisenstein's clichéd psychological portrait in mixed cartoon-prose form *I Was a Child of Holocaust Survivors.*[1] These texts vary considerably with regard to their aesthetic value; what they share, however, is generational inflection. That is to say, their authors write about the Holocaust in relation to its effects on multiple generations of one family; kinship in this subculture often brings with it an especially acute sense of obligation to one's progenitors. To put it yet another way, the memoirs in my corpus include the story of what happened to family members in the Shoah *and* the story of getting that story.

That dual structure prompts the specific investigation I want to conduct here: how such texts perform their relation to the factual, historical world. For it is the search for knowledge about history, if personal history, and commitment to sharing the history known and discovered that drives these endeavors in the first place. A further motivation for investigating these texts is that their double focus is often misapprehended; I diagnose it as one source of criticism of so-called second-generation texts, of which my memoirs must be considered one type.[2] Charges of "identity theft" (Franklin) and of claiming someone else's memories as one's own (Weissman 16–17) can only be made, I will argue, when a reader fails to appreciate that anchoring these authors' parents' stories in "real" history is partially accomplished by foregrounding how that history made itself felt in the authors' own lived experiences. For this reason, in addition to propagating the subgenre of "Holocaust family memoir," I will also propose the concept of "autobiography once removed" as a useful framework for encountering the texts in my corpus.

It is perhaps because of silences in my own family about what the previous generations had suffered in Greece during the Second World War that my thoughts while reading Holocaust family memoirs have been wondrous and admiring, not critical.[3] How did those children learn so much about what had happened to their parents in the first place? What difference does knowledge seem to make? How is it connected to writing itself? How is knowledge textualized and authenticated? I took a first step toward answering these questions by investigating two aspects of these memoirs: their paratexts, Gérard Genette's term for all those elements surrounding the text proper, for instance, the book's covers, its titles and subtitles, generic designations, dedications, prefaces and afterwords, blurbs, and so forth;[4] and the text itself, in its connection to what Dorrit Cohn has proposed we call the "referential level" or "data base," that is to say, "the more or less reliably documented evidence of past events out of which the historian fashions his story" (112).[5] Offered as memoirs, the texts in my corpus fall under Philippe Lejeune's "autobiographical pact," by which readers understand writers to be asserting the identity of the work's author, narrator, and protagonist (4–5). Lejeune's theories overlap with Cohn's when he asserts that both autobiography and biography are "*referential* texts," which like "scientific or historical discourse . . . claim to provide information about a 'reality' exterior to the text, and so to submit to a test of *verification*" (22, Lejeune's emphasis). In what he then designates as the "referential pacts" that life stories make with their readers—in differentiation to the specific version of text–reader pacts in scientific and historical discourse—Lejeune points out that "it is a supplementary proof of honesty to restrict it to the *possible* (the truth such as it appears to me, inasmuch as I can know it, etc., making allowances for lapses of memory, errors, involuntary distortions, etc.), and to indicate explicitly the *field* to which this oath applies (the truth about such and such an aspect of my life, not committing myself in any way about some other aspect)" (22, Lejeune's emphasis).

Several preliminary comments might be made about the "data base" and the related "referential pacts" of the works in my corpus. First, despite claims of some Holocaust deniers, the destruction of European Jewry is one if not the most documented series of events in the history of the world. However, the record-keeping-obsessed Nazis also put enormous effort into erasing their own criminal trail, especially once it was clear that they were not going to win the war (see Stark 192). Thus, documenting certain aspects of the Holocaust has been notoriously difficult. A second and related point is that many Holocaust family memoirs try to trace lives that were preserved precisely through targeted individuals' success in hiding or erasing signs of their (Jewish) existence. Not only generally chaotic circumstances or perpetrators' desire to save themselves from postwar retribution, then, but also survival strategies deployed by the subjects of these texts during the persecution may have been responsible for destroying documents that the offspring of the victims will later search for in vain. It is this reality about the Holocaust that inspired me to borrow Lisa Appignanesi's phrase for my essay title: "'when facts are scarce'" (224). With "facts" scarce, eyewitness testimony, that is, what the parents recount about their lives, plays a much larger role in these texts than it might in, say, historical biography. Eyewitness testimony is highly vulnerable to introduced information (see, for instance, Loftus 87), and yet it is, for many aspects of the Nazi Judeocide, the only "evidence" available. Third, the authors of the texts in my corpus certainly cannot be viewed—and usually do not view themselves—as neutral researchers or reporters. Their identities both as "individuals who were not there" and as "family members" make it particularly likely that the referential pacts they enter into with their readers will be highly inflected by stated or implicit caveats like Lejeune's: "the truth such as it appears to me," "inasmuch as I can know it," "making allowances for lapses of memory, errors, involuntary distortions, etc." (22). I intend my term "autobiography once removed" to signal not only generational distance but also, because of that distance, a likelihood of numerous such allowances and lapses. With documents so scarce and eyewitness testimony so qualified, how do these texts convince their readers of their veracity?

HOLOCAUST family memoirs rely heavily on the paratext for staking their claim to "a 'reality' exterior to the text," to quote Lejeune's phrase again. Strategies I will mention here include their subtitles, generic labels on the back cover, comments on the book flaps and copyright pages, comments on sources, documentary apparatus such as maps, and the inclusion of blurbs, testimonials to the testimony, if you will.

While the titles of books in my corpus—like the titles of most books—mainly try to reference the content in a dramatic, mysterious, or otherwise intriguing way, their subtitles often function to foreground the generational structure, as in the aforementioned "A Family Memoir" of Appignanesi's *Losing the Dead.* Helen Epstein explains her project in *Where She Came From* most explicitly through her subtitle: "A Daughter's Search for Her Mother's History." Michael Skakun subtitles *On Burning Ground* "A Son's Memoir," a label that almost exclusively bears the burden of communicating the generational structure since the father's wartime experiences comprise the bulk of the book (15–221). This proportion is similar in *The Hand of Fate,* in which the filial role is mainly one of amanuensis and editor, information that I solicited from Helen Gerzon Goransson in an interview but that can also be detected from information on the title page of *The Hand of Fate:* "Memoirs of George Gerzon as Told by Him to his Daughter, Helen (Gerzon) Goransson" (see, too, a similar statement on the copyright page). Anne Karpf's subtitle, "Living with the Holocaust," foregrounds personal experience, though the gerund also produces ambiguity as it could and probably does refer to both the parental and filial generations. Karpf's is the only edition that includes a generic label that sometimes appears on the back cover of books at the top or bottom: NON-FICTION is stated in bolded capital letters. Despite author-artist Spiegelman's virulent insistence that *Maus* is nonfiction (see the discussion in Hirsch 24 and 274n14), that word appears nowhere in the paratext of the 1991 two-volume edition. The prose on the cover flaps, however, elaborately foregrounds the factual basis of the volumes, making clear that the Art in the book shares an identity with the Art who penned it, for instance. The Library of Congress categories on the copyright pages reference the Holocaust and Poland in the same way that a history book on the subject would and furthermore include the label "biography." The Library of Congress information in Bernice Eisenstein's book similarly references her, the place where her life unfolded (Toronto), biography, and the Holocaust.

In addition to a generic label in the form of a subtitle or a designation somewhere on the exterior or copyright page pronouncing the book as a referential text, the works in my corpus use several other parts of the paratext to stake their claim to recounting factual material. In Helen Fremont's and Michael Skakun's memoirs, an explicit statement intones—oddly in much the same style as we have become used to seeing disclaimers at the end of films, that is, to their not being about real persons or events—that they *are* about real persons and events. The "Author's Note" on Fremont's copyright page asserts: "This is a work of nonfiction," and then continues, "I have changed the names, locations, and identifying characteristics of a number of individuals in order to protect their privacy. In some instances, I have imagined details in an effort to convey the emotional truths of my family's experiences" (unnumbered). Skakun's claim appears on the copyright page itself as a "Note to Readers" and explains in similar fashion: "Everything contained in this narrative is factual. The author has taken a small degree of license with such details as weather, occasional dialogue, and only minor particulars that do not detract from the veracity of this story" (unnumbered). I will return to the issue of "imagining" in my conclusion.

Sometimes Holocaust family memoirs include the kind of documentary apparatus we expect to see in scholarly histories or biographies, but not necessarily in memoir or autobiography. For example, Skakun includes a "Note on Spelling" that discusses "the variant spellings of names of Eastern European cities and towns" as "a product of the region's tumultuous history and frequent border changes" (unnumbered). Karpf places a glossary directly before the opening of her text proper (xiv–xvi) and defines there words of German, Yiddish, Hebrew, and English that refer to aspects of the Holocaust such as "Selektion" and "Shoah," or of Jewish culture or religion such as "matzo" and "shiva," that she considered potential stumbling blocks for the non-Jewish Britons she assumed would comprise the bulk of her audience. Karpf's text also contains endnotes with complete references for her sources. Epstein does not use notes but does include a selected bibliography. Directly before the text proper commences, she places a sober, simplified

map of "Central Europe around 1870" (2). Spiegelman allots maps a prominent place on the back covers of both volumes of *Maus*. Drawn by the artist
in the style of the book (though in color, not black and white), the maps show
critical places in which *Maus's* story will unfold—Poland and Rego Park, NY
(volume I), and Auschwitz-Birkenau and the Catskills (volume II). The similar graphics reinforce the connection between this paratextual element and
the text; even if subconsciously, the reader should use the maps' relation to
real locations to posit the text's relation to history.

I propose that some of the dedications of these books can be thought of
as serving to emphasize their authors' commitment to history, too. Michael
Skakun dedicates his memoir, for instance, in a manner that foregrounds
specific historical information and that brings the father's and son's personal
connection to the Holocaust to readers' attention before they have begun the
book proper:

> FOR MY FATHER
> *and in memory of*
> *Chaim Chaikel Skakun, my grandfather,*
> *who died during the Soviet occupation of eastern Poland in June 1940,*
> *and*
> *Chaja Elovich Skakun, my grandmother,*
> *murdered together with thousands of other Navaredkers on*
> *December 8, 1941.*
> (unnumbered)

Spiegelman deploys the dedication to further his work's connection to history particularly effectively by including a photographic portrait in the second volume of *Maus*. The photo labeled "For Richieu" conveys to readers
through the style of the clothing and hair not only the young age of his
brother at the time the picture was taken, but also the fact that this child lived
long ago (unnumbered). Readers of *Maus I* will already know, of course,
about Richieu's tragic death, poisoned by his caretaker when she fears her
and her charges' imminent deportation to Auschwitz (109). Richieu's photo
at the beginning of *Maus II* serves as a jarring reminder of that death and of
the connection of Spiegelman's two volumes to real lives.

Finally, under paratextual strategies announcing these books' relationship to the world of history and fact, I would like to mention promotional
blurbs that appear on front and back covers and sometimes in the initial
pages of the volumes as well. More than just convincing readers that these
books are worth reading because they are "good," many blurbs of the Holo-

caust family memoirs in my corpus anchor the books' referential level. Confirming the information on the cover and title page, the blurbs frequently
refer to the books' generic status. For instance, two of the blurbs on the back
cover of my edition of *Maus I* identify its genre in a way that makes apparent
its connection to history; to cite just one of these: Jules Feiffer pronounces
Maus not only "a remarkable work . . . brilliant, just brilliant," but also "at
one and the same time a novel, a *documentary,* a *memoir,* and a comic book"
(Spiegelman, *Maus I,* back cover, my emphasis). A quotation on the back of
The Hand of Fate seems to be included for the purpose of highlighting the
role of the daughter-writer, a role noted earlier as fairly invisible in the text
itself. The paperback edition of Helen Fremont's *After Long Silence* contains
twenty blurbs on the front and back covers as well as on three initial pages,
almost all of which include the word "memoir."

Beyond the specific content of their judgments, the very identity and
authority of the blurb writers occasionally vouchsafe the veracity of these family memoirs. The publishers of Skakun's *On Burning Ground* include across
the top of the cover of the paperback edition in large bold type an endorsement by Elie Wiesel: "What a life! This is a story that must be told." Wiesel's
name appears in similarly large bolded letters at exactly the center top of the
cover. It is not simply that Elie Wiesel is a famous person and his name one
that many readers will recognize that prompts the inclusion of such a quote.
Wiesel's endorsement would be additionally effective as an authenticating
strategy because he has long campaigned for the importance of personal
testimony and against "the literature of the Holocaust," going so far as to say
that "there is no such thing" [as Holocaust fiction] (7). Aware of this stance of
Wiesel, we can assume that if Skakun's story "must be told," it is nonfictional.
Similarly, when publishers decided to use blurbs by Eva Hoffman and by
Helen Epstein on Appignanesi's and Fremont's memoirs, respectively—even
though they are not as well known as, say, Feiffer or Wiesel—they did so at
least in part because of Hoffman's and Epstein's demonstrated interest in the
fates of children of survivors through their journalistic and book writing. I
surmise that the publishers counted on at least some readers picking up the
memoirs because they had been vetted by such experts as belonging to this
sphere.

ALTHOUGH authors might be involved in making particular decisions about
the paratext, editors and publishers usually play an active role in shaping
this part of any book as it can so directly affect marketing and sales. The
strategies I now want to consider were presumably more fully determined

by the authors since they concern the text proper, specifically the way these writers authorize themselves as individuals who know a lot about their parents' experiences during the Nazi persecution. I will try to shed light on this subject by focusing first on the sources of authors' knowledge about their parents' pasts and second on the ways in which those sources are referenced in the texts. Such ways include "global" procedures, by which the memoir writers authorize the entire discourse; "local" procedures, by which they reference the source for a specific narrated event or statement made in the discourse; and "regional" strategies, by which they authorize episodes or intermediate amounts of discourse. It is not practicable to keep the sources themselves and their appearances in the text strictly separated, and as I list concrete examples of the way the author documents her or his sources below, my readers will already begin to see how and when they are textualized.

The authors of Holocaust family memoirs learn about their parents' pasts in varied ways; in Cohn's terms, the nature of the data base that the referential level denotes is quite diverse. Considering all the texts in my corpus, I would place oral communication with the parents at the top of this list. Parental stories may have been heard or overheard repeatedly in childhood, as they were by Lisa Appignanesi and Michael Skakun. They may have been solicited explicitly by the offspring in adulthood, for instance, by Helen Fremont, to reveal parents' hidden pasts and confirm children's suspicions about those pasts. In many instances, the authors had been told some stories while children and had learned others—or other versions of the same—later in their lives, as appears to have been the case with Bernice Eisenstein, Helen Gerzon Goransson, Barbara Honigmann, Anne Karpf, and Art Spiegelman. Most readers will easily remember such scenes of adult offspring soliciting new or more detailed information from the survivor generation as they are depicted frequently throughout the two volumes of *Maus*. Information about parental pasts may also be acquired by the offspring through oral stories from other eyewitnesses to the original events, as when—to give a specific example from Spiegelman—Mala, Vladek's second wife, extends Vladek's account of the registering of Jews in the stadium at Sosnowiec (*Maus I*, 92). Lisa Appignanesi describes hearing stories from an entire network of Holocaust survivors on a regular basis during her childhood (18–22). As an adult, she also interviewed her older brother—a member of what Susan R. Suleiman has termed the 1.5 generation, "too young to have had an adult understanding of what was happening to them but old enough to have been there during the Nazi persecution of Jews" (372). Staszek may not have had "an adult understanding," and yet his memories of his childhood turn out to significantly aid his younger sister Lisa in decoding a few events that occurred toward the end of the war and during its immediate aftermath, events that their parents were reticent to discuss (Appignanesi 182–92). As for other types of eyewitnesses or eyewitnessing, Helen Epstein succeeds in locating and interviewing several friends and relatives of her parents. She could also take advantage of formally recorded testimony; before writing *Where She Came From,* Epstein had taken down an oral testimony from her mother for an oral history library in New York (314). Toward the beginning of *Losing the Dead,* Appignanesi recounts watching a video testimony her mother had given to a research team at McGill University (82–83).

Photographs and documents may be mobilized not only in the paratext (like the portrait of his deceased brother Richieu that Art Spiegelman uses as part of the dedication in *Maus II*) but also in the text proper to help tell the story—for instance, that of Art and his mother in the "Prisoner on the Hell Planet" section of *Maus I* (100)—and/or to explain how the author learned something. The thirty-two different images at the center of Epstein's *Where She Came From,* for instance, range from family photographs to reproductions of advertisements for family businesses to archival photos from wartime Prague and Theresienstadt that do not depict family members (unnumbered). Through these last, Epstein presumably learned about experiences which she assumes family members did endure but for which she could not locate personal evidence. Barbara Honigmann details the contents of numerous documents she has seen and incorporates into her text proper letters written by her mother, for instance, one from her mother to a biographer of Kim Philby's begging him not to mention her name in his work (113), and another to her writer-daughter Barbara entreating her to refuse interview requests on the subject of her mother's relationship to Philby (136–37). Authors learn more about their parents' pasts by explicitly searching elsewhere for documentary evidence beyond that located in the parental home; how such searches are conducted and what they turn up is reported by several authors, most notably by Appignanesi and Epstein. Sometimes documents are procured by mail, as those solicited by Helen Fremont and her sister (e.g., from Yad Vashem, 29); and sometimes they are sought in person when the adult child decides to travel to the European locations in which their parents' dramas unfolded. Such trips of "return" figure prominently in the family memoirs of Appignanesi and Karpf (to Poland), Epstein (to Austria and the Czech Republic), and Fremont (to the Ukraine). Conducting research by examining family documents already in their possession or by seeking out additional documents, eyewitnesses, and missing information by mail or in Europe is supplemented by authors' perusal of formal histories and of memoirs by persons who survived similar persecutions or who traversed some of the same spaces as the parents; Epstein assesses some memoirs listed in her selected bibliography as "most pertinent to my mother's story" (314; see, too, Eisenstein, e.g., 84–85).

While the family memoir writers point to the primary sources, they also authorize themselves in their texts as persons qualified to relate their parents' pasts. The passages in which they do so confirm my previous demonstration of the paratexts as foregrounding the memoirs as referential texts, that is, as having a relation to fact and history. The paratexts, we might say, offer the general message that the books are based in sources, and passages within the texts usually make that claim more explicitly by pointing to (a) specific source(s) and telling the story of how authors found the source and/or what they learned from it.

Similar to the paratext, some of these textualizations of working with the data base are "global," by which I mean that one act of citing a source presumably authorizes the entire discourse. In Michael Skakun's *On Burning Ground,* a short prologue of only four pages explains that the son heard from his father directly and repeatedly about his father's experiences trying to survive Nazi persecution: "It was every Friday at the Sabbath table that Father's narrative gifts flourished" (4); "He conveyed [his story of terror that defied all logic] with such emotional conviction that it became the substance of my life, until it achieved an immediacy as palpable as my own skin" (5). Having laid out from whom he had received this information and how thoroughly he knew it, Skakun-the-son begins to narrate Skakun-the-father's past in a fairly strictly chronological fashion, referring to the protagonist throughout as "Father." The son-narrator-author never mentions again how he acquired detailed knowledge of his father's survival, though he eventually reappears in the narrative at the book's conclusion to take up the issue of how he has wrestled with the burden of his father's impossible wartime choices (232–35). In other words, Skakun authorizes himself only once as teller of his father's tale on the basis of being the recipient of eyewitness testimony. Readers are left to deduce that all information included in the text derives from this source, which actually may not be the case (recall his proviso on the copyright page). The facts that Skakun begins with this authorization, that the narrative details follow, and that the narration centers on one character who is referred to as "Father" may strengthen readers' willingness to accept that the author-narrator-son could know the many things they read in *On Burning Ground.*

Other passages in the memoirs I'm considering read more like excerpts from history books in that they are not focused on personal experience, making it necessary for authors to establish how the information there can plausibly be known by them. When Anne Karpf raises the topic of her dis-comfort with the level of gratitude her parents displayed toward Britain—"I was touched but also always a little embarrassed . . ." (16)—she is covered by Lejeune's "autobiographical pact," since she is speaking about herself. But when she continues with a three-chapter discursus on British Jews, wartime British policy toward Jews, and life as an immigrant Jew in postwar Britain, or, as she describes it, when she places her "family's experiences into his-torical context" (167), she anchors the specific bits of information relayed there through standard referential practice for academic writing: notes—in fact, more than four hundred of them (318–40) for only eighty pages of text (165–245). In contrast to Skakun's unique indication of his single eyewitness source, Karpf points to her sources over and over again at the point where each one is relevant to her discourse; I consider this a "local" authenticating strategy.

To be sure, Karpf's text is the only one in my corpus that utilizes formal documentation procedures. However, other authors also frequently docu-ment locally how they know what they include in their texts by citing a source as it is relevant. The issue here is not so much a judgment that some sources legitimate better than others as it is the observation of authors' deci-sions about when, how, and how often to point to sources. I have already mentioned Spiegelman's repeated inclusion of the scene of his father giving testimony to him; similar strategies are found in other memoirs. For exam-ple, preceding the sections with notes, Anne Karpf not only tells the reader that she interviewed her parents but then also reproduces for the reader extended if edited quotations from those interviews, passages that look and read like transcripts in their layout and person of narration. Such passages completely disambiguate the origin of information and the subsequent first-person pronoun by including the eyewitness's name: "Josef Karpf: My father came from a large family of thirteen . . ." (18).

Though they may point to sources more subjective than the historical and academic studies to which Karpf's notes mainly refer us, or though they may look more familiar to us than the transcript style just quoted, even phrases such as "My father told me . . ." or "She said" or typographical marks such as quotation marks should be recognized as local authenticating strat-egies. They point to the source for the writers' knowledge—in these cases, to eyewitness testimony they have received. I would go so far as to say that such phrases function to communicate the preciousness of that knowledge received, the solicitation of which is often difficult in survivor families. Vir-tually all texts in my corpus stage difficult solicitations of information. One in Barbara Honigmann's memoir foregrounds these challenges by relating that when her mother was eighty years old, she finally decided to tell her daughter certain things about her past, only to then begin and stop, repeatedly claiming she didn't remember (112ff.).

Of course, to anchor each single piece of information in its source, particularly when so much comes from the same source, would be tedious for the writer and the reader.[6] Therefore, some writers mention the source only once in a section to authorize what presumably applies to all the information related there. The actual reference to the source might occur at the start, in the middle, or at the end of such a section. Neither limited to one fact nor extended to everything in the text, this strategy might best be labeled "regional." Helen Epstein's *Where She Came From* utilizes regional authentications particularly often. For instance, in a larger stretch of text describing the "first wholesale exclusion of Jews from Czech cultural life" (209)—something Epstein might have learned in history books, though she does not document locally as having done so—she narrates her mother Franci's and Franci's cousin Kitty's responses to this exclusion, including reflections on their physical appearance, and specifically their noses:

> Kitty's was small, straight, and unremarkable but Franci's was long and slightly hooked at the end: the sterotype of a "Jewish" nose. Its length and shape became the focus of all her frustration with the Nazi restrictions. "I thought if my nose were different," my mother later told me, "I could go to the movies." During that strange prewar summer, my mother talked her boyfriend, her parents, and one of Prague's few plastic surgeons into helping her obtain a nose job. (210)

The first statements are rather factual and the information related there might have been garnered by studying photographs. The next sentence, however, as the assessment of another person's feelings—"the focus of all her frustration"—mystifies. We wonder how Helen could know such a private matter until we get to the verbatim quotation which the daughter authenticates by anchoring it as an oral communication from her mother: "my mother later told me." Having read this, one can then consider the whole passage as authorized by eyewitness testimony: such a personal assessment about such a private emotion did indeed stem from the person who was doing the assessing, and it was shared by that person, the mother, with the daughter, who eventually wrote the passage. Epstein authorizes similarly other pieces of information by referring to things Franci had written: "'*Marie had undergone a subtle change*,' my mother would later write" (216). Here, both the italics and the phrase "my mother would later write" serve to authenticate by pointing to this specific information as having a specific source. On many occasions in Epstein's book, however, neither a local nor a regional indication of sources appears, and the reader might then need to assume that some thoughts and feelings or even statements about Franci's whereabouts or actions do derive from the mother, because they are globally authorized by Epstein's inclusion of her mother's autobiographical writings in the selected bibliography at the end of the text (315) or because they know Epstein talked at length with her mother about the past, including in a formal act of testifying.

The problem, of course, with multiple strategies of authentication, particularly given that some of them authorize indeterminate amounts of discourse and discourse to which they are not directly adjacent, is that the reader cannot always know the source for a particular event, dialogue, or thought. A reader's unsureness can be exacerbated by some authors' (global) announcements that they have "taken a small degree of license with such details as weather, occasional dialogue, and other minor particulars that do not detract from the veracity of this story" (Skakun, copyright page; see also Fremont unnumbered) or when they point (regionally) to "how *fantasy* works when facts are scarce" (Appignanesi 224, my emphasis), to now quote the full phrase from which my title stems. The door is left open to charges of fabricating something that *does* affect the veracity of the story, because none of these authors alert their readers (locally) to every instance of engaging their imaginations to fill in missing information, as none authorizes (locally) every fact for which they have indeed consulted a data base.

ALTHOUGH Fremont is probably the author in my corpus who learned the least amount directly from her parents, her poetic account of reconstructing her parents' past can serve to summarize the general process behind family memoirs and to bring together the main points of this essay:

> Over the next several months I gradually pieced together the story of my family: from my mother, anecdotes stripped of context, shrouded in mystery; from libraries, museums, and other survivors, I was able to fill in and add color to my mother's outline. And so the story began to take shape with information from several sources, stacked high like an enormous building, overlapping layers of history and family, fact and omission. (61)

As readers who have entered into an autobiographical pact with Fremont, that is, who assume that the author, narrator and protagonist share an identity and that the topic is the individual's own existence (Lejeune 4–5), we need not challenge her statement about her research project, and she need not authenticate it beyond writing in the first person, since she is relating something she herself did: "I gradually pieced together . . ." To consider now one of many counterexamples, when Fremont claims that her father's misshapen left arm "is a souvenir from the camps, a token of his time there, a little gift from the Gulag" (225), the statement no longer concerns the author's feelings, actions, or something she could have witnessed herself. Readers may rightly wonder: how does she know? Or to return to Cohn's terminology: through what data base has she come to know about her father's arm, and how does her text acknowledge her use of that data base?

Surely eyewitness testimony is the most likely source for this kind of information. After all, unlike a birth, arrest, deportation, or death, an accident or personal attack was not an occurrence to have created a paper trail during the Nazi assault on European Jewry or in the Soviet prison camp system where this particular event transpired. That's not just a guess, of course. Having read the book, I know that when she was a child, Fremont had discovered an old newspaper article that reported that her father's arm had been broken in a Soviet camp by prisoners trying to steal his clothes from him (226); Fremont had then immediately queried her mother who confirmed that this was true (226); years later her father himself told her about being jumped by other prisoners (228). In other words, Fremont the narrator reveals that she learned of this particular episode in multiple ways, through a written account and two oral communications, one from an eyewitness, the protagonist of this episode, her father, and one from an intimate of the eyewitness, her mother.

The question remains: Why does the *reader* accept this as a true story from the past? The author refers to them, vouches for them, by putting them into first-person statements in her book. To quote now instead of to paraphrase: "I found an article . . ." (225); "I went to my mother with the article . . ." (226); "When I was in college in 1975, my father told me more about his arm" (228). Notice how even the oral interaction with the eyewitness is subsumed into a sentence about the self: "When *I* was in college . . . my father told me . . ." In such instances—and there are so many in my corpus that I could not possibly cite them all here—we should notice that information is authorized not by foregrounding the actual source but by narrating *the author's experience of encountering the source.* This strategy makes sense given the generational structure of these texts and their multiple plots, time frames, and goals: as mentioned at the beginning of this essay, most authors concentrate on their parents' pasts and include information about their own childhoods and their searches to learn more about their parents. I return here, too, to the generic point. We might conceptualize at least passages like Fremont's on her father's arm as "autobiography once removed" rather than as strictly biography or history. These texts are narrated in the first person and located in a book with the offspring's name on the cover, and thus the veracity of the content of these statements falls under the autobiographical pact. To put it otherwise, once attributed to the self, the knowledge need not be authorized in an additional way, and in fact in myriad instances authors of my family memoirs do not authorize such information in any other way.

We can use my generic idea of "autobiography once removed" to shed light on an ethical point, that is, on accusations that the second generation believes that its "'experiences' of the Holocaust are just as valid as those of the survivors" (Franklin 31) or misreadings of Hirsch's concept of post-memory as claiming that children of survivors "have memories of living these experiences" (Weissman 17). These charges are preposterous in their generalizing and, in any case, constitute a mischaracterization of the family memoirs I have been examining. These books' numerous and sometimes overlapping authenticating strategies in the paratext and text proper demonstrate that authors do assert and do partially account for a relation between their works and verifiable history. They mobilize various strategies for doing so. Furthermore, these authors are sometimes writing as autobiographers and sometimes as biographers. However, as I hope my discussion above and the "once removed" part of my term demonstrate, occupying both roles facilitates authors' *slippage* between authenticating strategies readers might consider as more appropriate to one genre or the other. As in the (re)framing of information we observed in Helen Fremont's account of learning the history of her father's mangled arm, the knowledge about the parent may stay in the form of autobiography even as it reports something that mainly concerns the survivor-parent. Family memoirs shift easily and frequently between what happened to the parent and how "I" learned the information. Naturally, an individual reader may be more interested in learning about surviving the Nazi Judeocide than about surviving growing up in a household with a survivor. My point here would be that for many if not all of my authors these two things are connected: surviving in such a household involves (eventually) learning more about what happened in the past. These memoirs and their authenticating strategies thematize this tangled connection.

I want to conclude by claiming an ethical and practical role for well-written books about the story of getting the story. For one thing, such narratives can inspire and have inspired other individuals to undertake searches that may then be personally beneficial to them. Why, as a society, should we count that as nothing? Perhaps even more importantly, and certainly to the point of this entire volume, soon such books may be the only new sources for making the acquaintance of survivors in something close to the fullness of their personalities and the contradictions and fragilities of their lives. Family memoirs will be one of few sources for making clearer to us aspects of the Nazi persecution that are likely to seem more fantastical with the passage of time. The stories that someone like Helen Epstein can tell about her mother's internalization of Nazi racial ideas and the extremes to which she therefore went to try to pass as Aryan according to those ideas are different stories from the ones we are likely to receive through an oral interview with the parent conducted by a stranger or even, I would suggest, in a memoir written by the parent. Helen Fremont runs to ask her mother about the article on her father because she is shocked to think of her father as a victim and because she read there that someone tried to take his clothes away from him: "It didn't occur to me that they wanted his clothes for themselves, for warmth. This was *beyond my imagination* as I sat in my parents' warm home, well-clothed. I could not picture anyone (much less my father) that cold" (226, my emphasis).

To frame the story in terms of herself and her own incredulity at the possibility of one human being feeling so frozen that s/he would not only steal but maim another human being is not to steal the parents' identity, nor is it to claim that the second generation's experiences are "just as valid." It is, rather, to reenact a scene of the tremendous task for those who were not there—that will soon be all of us—of engaging precisely our imaginations to come to knowledge of what the persecuted experienced and how they felt about it. If we still have hopes of learning lessons from the Shoah, these memoirs offer valuable examples of trying to bridge a chasm through research and fantasy that will only loom larger "after testimony."

Notes

1. Some texts that resemble my family memoirs include Sarah Kofman's philosophical essay *Paroles suffoquées* for its inclusion of a critical document about her father's death (the deportation lists). As her memoir *Rue Ordener, Rue Labat* makes clear, though, Kofman is herself a survivor and her father a murdered victim. *Lost in Translation* focuses on Eva Hoffman's own experiences as an immigrant, not as the child of survivors that she in fact is. She writes from this identity position briefly and movingly in *After Such Knowledge*, but this text is much more of a sociological analysis than a narrative. Marianne Hirsch and Leo Spitzer's *Ghosts of Home* could be considered also as a mixed genre, with some more analytical and some more narrative elements; the book's blurb labels it, among other things: a "communal memoir." Carl Friedman's *Tralievader* [*Nightfather*] takes up many of the issues of my family memoirs and is written from the first-person

perspective of the daughter of survivors, but its author clearly labels it "fiction." Daniel Mendelsohn's *The Lost* resembles perhaps most closely other texts in my corpus; I ultimately decided not to include it here since Mendelsohn's nuclear family was safely living in the United States throughout the Holocaust, and he investigates the fates of individuals he had never known. It should count as one of Stark's "postmemorial" books, though (Stark 202).

2. Hypotheses about the psychological effect of the Holocaust on survivors' offspring began essentially at the same time that the concept of "survivor syndrome" was proposed, that is in the 1950s and 60s (see Solkoff; and Bergmann and Jucovy). Interest in so-called second-generation literature began several decades later and has primarily concerned itself with fictional texts about the Holocaust and its legacies (see Berger and Berger; McGlothlin; and Sicher). The most important theoretical development came from Marianne Hirsch and her proposal of the term "postmemory" to identify "an intersubjective transgenerational space of remembrance, linked to cultural or collective trauma which is not strictly based on identity or on familial connection" (Hirsch and Kacandes 14; also Hirsch). Distinguishing memoirs from fictional writing has begun only quite recently (e.g., Kacandes 243–44).

3. Inspired by Holocaust family memoirs, I eventually wrote about those silences and how I learned more about what lay behind them (Kacandes).

4. The specific examples I give here of "paratext" Genette actually lists under the subcategory of "peritext," which he distinguishes from "epitext"—writings related to the text such as reviews, journals, or correspondence about it; for Genette peritext and epitext constitute the paratext. In a recent meeting of the International Society for the Study of Narrative (Birmingham, June 2009), however, it was agreed that in practice, most narratologists do not distinguish between the two subtypes and that Genette's umbrella term is the one in circulation.

5. Thus Vladek Spiegelman's account of the function of the Auschwitz-Birkenau death machinery in the second volume of *Maus* can be checked against the Nazis' own architectural plans (see Dwork and Pelt), against clandestine photos (see Didi-Huberman), or against other eyewitness testimony (see Gradowski, Lengyel, Levi). In contrast, the layout of Trachimbrod cannot be verified anywhere, as it "exists" only in Jonathan Safran Foer's novel *Everything Is Illuminated*. The shtetl's streets, therefore, have a textual rather than a referential existence. To be sure, fictional texts can include reference to places and events whose existence can be verified in the available historical record. Rachel Seiffert's poignant novel *The Dark Room*, for instance, depicts prewar, wartime, and postwar Germany and Eastern Europe, including mentions of real persons, places, and events. However, because of the paratextual apparatus, the message given to us by the work about its genre (e.g., its designation as "fiction" on the copyright page), readers' horizon of expectation does not include querying each element in Seiffert's novel, even if some of the details it utilizes are "true," in the sense of "verifiable in documents or archives."

6. That is, unless one is as talented a writer as W. G. Sebald, who foregrounds the issue of transmission of knowledge by repeatedly anchoring the discourse in phrases that specify who said what to whom: "sagte Vera zu mir, sagte Austerlitz . . ." [Vera said to me, said Austerlitz] (250). Sebald did not give a generic label to his work *Austerlitz*, but no researcher has yet disproved that he meant it as a novel. The frequency with which the narrator and characters point to oral transmission comes across to the readers, I would suggest, as one of *Austerlitz*'s literary features; the inquits sound like poetic refrains.

Works Cited

Appignanesi, Lisa. *Losing the Dead. A Family Memoir.* London: Chatto & Windus/Random House, 1999.

Berger, Alan L. and Naomi Berger, eds. *Second Generation Voices: Reflections by Children of Holocaust Survivors and Perpetrators.* Syracuse: Syracuse University Press, 2001.

Bergmann, Martin S. and Milton E. Jucovy, eds. 1982. *Generations of the Holocaust.* New York: Columbia University Press, 1990.

Cohn, Dorrit. *The Distinction of Fiction.* Baltimore and London: The Johns Hopkins University Press, 1999.

Didi-Huberman, Georges. *Images malgré tout* [*Images after All*]. Paris: Seuil, 2003.

Dwork, Debórah and Robert Jan van Pelt. *Auschwitz: 1270 to the Present.* New York: W. W. Norton, 1996.

Eisenstein, Bernice. *I Was a Child of Holocaust Survivors.* New York: Riverhead (Penguin), 2006.

Epstein, Helen. *Where She Came From: A Daughter's Search for Her Mother's History.* Boston and New York: Little, Brown and Company, 1997.

Foer, Jonathan Safran. *Everything Is Illuminated.* New York: Houghton Mifflin, 2002.

Franklin, Ruth. "Identity Theft: True Memory, False Memory, and the Holocaust." *The New Republic* (May 31, 2004): 31–37.

Fremont, Helen. *After Long Silence. A Memoir.* New York: Dell Publishing/Random House, 1999.

Friedman, Carl. *Tralievader* [*Nightfather*]. Amsterdam: Uitgeverij G.A. van Ooorschot, 1991.

Genette, Gérard. *Paratexts: Thresholds of Interpretation.* Trans. Jane E. Lewin. Cambridge and New York: Cambridge University Press, 1997.

Gerzon, George and Helen Gerzon Goransson. *The Hand of Fate. Memoirs of George Gerzon as Told by Him to His Daughter.* Dover, NH: Odyssey Press, 1999.

Goransson, Helen Gerzon. Telephone interview. March 22, 2004.

Gradowski, Salmen. *Au coeur de l'enfer: Document écrit d'un Sonderkommando d'Auschwitz—1944.* Edited by Philippe Mesnard and Carlo Saletti. Paris: Kimé, 2001.

Hirsch, Marianne. *Family Frames: Photography, Narrative, and Postmemory.* Cambridge, MA: Harvard University Press, 1997.

Hirsch, Marianne and Irene Kacandes. "Introduction." In *Teaching the Representation of the Holocaust,* edited by Marianne Hirsch and Irene Kacandes, 1–33. New York: Modern Language Association, 2004.

Hirsch, Marianne and Leo Spitzer. *Ghosts of Home. The Afterlife of Czernowitz in Jewish Memory.* Berkeley: University of California Press, 2010.

Hoffman, Eva. *After Such Knowledge: Memory, History, and the Legacy of the Holocaust.* New York: Public Affairs, 2004.

———. *Lost in Translation: A Life in a New Language.* New York and London: Penguin Books, 1989.

Honigmann, Barbara. *Ein Kapitel aus meinem Leben.* München: Carl Hanser Verlag, 2004.

Kacandes, Irene. *Daddy's War: Greek American Stories.* Lincoln: University of Nebraska Press, 2009.

Karpf, Anne. *The War After: Living with the Holocaust.* London: Minerva/Random House, 1996, 1997.

Kofman, Sarah. *Paroles suffoquées*. Paris: Éditions Galilée, 1987.

———. *Rue Ordener, Rue Labat*. Paris: Éditions Galilée, 1994.

Lejeune, Philippe. *On Autobiography*. Edited by Paul John Eakin. Translated by Katherine Leary. Minneapolis: University of Minnesota Press, 1989.

Lengyel, Olga. *Five Chimneys: The Story of Auschwitz*. 1946. New York: Fertig, 1995.

Levi, Primo. *Survival in Auschwitz*. Trans. Stuart Woolf. New York: Collier, 1961.

Loftus, Elizabeth. *Eyewitness Testimony*. 1979. Cambridge, MA: Harvard University Press, 1996.

McGlothlin, Erin. *Second-Generation Holocaust Literature: Legacies of Survival and Perpetration*. Rochester, NY: Camden House, 2006.

Mendelsohn, Daniel. *The Lost: A Search for Six of Six Million*. New York: HarperCollins, 2006.

Sebald, W. G. *Austerlitz*. 2001. Frankfurt am Main: Fischer Taschenbuch Verlag, 2003.

Seiffert, Rachel. *The Dark Room*. New York: Pantheon Books, 2001.

Sicher, Efraim, ed. *Breaking Crystal: Writing and Memory after Auschwitz*. Urbana: University of Illinois Press, 1998.

Skakun, Michael. *On Burning Ground. A Son's Memoir*. New York: St. Martin's Press, 1999.

Solkoff, Norman. "Children of Survivors of the Nazi Holocaust: A Critical Review of the Literature." *American Journal of Orthopsychiatry* 51, no. 1 (1981): 29–42.

Spiegelman, Art. *Maus: A Survivor's Tale*. Vols. 1 and 2. New York: Pantheon Books, 1991.

Stark, Jared. "Broken Records: Holocaust Diaries, Memoirs, and Memorial Books." In *Teaching the Representation of the Holocaust*. edited by Marianne Hirsch and Irene Kacandes, 191–204. New York: Modern Language Association, 2004.

Suleiman, Susan Rubin. "The 1.5 Generation: Georges Perec's *W or the Memory of Childhood*." In *Teaching the Representation of the Holocaust,* edited by Marianne Hirsch and Irene Kacandes, 372–85. New York: Modern Language Association, 2004.

Webster's New Collegiate Dictionary. 9th ed. "Memoir." Def. 2a., 1986.

Wiesel, Elie et al. *Dimensions of the Holocaust*. Evanston: Northwestern University Press, 1977.

Weissman, Gary. *Fantasies of Witnessing: Postwar Efforts to Experience the Holocaust*. Ithaca: Cornell University Press, 2004.

CHAPTER 9

Objects of Return

MARIANNE HIRSCH

> Edek resumed his digging. He dug and he dug. Half of the outhouse's foundation now seemed to be exposed. Edek got down on his knees, and dug a hole at the base of the foundations. Suddenly he stiffened.
>
> "I think I did find something." Everyone crowded in. . . .
>
> He reached under the foundation and dug around with his fingers. He was lying stretched out on the ground.
>
> "I got it," Edek said breathlessly. He pulled out a small object, and began removing the dirt from its surface. The old man and woman tried get closer.
>
> "What has he got? What has he got?" the old woman said. . . .
>
> Edek got up. He had cleaned up the object. Ruth could see it. It was a small, rusty, flat tin. "I did find it," Edek said, and smiled.
>
> —Brett, *Too Many Men* 514

Incongruous Objects

At the end of Lily Brett's 1999 novel, *Too Many Men,* Edek and his Australian-born daughter Ruth return one more time to Kamedulska Street in Lódz where Edek had grown up as a small boy and young man in the 1920s and 30s. They had already been there several times and, each time, had discovered additional objects that provided clues to Edek's and his family's past. Ruth had gone there by herself to buy, for inordinate sums of money, her grandmother's tea service and other personal items that the old couple living in the apartment that had been Edek's brought out for her in a slow and emotionally torturous process of extortion. But after traveling on from Lódz to Kraków and then to Auschwitz, where Edek and his wife Rooshka had survived the war, Edek insisted on returning to Lódz and to Kamedulska Street once more to retrieve an additional item of immense personal value. "Did they find gold?" the neighbors kept asking, but the old couple had already searched every inch of ground and had come up empty. To his great joy, Edek does find the precious object buried in the ground: it is "a small, rusty, flat tin" (514).

It isn't until later, at their hotel, that Edek opens the small tin. Ruth

> could feel the dread in her mouth, in her throat, in her lungs, and in her stomach. . . . The tin held only one thing. Edek removed the object from the tin. It was a photograph. A small photograph. . . . It was a photograph of her mother. . . . Rooshka was holding a small baby. The small baby was Ruth. . . .
>
> "It does look like you," Edek said. "But it is not you." Ruth felt sick (518)

Edek then proceeds to tell Ruth a story concerning her parents that she had never heard before. After liberation, Edek and Rooshka had found each other again and had had a baby boy in the German DP camp Feldafing. The baby had been born with a heart problem that required a kind of care that these stateless Auschwitz survivors were not in a position to provide. At the advice of their doctor, they made the excruciating decision to give him up to a wealthy German couple for adoption. Before giving him away, Edek had taken a photograph of the baby. Rooshka, however, "'was angry. She did say that if we are going to give him away, he will be out of our lives, so why should we pretend with a photograph that he is part of us. . . . Mum did tell me to throw away the photograph. But I did not want to throw it away'" (524). Edek gave the photo to his cousin Herschel who was going back to Kamedulska Street, which, he believed, "'was still more his home than the barracks.'" Herschel took the photo with him and, discovering that this could, in fact, never again be his home, buried it in the yard under the outhouse before returning to the DP camp.

Too Many Men belongs to a genre of Holocaust narrative that has been increasingly prevalent in recent years: the *narrative of return,* in which a Holocaust survivor, accompanied by an adult child, returns to his or her former home in Eastern Europe, or children of survivors return to find their parents' former homes, to "walk where they once walked." Memoirs by these children of survivors dominate this narrative genre, but *Too Many Men* provides a rich fictional example and the chance to discuss the characteristics of return plots that are generally punctuated by images and objects that mediate acts of return.[1]

Narratives of return are quest plots holding out, and forever frustrating, the promise of revelation and recovery; thus Edek's discovery of the metal tin and the baby's photograph offers a rare epiphanic instant in this genre. And yet, characteristically perhaps, this moment of disclosure and satisfaction serves only to raise another set of questions that defer any possibility of narrative closure. Why, when Edek's baby was born after liberation, in Germany, was his photo taken back to Lódz, to Kamedulska Street, to be buried there? And why does Edek spend such enormous sums of money and effort to go back to his former home one more time to search for and to retrieve the photograph? Why, if the photo is so important to him, does he not dig for it on his first visit? Why, in fact, does he wait? Narratives of return, like *Too Many Men,* abound in implausible plot details such as these. What, actually, does Ruth find out about her parents and about herself when her father succeeds in unearthing the photo of her lost brother? What can these moments of narrative fracture and incongruity tell us about the needs and impulses that engender return in different generations and about the scenarios of intergenerational transmission performed in and by acts of return?[2]

In this essay, I read Brett's novel alongside two other works that clarify the incongruities, the implausibilities and impossibilities, and the fractured shapes characterizing the impulse to return and the narrative and visual enactments of return: Palestinian writer Ghassan Kanafani's 1969 novella *Return to Haifa,* a work that deals not with the Holocaust but with the Nakba, and the Eurydice Series of Bracha Lichtenberg-Ettinger, an Israeli visual artist who is the daughter of Holocaust survivors. These three works enable us to look, in particular, at the role that objects (photographs, domestic interiors, household objects, items of clothing) play in return stories, marking their sites of implausibility and incommensurability. Objects, lost and again found, structure plots of return: they can embody memory and thus trigger affect shared across generations. But as heavily symbolic and over-determined sites of contestation, they can also mediate the political, economic, and juridical claims of dispossession and recovery that often motivate return stories.

Read together, these three works stage the impulse to return as a fractured encounter between generations, between cultures, and between mutually imbricated histories. From Australia, New York, and Israel to Poland and back, from the West Bank to Haifa, from a layered present to a complicated past, return is desired as much as it is impossible. In focusing on the figure of the lost child, however, these works expose the deepest layers of the contradictory psychology of return and the depths of dispossession that reach beyond specific historical circumstances. How can different histories that expose children to danger and abandonment be thought together, without flattening or blurring the differences between them? Perhaps in a feminist, *connective* reading that moves between global and intimate concerns by attending precisely to the intimate details, the connective tissues and membranes, that animate each case even while enabling the discovery of shared motivations and shared tropes. Such a feminist reading, as I see it, pays attention to the political dimensions of the familial and domestic and to the gender and power dynamics of contested histories. It foregrounds affect and embodiment and a concern for justice and acts of repair. It is *connective* rather than *comparative* in that it eschews any implications that catastrophic histories are comparable, and it thus avoids the competition over suffering that comparative approaches can, at their worst, engender.

In Kanafani's text, a Palestinian couple drives from Ramallah to the house in Haifa that they were forced to leave in 1948. It is June 1967, twenty years later, and Said S. and Safiya join many of their neighbors and friends curious to revisit the homes they had left behind and that they were allowed to visit after the Israeli annexation of the West Bank and the opening of the borders. As they approach Haifa, Said S. "felt sorrow mounting from inside him . . . No, the memory did not come back to him little by little, but filled the whole inside of his head, as the walls of stone collapsed and piled on top of each other. Things and events came suddenly, beginning to disintegrate and filling his body" (99). Return to place literally loosens the defensive walls against the sorrow of loss that refugees build up over decades and that they pass down to their children. Just as Ruth responds to the photograph in *Too Many Men,* so Said S. and Safiya respond viscerally, with trembling, tears, sweat, and overpowering physical feelings of torment. As the couple approaches their former house, the streets they cross, the smells of the landscape, the topography of the city—all trigger bodily responses that are not exactly memories, but reenactments and re-incarnations of the events of the day in 1948 when they left their home. The past overpowers the present, "suddenly, cutting like a knife" (102), and we are with Said S. in 1948 as he desperately attempts to get back to his wife through the bullets and confusion on the city streets; we also see her haste to get to him and her inability to fight her way back through the flood of refugees to the house where her baby Khaldun remains asleep in his crib, tragically left behind. Later that day, offshore, as the boats take them away from Haifa, "they were incapable of feeling anything" (107). The loss is so overwhelming that for twenty years, Khaldun's name is rarely pronounced in their house, and then only in a whisper. Their two younger children do not know about their lost brother. And even as they drive toward Haifa together in 1967, neither Said S. nor Safiya, who talk about everything else during the journey, "had uttered a syllable about the matter that had brought them there" (100). On the surface, the trip is about seeing their house again—as they say, "just to see it" (108).

Both of these fictional works represent refugees' and exiles' re-encounter with the material textures of their daily lives in the past.[3] "Habit," Paul Connerton writes in his book *How Societies Remember*, "is a knowledge and a remembering in the hands and in the body, and in the cultivation of habit it is our body which 'understands'" (95). In returning to the spaces and objects of the past, displaced people can remember the embodied practices and the incorporated knowledge that they associate with home. When Said S. slows his car "before reaching the turn which he knew to be hidden at the foot of the turn" (Kanafani 11), when he "looked at all the little things which he knew would frighten him or make him lose his balance: the bell, the copper door knocker, the pencil scribblings on the wall, the electricity box, the four steps broken in the middle, the fine curved railing which your hand slipped along," he reanimates deep habits and sense memories. Ordinary objects mediate the memory of returnees through the particular embodied practices that they re-elicit. And these embodied practices can also revive the affect of the past, overlaid with the shadows of loss and dispossession.

Said and Safiyah notice every detail of the house, comparing and contrasting the present with the past "like someone who had just awoken from a long period of unconsciousness" (112). Much remained exactly the same: the picture of Jerusalem on one wall, the small Persian carpet on the other. The glass vase on the table had been replaced with a wooden one, but the peacock feathers inside it were still the same, though of the seven feathers that had been there, only five remained. Both wanted to know what happened to the other two.

Somehow, those two missing feathers become signifiers of the incommensurability of return—a measure of the time that had passed and the life lived by other people and other bodies in the same space and among the same objects. Emerging from this bodily re-immersion in his former home, Said S. begins to realize that, for years, other feet have shuffled down the long hallway, and others have eaten at his table: "How very strange! Three pairs of eyes all looking at the same things . . . and how differently everyone sees them!" (113). In Kanafani's novella, the third pair of eyes belong to Miriam, the wife of the deceased Evrat Kushen, both of them Holocaust survivors who had been given the house by the Jewish Agency only a few days after Said S. and Safiya left it.[4] "[A]nd with the house, he was given a child, five months old!" (120), Miriam tells Said S. and Safiya as they sit in the living room that all three of them consider their own. Miriam also tells them how she had been ready to return to the Italian DP camp to which they had been sent after the war because of the disturbing scene she had witnessed during those days in 1948: Jewish soldiers throwing a dead Arab child, covered with blood, into a truck "like a piece of wood." When they adopted the baby, Evrat Kushen hoped that his wife would be able to heal from the shock of that vision.

As Said S. and Safiya discuss whether to wait for the return of Khaldun who had been raised by his Jewish parents as Dov, or whether to leave immediately, accepting the fact that their son had irrevocably been taken from them, they surprisingly equate their child with the house that had been, and was now no longer, theirs. Both house and child are invested with agency and power—to accept or to deny their former owners/parents. As Said tells Safiya, "'Don't you have those same awful feelings which came over me while I was driving the car through the streets of Haifa? I felt that I knew it and that it had denied me. The same feelings came over me when I was in the house here. This is our house. Can you imagine that? Can you imagine that it would deny us?'" (123). What could figure the enormity of their dispossession as powerfully as the loss of a child, or a child's refusal to recognize his parents? When Khaldun/Dov finally appears on the scene, he is wearing an Israeli uniform.

Although, in Kanafani's novella, the lost child structures the story of return, the novella's plot does not fully motivate the loss of Khaldun: we are told that Safiya tried, desperately, to return to the house to fetch her baby—but how, we cannot help wondering, could she have left him there in the first place? This narrative implausibility is compounded by other textual incongruities, most notably Dov's revelation that "they" (his parents) only told him "three or four years ago" (131) that he was not their biological son, even though he said earlier that "my father was killed in Sinai eleven years ago" (129).[5] Is this a mistake on Kanafani's part or an indication of the son's very belated acceptance of his adoption? These implausible elements of the story and the questions they raise produce moments of fracture in which different plot possibilities are overlaid on one another with no possible resolution. They can be motivated only on the level of fantasy and symbol—as the measures of a failed maternity and paternity in a time of historical extremity and as emblems of the radical dispossession that is the result of Israeli occupation.

For Said S. and Safiya, as for Edek and Rooshka in *Too Many Men*, the lost child remains a shameful and well-kept secret, haunting and layering the present. When Edek regrets giving his baby up for adoption and worries that he had made the wrong decision, Ruth attempts to alleviate her father's guilt by insisting, "You did nothing wrong" (Brett 526). Here, also, extreme historical circumstances fracture family life and disable parental nurturance. Just as Said S. and Safiya need to return to their former home and to reencounter the objects that trigger bodily memories and with them the emotions of inconsolable loss they had so long suppressed, so Edek needs to find the photograph of his baby son if he is to tell the story to his daughter. More than her grandmother's tea service that Ruth buys from the old couple at an exorbitant price, more than her grandfather's overcoat and the photographs that are in one of its pockets, the photo of the lost child figures the expulsion from home and the impossibility of return. In the narrative, we need to wait for its revelatory power; we need to witness the progressive discovery that Edek and, with him, Ruth undergo. Suspense, partial disclosures, and delayed revelations structure the plot: several scenes of digging have to precede the unearthing of the small tin can. In both texts, the loss of the child, associated with guilt and shame, is deeply suppressed. It can be brought into the open and confronted only gradually, by crossing immense temporal and spatial divides.

For Edek, the photograph becomes the medium of a narrative shared across generations. Ruth wonders why her parents had never told her about her baby brother and insists that this is *her* story as much as it is her mother's and father's: "It was impossible to grow up unaffected. The things that happened to you and to Mum became part of my life. Not the original experiences, but the effects of the experiences'" (527). It is these effects that motivate Ruth's journey to Poland, her need to imagine her parents' lives, her tireless search for every object and every detail of their past. They motivate her repeated returns to Kamedulska Street and her need to go there with her father. And, through a process of unconscious transmission of affect, they motivate a recurrent nightmare that plagues Ruth throughout her trip to Poland, before she ever sees the photo or learns about her lost brother: "She had had one of her recurring nightmares. The worst one, the one in which she was a mother. The children were almost always babies. . . . In these dreams she lost her babies or starved them. She misplaced them. Left them on trains or buses. . . . The abandonment in her dreams was never intentional. She simply forgot that she had given birth to and brought home a baby. When in her dreams she realized what she had done, she was mortified" (113). How does the act of returning to place and how do the objects found there inflect the process of affective transmission that so profoundly shapes the postmemory of children of exiles and refugees?

Returning Bodies

In her latest book on memory, *Der lange Schatten der Vergangenheit* (*The Long Shadow of the Past*), the German critic Aleida Assmann reflects on the role of objects and places as triggers of bodily or sense memory.[6] Invoking the German reflexive formulation of "ich erinnere mich" ("je me souviens") she distinguishes what she calls the verbal and declarative, active *ich-Gedächtnis* (I-memory) from the more passive *mich-Gedächtnis* (Me-memory) appealing to the body and the senses rather than to language or reason.[7] Assmann's *mich-Gedächtnis* is the site of involuntary memory that is often activated and mediated by the encounter with objects and places from the past. Scholars of memory sites, such as James Young and Andreas Huyssen, have been skeptical of what they deem a romantic notion that endows objects and places with aura or with memory. In response, Assmann specifies that although objects and places do not themselves carry qualities of past lives, they do hold whatever we ourselves project onto them or invest them with. When we leave them behind, we bring something of that investment along, but part of it also remains there, embedded in the object or the place itself. Assmann uses the metaphor of the classical Greek legal concept of the *symbolon* to conceptualize this. To draw up a legal contract, a symbolic object was broken in half, and one of those halves was given to each of the parties involved. When the two parties brought the two halves together at a future time, and they fit, then their identity and the legal force of the contract could be ratified. Return journeys *can* have the *effect* of such a reconnection of severed parts, and, if this indeed happens, they can release latent, repressed, or dissociated memories—memories that, metaphorically speaking, remained behind, as it were, concealed within the object. And in so doing, they can cause them to surface and become re-embodied. Objects and places, therefore, Assmann argues, can function as triggers of remembrance that connect us, bodily and thus also emotionally, with the object world we inhabit (122). In her formulation, the *mich-Gedächtnis* functions as a system of potential resonances, of chords that, in the right circumstances—during journeys of return, for example—can be made to reverberate.

But can the metaphor of the *symbolon* cover cases of massive historic fractures, such as the ones introduced by the Shoah and the Nakba? Would not contracts lose their legal force in such cases, so much so that the pieces would no longer be expected to fit together again? Worn away not only by time but also by a traumatic history of displacement, forgetting, and erasure, places change and objects are used by other, perhaps hostile, owners, and over time they come to merely approximate the spaces and objects that were left behind. Cups and plates chip, peacock feathers disappear, wooden vases replace glass ones, and keys to houses, obsessively kept in exile, no longer open doors. "Home" becomes a place of no return.

And yet, embodied journeys of return, corporeal encounters with place, do have the capacity to create sparks of connection that activate remembrance and thus reactivate the trauma of loss. In the register of the more passive *mich-Gedächtnis,* or of the "repertoire," they may not release full accounts of the past, but they can bring back its gestures and its affects. Perhaps the sparks created when the two parts of a severed power line touch ever so briefly constitute a more apt image for this than the ancient *symbolon* cut in half. The intense bodily responses to the visits of return that we see in both of these novels testify to the power of these sparks of reconnection that increase expectation and thus also intensify frustration.

The powerful bodily memory engendered in return is compounded in these narratives by the trope of the lost child that clarifies the enormity of the stakes involved. In contrast to Brett and Kanafani, W. G. Sebald's *Austerlitz,* which contains another paradigmatic narrative of return, reverses the generations by staging the return of the lost amnesiac child in search of his parents and his own past self. Here too, bodily symptoms signal found sites and engender moments of reconnection, often without cognitive recognition: "I could tell, by the prickling of my scalp . . ." Austerlitz says of a scene that was "brought back out of my past" (151). "[I]t was as if I had already been this way before and memories were revealing themselves to me not by means of any mental effort but through my senses" (150). When he is handed the photo of the little page boy and is told "this is you, Jacquot" (183), Austerlitz is "speechless and uncomprehending, incapable of any lucid thought" (184). "I could not imagine who or what I was" (185), he repeats. In the face of expulsion and expropriation—especially childhood expulsion—home and identity are in themselves implausible, and objects remain alienating and strange.

Generations and Surrogations

The impossibility and implausibility of return is intensified if descendants who were never there earlier return to the sites of trauma. Can they even attempt to put the pieces together, to create the spark? Or is the point of connection, including the physical contact with objects, lost with the survivor generation? What if several generations pass? What if traces are *deliberately*

erased and forgetting is *imposed* on those who are abducted or expelled, as
Saidiya Hartman asks in her moving memoir of "return" to the slave routes
of Ghana, tellingly titled *Lose Your Mother?* Her narrative, like other second-
and subsequent-generation stories of return, attempts to reclaim memory
and connection to the objects and places of the past, even while making
evident the irreparability of the breach. Narrative incongruity in fictional
accounts may well serve the purpose of signaling the fractures and implausibilities underlying both home and return in the autobiographical and fictional accounts of postmemorial generations that have inherited the loss.
And images, objects, and places function as sites where these implausibilities
manifest themselves.

In *Too Many Men,* Ruth says to Edek that "so much of what happened in
your life became part of my life" (Brett 526). Along with stories, behaviors,
and symptoms, parents do transmit aspects of their relationship to places
and objects from the past to their children. Ruth had wanted to visit Poland
the first time "just to see that her mother and father came from somewhere.
To see the bricks and the mortar. The second time was an attempt to be less
overwhelmed than she was the first time. To try and not to cry all day and
night. . . . And now she was here to walk on this earth with her father" (5).
He identifies places and objects, gives her information, but also, together,
they are able to relive the most difficult and painful moments of his past—to
transmit and to receive the sparks of reconnection. These are often provocative and disturbing, as when Said S. and Safiya confront Dov with the reality of his double identity, or when Ruth cannot evade the running mental
dialogue with Rudolf Hoess, the commandant of Auschwitz whose voice,
implausibly again, addresses and argues with her as soon as she arrives in
Poland, from the dead, or, as he presents it, from "Zweites Himmel Lager"
[Second Heaven Camp], as part of his own rehabilitation program.

This need on the part of the child born after the war, and after the moment
of expulsion and expropriation, to visit the places from which her parents
were evicted provides another explanation for cousin Herschel's return and
burial of the baby's photograph in Lodz in *Too Many Men.* It comes from
a yearning to find a world *before* the loss has occurred, before the Rudolf
Hoesses dominate the scene—from a need for an irrecoverable lost innocence that descendants of survivors imagine and project.

With the small tin and the photo inside it, Edek is unearthing more than
his own repressed feelings of loss. He is demonstrating to Ruth her own surrogate role: she is not the first child to "return" "home" to Lódz; the baby had
already come back before she did, albeit in the guise of a photo. As Joseph
Roach argues in *Cities of the Dead,* cultural memory of loss works through a

genealogical network of relations we might think of as surrogation: memory is repetition but always with some change, reincarnation but with a difference. Those of us living in the present do not take the place of the dead but live among or alongside them. In encountering the baby's photo, Ruth comes to understand her role as surrogate. The lost brother's photo is literally dug up from under the foundation of the house. His image, *like* and also *unlike* her, emerges as the fantasmatic figure shared by all children of survivors who tend to think of themselves as "memorial candles"—stand-ins for another lost child, who becomes responsible for perpetuating remembrance, for combating forgetting, for speaking in two overlapping voices.[8]

The structure of surrogation functions even more literally in Kanafani's text. The children Said and Safiya have after losing Khaldun are called Khalid and Khalida. These children do not know about their brother. And yet, on some level they may have learned that in the familial economy of loss, they are taking his place. At the end of the novel, Said emotionally authorizes Khalid to take up arms for Palestine, to win back the home from which they were evicted. Mythically, brother will fight against brother.

Reading these two texts connectively, however, shows how differently memory can function in the different contexts in which journeys of return take place. When Edek returns to Kamedulska Street, the old couple residing there worries that he plans to reclaim his property. Nothing could be further from his intentions: Edek and Ruth are there to find the past not the present. Even though Edek enjoys the food of his youth and feels at home in his language, he is uninterested in Poland and cannot wait to leave it. Ruth could not imagine living there: her project is one of mourning and psychic repair, not recuperation of the past. Bringing her grandmother's tea service to New York promises to reconnect some of the disparate parts of her life, to find continuity with a severed past—not to bring it into the present. But Hoess's constant whisper, overlaid onto her musings about her parents' and grandparents' world of before, shows her how much the past and also the future are dominated and overshadowed by the incontrovertible fact of the genocide. No revelation or recovery can heal the breach.

In Kanafani's text, we see an entirely different economy at work. "'You can stay for a while in our house,'" Said S. says to Miriam and to Dov as he leaves. It is *his* house and he imagines that his son Khalid will help recover it. Khalid had wanted to join the *fedayeen,* to become a guerilla and sacrifice his life for the struggle, but his father and mother had been opposed. Now, driving back to Ramallah, Said hopes that his son has left while they were away. Memory serves a future of armed struggle and resistance here, not one of mourning or melancholy. And return serves the cause of legal and moral claims of recovery in a context in which the conflict continues and resolution cannot yet be envisioned.

But the fantasmatic structure of surrogation functions in a more disturbing and open-ended fashion as well. In both texts, the lost child's survival is, for a while at least, submerged in ambiguity. Said S. and Safiya do not know whether they will find Khaldun when they return to Haifa. Ruth harbors fantasies of searching for and finding her lost brother, and in fact the novel, implausibly again, holds out that possibility: a German woman Ruth meets on her trip tells her about a young Christian German man named Gerhard who looks exactly like her and who, though German, identifies profoundly with Jews. At the end of the novel, Ruth, in a fantasy of recovering her lost brother, sets out to search for Gerhard. Could the lost child, then, function in these texts alongside the logic of the uncanny—as the embodiment of childhood innocence and hope irrevocably lost with war and dispossession? In this schema, surrogation would work backward toward a primordial past, rather than forward into the future, and Edek, as well as Said S., would be finding not their sons but their own childhood selves—lost, unprotected, neglected, forgotten, and repressed, but returning, perpetually and uncannily, to haunt a tainted present and to hold out the vision of an alternative ethical and affective future.

Visual Returns

I turn now to a third body of works that exhibit a visual aesthetics of return characterized by fracture, overlay, and superimposition. The works by Bracha Lichtenberg-Ettinger, a second-generation Lacanian psychoanalyst and feminist visual artist, allow us to measure the political and psychic implications of the repetitions and irresolutions of return.

In her Eurydice Series, produced between 1990 and 2001, Ettinger goes back to a street in Lódz at a moment "before" the Shoah. A 1937 street photograph of Ettinger's parents from the Polish city of Lódz (see figure 1) has become an obsessive image that recurs throughout her visual work in many iterations. In the image, her young, smiling parents are energetically walking down a street in their town, exuding comfort and safety. They are happy to look and be looked at, to display and perform their sense of belonging in this city and its urban spaces. In a label on her website, the artist informs viewers that, unlike her parents, the friend walking on the street with them was later killed by the Nazis. The image of her young parents taken before her own birth appears in Ettinger's Euridyce Series superimposed onto another

Figure 1
Street photo Lódz, 1937.

image, a washed-out photograph of her own childhood face (see figure 2). The child's smile is covered, almost erased, by the mother's smiling figure. The prewar stroll through the city, the couple walking toward a future they could not yet imagine, bleeds into the face of the child who grew up in a distant place, dominated by stories and histories that preceded her birth. Here, in overlay fashion, are the past and the present, two worlds that the postwar child longs to bridge: the world her parents once knew—where the Holocaust had not yet happened—and her own world, "after Auschwitz." In projecting her own face onto and into the spaces of the past, Ettinger absorbs some of the embodied practices of that past moment, enacting a kind of return journey in photographic mode. This journey is characterized by similar structures of superimposition and overlay as Brett's and Kanafani's fictions. Past and present coexist in layered fashion, and their interaction is dominated by objects that provoke deep bodily memory and the affects it triggers.

Thus, in Ettinger's composite images, the Lódz street photo of her parents and the image of her childhood face are often juxtaposed, overlaid, or blended with yet a third image—a disturbing, well-known photograph of a group of naked Jewish women, some holding children, herded to their execution by Einsatzgruppen in Poland. This image, no doubt taken by one of the Nazi photographers who accompanied the Einsatzgruppen, serves as the basis for Ettinger's Eurydice Series. This is not a space to which one would want to return; it is the antithesis of "home."

For this artwork, Ettinger made reproductions of various details of the Einsatzgruppen photo, which she then ran through a photocopier, enlarged, cut into strips, mounted on walls, and tinted with India ink and purple paint to a point where all details are washed out or made virtually invisible (see figure 3). The juxtapositions of the Lódz and Einsatzgruppen photos—one taken by a prewar street photographer, a fellow citizen, the other snapped and shaped by the annihilating Nazi gaze conflating the camera with the gun— illustrate the child's deep fear of parental impotence in a time of extremity that dominates all the texts under discussion. They illustrate the underside of return, the fear that violence will be repeated, that, as in Eurydice's backward look, return will prove to be deadly. As objects emerging from the past, the superimposed images contain and activate those fears, and Ettinger mobilizes them in her superimpositions.

The women walking toward their death, holding their babies, suffer the ultimate failure of parental care: they cannot protect their children, or themselves, from annihilation. They are witnesses and victims of the ultimate breach of a social contract in which adults are supposed to protect infants

Figure 2
Bracha Lichtenberg-Ettinger, "Mamalangue—Borderline conditions and pathological narcissism," no. 5.

Figure 3
Bracha Lichtenberg-Ettinger, Eurydice, no. 5.

rather than murder them. In these composite images (see figure 4), the artist, as child, becomes the surrogate of the dead baby; the infant held by the
mother in the picture becomes, by implication, her own phantom sibling or
her fragile child self.

In the Eurydice images, the photos from "before" cannot be separated
from the photos taken "during" and "after" the destruction. As a child born
after the war—a child who might easily never have been born at all had her
parents' fates taken a slightly different turn—Ettinger is unable to return to
the spaces from "before" without the superimposed, layered, screen image
of the atrocity "during." The prewar photo from the family album—from
the seemingly protected intimate and embodied space of the family and its
repertoires—cannot be insulated from the collective, anonymous images in
the killing fields, and the child born after the war is inevitably haunted by
the phantom sibling. The two kinds of images, and the three temporalities,
are inextricably linked. In this way, Ettinger's juxtapositions forge a powerful, anti-nostalgic idiom for the postmemorial subject. Return, even metaphoric return, cannot jump over the breach of expulsion, expropriation, and
murder.

In foregrounding and recasting Eurydice into the maternal figure who
lost her child, Ettinger, moreover, is reframing the father/son and father/
daughter perspectives presented in Kanafani's and Brett's novels. Ettinger's
Eurydice is the maternal figure who returns from Hades having witnessed
the loss of her child. In her powerful reading of the Eurydice Series, Griselda
Pollock sees Eurydice as the woman precariously alive "between two deaths":
for the women in the ravine, this is the brief moment between being shot by
the camera and by the gun. Eurydice's story is no doubt the prototypical narrative of impossible return. For Pollock, however, Ettinger, the daughter artist, is reframing the Orphic gaze of no return in favor of an aesthetic of what
Ettinger calls "wit(h)ness" and "co-affectivity."[9] In subjecting her original
images to technologies of mechanical reproduction, in degrading, recycling,
reproducing, and painting over them, Ettinger underscores the distance and
anonymity of the camera gaze. But, at the same time, she allows all of these
images to invade, inhabit, and haunt her, and she therefore inscribes them
with her own very invested act of looking, exposing in the images her own
needs and desires—her own fears and nightmares. In Pollock's reading, the
purple paint is a physical touch that marks the images with "the color of
grief" (175).

But more still is at stake in a few of the images from this series that
include yet one more level of superimposition. The grid in the image in figure 5 is of a World War I map of Palestine, and of aerial views of Palestinian

Figure 4
Bracha Lichtenberg-Ettinger, Eurydice, no. 37.

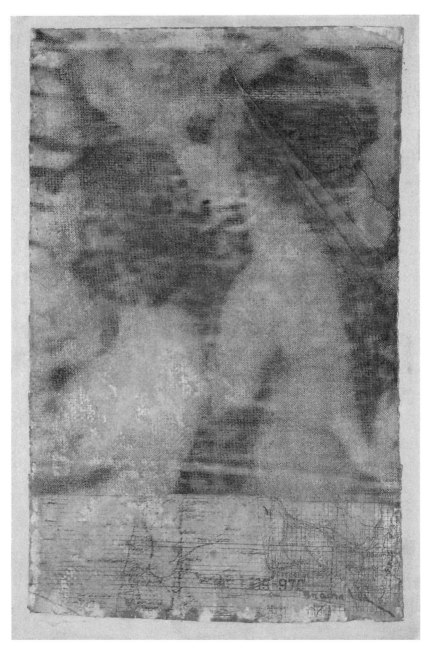

Figure 5
Bracha Lichtenberg-Ettinger, Eurydice, no. 2.

spaces taken by German warplanes during World War I when Palestine was occupied by the British. Ettinger, born in Israel after World War II, has inherited other traces of loss—traces of Palestinian spaces that she maps onto the spaces of Polish streets before World War II.

These competing spaces and temporalities become part of a multilayered psychic grid, unconsciously transmitted, merging geography and history and challenging any clear chronology or topography of return. The views are aerial shots taken by military airplanes. In including them in her own family image, Ettinger dramatizes, in a closer and more intimate manner, the irreconcilable stakes of memory and return. The spectral unconscious optics that emerge in her composite images blend the spaces of the individual journey of return with a larger global awareness of contested space and competing geopolitical interests.[10] Hers is an enlarged map that incorporates the losses of the Shoah into a broader intertwined psychology and geography of irrecoverable loss. The illegibility of her works, moreover, and the multiple generations they have undergone in the process of copying and reproduction, signal the loss of materiality that the objects and images have suffered in the multiple expulsions which they survived in faded and sometimes unrecognizable form.

Sequellae

Ettinger's layered compositions use the image of the fractured family and the lost or murdered child in the service of a political reading in which the structure of surrogation produces a layered memory that can recall and call attention to multiple losses across unbridgeable divides. The figure of the lost child and the textual implausibilities it engenders complicate and subvert the temporal and emotional trajectories of return narratives. A spectral figure that cannot be neatly integrated into the plot, it haunts the return story sprouting into series, subplots, projections, overlays, and sequels.

Just as the return plot of *Too Many Men* is punctured by the voice and implausible sub-plot of Rudolf Hoess, the primary plot of *Return to Haifa* is also interrupted by a long subplot. Said S. tells Safiya about a neighbor, Faris al Labda, who went back to his old home in Jaffa to find the picture of his martyred brother Badr still hanging in the house they had left. The picture inspires the brother who finds it, and the Israeli Arab family who has been living in the house, to take up arms for Palestine.

Both texts have also sprouted sequels. Brett's sequel to *Too Many Men*, the 2006 *You've Gotta Have Balls*, renamed *Uncomfortably Close* in the paperback edition, takes Ruth and her father back to New York. Kanafani, killed in an Israeli reprisal raid in 1972, could not, of course, write a sequel to *Return to Haifa,* but several adaptations and sequels have appeared in Israel, producing overlay reinterpretations of the original. These Israeli rewritings and stage adaptations use Kanafani's text in the service of fantasies of peace and reconciliation, covering over the breaches and angers that shape the original. Most notable is Iraqi–Israeli novelist Sami Michael's 2005 novel *Doves in Trafalgar*—a work that did not initially acknowledge its debt to Kanafani and that features the two mothers in the narrative. Michael's novel ends with the son Zeev's dream of "a federation between two nations . . . with two flags and one common currency."[11] The 2008 theater production of *Return to Haifa adapted* by Boaz Gaon and staged on the occasion of Israel's sixtieth anniversary "wanted to offer an opening for something else to happen." Gaon claims to find in the novella "a moment of grace where perhaps they could become one family" (Harrison).

In contrast to these recent rewritings, I have read return stories precisely for the implausibilities and incongruities, the fractures that foreclose resolution and reconciliation. Ettinger's series conform to this structure of irresolution. The Eurydice Series returns to the same images and the same themes obsessively, again and again. But this is not an art of endless melancholy and perpetual return. I prefer to see the different images in the series, the recurring dreams and nightmares, the multiple plots and subplots in the novels, as versions or approximations—drafts of a narrative in process, subject to revision. It is an open-ended narrative that embraces the need for return and for repair, even as it accepts its implausibility.

Notes

This chapter will also appear in my own book *The Generation of Postmemory: Writing and Visual Culture after the Holocaust (New York: Columbia University Press, 2012)* and in *The Global and the Intimate,* ed. Geraldine Pratt and Victoria Rosner (New York: Columbia University Press, 2012). I am very grateful to Bracha Lichtenberg-Ettinger for permission to reproduce her artwork. Thanks also go to a number of colleagues for their helpful suggestions on the draft manuscript: Lila Abu-Lughod, Carol Bardenstein, Sidra DeKoven Ezrahi, Saidiya Hartman, Jean Howard, Martha Howell, Dorothy Ko, Jakob Lothe, Nancy K. Miller, James Phelan, Victoria Rosner, Susan Rubin Suleiman, Carol Sanger, and Leo Spitzer.

1. On the contemporary phenomenon of return and its recent prevalence, see Hirsch and Miller.

2. On implausibility, see Miller.

3. See Hirsch and Spitzer, "The Tile Stove" and *Ghosts of Home,* for a related analysis of the embodied qualities of return journeys.

4. Miriam is one of the first Jewish–Israeli characters in Palestinian literature, and a remarkably sympathetic one.

5. I am grateful to Amira Hass for pointing this incongruity out to me.

6. See especially 119–37.

7. Assmann's distinction is comparable to Diana Taylor's recent theorization of a distinction between the "archive" and what she terms "the repertoire"—that set of stored behaviors and embodied practices that exceed the conventional structures of the cultural archive. But while Taylor specifically writes about cultural memory, Assmann's distinction here is centered on individual embodied recall.

8. The phantom sibling, or "memorial candle," is a ubiquitous and determining figure in narratives of massive trauma and loss. See, especially, Richieu in Art Spiegelman's 1986 Maus, but also, more recently, the figure of Simon in Phillippe Grimbert's novel and Claude Miller's 2008 film based on it, A Secret. On the notion of "memorial candle" see Wardi. See also Hirsch, Family Frames. On "replacement children," see Schwab.

9. See especially Pollock; and Lichtenberg-Ettinger, 1997, 2001.

10. On unconscious optics see Benjamin; and Hirsch.

11. See Karpel for a full account. Michael's novel has not been translated into English.

Works Cited

Assmann, Aleida. *Der lange Schatten der Vergangenheit: Erinnerungskultur und Geschichtspolitik.* Munich: C. H. Beck, 2006.

Benjamin, Walter. "The Work of Art in the Age of Mechanical Reproduction." In *Illuminations,* translated by Harry Zohn. New York: Harcourt, Brace & World, 1968.

Brett, Lily. *Too Many Men.* New York: HarperCollins Perennial, 2002.

———. *You Gotta Have Balls.* New York: William Morrow, 2006.

Connerton, Paul. *How Societies Remember.* Cambridge: Cambridge University Press, 1989.

Harrison, Rebecca. *Review of "The Return to Haifa." Ha'aretz,* April 15, 2008.

Hartman, Saidiya. *Lose Your Mother: A Journey along the Atlantic Slave Route.* New York: Farrar, Strauss and Giroux, 2007.

Hirsch, Marianne. *Family Frames: Photography, Narrative and Postmemory.* Cambridge, MA: Harvard University Press, 1997.

Hirsch, Marianne and Nancy K. Miller, eds. *Rites of Return: Diaspora Poetics and the Politics of Memory.* New York: Columbia University Press, 2011.

Hirsch, Marianne and Leo Spitzer. "The Tile Stove." *WSQ* 36, nos. 1 and 2 (Spring/Summer 2008): 141–50.

———. *Ghosts of Home: The Afterlife of Czernowitz in Jewish Memory.* Berkeley: University of California Press, 2010.

Huyssen, Andreas. *Present Pasts: Urban Palimpsests and the Politics of Memory.* Stanford: Stanford University Press, 2003.

Kanafani, Ghassan. *Palestine's Children: Return to Haifa and Other Stories.* Translated by Barbara Harlow. London: Heinemann, 1984.

Karpel, Dalia. "With Thanks to Ghassan Kanafani." *Ha'aretz,* April 15, 2005.

Lichtenberg-Ettinger, Bracha. *Que dirait Euridyce? [What would Eurydice Say?] Emmanuel Levinas en/in Conversation avec/with Bracha Lichtenberg-Ettinger.* Amsterdam: Kabinet in the Stedeijk Musem, 1997.

———. *The Eurydice Series*. Edited by Catherine de Zegher and Brian Massumi. New York: The Drawing Center's Drawing Papers 24, 2001.

Miller, Nancy K. "Emphasis Added: Plots and Plausibilities in Women's Writing." *PMLA* 96, no. 1 (January 1981): 36–48.

Pollock, Griselda. "Inscriptions in the Feminine." In *Inside the Visible: An Elliptical Traverse of 20th Century Art*. Cambridge, MA: The MIT Press, 1996.

Roach, Joseph. *Cities of the Dead: Circum-Atlantic Performance*. New York: Columbia University Press, 1996.

Schwab, Gabriele. *Haunting Legacies: Violent Histories and Transgenerational Trauma*. New York: Columbia University Press, 2010.

Sebald, W. G. *Austerlitz*. Translated by Anthea Bell. New York: The Modern Library, 2001.

Taylor, Diana. *The Archive and the Repertoire: Performing Cultural Memory in the Americas*. Durham: Duke University Press, 2003.

Wardi, Dina. *Memorial Candles: Children of the Holocaust*. New York: Routledge, 1992.

Young, James E. *The Texture of Memory: Holocaust Memorials and Meaning*. New Haven: Yale University Press, 1993.

CHAPTER 10

Narrative, Memory, and Visual Image

W. G. Sebald's Luftkrieg und Literatur and Austerlitz

JAKOB LOTHE

One essential reason why the German–British author W. G. Sebald's prose works are not only peculiarly unclassifiable but also unusually compelling is the way in which their textual surface is interrupted by uncaptioned black-and-white photographs and other visual images. This essay will explore how Sebald responds to the historical events of the Second World War and the Holocaust by using such visual images as integral parts of his narratives. I will focus on two of his books, *Luftkrieg und Literatur*,[1] a collection of essays first published in German in 1999, and *Austerlitz*, the strange novel that appeared in 2001. I will discuss two visual images presented in the first essay of the former book and then proceed to comment on three images that appear toward the end of the latter. In each case, I link the visual images to the narrative discourse in which they are situated and of which, I argue, they form an integral and important part. The critical aim of my discussion is to show how the interplay of verbal text and visual image serves not only to obliquely present Sebald's abiding preoccupation with the war and the Holocaust but also to urge the reader to reflect on the temporal reach of these historical events, not least the significant absences they generated in individual lives.[2]

Before turning to Sebald, I want to make four observations on the aesthetic and ethical effects of visual images presented in verbal narrative.[3] These brief comments on a complex issue are related to, and inspired by, the discussion that follows. My obvious yet important first point is that once a visual image is included in a verbal text, we are confronted not just with what we can term two different media but also with a constellation of, and opposition between, two aesthetic and communicative registers. Simply put, the reader also becomes a viewer, and the fact that we are looking at a photo when reading a verbal narrative does something to the way we read both the verbal text next to the photo and the whole narrative. As Silke Horstkotte notes in an essay titled "Photo-Text Topographies," a photo-text topography indicates "a spatial dimension which the photos introduce into the linearity of verbal narrative" (50). In a narrative like *Austerlitz* this spatial dimension is added to, or superimposed on, that of the verbal narrative itself. Literature, and not least fictional literature, has a topography of its own—a spatial dimension at once linked and opposed to the temporal one.[4] The topography of a photo-text, or what J. W. T. Mitchell calls "imagetext" (83), is thus a combination of two topographies, one verbal and one visual, and our construction of the former (an integral and essential part of the reading of fiction) may be supported or complicated by our understanding of the latter. Thus the relation of the topographies can vary across a wide spectrum with total reinforcement at one end and complete conflict at the other.

Second, since we conventionally relate a photograph to our experience of the external, physical world, the encounter with a photo when reading a verbal narrative, and especially a fictional one, raises the issue of authenticity. Broadly, two dimensions are activated here. If one purpose of the narrative is to say something about historical reality (historical events, characters, processes), a photograph can support that purpose. But if, not least in a fictional narrative, the author wants to exploit the ambiguity of the photograph, he or she can make it part of "an elaborate play with interdiscursive (intertextual, intermedial, and intericonic) allusions" (Horstkotte 50), thus problematizing the notion of authenticity. Interestingly, the two dimensions need not necessarily exclude each other; rather, they may coexist in curiously alogical fashion. One illustrative example of this kind of combination, which presents the reader (and viewer) with a considerable interpretive challenge, is that of the photographs of Vita Sackville-West included in the first edition of one of the major fictional biographies of the twentieth century, Virginia Woolf's *Orlando* (1928).

Third, since, as indicated already, the presentation and layering of space in incorporated photos and other visual images can relate in different ways to the topography and storyworld evoked in the verbal narrative, issues of narrative are highlighted. I identify two such issues, both of which are possessed of aesthetic as well as ethical aspects. The first aspect is located at the intersection of narrative, reading, and viewing. If we are confronted with a visual image when reading a verbal narrative, our reading of the verbal text is temporarily suspended as we look at the image and wonder about its relevance and significance. Seen thus, there is a sense in which the visual image has the potential to disrupt the previous narrative progression but also the potential to enrich it. And yet the image, the textual picture we are looking at, can itself include narrative features—features that may be convergent with, accentuated by, or opposed to the surrounding verbal narrative. Such an imbrication of visual and verbal elements becomes particularly noticeable if, as in the case of Sebald, the textual pictures are uncaptioned, thus in a way making the verbal text an extended caption and, conversely, turning the pictures into an oblique commentary on the verbal text. This dimension of the first aspect blends into the second: who or what are the narrative agent(s) responsible for the visual images? If we use the verbal narrative as our interpretive starting point, is the relationship between the author and the narrator different as far as the textual pictures are concerned?

Fourth, while most visual images are imbued with an aesthetic aspect, the ethical dimension may be more implicit and may to a larger extent depend on the reader's interpretive activity. Unsurprisingly, as far as the Holocaust is concerned it is a matter of considerable debate how photographs and other visual images of this historical event can, and should, be presented. As Anette H. Storeide notes in her contribution to this volume, "an unwritten rule has been that the images should not be shown at the expense of the victims and not satisfy the audience's need or greed for sensations and shocking images." This issue is interestingly linked to both of the narratives that I now proceed to discuss. One reason why the question is important is that it highlights the narrative dimension of photographs of this kind: when a viewer is looking at a photo from, say, Auschwitz, his or her more or less accurate or comprehensive narrative of Auschwitz is activated; moreover, he or she is forcefully reminded of the close, in this case even insistent, interplay of visual image, narrative, and historical as well as personal memory.[5]

Born in a hamlet in the Bavarian Alps in 1944, Sebald was literally as well as metaphorically a child of the Second World War. After the German capitulation in May 1945 his father, a soldier in the Wehrmacht (the German army), was detained in a prison camp in France for two years. When he finally returned to his family in 1947, Sebald's father, who hardly ever spoke about his war experiences, was not recognized by his three-year-old son. Whether the difficult relationship with his father was one reason why Sebald later decided to leave Germany we do not know. After having studied German and comparative literature at the University of Freiburg and in French-speaking Switzerland, Sebald emigrated to Britain in 1966. After that he spent most of his time in Norwich, writing and teaching at the University of East Anglia and becoming the first director of The British Centre for Literary Translation. His writings stretch from his MA thesis on Carl Sternberg and Alfred Döblin, via essays on German and Austrian literature, to the more personal essays and the book of poetry titled *Nach der Natur*.[6] In the 1990s Sebald's writing moved closer to fiction, and *Austerlitz* has often, though never by Sebald himself, been referred to as a novel. Tragically, since he was killed in a traffic accident in 2001, this major work was to become his last book. Both generally and with a view to *Austerlitz* in particular, the passage from *Luftkrieg und Literatur* that I will consider in this essay marks an important stage in Sebald's development as a writer.

Even though *Luftkrieg und Literatur* assumes documentary form, it is not generically simple. The two first chapters consist of lectures Sebald delivered in Zürich in the autumn of 1994. Two related purposes of these lectures were, first, to argue that postwar German literature had failed to address the massive destruction of German cities and the killing of German citizens in the last years of the war, and, second, to provide a belated account of, and reflection on, this vexed issue. While, unsurprisingly, the language of these lectures is predominantly argumentative, in the third chapter the discourse's narrative dimension is strengthened. Here Sebald reflects on the reactions to his Zürich lectures. The shift to a more narrative mode is accompanied by, and partly the result of, the inclusion—or perhaps rather intrusion—of elements of autobiography. Few passages in Sebald are more painfully autobiographical than the long second paragraph of chapter 3. Here aspects of narrative, memory, and photographic image are suggestively combined, thus producing rich thematic effects.

At the beginning of this paragraph, which is at the center of my critical attention and blends into my first quoted passage, Sebald makes an unusually explicit statement on the effect that visual images of the war can have on him. "When I see photographs or documentary films dating from the war," he notes, "I feel as if I were its child, so to speak, as if those horrors I did not experience cast a shadow over me, and one from which I shall never entirely emerge" (71). He then goes on to link this observation to a book published in 1963 on the history of a small hamlet in Bavaria, the region where he grew up. As we can see in figure 1,[7] the page that Sebald reproduces from this book shows two photos: an idyllic landscape and a small, laughing girl. The page includes two caption-like comments placed next to the photos. Sebald presents, in English translation, the first of these comments: "The war took much from us, but our beautiful native landscape was left untouched, as flourishing as ever." For Sebald, however, the photos are blended with "images of

Und allmählich schritten wir wieder – begleitet vom Lachen unserer Kinder – in eine hoffnungsfrohe Zukunft.

Viel hat uns der Krieg genommen, doch uns blieb – unberührt und blühend wie eh und je – unsere herrliche Heimatlandschaft.

de ein Jahr alt und kann also schwerlich auf realen Ereignissen beruhende Eindrücke aus jener Zeit der Zerstörung bewahrt haben. Dennoch ist es mir bis heute, wenn ich Photographien oder dokumentarische Filme aus dem Krieg sehe, als stammte ich, sozusagen, von ihm ab und als fiele von dorther, von diesen von mir gar nicht erlebten Schrecknissen, ein Schatten auf mich, unter dem ich

77

Figure 1
Page 77 of *Luftkrieg und Literatur*

destruction—and oddly enough, it is the latter, not the now entirely unreal idylls of my early childhood, that make me feel rather as if I were coming home." (71)

Considered as an integral part of *Luftkrieg und Literatur,* this textual picture is important for two related reasons. The first reason is suggested by the formal and semantic elements of the picture itself. We note the rhetorically effective way in which the two captions not only comment on the photos but are also commented on by the verbal discourse into which they are incorporated. This comment also applies to the second caption, that is, the one positioned to the left of the laughing girl, "And gradually we move on—accompanied by the laughter of our children—into a hopeful future" (my translation from the German). If separated from the surrounding narrative and considered as captions only, these two sentences reveal an attitude that is naïvely optimistic and willfully vague about "the war." When read as part of Sebald's discourse, however, the words accompanying the pictures—even more than the photographic images themselves—become ironically ambiguous. I identify two facets of this ambiguity, which is thematically productive and considerably strengthens the picture's narrative dimension. First, the noun "the war"/"der Krieg" may refer not just to the Second World War but also to the first. Although this link may be rather weak, it is supported by the second facet: the picture of the little girl strikingly calls to mind the way in which girls and young women were presented by Nazi propaganda in the 1930s. Significantly, this association on the part of the reader, and perhaps also Sebald, becomes possible only as a result of the visual image—neither the caption nor Sebald's verbal discourse refers to the prewar period. The photo of the laughing girl accentuates the irony of Sebald's observation, while at the same time furthering the discourse's narrative and thematic complexity. The textual reference to "images of destruction" (which are not presented or reproduced visually) colors our reading of both the visual image of the beautiful landscape and of the laughing girl. As readers who also become viewers, we see these visual images and simultaneously imagine war's destruction.

The second reason why this picture is important is that it provides the starting point for, as well as an elegant transition to, the concluding part of the paragraph and its incorporated photograph. The English translation of the passage accompanying the photo reads thus:

> I know now that at the time, when I was lying in my bassinet on the balcony of the Seefeld house and looking up at the pale blue sky, there was a pall of smoke in the air all over Europe, over the rearguard actions in east

and west, over the ruins of the German cities, over the camps where untold numbers of people were burnt, people from Berlin and Frankfurt, from Wuppertal and Vienna, from Würzburg and Kissingen, from Hilversum and The Hague, Naumur and Thionville, Lyon and Bordeaux, Kraków and Łódź, Szeged and Sarajevo, Salonika and Rhodes, Ferrara and Venice— there was scarcely a place in Europe from which no one had been deported to his death in those years. I have seen memorial tablets even in the most remote villages on the island of Corsica reading "Morte à Auschwitz" or "Tué par les Allemands, Flossenburg 1944." I saw something else in Corsica too—if I may be permitted a digression: I saw the picture from my parents' bedroom in the church of Morosaglia, a half-decayed edifice with a dusty, pseudo-Baroque interior. It was a bluish oleograph in the Nazarene style, showing Christ before his Passion seated deep in thought in the moonlit, nocturnal Garden of Gethsemane. The selfsame picture had hung over my parents' conjugal bed for many years, and then at some point it disappeared, probably when they bought new bedroom furniture. And now here it was again, or at least one exactly like it, in the village church of Morosaglia, General Paoli's birthplace, leaning against the plinth of an altar in a dark corner of one of the side aisles. My parents told me that just before their wedding in 1936 they had bought their picture in Bamberg, where my father was transport sergeant in the cavalry regiment in which the young Stauffenberg had begun his military career ten years earlier. Such is the dark backward and abysm of time. Everything lies all jumbled up in it, and when you look down you feel dizzy and afraid. (71–74)

Relating this passage and its textual picture to our concern with narrative and memory, we can start by noting how the narrator's, and Sebald's, associative train of thought gradually brings him closer to the key words "deported to his death." In Sebald's original German, the concluding part of the sentence (following all the place names) reads: "—kaum ein Ort in Europa, aus dem in diesen Jahren niemand deportiert worden wäre in den Tod" (78) ("— there was scarcely a place in Europe from which no one had been deported to his death in those years").[8] The subjunctive in the passive construction "deportiert worden wäre" is doubly significant: while the passive reminds us that they were deported by somebody, that is, the Nazis, the subjunctive form *wäre* refers to "niemand"/nobody, thus indicating that in spite of the narrator's wish, deportations actually occurred in all of these places. The double negation affirms a historical truth.

The association of names prompted by the first picture brings the narrator into touch with the second one, which then takes over as the narrative's primary point of reference. I do not find it necessary to distinguish between the narrator and Sebald here. What is important, however, is to note how suggestively, almost imperceptibly, three constituent elements of the narrator's experiential self are blended. James Phelan has usefully drawn attention to the ways in which, in much autobiographical narrative, the "I" "will sometimes speak from the perspective of her former self, thereby making the communication shift from the direct to the indirect" (1). In this passage, the narrator is speaking from two perspectives of his former self: while at the beginning the "I" is looking up at the "pale blue sky" (71) from the balcony of his parents' home in Bavaria, the "memorial tablets" (73) which he refers to are clearly seen not only in a "remote" place but also at a much later stage of his life. Moreover, since Sebald's own perspective as narrator at the time of writing is not totally eliminated, it is added to, or perhaps rather infiltrated by, the other two.

The documentary feature of this variant of first-person account serves to delineate its narrative purpose. It also strengthens the narrative's autobiographical dimension, which has two distinctive features in this paragraph. On the one hand, the narrator is induced by the idyllic scene from the Bavarian countryside to think of the many places from which people, in large part Jews, were deported to Nazi concentration and extermination camps. On the other hand, or rather as a digression (*Abschweifung*) from his train of thought, the narrator takes the reader into his parents' bedroom. I am not claiming that looking at this picture (see figure 2) makes us feel voyeuristic. But I am suggesting that the addition of this second autobiographical facet brings the reader embarrassingly and almost painfully close to Sebald's difficult relationship and lasting preoccupation with his parents, his Bavarian home, his past, and the Holocaust.

It is characteristic of Sebald's narrative art that the transition from the first to the second autobiographical facet is provoked by his associative interlinking of two physical objects seen in the same place, that is, Corsica: first the "memorial tablets" and then the oleograph in the church of Morosaglia which he identifies as "the picture from my parents' bedroom" (73). To these two elements of space are added the geographical names of Auschwitz and Flossenburg, yet in Sebald's discourse all of these places are immediately temporalized. The memorial tablets are related both to the time of his visit and to 1944; the painting of Christ in Gethsemane is related not just to his parents' bedroom but also to the time when he (the narrator/Sebald) was a child, perhaps sleeping in the same room. Thus the atrocities of the Holocaust force themselves into the author's most private sphere. This narrative association of historical events and personal memory is strengthened by the

rosaglia, auch noch gesehen habe – diese Abschweifung
sei erlaubt –, war das Schlafzimmerbild meiner Eltern,
einen Öldruck, Christus darstellend in nazarenerhafter
Schönheit, wie er vor Antritt seiner Passion im nacht-
blauen, vom Mond beschienenen Garten von Gethsemane sitzt in tiefer Versonnenheit. Viele Jahre hindurch war
dieses Bild über dem Ehebett der Eltern gehangen, und
irgendwann war es dann abhanden gekommen, wahr-
scheinlich als eine neue Schlafzimmergarnitur ange-
schafft wurde. Und jetzt stand es, oder zumindest genau
das gleiche, hier in der Dorfkirche von Morosaglia, dem
Heimatort des Generals Paoli, in einer finsteren Ecke an
den Sockel eines Seitenaltars gelehnt. Meine Eltern er-
zählten mir, sie hätten es 1936, kurz vor ihrer Hochzeit,
gekauft in Bamberg, wo der Vater Schirrmeister im sel-
ben Kavallerieregiment war, in dem zehn Jahre zuvor der
junge Stauffenberg seine militärische Laufbahn angetre-
ten hatte. Solcher Art sind die Abgründe der Geschichte.

Figure 2
Page 79 of *Luftkrieg und Literatur*

reference to Bamberg, where Sebald's parents had bought the picture in 1936. Sebald's father was a transport officer in Bamberg at the time, and exactly here "the young Stauffenberg had begun his military career ten years earlier" (74). This information is historically correct: Claus Schenk Graf von Stauffenberg, born 1907, entered the so-called *Reiterregiment* in Bamberg in 1926. Stauffenberg later played a key role in the attempt to assassinate Hitler in 1944; when this attempt failed, he was caught and executed.

It would be misleading, however, to claim that it is the connection between Sebald's father and Stauffenberg that leads the narrator to make the observation on time and history at the end of the passage. Although inspired by it, this generalized comment is generated by the narrative's implications and thematic thrust. The picture inserted into the middle of the paragraph simultaneously prompts and silently accompanies the narrator's observation, serving as an obscure visual illustration of it. Considered as a photograph, the picture is not a good one; it seems amateurishly contrived and there is no way we as readers can decide whether it is authentic or not. That is not the main issue here, however. What is essential from my critical perspective is the picture's narrative and thematic function in this particular paragraph, and as an integral part of *Luftkrieg und Literatur*. Seen in this light, it is arguably very significant. Since the photo shows a bedroom with a painting on the wall, the visual medium of painting is added to that of photography; and the defining features of both these variants of visual representation simultaneously enrich and complicate our reading of the verbal text. As the photograph shows both a bedroom and a painting, two elements of space are presented as one. Yet there is a tension between them. Accentuated by the different forms of visual media (photograph and painting), this tension is generated in large part by the contrast between the temporal positioning of the bedroom in the late 1940s and the image of Christ in Gethsemane almost 2,000 years earlier. This constellation of two spatial images held together in one spatial frame considerably strengthens the photograph's temporal dimension, while also accentuating the religious (Catholic) dimension of Sebald's childhood milieu. It is significant that, as described by the narrator, Christ is not only alone but "seated deep in thought." It is as though the narrator is identifying, and even accentuating, a distinctly melancholic aspect of the painting—an aspect imbued with a sense of loneliness and powerlessness. Thus the content of the visual image contributes to the dizziness and fear associated with looking at the past. Markus Weber has suggested that, for Sebald, pictures do not document reality but rather indicate the narrator's searching movement. Weber's term *Suchbewegung* (68) is suggestive, and his point would seem to be supported by this picture. The movement is not just into the past, since the "abysm of time" also brings the past closer. There is a strong sense in which the visual image documents reality not only as *remembered* by the narrator but also as *experienced* by him at the time of seeing the picture in the church in Morosaglia. What he sees in the church is not the photo but the painting in it; thus he is reminded of his childhood by looking at a work of art—an object that is made, created, rather than mechanically reproduced. And yet the painting is of course reproduced here, in the photo, thus adding one more complication.

Turning to *Austerlitz,* a perhaps obvious yet important first point to make is that since this long narrative is closer to the novel than to autobiography, the effects of its insistent linking of verbal discourse and visual image both resemble and differ from those noted in *Luftkrieg und Literatur.* As in the latter book, the verbal discourse of *Austerlitz* is punctuated by visual images, which are here not just photographic but also graphic and filmic. I will discuss the way in which three different textual pictures—a map, a frozen video image, and the photo of a railway station—influence and shape our understanding of the three passages of verbal discourse into which they are inserted and from which neither author nor reader—or, inside the fictional universe of *Austerlitz,* neither narrator nor character or narratee—is able to dissociate them.

One important reason why the visual images in *Austerlitz* both resemble and differ from those in *Luftkrieg und Literatur* is generic. I have described the chapter from the latter book as a blend of essay, commentary, and autobiography. Even though we must be wary of collapsing these generic categories into one, they all purport to refer to, and thus represent, aspects of the real world—such as Sebald's reflections on the reactions to his Zürich lectures or the account, albeit selective, of aspects of his childhood in Bavaria. The essential point to make here is that in this discourse the embedded photographs confirm, rather than complicate, its nonfictional character. I am making this point in spite of the fact that the photo of the bedroom of Sebald's parents may be "constructed," and thus in one sense fictional. One of photography's defining features, and also one of the strongest conventions associated with this medium, is its capacity to visually represent a segment of physical reality at a given point in time. Seen thus, photography is a marker of nonfictionality, and not just in *Luftkrieg und Literatur* but also in *Austerlitz.* In the latter text, however, the relationship between visual image and verbal discourse is more complex, also in the sense of being more problematic and presenting the reader with considerable interpretive challenges. The reason is that in contrast to *Luftkrieg und Literatur,* the verbal discourse of *Austerlitz* is possessed of several signposts of fictionality. Even though there is no theoretical consensus as to whether any combination of linguistic usages or narrative and literary devices can unambiguously indicate fictionality, David Gorman is right to note, in his helpful entry on "Theories of Fiction" in the *Routledge Encyclopedia of Narrative Theory,* that the combination of such signposts at least makes a text more likely to be fictional. Two signposts of fictionality in this novel (I will call it a novel, though it is a strange and highly original one) are extensive use of dialogue and what Gorman calls "distinguishability" of narrator from author.

As my reading of the three visual images in *Austerlitz* turns on the way in which they are embedded in a verbal discourse, I need to briefly indicate how the narrative is established and sustained. The main character of *Austerlitz* has grown up ignorant of his past, and many years after the Second World War he is forced to explore what happened to him and his parents, both of whom were Jews and in all probability victims of the Holocaust.

This is how the novel begins: "In the second half of the 1960s I travelled repeatedly from England to Belgium, partly for study purposes, partly for other reasons which were never entirely clear to me, staying sometimes for just one or two days, sometimes for several weeks" (1). On a first reading, we may think that the first-person narrator, the "I" who travels "repeatedly from England to Belgium," is identical with Austerlitz. Yet although, as it turns out, there is a peculiarly strong resemblance between the first-person narrator and the novel's main character—who also becomes eventually a main narrator—this beginning is actually a frame narrative whose function is to establish a narrative situation in which the two can meet and in which Austerlitz can talk.

Sebald's use of a frame narrator can be linked to a tradition of such narrators in literary fiction. With a view to the narrative and thematic fabric of *Austerlitz,* the gains of employing a frame narrator are considerable, and they strikingly resemble the effects of Joseph Conrad's use of a frame narrator in *Heart of Darkness.* Conrad's famous novella from 1899 is one of the strongest intertexts in *Austerlitz.* In both narratives, the main narrator is introduced by a frame narrator, who then becomes a keenly interested listener or narratee. Moreover, in *Austerlitz* as in *Heart of Darkness,* the frame narrator's relative conventionality renders him more reliable, thus making it easier for us to believe Austerlitz's story, which the frame narrator reports to us as readers. This narrative strategy creates a tentacular effect: we are drawn into the narrative in a manner comparable to the way in which the frame narrator is irresistibly attracted to Austerlitz's account. And one of the elements that attract him, and the reader, is Austerlitz's pictures. In *Story and Situation,* Ross Chambers draws attention to the manner in which, at a deep and frequently unthematized level, the narrator's motivation to narrate is complemented by the narratee's readiness to listen, and he notes that for both parties, possibilities of gain as well as risks of loss are involved (51). The narrative situations in *Austerlitz* offer ample illustrations of this important point. For example, by telling fragments of his story Austerlitz risks confirming his sense of loss and estrangement, yet his narration may enable him to negotiate that loss. By listening to the story, the narratee risks losing, or being drawn out of, a comfortable position of ignorance; yet the fact that he not only listens to but also retells what Austerlitz has told him suggests a learning process, and thus the possibility of gaining essential knowledge.

Even though both the frame narrator and Austerlitz are presented as fictional characters, the pictures Austerlitz takes—and at least some of which, the reader assumes, are presented in the book—seem to refer to the same physical reality as those included in *Luftkrieg und Literatur.* And yet we read them differently, since the pictures in *Austerlitz* simultaneously oppose and are colored by the fictional verbal discourse in which they are embedded, and from which Sebald makes it exceedingly difficult to disentangle them. During one of their first conversations in the railway station in Antwerp, "Austerlitz took a camera out of his rucksack, an old Ensign with telescopic bellows, and took several pictures of the mirrors, which were now quite dark, but so far I have been unable to find them among the many hundreds of pictures, most of them unsorted, that he entrusted to me soon after we met again in the winter of 1996" (7). If Austerlitz's narrative is relayed to the reader via the frame narrator, so, it seems, are his pictures.

In an insightful comment on *Heart of Darkness,* Tzvetan Todorov has said of Marlow's narration that it spirals toward a thematic core or center, which, however, turns out to be empty (167, 169). There is a sense in which this description applies to Austerlitz's narration too, and the three textual images to be discussed support the notion of gravitating toward a nightmarish vacuity. A Czech Jew, Austerlitz escaped from the Nazis in the summer of 1939, on a *Kindertransport* to Britain. Austerlitz's father, Maximilian, fled to France, while his mother, Agáta, remained in Czechoslovakia together with Věra, a non-Jewish friend of the family. As Austerlitz's search for his parents now, many years later, takes him "further and further east and further and further back in time" (262–63), his conversations with Věra, with whom he resumes contact, make him believe that his mother was interned in Terezín (the German name is *Theresienstadt*) in late 1942 (281) and then "sent east in September 1944" (287).[9] Accordingly, Austerlitz, with typical thoroughness, studies an 800-page book "which H. G. Adler, a name previously unknown to me, had written between 1945 and 1947 in the most difficult of circumstances, partly in Prague and partly in London, on the subject of the setting up, development and internal organization of the Theresienstadt ghetto . . ." (327). In the German edition of *Austerlitz,* this sentence is divided into two by this textual picture, shown in figure 3.

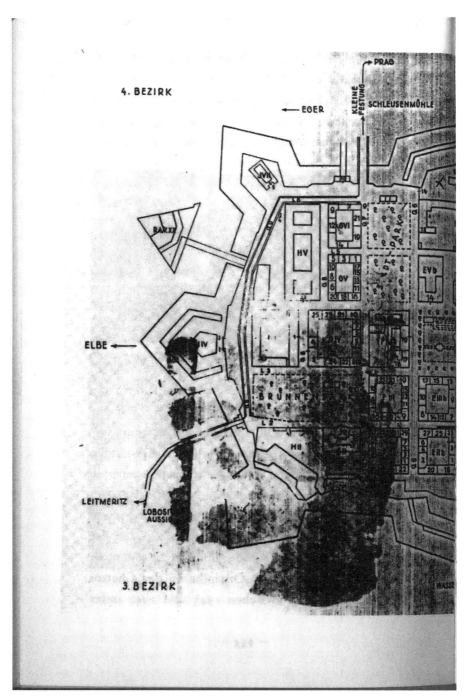

Figure 3
Pages 336–37 of *Austerlitz*

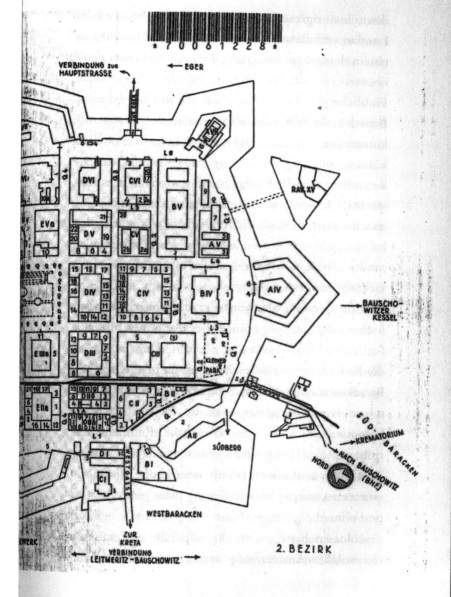

VERBINDUNG zur HAUPTSTRASSE

← EGER

VERBINDUNG zur HAUPTSTRASSE

DVI

CVI

BV

RAK XV

EVa

DV   19

CV

AV

DIV   CIV

BIV

AIV

→ BAUSCHO-WITZER KESSEL

EIIIa

DIII

CIII

KLEINER PARK

EIIa

DII

CII

BII

AII

SÜDBERG

SÜD-BARACKEN

→ KREMATORIUM

NORD

→ NACH BAUSCHOWITZ (BHF)

DI

BI

CI

WESTBARACKEN

ZUR KRETA

VERBINDUNG LEITMERITZ-BAUSCHOWITZ

← →

2. BEZIRK

An illustrative example of Sebald's technique of integrating visual images into his verbal discourse, this map invites three comments. First, although not a photograph, this textual picture has a topographical dimension in that it indicates—and makes Austerlitz, the frame narrator, and the reader visualize—an element of space, a place complete with streets, houses, and a surrounding border. However, as our knowledge that this place was a concentration camp during the Second World War blends into our impression of its topographical shape, it is temporalized and linked to our own history. Second, as if preempting such a reading of the map, Austerlitz makes an attempt to qualify or counter it by stating that "because in its almost futuristic deformation of social life the ghetto system had something incomprehensible and unreal about it . . ." (331). This is as close as the verbal discourse in *Austerlitz* comes to being a caption, or caption-like. Third, like most maps, this one too has names written on it. Names, as we well know, have to be read; and two general names in particular become semantically loaded in the context of the proper names to which they are linked and of the verbal narrative in which they are situated: "(BHF)" [railway station] and "KREMATORIUM." "BHF" signifies both Austerlitz's restless train journeys across Europe and those of countless Jews being deported to the extermination camps; "KREMATORIUM" is repeated in the main text when the frame narrator reports that the "incinerators of the crematorium, kept going day and night in cycles of forty minutes at a time, were stretched to the utmost limits of their capacity, said Austerlitz" (337).

The protagonist and main narrator Austerlitz makes this comment in the middle of the novel's longest sentence, which stretches from page 331 to page 342. Through this long, convoluted sentence, Austerlitz's first-person narrative—relayed to the reader via the frame narrator—makes a sustained attempt to move beyond the sterile surface of the map, groping for a different kind of sign that could possibly affirm, for him, the existence of his mother in the camp. At the very end of the ten-page sentence, Austerlitz suddenly mentions that, according to Adler, the Nazis made a film at Theresienstadt, a film Adler never saw "and thought it was now lost without trace" (342). However, Austerlitz eventually manages to obtain "a cassette copy of the film of Theresienstadt for which I had been searching" (343). Watching the film, he cannot see his mother, Agáta, anywhere. But then he gets the idea of having a slow-motion copy made. Watching this artificially extended version, he notices the face of a young woman in the backdrop. The visual image is accompanied by this passage:

Around her neck, said Austerlitz, she is wearing a three-stringed and delicately draped necklace which scarcely stands out from her dark, high-necked dress, and there is, I think, a white flower in her hair. She looks, so I tell myself as I watch, just as I imagined the singer Agáta from my faint memories and the few other clues to her appearance that I now have, and I gaze again and again at that face, which seems to me both strange and familiar, said Austerlitz, I run the tape back repeatedly, looking at the time indicator in the top left-hand corner of the screen, where the figures covering part of her forehead show the minutes and seconds, from 10:53 to 10:57, while the hundredths of a second flash by so fast that you cannot read and capture them. (350–51)

As it turns out, this woman is probably not Agáta, since Věra cannot recognize her. Nor does Austerlitz himself seem to be certain of her identity, as words such as "imagined" and "faint memories" indicate. The failure of identification is revealing. My main concern, though, is the presentation and effect of the image. Unusually for *Austerlitz,* the textual image inserted into this passage is filmic. This means that, in concert with this medium's conditions of production (that is, making a film), what we are looking at here is just one frame out of the 24 frames per second that our eyes need to be exposed to in order to experience an optical illusion of movement. The temporal dimension of the filmic image is insistent in a way that that of a photograph is not, and here it is visually presented in the form of the numbers indicating the day, month, and year of the recording of the tape, as well as the time (close to eleven minutes) played and seen so far.

And yet what we are looking at is a frozen image, an image that insists on moving and yet stands still, suspended in time and space. It is as though Austerlitz, or Sebald, or the frame narrator, is attempting to stabilize or temporarily halt a fleeting, moving image by freezing it in time—first by having the slow-motion copy made and then by making the still copy. Avi Kempinski finds that by running "the tape back repeatedly," Austerlitz evokes Roland Barthes's notion of the "defeat of Time" (96) in historical photographs; Austerlitz seems to experience a *punctum* whose uncoded intensity and "power of expansion" (Barthes 45) lead him to believe that the woman in the photo may be his mother.[10] Kempinski is correct to note that "despite this attempt to resuscitate the mother-image through the 'defeat of time,' this faint image ultimately betrays a face, but not the mother's" (466). The two faces in the image seem to be approaching the viewer from an unknown place somewhere in the past, and the lack of textual commentary on the man in the foreground of the still seems conspicuous. He appears to be unknown, yet he may irresistibly remind Austerlitz of his lost father. Although there is something ghostlike about the appearance of the two faces, they do add a human dimension to the map of Theresienstadt, the place where these two human

alten Herrn, dessen kurz geschorenes graues Haupt die rechte Hälfte des Bildes ausfüllt, während in der linken Hälfte, etwas zurückgesetzt und mehr gegen den oberen Rand, das Gesicht einer jüngeren Frau

erscheint, fast ununterschieden von dem schwarzen Schatten, der es umgibt, weshalb ich es auch zunächst gar nicht bemerkte. Sie trägt, sagte Austerlitz, eine in drei feinen Bogenlinien von ihrem dunklen, hochgeschlossenen Kleid kaum sich abhebende Kette um den Hals und eine weiße Blumenblüte seitlich in ihrem Haar. Gerade so wie ich nach meinen schwachen Erinnerungen und den wenigen

Figure 4
Page 358 of *Austerlitz*

beings were at the time of the shooting of the film. The image contributes to, and further extends, Austerlitz's attempt to understand at least something of the terrible conditions under which the inmates of the camp lived. As Marianne Hirsch has shown in *Family Frames,* the appearance of faces, human beings, in a photograph prompts a form of narrativization of it—not least if it is one of a family member. In this textual picture, narrativization is accentuated partly by the way in which time and space play equally important roles in film, partly by the imprint of temporal markers (numbers) on the frozen image.

We have noted that although the visual images in *Austerlitz,* in common with those in *Luftkrieg und Literatur,* seem to refer to physical reality, we read them differently because of the fictional verbal discourse into which they are integrated. One of the ways in which Sebald makes it difficult to disentangle this frozen filmic image from the fiction in which it is embedded is that Austerlitz thinks he can recognize his mother, Agáta, in a historical film made at Theresienstadt by the Nazis.[11] As it would seem impossible for a fictional character such as Austerlitz to recognize his mother in a documentary film about people in the real world, there is a sense in which the historical film is fictionalized—even though it links Austerlitz to historical reality. Moreover, fictionalization is also very much part of the film itself: as a Nazi propaganda film it presents a picture of Theresienstadt that is entirely false. Before making the film, the Nazi authorities fixed up the camp and arranged cultural activities to give the appearance of a happy community; after the filming ended, the camp slipped back into its cruel routine. In the fictional world of the novel, Austerlitz thinks that Agáta was "sent east in September 1944" (287); in historical reality, both before and after shooting the film at Theresienstadt, the Nazis deported a large number of the camp's inmates to Auschwitz. Accentuating the novel's ethical dimension, Sebald's incorporation of the documentary into the fiction of *Austerlitz* testifies to a powerful concern on his part not just with the relations between history and fiction but also with the relations between truth and falsity: the documentary has a historical existence but its purpose was not to fictionalize but to lie, whereas Sebald's narrative is fictional but its purpose is to capture truths that the documentary either denies or neglects. Indeed, the Nazi film does not really merit the term "documentary," even if, as Sebald demonstrates, documentary evidence of some sort may be obtained from it through an oppositional reading.

Just after the presentation of this image, Austerlitz tells his narratee, who has been listening patiently for a long while, that "he was now about to go to Paris to search for traces of his father's last movements" (354). If the visual image of the woman from Theresienstadt is as close as Austerlitz thinks he is

able to come to his mother, the last one I want to discuss is a forceful visual
representation of his search for his father (see figure 5).

Linked to this visual image is the following paragraph:

> Curiously enough, said Austerlitz, a few hours after our last meeting, when
> he had come back from the Bibliothèque Nationale and changed trains at
> the Gare d'Austerlitz, he had felt a premonition that he was coming closer
> to his father. . . . an idea came to him of his father's leaving Paris from this
> station, close as it was to his flat in the rue Barrault, soon after the Germans
> entered the city. I imagined, said Austerlitz, that I saw him leaning out of
> the window of his compartment as the train left, and I saw the white clouds
> of smoke rising from the locomotive as it began to move ponderously away.
> (404–6)

Reading these lines and looking at this textual picture, the reader has a sense
of the narrative coming full circle, for one of the first images of *Austerlitz* is
also one of a railway station. Moreover, the name of the railway station at
Antwerp, *Salle des pas perdu* (Hall of Lost Steps), can equally be linked to the
Gare d'Austerlitz, whose name is blended with one significant aspect of the
protagonist's name. As the frame narrator tells us that Austerlitz takes several
photographs in the *Salle des pas perdu,* he may have taken this one too.

Significantly, there are no people in this photo—just a large hall and two
trains, one on each side of the hall. We assume that it is a photo of the Gare
d'Austerlitz, but we cannot be sure, and probably are not meant to be. This
kind of ambiguity is thematically productive: the image induces us to think,
first, of Austerlitz imagining his father traveling out, *aus,* escaping from the
Nazis in 1940 and yet, we suspect, ending up in a concentration camp a few
years later. Second, the image also invites us to think of this railway station
as one of many sites of deportation. The German words *Zug* and *Bahn/Eisen-
bahn* are semantically loaded for Sebald, as are the various references to trains
and railways throughout *Austerlitz.* On the one hand, they signal voluntary
travel and possible escape (as in the case of Austerlitz himself); on the other
hand, they are inextricably linked to the transport of Jews to the concentration and extermination camps. Giving a visual anchorage to one of the novel's
most important leitmotifs, this last image is suggestively linked to the one
from Theresienstadt just discussed. While the first one gives us an image of
two humans with textual commentary about Austerlitz's effort to identify the
woman as his mother, the second gives us an image without any humans but
with commentary about Austerlitz's imagining his father leaning out of the
window of a train leaving the station. The first juxtaposition of image and text

vor von einem Mitarbeiter des Dokumentationszentrums in der rue Geoffroy-l'Asnier eine Nachricht erhalten habe, derzufolge Maximilian Aychenwald Ende 1942 in dem Lager Gurs interniert gewesen sei, und daß er, Austerlitz, diesen weit drunten im Süden, in den Vorbergen der Pyrenäen gelegenen Ort nun aufsuchen müsse. Sonderbarerweise, so sagte Austerlitz, habe er wenige Stunden nach unserer letzten Begegnung, als er, von der Bibliothèque Nationale herkommend, in der Gare d'Austerlitz umgestiegen

sei, die Vorahnung gehabt, daß er dem Vater sich annähere. Wie ich vielleicht wisse, sei am vergangenen Mittwoch ein Teil des Eisenbahnverkehrs wegen eines Streiks lahmgelegt worden, und in der aufgrund dessen in der Gare d'Austerlitz herrschenden ungewöhnlichen Stille sei ihm der Gedanke gekommen, der Vater habe von hier aus, von diesem seiner Wohnung in der rue Barrault zunächst gelegenen Bahnhof, Paris verlassen bald nach dem Einmarsch der Deutschen. Ich bildete mir ein, sagte Austerlitz, ihn

Figure 5
Pages 410–11
of *Austerlitz*

leads to the conclusion that the woman is not his mother, while the second emphasizes the gap between what is known and what is imagined. In different ways the combinations of visual image and verbal text underline the same larger point about the absence in Austerlitz's knowledge—and in his life.

Concluding, I link my observations on these three textual pictures in *Austerlitz* to those made on the three photographs from *Luftkrieg und Literatur.* Even though these images would appear to support Mieke Bal's notion of making "discourse a partner, rather than dominant opponent, of visuality" (288), we must not forget that, as we have seen, the visual images' narrative and thematic functions vary considerably. Broadly speaking, the relationship between visual image and verbal discourse is less obvious, and more indirect, if this discourse is fictional. And yet the map of Theresienstadt, the frozen filmic image of two of the camp's inmates, and the photo of Gare d'Austerlitz serve to anchor the constructed story of the fictional character Austerlitz in historical reality. Aided by his fictional narrator, Sebald manages to make some contact with aspects of his past, the war, and the Holocaust that would otherwise have remained out of reach.

All the visual images discussed here, and not least the last one from *Luftkrieg und Literatur,* contribute significantly to the two texts' multidimensionality of narrative and thematic purpose not only by altering the verbal meaning but, more importantly, by extending and enriching that meaning. Since the photograph of the bedroom of the narrator's parents is placed in the narrative of Sebald's familial history, and since that history is available to him essentially through associative, narrativized memory, the temporal and spatial variants of distance observable in the photo simultaneously reflect and intensify the narrator's sense of being permanently removed from something or somebody he cannot possibly retrieve but still needs to go on searching for. The visual images in *Austerlitz,* and the passages of which they become integral parts, reveal narrative fiction's unique capacity to make a strong, generalized statement about human action—ranging from mass murder on the one hand to the importance of not forgetting those murders on the other.

In *Luftkrieg und Literatur* as in *Austerlitz,* the visual images confirm and intensify the narratives' ethical dimension. In the novel's fictional discourse, the ethical facet is closely linked to, and developed through, Austerlitz as character narrator. Austerlitz keeps searching for his parents because he feels he has a moral obligation to do so and because he has an existential need to search for his own past. The novel's ethical thrust is perhaps even stronger for the frame narrator, who feels compelled to listen to Austerlitz as a kind of moral duty of learning and also of witnessing by passing on Austerlitz's story to the reader. Shoshana Felman and Dori Laub put emphasis on the important role of the listener in testimony (57–59)—in an important way, the frame narrator and via him the reader are placed into that role here. Thus the novel has two main narrators, since Sebald makes the entire narrative depend on a frame narrator who is German and who as a German born at the end of the war comes distressingly close to awful crimes he did not commit.[12] While Austerlitz is drawn toward the victims of the Holocaust, the frame narrator seems unable to reassuringly distance himself from the perpetrators responsible for the crime.[13] The photograph of the empty railway station—be it the Gare d'Austerlitz or an anonymous site of deportation or both—is a forceful visual reminder of the novel's ethical dimension, effectively relayed to the reader via the frame narrator as Austerlitz's narratee. In our example of nonfictional, autobiographical discourse the ethical dimension becomes particularly noticeable in the narrator's associative linking, in the village in Corsica, of the "memorial tablets" of Holocaust victims and "the picture from my parents' bedroom" (73). It is significant that, in common with most autobiographies or fragments of autobiography, this narration is in the first person. As a first-person narrator is involved in the plot, it becomes more difficult for him or her to remain at a comfortable distance from that plot. Although Sebald was born during the war, this narrative association suggests that in a distressing sense his father's service in the Wehrmacht brings him, the first-person narrator Sebald, problematically close to wartime actions making possible, and including, the Holocaust. The reference to Stauffenberg, whose moral decision to attempt to assassinate Hitler cost him his life, further strengthens the passage's ethical dimension. So does the painting in the photograph: Jesus, immobile and in a moment of doubt, is also facing an ethical dilemma at this difficult stage of the narrative of His Passion. Although this kind of affinity should not be exaggerated, it suggests, in combination with the other aspects we have noted, Sebald's narrative method of linking together apparently disparate elements of space and time.

Notes

1. The title of the German original is preferable to the English one, *On the Natural History of Destruction*. However, quotations from this book as well as *Austerlitz* are from the English translations by Anthea Bell.

2. Three helpful collections of essays on Sebald are Görner, *The Anatomist of Melancholy;* Long and Whitehead, *W. G. Sebald;* and Patt, *Searching for Sebald.* Two important monographs are McCulloh, *Understanding W. G. Sebald;* and Long, *W. G. Sebald.* In addition to the contributions to Patt's volume, four essays dealing specifically with the issue of visual images and narrative in Sebald are Shaffer, "W. G. Sebald's Photographic Narrative";

Duttlinger, "Traumatic Experience"; Kilbourn, "Architecture and Cinema"; and Horstkotte, "Photo-Text Topographies."

3. I use the terms "visual image" and "textual picture" synonymously to indicate photographs and photocopied matter (e.g., an illustration or a map) presented in, and thus made a part of, a verbal text. Even though such images are generically and aesthetically very different from the images formed in, and by, verbal language, the interpretive activity prompted by the reading of Sebald can establish points of contact between the two main variants.

4. In *Topographies* J. Hillis Miller gives a detailed account of the complexity of the term; see especially 3–5. I make more comments on the spatial aspect of narrative fiction in my "Space, Time, Narrative."

5. Two helpful books on narrative and memory are King, *Memory, Narrative, Identity;* and Rossington and Whitehead, *Theories of Memory.*

6. The English translation by Michael Hamburger, *After Nature,* appeared in 2001.

7. Since the positioning of the photos is inaccurate in the English editions of *Luftkrieg und Literatur* and *Austerlitz* compared to the original German ones, illustrations of pages with photographs or other images inserted into the body of the text are taken from the German editions. Quotations from the passages associated with the images, however, are from the English translations by Anthea Bell.

8. Although Anthea Bell's translation is generally good, it needs to be pointed out that Sebald's *niemand* (nobody) refers not just to people deported to "his death" but also "her death." Large numbers of women were deported from locations across Europe, and their chance of surviving a camp like Auschwitz was even smaller than that of the men.

9. A specific and historical camp, Theresienstadt is at the same time representative of the concentration and extermination camps constructed and run by Nazi Germany. Of all the camps, Auschwitz has come to symbolically represent the Holocaust, and it is hardly coincidental that the first three and last three letters of the names Austerlitz and Auschwitz are identical. See my "Narrative, Genre, Memory," 117.

10. While in *Camera Lucida* the concept of *studium* refers to the cultural, linguistic, and relatively conventional interpretation of a photograph, *punctum* denotes the wounding, intensified, subjective, and personally touching detail that establishes a more direct relationship with the object or person within the photo. See Barthes, 26–27.

11. The film's original title is *Der Führer schenkt den Juden eine Stadt* (*The Führer Gives a City to the Jews*), written and directed by the Jewish actor Kurt Gerron. Forcing Gerron to make the film, the Nazi authorities promised him his life. Filming started on August 16, 1944, and was completed on September 11 of that year. After that, Gerron was deported to Auschwitz, and he was gassed in Birkenau on October 28, 1944. See The Holocaust Education & Archive Research Team, http://www.holocaustresearchproject.org/toc.html. Surviving footage of the film, a portion of which can be seen on YouTube, is about twenty minutes long. The YouTube excerpt includes the filmic image of the man and woman presented on page 351 of the novel and discussed in this essay. See http://www.youtube.com/watch?v=Hp_KaenGnDM.

12. Although the frame narrator lives in England, he tells the reader, "I returned to Germany at the end of 1975, intending to settle permanently in my native country, to which I felt I had become a stranger after nine years of absence" (45). The number "18.5.44" (415), which the frame narrator mentions on the novel's last page, is Sebald's birth date.

13. If, as Charles L. Griswold observes in *Forgiveness*, "forgiveness requires reciprocity between injurer and injured" (xvi), the conversations between the frame narrator and Austerlitz reveal, as I argue in a different essay ("Forgiveness, History, Narrative,"), elements of such reciprocity, which simultaneously highlight the need for forgiveness and demonstrate the problems or limitations of forgiveness. In the narrative dynamics of *Austerlitz* these elements are blended with, and thus in one sense qualified by, friendship, trust, and a melancholic sensation of the past's pervasive present.

Works Cited

Bal, Mieke. *Reading "Rembrandt": Beyond the Word-Image Opposition*. Cambridge: Cambridge University Press, 1991.

Barthes, Roland. *Camera Lucida: Reflections on Photography*. Translated by Richard Howard. London: Jonathan Cape, 1982. First published as *La Chambre claire: Note sur la photographie*. Paris: Éditions du Seuil, 1980.

Chambers, Ross. *Story and Situation: Narrative Seduction and the Power of Fiction*. Manchester: Manchester University Press, 1984.

Duttlinger, Carolin. "Traumatic Experience: Remembrance and the Technical Media in W. G. Sebald's *Austerlitz*." In *W. G. Sebald: A Critical Companion*, edited by J. J. Long and Anne Whitehead, 155–71. Edinburgh: Edinburgh University Press, 2004.

Felman, Shoshana and Dori Laub. *Testimony: Crises of Witnessing in Literature, Psychoanalysis, and History*. New York: Routledge, 1992.

Gerron, Kurt. *Der Führer schenkt den Juden eine Stadt* [*The Führer Gives a City to the Jews*]. Written and directed by Kurt Gerron. Filmed at Theresienstadt, August16–September 11, 1944. http://www.youtube.com/watch?v=Hp_KaenGnDM. Accessed August 22, 2011.

Gorman, David. "Theories of Fiction." In *Routledge Encyclopedia of Narrative Theory*, edited by David Herman, Manfred Jahn, and Marie-Laure Ryan, 163–67. London: Routledge, 2005.

Griswold, Charles L. *Forgiveness: A Philosophical Exploration*. Cambridge: Cambridge University Press, 2007.

Görner, Rüdiger, ed. *The Anatomist of Melancholy: Essays in Memory of W. G. Sebald*. München: Iudicium Verlag, 2003.

Hain, Hans-Joachim. "Leerstellen in der deutschen Gedenkkultur: Die Schreitschriften von W. G. Sebald und Klaus Briegleb." *German Life and Letters* 57, no. 4 (October 2004): 357–71.

Hirsch, Marianne. *Family Frames: Photography, Narrative, and Postmemory*. Cambridge, MA: Harvard University Press, 1997.

Holocaust Education & Archive Research Team. http://www.holocaustresearchproject.org/toc.html. Accessed August 22, 2011.

Horstkotte, Silke. "Photo-Text Topographies: Photography and Representation of Space in W. G. Sebald and Monkia Maron." *Poetics Today* 29, no. 1 (Spring 2008): 49–78.

Kempinski, Avi. "'Quel Roman!' Sebald, Barthes, and the Pursuit of the Mother-Image." In *Searching for Sebald: Photography after W. G. Sebald*, edited by Lise Patt, 456–71. Los Angeles: The Institute of Cultural Inquiry, 2007.

Kilbourn, Russell J. A. "Architecture and Cinema: The Representation of Memory in W. G.

Sebald's *Austerlitz.*" In *W. G. Sebald: A Critical Companion,* edited by J. J. Long and Anne Whitehead, 140–54. Edinburgh: Edinburgh University Press, 2004.

King, Nicola. *Memory, Narrative, Identity: Remembering the Self.* Edinburgh: Edinburgh University Press, 2000.

Long, J. J. and Anne Whitehead, eds. *W. G. Sebald: A Critical Companion.* Edinburgh: Edinburgh University Press, 2004.

Long, J. J. *W. G. Sebald: Image, Archive, Modernity.* Edinburgh: Edinburgh University Press, 2007.

Lothe, Jakob. "Narrative, Genre, Memory: The Title of W. G. Sebald's Novel *Austerlitz.*" In *Comparative Approaches to Nordic and European Modernisms,* edited by Mats Jansson, Janna Kantola, Jakob Lothe, and H. K. Riikonen, 109–26. Helsinki: Helsinki University Press, 2008.

———. "Space, Time, Narrative: From Thomas Hardy to Franz Kafka and J. M. Coetzee." In *Literary Landscapes: From Modernism to Postcolonialism,* edited by Attie de Lange, Gail Fincham, Jeremy Hawthorn, and Jakob Lothe, 1–18. New York: Palgrave Macmillan, 2008.

———. "Forgiveness, History, Narrative: W. G. Sebald's *Austerlitz.*" In *The Ethics of Forgiveness: A Collection of Essays,* edited by Christel Fricke, 179–96. New York: Routledge, 2011.

McCulloh, Mark R. *Understanding W. G. Sebald.* Columbia: University of South Carolina Press, 2003.

Miller, J. Hillis. *Topographies.* Stanford: Stanford University Press, 1995.

Mitchell, J. W. T. *Picture Theory: Essays on Verbal and Visual Interpretation.* Chicago: University of Chicago Press, 1994.

Patt, Lise, ed. *Searching for Sebald: Photography after W. G. Sebald.* Los Angeles: The Institute of Cultural Inquiry, 2007.

Phelan, James. *Living to Tell about It: A Rhetoric and Ethics of Character Narration.* Ithaca: Cornell University Press, 2005.

Rossington, Michael and Anne Whitehead, eds. *Theories of Memory: A Reader.* Edinburgh: Edinburgh University Press, 2007.

Sebald, W. G. *Nach der Natur: Ein Elementargedicht.* Photographs by Thomas Becker. Nördlingen: Greno, 1988.

———. *Luftkrieg und Literatur.* Frankfurt am Main: Fischer Verlag, 2005. First published by Carl Hanser Verlag, 1999.

———. *After Nature.* Translated by Michael Hamburger. New York: Random House, 2002.

———. *On the Natural History of Destruction.* Translated by Anthea Bell. New York: The Modern Library, 2004.

———. *Austerlitz.* Frankfurt am Main: Fischer Verlag, 2003. First published by Carl Hanser Verlag, 2001.

———. *Austerlitz.* Translated by Anthea Bell. London: Penguin, 2002.

Shaffer, Elinor. "W. G. Sebald's Photographic Narrative." In *The Anatomist of Melancholy: Essays in Memory of W. G. Sebald,* edited by Rüdiger Görner, 51–62. München: Iudicium Verlag, 2003.

Todorov, Tzvetan. "Connaissance du vide: *Coeur des ténèbres.*" In *Les Genres du discours,* 161–73. Paris: Seuil, 1978.

Weber, Markus R. "Die fantastische befragt die pedantische Genauigkeit: Zu den Abbildungen in W. G. Sebalds Werken." *Text+Kritik: Zeitschrift für Literatur,* Heft 158 (April 2003): 63–74.

CHAPTER 11

Which Narrative of Auschwitz?

A Narrative Analysis of Laurence Rees's Documentary Auschwitz: The Nazis and 'the Final Solution'

ANETTE H. STOREIDE

Introduction

The documentary *Auschwitz: The Nazis and 'the Final Solution'* was aired on the occasion of the sixtieth anniversary of the end of the Second World War. The main topics of the series are, first, the planning and building of the concentration and extermination camp Auschwitz and, second, the perpetrators' motives; the latter is part of an attempt to explain why Auschwitz was built and made into "the site of the largest mass murder in history," a statement often quoted throughout the series.

The creative director of the history programs at the BBC, Laurence Rees, wrote and produced this six-part documentary, a coproduction of the British BBC and the American KCET, an independent public television station. The American title of the documentary is *Auschwitz: Inside the Nazi State*. Rees is also the author of the accompanying book *Auschwitz: The Nazis and 'the Final Solution.'* A BBC survey presented as part of the press release before the airing of the documentary in 2005 stated that a large part of the British population knew little or nothing about Auschwitz and the Second World War (BBC Press Office). Thus, one expressed intention behind the documentary was to transmit knowledge of the Nazi mass murder to a broader and also younger audience.

The series is based on up-to-date research. The opening of the former Soviet archives, where among other aspects the complete building plans of

Auschwitz were discovered, has given historians new and important sources for research on the Second World War. This new knowledge is reflected in the series. A team of experts on the Holocaust, including the well-known historian Ian Kershaw, provided support and advice during production. As part of the documentary's pedagogical aspect, Learning Resources were published on the Internet (http://www.pbs.org/auschwitz/).

The historical facts presented in the documentary were well known to historians when the series was broadcast in 2005. It can be viewed as a summary of the current research and knowledge of the Nazi persecution and mass extermination, with focus on the events in Auschwitz, available sixty years after the end of the Nazi era. Promoted as the "definitive screen history of the evolution of Auschwitz" in which "the reality of life in the camp is exposed in unflinching detail" (according to the text on the back cover of the DVD), the documentary contributed to making the latest historical research available to a wider public with no or limited academic interest in historical research on the Second World War. As the series was aired, it became very popular in several European countries. Although it may come as a surprise that a documentary on a historical subject would attract that much attention, the public's interest in the Second World War and the Nazi regime has hardly faded, and the year 2005 also marked the sixtieth anniversary of the end of the Nazi dictatorship. This essay will argue that the narrative strategies used by Rees to construct this narrative of Auschwitz—especially the implementation of dramatized scenes and the intensive emotional and dramatic aspect, which will be a main focus of the essay—may have contributed significantly to the documentary's widespread success and made the history of Auschwitz and the Holocaust "available" to new generations of viewers. The application of these key narrative strategies, which are important pop-cultural features, may have promoted the emotional involvement and interest of a wider audience. Although Rees's series proved successful, however, its effect was not comparable to that of the American TV series *Holocaust* (1978)—a hugely popular series that also introduced "the Holocaust" as a common term for the Nazi genocide. Furthermore, the two series differ significantly in the adaptation of historical reality (I will elaborate on this point later). While the American TV series does not present reenacted scenes, Laurence Rees's series is presented as a documentary, but at the same time it contains a wide implementation of reenacted scenes and even credits a drama director. Thus, a major critical concern of this essay is the use and consequence of implementing reenactments in documentaries.

The possibility of establishing a narrative of a traumatic experience such as the Nazi mass murder has been widely discussed. Appropriating Jürgen

Habermas's definition of the term "Holocaust" (Habermas, in Feuchert 5ff.), the thesis of the unspeakability of the Holocaust dominated philosophical and literary perspectives for many years. However, since the 1980s there has been a growing focus on memory, and the perspective of research on memory has turned from *which* memories are depicted to *how* memories are constructed. One of the main foci in research on testimonies of survivors in the last years concerns more *how* the memories are narrated and represented as text than *which* memories of persecution and imprisonment the survivors present. One of the initiators of this perspectival shift, Lawrence L. Langer, calls it the second phase of reaction to the Holocaust ("Die Zeit der Erinnerung" 53). The phase of questioning the representation is followed by a phase of analyzing the representation.

Responding to this new trend of research, this essay focuses on *what* narrative is presented of Auschwitz and *how* this narrative is presented. I thus use the inclusive definition of narrative given by Jens Brockmeier and Rom Harré, who consider narrative as an "ensemble of linguistic, psychological, and social structures, transmitted cultural-historically, constrained by an individual's level of mastery and by his/her mixture of communicative techniques and linguistic skills" (41). I transfer this definition to filmic representation in which not only the verbal (spoken and written) discourse about the history of Auschwitz has to be considered, but also the complex combinations of images and sound (including music). I use this extended definition of narrative to emphasize that the historical, political, and cultural context of a narrative cannot be separated from the narrative itself. Each narrative is a social construction dependent upon the context of its narration, and Rees's narrative of Auschwitz not only contains knowledge on the historical events in and concerning Auschwitz, but is also constructed under certain political and cultural conditions sixty years after the liberation of the camp and the capitulation of Nazi Germany. These aspects, and not only the facts about Auschwitz, also need to be considered in an analysis of Rees's narrative.

Considering the series as an attempt to establish a narrative of Auschwitz sixty years after the end of the Nazi era, I will examine the combination of the images (photos, film, original recordings, dramatized scenes), music, interviews (with both surviving victims and perpetrators), and the speaking voices (both of the main narrator and of the interviewed persons). I will consider the filmic construction of the narrative by analyzing the narrative strategies, focusing mainly on the combination of documentary strategies and dramatization. Important questions include: Why does the director implement dramatizations in this attempted documentary? What effects do such strategies have in and on a documentary? Moreover, which situations are being dramatized and which are not? The extensive use of dramatization in this series blurs the limit between documentary and historical drama. Main points argued in this essay are that the series therefore in many aspects can be interpreted as a "docudrama" and that its conception as a drama of this kind may have contributed significantly to its widespread international success.

The Narrative of Auschwitz according to Laurence Rees

Rees's narrative contains six parts, each running approximately fifty minutes. The six parts are titled 1) "Surprising Beginnings," 2) "Orders and Initiatives," 3) "Factories of Death," 4) "Corruption," 5) "Frenzied Killing," and 6) "Liberation and Revenge." The narrative represents a temporal chronological construction mainly from April 1940 in Poland until approximately the trial of Adolf Eichmann in 1961. The beginning is defined with the preliminary considerations of establishment of the camp. The end is less definite because it refers to various aspects of the postwar period and to what happened to some of the survivors without specifying the time of event. Recent retrospective reflections are incorporated into the narrative through the interviewees. In addition to this main focus, recent footage of Auschwitz and other sites and places—as well as recent interviews with perpetrators, victims, and others involved—represent a different time level as well as an aspect of topicality. The narrative switches in time mainly for two reasons: the pictures from "then" (both original and reenacted) and the interviewees. As we shall see, they are "telling and commenting" on the story in retrospect.

The first episode, "Surprising Beginnings," presents the development of Auschwitz from April 1940 until the decision to build Birkenau in the winter of 1940–41. This part starts with the establishment of Auschwitz I through the decision to use existing barracks earlier used by the Polish army as a site of imprisonment for prisoners of war (POWs) and Polish political prisoners. Early in the program, the interest of the German company IG Farben, a chemical industry conglomerate, is presented in a dramatized scene that shows people visiting the site as part of an intended industrial expansion. The voice-over narrator issues a "warning": the situation will get worse. It is clearly stated that the establishment of IG Farben and the war against the USSR resulted in a radicalization of the Nazi policies against the Jews and other victims. This part of the first episode also tells of the exploration of different ways of murdering prisoners, which led to the application of the gas

Zyklon B for mass killings. Although these historical facts may be expected to be part of "common knowledge," the first episode is constructed around the presentation of basic information and the indication of later developments ("it gets worse"; "this came to be the site of the greatest mass murder"). Although dealing with what can be considered as well-known historical facts and events, the documentary's attempts to trigger suspense through warnings, remarks, and hints of the advancing catastrophe are comparable to strategies routinely implemented in popular drama.

The second part, "Orders and Initiatives," describes the development of the camp Birkenau from 1941 until the Wannsee Conference on January 20, 1942. This part shows that the combination of orders from above and initiatives from below led to the development of Auschwitz as a site of industrial genocide. The focus remains on what proved to be the preamble to industrial mass murder in Auschwitz–Birkenau: the ghetto of Łódź, Chełmno, and mass killings in Eastern Europe, as well as experiments on Soviet POWs in Auschwitz I. Part 2 ends by concluding that the phase of testing and experiments with gas ended in the early weeks of 1942. Now permanent buildings for gassing were constructed in Birkenau, and Jews from all Europe were to be brought there to be gassed. Parts 1 and 2 of the series thus describe the preparations leading toward the industrial genocide, and hence toward the so-called narrative peak.

"Factories of Death," part 3, presents the widespread Nazi persecution of the Jews, leading to arrests and deportations even from remote parts of the occupied territories such as the British Channel Islands, the island of Corsica in the Mediterranean, and the city of Tromsø in Northern Norway. This third part of the documentary presents the camps of Bełżec, Sobibór, and Treblinka as they operated in 1942. On the one hand, these camps are seen as preparing the ground for Auschwitz; on the other hand, they are said to come even closer to the "final solution" than Auschwitz because they were pure killing factories where 99 percent of the prisoners died within two hours of arrival.

The fourth part, "Corruption," focuses on the "crucial phase of Auschwitz in 1943" as the camp developed into the "site of the largest mass murder in history"—a remark repeated several times throughout the series. Thus the emphasis is put on the result, the mass murder, rather than on the perpetrators or the victims. The year 1943 is described as the "bloom year for the Nazis," presenting a grotesque contrast to the camp inmates' horrific conditions. The development of sub-camps and the exploitation of the prisoners as slave labor in the armament industry are mentioned, but the main focus remains on the corruption in the camp, the Canada command (where the belongings of the victims were sorted and stored), and the thefts among the SS guards and the soldiers.

Part 5, "Frenzied Killing," presents the year 1944 as a period of massive extermination in Birkenau. This part marks the "peak" of the narrative: the industrial genocide, which has been announced several times in the preceding parts. Thus, the first four parts of the documentary illustrate the stages of the dynamic process of Birkenau's development toward becoming the site of "the greatest mass murder." In 1944 the construction of four large cremators with gas chambers was completed, as well as the railway line leading directly into the camp. The result was that the mass murder could be carried out more effectively. Part 5 shows the year 1944 as marked by both the peak of the murders in Birkenau and the breakdown and chaos in the camp.

The sixth and last part of Rees's narrative, "Liberation and Revenge," presents the evacuation of Birkenau and the Soviet liberation of the camp on January 27, 1945, also applying archival footage. Main topics of the last part include the fighting in Berlin, the liberation of Bergen-Belsen (incorporating some of the original footage), the punishment of the perpetrators (e.g., Rudolf Höss), and survivors returning to their prewar homes.

Significant Aspects of Rees's Narrative

When one is analyzing Rees's narrative of Auschwitz, it is important to consider both what is told and what is not told. One important achievement of Rees's narrative presentation is the correction of the stereotypical, popular, and static image of Birkenau through a sustained focus on the *phases* of genocide and the *process* that led to the genocide and transmitting this important point to a broader public. Placing Auschwitz I–III in the context of other camps, and illustrating the dynamic process of the Holocaust, the series thus provides a more nuanced view than stereotypical presentations, which tend to highlight the singularity of Auschwitz as the center of mass murder.

Rees's presentation of Birkenau as one of the last camps with massive killing capacity has been interpreted as a correction of myth, but this knowledge has been an essential part of the "historians' narrative" of Auschwitz and the Holocaust for several years (e.g., as presented in Raul Hilberg's *The Destruction of the European Jews*). However, Rees's documentary series may have added this aspect to the "public or popular narrative" of the Holocaust, which has been dominated by a narrow-minded focus on Auschwitz as the singular, the unique, place of mass murder.

The enormous number of Nazi camps, especially in Eastern Europe, and the heterogeneity of the victims are two important aspects of the Holocaust that are often ignored. An asset of Rees's documentary is its mediation of knowledge of death camps other than Auschwitz, and also of victims other than the Jews, because the Nazi genocide is often stereotypically reduced to the gassing of Jews in Auschwitz. For example, the fate of the European Gypsies is often forgotten in the public narrative of Auschwitz, and it is to Rees's credit that he does not do so but instead pays close attention to the *Porrajmos* (the Nazi genocide of the Gypsies). An important part of the fifth installment presents the Gypsies killed in Birkenau: 20,000 out of 23,000 Gypsies brought to Birkenau were murdered. They "suffered more proportionally than any group apart from the Jews," the documentary states. The Gypsy camp was destroyed in the course of one night in the night of August 2, 1944, when all remaining inmates were killed in crematorium V.

Part 2, for example, highlights topics that are controversial and parts of so-called grey zones in a moral narrative of right and wrong, of good and evil. These include the Jewish leadership forced to cooperate with the Nazis in running the ghetto of Łódź as well as the leader Rumkowski's abuse of power, including deporting people who opposed him and sexually abusing female inmates. In this way the series makes us aware of difficult topics and questions that have often been repressed. Although these aspects hardly present new facts, to a large extent they have been taboo outside historical research.

The series also does important work in showing the problems that survivors faced when returning to their prewar homes in Eastern European countries, such as their frequent failure to regain their property and, incredibly, meeting widespread anti-Semitism. The persistent hatred against the Jews is presented as a problem especially for survivors in Eastern Europe. One may query, though, whether this was only a problem in Eastern Europe: it has been well documented that many returning prisoners faced the same problems in countries such as Norway, France, and the Netherlands. For example, not until the last ten years has there been any attempt to recognize the Norwegian responsibility for the deportation and extermination of the Norwegian Jews—only 34 out of 771 deportees survived—and not until 1997 did the Norwegian government pay compensation for confiscated Jewish property during the time of Nazi occupation (1940–45). Providing a striking contrast to the problems of many survivors, the documentary tells of the good life of many Nazi perpetrators in postwar Germany, for example, the interviewed Oskar Gröning who was an SS guard in Auschwitz. The Nuremberg Trial of Major War Criminals found the SS to have been a criminal organization. Like many other members of the SS, however, Gröning, although identified, was never punished for his actions. Focusing on events such as the Eichmann trial, this part of the series rightly stresses that most perpetrators, around 90 percent, were never put on trial. Surprising, though, is the focus on Rudolf Höss, who is presented in the series as the main persecutor, whereas Adolf Hitler and the other leading Nazis remain in the background. Nor does the series elaborate on the postwar reintegration of Nazis. In actual fact, most Nazis could continue their professional positions and personal lives after the downfall of the Third Reich without encountering great difficulties because of their Nazi past (Storeide 96ff.). In 1949 and 1954 West Germany adopted two acts: 1) the so-called amnesty laws, which promoted and reinforced the reintegration into society of a number of "minor offenders" and people with a Nazi past; and 2) the so-called 131 Act of 1951 that enabled many employees in the judiciary and public administration to continue their jobs despite their connections with the Nazi regime.

The word "beginnings" in the title of part 1 of Rees's narrative suggests the establishment, initial experiments, and planning of Birkenau—the preparation of what was to become the largest industrial genocide the world has seen. But was it really surprising? The radicalism of Nazi ideology and actions against people considered "unworthy of life" was more than clear in 1940: the Nazi persecution of their political opponents started immediately after they gained power in January 1933; concentration camps had existed for seven years; the racial laws that established the legal basis for discrimination against and persecution of Jews were adopted in Nuremberg in 1935; and the killings of so-called disabled persons had been going on for a long time. Yet "surprising" may also refer to the fact that Auschwitz originally was established as a camp for Polish prisoners, and not for Jews, whereas Auschwitz today is most "famous" for being the site of the "largest mass murder of the European Jews." However, establishing an important link between the Nazi mass murder program and the later mass murder with gas, part 1 also presents the beginning of the testing of gas for purposes of murder in barrack B11 in Auschwitz.

When a narrative of Auschwitz is constructed, it is also important to consider what is *not* included. A major weakness of Rees's narrative is that it fails to appreciate the significant role of German industry in the Holocaust. The presentation of economic aspects of the Auschwitz camp complex focuses on the corruption and the thefts in the camp (part 4). The fourth part, which presents the year 1943, also concentrates on sexual abuse of female prisoners, on Mengele's experiments performed on twins, and on the countries that did not cooperate in the deportation of Jews: Italy, Bulgaria, Romania, and especially Denmark. A major flaw of the narrative is that it does not

clearly show that the years 1943–44 were marked by a widespread cooperation between German industry, especially the armament industry, and
many camps where prisoners were exploited as slave laborers. During these
two years, the net of sub-camps and satellite camps where prisoners had to
work as slaves expanded fast. Even though the role that IG Farben played in
establishing Auschwitz is stated in part 1, the company's responsibility for
the construction of this site of mass murder is to a large extent ignored in
Rees's narrative of Auschwitz. The industry's contribution and the existence
of Monowitz, a camp that operated in close relation with Birkenau, are hardly
mentioned. The camp Monowitz is referred to only once, and then only in
connection with the Allied bombing. Yet this camp was in charge of a large
number of sub-camps where prisoners were abused as forced laborers; many
of them died because of the inhuman working conditions. Rees's failure to
recognize the great impact that German industry exerted on the development of Auschwitz and other concentration camps may induce the viewer
to consider Rees's narrative as an acquittal of industry—industry that gained
substantial benefits from the exploitation of inmates as slave labor and from
extensive economic and industrial cooperation with the Nazi regime (Orth
48ff.; Zimmermann 730ff.). Since Rees's narrative completely ignores the
camps as sites of slave labor, it fails to bring out the close connection between
the economic aspects and the mass murder that took place in the numerous
Nazi camps. It also fails to question what German civilians knew of the ongoing political and racial persecution and genocide and the role that so-called
ordinary people played in the Holocaust. The German interviewees are former soldiers and members of the SS; to give a broader presentation of the
"German perspective," Rees might also have interviewed German civilians
such as housewives and children.

The Filmic Construction of a Narrative of Auschwitz

Important narrative aspects of Rees's documentary are the use of contrasts,
various narrative voices, and the implementation of dramatization and reenactments—strategies that may promote the emotional involvement and
interest of a broader audience.

The Use of Contrasts

The application of contrasts represents an important strategy of narration in
this documentary. The use of contrasts may promote the emotional involve-

ment of the audience and reinforce the impression of brutality and suffering. The main contrast lies between the lives of the perpetrators and those of the victims, that is, between life itself and the threat against and extermination of life. One significant effect of Rees's use of this kind of contrast is to highlight the perpetrators' brutality and careless attitude to the victims, including their pain and the terrible conditions they lived under. There is an enormous gap between the comfort of Höss and his family and the appalling conditions of the prisoners, between Höss's apparently happy and peaceful family life and the experiments with gas, and between the singing at the perpetrators' parties and the cruelty of the camps. Furthermore, the stories told reinforce the crucial contrast between the Nazis' conspicuous lack of empathy and the suffering among the prisoners. This contrast is highlighted by using quotations from Rudolf Höss's autobiographical report (which conveys his ignorance of the fact that his actions actually were crimes and that he committed crimes against humanity) as "comments" on the victims' suffering, which is presented by either reenacted or original footage or interviews.

In some passages the documentary constructs contrasts by making surviving victims tell stories in which the brutality, dehumanization, fear, and suffering are opposed to the ignorance and neglect—and in many cases continuing anti-Semitism—of former perpetrators. One illustrative example is the presentation of mass executions of more than 10,000 Ukrainian Jews in August 1941 (part 1). In this scene there is a strong opposition between the surviving victim Vanyl Valdeman and the perpetrator Hans Friedrich. The interview with the former SS guard Friedrich, who took part in such mass shootings, makes abundantly clear that he is still an anti-Semite who even talks openly about his hatred against Jews. The image shifts from the interviewee Friedrich to reenacted images of soldiers, scenes in which shots can be heard, followed by images of cartridge cases falling down. One reason why focalization remains on the SS guards may be that most original footage approximates the perpetrators' perspective as they are dealing with their victims. Here, however, the viewer can see the perpetrators in action. The reenacted footage then shifts to original footage of naked people before the execution squad and naked bodies in mass graves.

Telling about his participation in the execution, Friedrich states that he did not feel anything—he just focused on secure hits. When the female interviewer (whose voice we hear) asks him directly about his feelings, he repeats that he did not feel anything at all because of his lifelong hatred against the Jews. In his childhood, his family was cheated by some Jews, he says, and that is why he hates them. He confirms that the people he shot did not have anything to do with those who cheated his family. But they were Jews, and that is why he did not feel anything, he concludes. As a contrast to this perpetrator's lack of regret, the Jewish survivor Valdeman tells about his and his mother's escape from the ghetto and their rescue by local villagers and about the extermination of the Jews in Eastern Europe. The contrast between the victim and the perpetrator, combined with the brutality of the images and the survivor's story of the victims' suffering, may serve to enhance the viewer's emotional engagement. Similar constructed sequences are observable throughout.

The series implements interviewees from both sides, both victims and perpetrators. For many years it was a crucial point whether the perpetrators' stories could be told in this way, without being contradicted. In Rees's documentary the perpetrators are given the chance to tell their story without obstacles and, as I have shown with reference to Friedrich, may state their lack of regret. But the archival footage and the victims' testimonies provide an effective contrast to the stories and attitudes of the perpetrators, highlighting them as grotesque.

In some cases the documentary contrasts the "then" of the Second World War and the "now" of the filmmaker and viewer. It contains scenes in which the horrible stories of what occurred in the camps represent a glaring contrast to the beautiful landscapes of the sites pictured today. This construction method is, for example, implemented in the presentation of the death camp Chełmno (part 2): A female survivor tells about the ghetto of Łódź, at the same time original footage is presented. Then there is a shift to reenactments of the Nazis' planning of Chełmno; the planning of this extermination camp was the result of the overcrowding of the ghetto in Łódź and the need for more space. Rees presents a reenacted scene in which Herbert Lange, an SS officer who had been involved in the murder of disabled people in East Prussia and had participated in using gas vans for killings, is being driven in his car to his "new mission"; Lange talks about the tasks that await him. Then the narrator's voice takes over, stating that the purpose of Chełmno was to exterminate Jews in order to create more space in Łódź and concluding that Chełmno was not the only such place at this time. Providing a thought-provoking contrast to this chilling story, the footage changes to images of the peaceful and beautiful scenery as it looks today. Stressing the inordinate brutality of the events, this shift in footage may reinforce the audience's emotional engagement in the story. Thus, the recently recorded footage does not signal recovery, although the landscape obviously has recovered and the sites of the atrocities are no longer visible. Rather, it creates a feeling of a peaceful community whose life was abruptly ruined by the Nazis, thus accentuating the contrast between an innocent nature and the danger of fanatic culture. This strategy calls Claude Lanzmann's masterpiece *Shoah* strikingly to mind,

although Lanzmann distanced himself from any implementation of dramatization in his documentary work.

Another narrative strategy of the documentary concerns oppositions
between the images shown and the narrating voice, either that of the main
narrator or that of one of the interviewees. This method is used, for example,
at the beginning of part 3. The images show Paris, the Eiffel tower, German
soldiers eating grapes, and people promenading. While a joyful French song
is being played, the main narrator tells about the deportation of the French
Jews; as he does so, the image changes to a recent picture of Paris by night.
Then the perspective changes again as a female survivor is describing her
own arrest in Paris. While her story is told, the image shown on the screen
changes from Paris today to a dramatized scene of French policemen running upstairs to an apartment to arrest someone. The woman's brother also
serves as a narrator in this story. The topic is the arrest of Jews in France. The
narrative strategy is a blend of stories told by survivors, original footage from
the French camp Drancy, and reenacted scenes of arrests made by the French
police. Contrasting with this deportation story, images show the happy life
of German soldiers in Paris during the war and stereotypical, well-known
images of Paris by night. A similar strategy is implemented in the story of
the war in the Channel Islands (part 3). Presenting a holiday paradise, the
footage establishes a stark contrast to the narrator's and the witnesses' stories
about the registration and the deportation of local Jews in Guernsey.

The music applied, not only in these sequences but also throughout the
series, may further and support the audience's emotional engagement, not
only through its recurrent theme, but also by means of modulations of light
and heavy chords, reminding the viewer of marching soldiers. The music
seems to be implemented in ways that support Rees's elaborate use of contrasts. For instance, while the visual images of Paris at the beginning of part 3
are made more joyful by the accompanying happy music on the soundtrack,
the story told elaborates on the tragic story of the deportation of Jews from
France.

The Narrating Voices

Rees's documentary contains a variety of narrating voices. I have mentioned
Rees's use of an unidentified narrator. Performing a key role in the documentary, this narrator has different functions. First, he serves as introducer,
inviting the viewer into and guiding him or her through the documentary.
Thus this narrator, whose narrative characteristics largely fit those of voice-

over, fills in the gaps between the images (both original and reenacted). Second, he comments on pictures we see and on stories we are being told (also by interviewees). Finally, he serves as the expert stating facts and statistics.

The interviewees have different roles too. When interviewed, the surviving perpetrators and victims are pictured sitting in a chair, shown from the waist-up and looking straight into the camera. In this way, they are, first, telling their stories when communicating "directly" with the viewer. Second, since their narratives are linked to the original or reenacted footage, the survivors serve as commentators on the images we see. This aspect of the interviewees' narrative role is often contrastive because their stories are those of brutality and suffering while the footage shown may be peaceful images of the beautiful present-day landscapes today (cf. the discussion above of the filmic presentation of Chełmno). Third, the interviewees comment on their own stories or other events.

In some of the dramatized scenes the actors playing the historical characters speak as if history repeats itself in front of the eyes of the public. These dialogues and fragments of speech are partly based on historical documents such as reports and letters, partly constructed from what we know was the result of, for example, a meeting. The latter variant means that a fictional element has been added to the attempted documentary, because although the result of a meeting may be known, the discussions, gestures, and so forth, almost invariably remain in the dark. This does not mean that the presented stories are untrue, but it shows that elements of imagination are implemented in the documentary. Fiction (from the Latin noun *fictio* and the verb *fingere,* "to invent or construct") is traditionally defined as any narrative invented by the author. Clearly, Rees did not invent the narrative of Auschwitz—it refers to historical facts and events. To a certain extent and in certain situations, however, fictional elements are implemented in Rees's reenactments. They are no doubt based on facts, but because of the limited knowledge and lack of information of some situations, meetings, discussions, and so on, certain aspects have been invented and therefore represent fictional elements of the documentary, although they are constructed as close to the historical reality as possible.

The readings from Höss's autobiographical report by an unknown voice are also part of the narrating voices. In Rees's documentary, Höss's report functions as a transmitter of facts, especially about Auschwitz and the events that occurred there. This kind of function is linked to, and supported by, the value and reliability of the information, which many historians attribute to the genre of memoir. In this particular case, however, it is questionable whether an autobiographical report can be identified as the truth or as a reliable source of what actually happened, for the documentary also uses the report as evidence of Höss' guilt as a perpetrator and as a contrast to stories told by victims. Considered as a contrastive narrative, the report represents an insensible and non-regretful speech given by one of the main perpetrators, who in Rees's narrative functions as the main perpetrator of all the Nazis responsible for the Holocaust.

Beginning and End

The beginning and ending represent crucial aspects of any narrative. Rees's documentary opens with a long shot of Birkenau today, showing a huge, almost empty landscape. Some barracks are still intact, some ruins remain, and it is green and quiet. This opening shot slowly blends into a dramatized computer-reconstructed image of how the camp looked when it was in operation during the Second World War. A narrative voice announces that "this is the story of the evolution of Auschwitz and the motives of the perpetrators." The word "evolution" is somewhat unexpected given that it has various connotations, including that of "natural development," whereas the development of Auschwitz was intentional and pursued by human beings, which is also one of the main points of Rees's narrative. The camera's focalization is comparable to the eye of the viewer. It takes the viewer down to the gas chamber, and the screen goes dark, as if the viewer is captured in the darkness of the chamber. This technique—which is similar to that of other scenes in which the camera's perspective approximates that of the viewer, thus serving as the public's eye—may create an emotional engagement and enhance the impact on the audience.

At the end of the last part of the series, there is a similar shot of the site of Birkenau today. The narrator announces that of the 1.3 million people sent to Auschwitz–Birkenau, 1.1 million were killed. Recent footage of the remaining railway tracks, the wood, the barracks, and the main entrance with its watchtower pass the screen while the narrator's voice elaborates on the numbers of the different groups of victims. Dan Diner has argued that there can be no narrative of the Holocaust, only statistics ("Gestaute Zeit" 126; "Vorworth des Herausgebers" 9). As if to bear out this point, the main narrator of Rees's narrative sums up the tragic statistics of Auschwitz. Then archival footage of Jews on the way to the gas chamber is presented, and a female survivor's voice identifies her aunt with four children in the footage. In this way, the horror and immense dimension of Auschwitz and the Nazi genocide are personalized and taken into the context and narrative of a family. The statistics contain someone's aunts, uncles, brothers, sisters, mothers, fathers, and children. The narrative ends by focusing on Birkenau. The image changes again, presenting recent footage of the destroyed crematoria of Birkenau. Through computer graphics, this image changes to one computer-reconstructed image of a crematorium with a gas chamber reconstructed as one of the crematoria put into operation in 1944. Rees's narrative of Auschwitz closes with the narrator's voice stating that the ruins remain as a "reminder of what human beings are capable of"—Auschwitz was the result of an intended construction process and of the Nazis' firm determination to exterminate millions of human beings.

Visual Aspects and the Use of Reenactments

The visual aspects of Rees's documentary include, first, *archival footage* as expected of a documentary, a convention that Claude Lanzmann, among others, famously worked against in *Shoah*. Rees's documentary features a collection of original recordings, both pictures and film, made by perpetrators, victims, and the Allied forces. Second, the documentary presents a surprisingly large number of *dramatized scenes*. The filmmakers seem to have been seeking to fill in the gaps in the narrative by incorporating reenactments of the "missing" sequences.

Holocaust documentaries have conventionally limited the representation to original recordings, material, and interviews with participants. They have strictly avoided dramatizations and fictionalizations often interpreted as strategies typical of the fiction film in opposition to documentary film. Since, as indicated already, Rees's documentary makes extensive use of reenactments, important questions in my further analysis are: Why does Rees implement dramatizations in this attempted documentary and what effects do they have? Furthermore, which situations are being dramatized and which are not—what principle of selection is operative here?

An important aspect of the discussions of the Holocaust is whether and how this genocide can be represented. The so-called image ban or aniconism (*Bilderverbot*) implies that every imagination necessarily becomes a banalization and a twisting of the historical event (Oster and Uka 251ff.). Elie Wiesel and Claude Lanzmann are both prominent representatives of those who have connected the image ban on cinematic presentations with the aniconism of the Old Testament, and thus added restrictions on how the Holocaust can be represented as film. Wiesel has opposed any kind of fictionalization and dramatizations of the Holocaust (314). And Lanzmann

clearly turned against the use of both original photography and film footage and dramatized sequences when he made *Shoah,* a film also made as
a response to the American television series *Holocaust* (1978). Lanzmann
criticized the latter for its fictionalization that turned the Holocaust into a
soap opera and represented a violation of the aniconism of the Holocaust
(Reichel 295, 299). *Shoah* differs from most documentaries on the Second
World War by its renunciation of both archival footage and reenactments.
Concentrating on interviews with surviving victims, bystanders, and perpetrators, it consists solely of present footage of the sites the witnesses talk
about.

Important questions concern which photos and images of the Holocaust
can be presented and how the detailed descriptions of the Holocaust are
deemed acceptable. An unwritten rule has been that the images should not
be shown at the expense of the victims and should not satisfy the audience's
need or greed for sensations and shocking images. After the publication of
Daniel Jonah Goldhagen's *Hitler's Willing Executioners,* there has been a radicalization of detailed presentations of violence, abuse, and murder (Krankenhagen 202). Containing a large number of close-up realistic depictions
of torture, suffering, and killing, Goldhagen's study attracted considerable
attention when it was published in 1996. The interest in his book may have
promoted a change in the perception of the image ban or aniconism of the
Holocaust.

A documentary deals with historical events, facts, and nonfiction. Even
though the term "documentary" is often used synonymously with the terms
"document" and "documentation" (Sørenssen 14–17), however, it is crucial
to remember that a documentary is a *construction* of scenes, focalization,
time, and narration that separates it from what actually occurred. Since a
documentary is a selection and construction of a narrative of the reality
it seeks to present, it is an *interpretation* of historical reality. The events to
be presented are part of a past that cannot be reached but instead must be
constructed from the present, relying on the "ruins of memory" (Langer,
"Holocaust Testimonies" 1991) and on remaining documentation. Inevitably,
gaps exist between the past and what we can possibly know about it. Such
gaps between historical events and present knowledge of these events can be
reduced by using a main narrator and by interviewing persons involved.

Rees's documentary is distinguished precisely by the use of dramatizations as a way to overcome the narrative gaps. The reenactments enable
Rees to visually present situations and events that have not been preserved
through original recordings and documents. At the same time, the reenactments blur the line between fiction and nonfiction, thus incorporating a

fictional element into the attempted documentary, as I have mentioned already. Rees constructs his narrative on extensive historical research, but events that we do not have full knowledge of are reconstructed through reenactments. This does not make Rees's narrative a fiction because it deals with real historical events that are reconstructed as accurately as possible. However, since the dramatized scenes require imaginative representation where historical knowledge is missing, fictional elements are inevitably implemented in the documentary.

The dramatized scenes are reconstructed in a manner that makes them appear as realistic as possible. As stated by Rees himself, the reenactments are based on research on, for example, the shape of the rooms; they are also indebted to primary source documents such as minutes or protocols from meetings; letters; diaries; and trial testimonies by or interviews with participants (Gallagher 2004). For example, the reenacted meeting before the invasion of the Soviet Union (part 1) is based on the original minutes of the meeting. Yet there will always be a gap between the past historical event and the filmic reconstruction of an event, no matter how accurate the film aims to be; thus fictional elements have to be added. One difficulty concerning the reenactments in Rees's documentary is that since the reenacted parts are often filmed in black and white, in many cases it can be difficult for a viewer without some relevant historical knowledge to decide whether the footage is original or dramatized.

The dramatized sequences present events, meetings, and situations, but they do not show prisoners in gas chambers or in similar situations of abuse and suffering. In the case of the reenacted scene of the mass shootings of Ukrainian Jews already discussed, the reenactment concerns the SS guards lining up and the dropping of the cartridge cases. These images were perhaps chosen because a reenactment of the victims being shot may have been seen as a violation of the aniconism of the Holocaust and as disrespect toward the victims. Instead, Rees has implemented original footage of people before an execution and of naked bodies in a mass grave. Yet although aniconism is often neglected, Rees obviously imposes limits on representation when it comes to the reenacted parts, especially those concerning the victims of the Holocaust.

As a counterpart to Rees's documentary and hence to aniconism, I want to briefly comment on another BBC documentary. Written by Andrew Bampfield and directed by Richard Dale et al., *D-Day 6.6.1944* (2004) goes even further than Rees both in the implementation of reenacted scenes and in the dramatization of scenes where people are suffering and/or dying—for example, in the presentation of the Allied forces' landing on Omaha Beach on June 6, 1944, and the liberation of the city of Caen. Both events are presented by the use of original footage and reenacted scenes. Some of the reenacted scenes are very detailed in showing pain and suffering and injuries and damage. Furthermore, in this documentary the stories of the interviewed survivors, Allied soldiers and Germans alike, are partly reenacted, and the interviews of the survivors serve in many cases as comments or elaborations on the reenactments. As the reenacted scenes in *D-Day 6.6.1944* are shot in color and unambiguously reenacted, there is hardly a risk of a mix-up between the film's original and dramatized footage. For this reason, Dale's *D-Day 6.6.1944* is more easily associated with the genre of docudrama than is Rees's narrative.

In addition to reenactments, Rees uses specially commissioned computer images to fill in the information gaps of his documentary. These narrative techniques are used to present the gas chambers: the scenes are constructed through an extended focalization in which the camera serves as the eye of the public, taking them into the door of a reconstructed crematorium building, down the stairs, and into the waiting room, making them look around the room, enter the gas chamber, turn around to the door which is closed—and then it gets dark. This scene is repeated with a few changes throughout the series, marking, for example, the end of part 2. The gassing was an "event without witnesses" (Laub 80) where the "real witnesses" were murdered (Agamben 31–33; Levi 83–84). However, by using computer graphics, Rees's filmically constructed narrative shows us the inside of the gas chambers, thus attempting to fill in the gaps in the narrative of Auschwitz.

The repetitively displayed images of the gas chambers from inside can be viewed as violations of the aniconism of the Holocaust and as a presentation of images of the "event without witnesses," even though the actual gassings are not dramatized. These reconstructed scenes of the gas chambers may function as important emotional triggers for the audience, also prompting the question of how far one should go in applying strategies of emotionalization in order to attract the audience's attention. Although it is important to evoke interest and involvement to further and enhance the viewer's empathy with the victims, sensational and shocking effects should never be promoted for their own sake. As I have shown, Rees clearly imposes ethical limits of representation on his film, although on several occasions he neglects aniconism in general.

The strategy of reenactment blurs the limit between fiction and nonfiction and separates Rees's documentary from documentation, also removing it from the transmission of the "pure document" as attempted, for example, in Lanzmann's *Shoah*. Different as they are, both films are interestingly linked to Steven Spielberg's historical drama *Schindler's List* (1993), which presents the story of the German industrialist Oscar Schindler who saved over 1,000 Jews during the war. Spielberg's hugely popular film adapts aspects from the documentary genre. It is made almost completely in black and white, but at the end the images switch to color and the viewer is presented with the real "Schindler-Jews" (not actors) standing at Schindler's grave in Jerusalem. This documentary scene may serve to justify and authorize Spielberg's film as authentic and real. Lanzmann criticized the film for showing images of the Holocaust that do not exist, for example, the gas chambers (Reichel 313). This aspect is radicalized in Rees's documentary where the camera acts as the audience's eyes, thus taking us as viewers into the gas chambers and even showing when the doors are shut. While *Schindler's List* uses documentary codes to enhance the authenticity of the film, Rees's documentary employs dramatic elements to fill the gaps of the visual narrative of Auschwitz.

Rees's focus on historical research and primary sources, as well as the implementation of original footage and interviews with survivors of both sides, make his documentary different from the American fictional television series *Holocaust* (1978). In many ways Rees's series is situated between two important Holocaust series, being more nonfictional than *Holocaust* (and also *Schindler's List* where the fictional aspect concerns the form as a historical drama, not the story told) and more fictional than *Shoah* because of the dramatizations. I conclude by considering Rees's series partly as a "docudrama" because of the extensive use of reenactment. To the extent possible, the reenacted footage is based on realism. Yet in the presentation of meetings, for example, fictional elements are inevitably implemented because of the lack of information. The story of Auschwitz is a true story, and Rees's narrative contains a large amount of information collected from primary and secondary sources. For Rees, however, reenactments take over where the archive does not exist.

The problem of reenactments concerns the following aspects: First, in many cases it is difficult to decide which recordings are original and which are dramatized scenes with a view to a large and heterogeneous audience. The series was made to reach a wider public, and the dramatizations are a way of attracting the attention of different kinds of viewers. And yet we have seen that, not least because the reenactments are in black and white, people without basic knowledge of the Holocaust can find it difficult to separate the reenacted scenes from original recordings; thus reenactments are potentially misleading. Second, there are methodological and ethical problems linked to the aspects of entertainment on the one hand and historical information and rational thinking on the other. Emotional engagement does not necessarily further critical reflection on the topic of the Holocaust. Leading the audience behind a curtain, the series blurs the difference between original and reenacted images and scenes, and in several cases the reenacted scenes lead to confusion about source materials and references. The effect is similar to that of a history book without footnotes, written for an audience without background knowledge. If the dramatized scenes were not shot in black and white or marked as dramatizations in some way—as in *D-Day 6.6.1944*—the potential confusion would have been avoided. Crucially, narrative strategies as such are not a topic of discussion in the series; it does not comment or reflect on the gains and problems of the narrative strategy employed. Even though it might be difficult to do this, the absence of such reflections removes the series from a main concern of film and literature on the Holocaust (Krankenhagen 181–85; Langer, "Die Zeit der Erinnerung" 53). In Bill Nichols's terms, Rees's film can be characterized as documentary in the participatory mode because of the use of interviews and archival footages, but at the same time it has important expository segments because of a narrator's verbal commentary (33–34, 105–109, 115–24). The reflexive mode, though, is neglected and completely absent in the series (34–35, 125–30).

The third visual aspect of the series—footage of present-day sites and landscapes that play an important part in the strategy of contrasts—has been discussed already. A fourth visual aspect consists of the interviews in which the interviewees, both former victims and perpetrators, are sitting in a chair in their own living room, telling their stories. Reaffirming and strengthening both the link and the contrast between "now" and "then," these interviews further increase the impression of the brutality and suffering of the "then"— the Second World War and the Holocaust. The witnesses of both sides serve as transmitters of the past, telling their stories with hindsight "now" and also commenting and reflecting on the gruesome events of the past.

"Auschwitz" Revisited?

In conclusion, we may ask how Rees's narrative—in both form and content— is related to other narratives on Auschwitz. This narrative contributes to the mediation of important aspects of the "historian's narrative"—aspects that to some extent had been taboo—for a more general public, using popular transmission techniques such as reenactment, repetition, drama, excitement, emotions, and so forth, which move the documentary toward the genre of docudrama. While the extensive use of reenactments in this presentation of the history of Auschwitz may have triggered the attention and interest of a larger audience, it problematically blurs the distinction between fiction and nonfiction and between drama and documentary.

One fundamental problem in constructing a narrative of Auschwitz more than sixty years after its liberation is the absence of presence. For many years the survivors have represented a link between the past and the present. In a few years there will be no survivors left. Reenactments may serve as an alternative strategy to create presence for the past.

Presenting important facts about the development of the Holocaust as a process with different phases and a complex of camps, Rees's documentary draws the viewer's attention to "grey zones" of the camp system such as brothels, corruption, and *Sonderkommandos,* and to the insufficient legal persecution of Nazi criminals. Important as it is, this focus on "sensational" aspects of the story of Auschwitz must not suspend the transmission of general facts. Unfortunately, Rees's narrative of Auschwitz comes close to acquitting German industry, which actually played an important role in the exploitation and killing of many hundreds of thousands of enslaved laborers. The series' most significant contribution is the transmission of new historical knowledge to a broader, and specifically to a younger, audience, and the presentation of the Nazi genocide not as the killings of madmen but as the result of a rational and logical decision process led by human beings.

Works Cited

Agamben, Giorgio. *Was von Auschwitz bleibt: Das Archiv und der Zeuge (Homo sacer III).* 1998. Frankfurt am Main: Suhrkamp, 2003.

Bampfield, Andrew and Richard Dale et.al. *D-Day 6.6.1944.* TV series. United Kingdom: BBC, 2004.

BBC Press Office. *Auschwitz: The Nazis and the 'Final Solution.'* 2004. http://www.bbc.co.uk/pressoffice/pressreleases/stories/2004/12_december/02/auschwitz.shtml. Accessed June 4, 2009.

Brockmeier, Jens and Rom Harré. "Narrative: Problems and Promises of an Alternative Paradigm." In *Narrative and Identity: Studies in Autobiography, Self and Culture,* edited by Jens Brockmeier and Donald Carbaugh, 39–58. Amsterdam and Philadelphia: John Benjamins, 2001.

Chomsky, Marvin J. *Holocaust.* TV series. United States: CBS, 1978.

Diner, Dan. "Gestaute Zeit: Massenvernichtung und jüdische Erzählstruktur." In *Kreisläufe: Nationalsozialismus und Gedächtnis,* edited by Dan Diner, 123–39. Berlin: Berlin Verlag, 1995.

———. "Vorwort des Herausgebers." In *Zivilisationsbruch: Denken nach Auschwitz,* edited by Dan Diner, 7–13. Frankfurt am Main: Fischer, 1988.

Feuchert, Sascha. "Einleitung." In *Holocaust-Literatur Auschwitz,* edited by Sascha Feuchert, 5–40. Stuttgart: Philipp Reclam, 2000.

Gallagher, Patrick. "Historians Play Major Role in New Documentary on the Holocaust." *American Historical Association.* November 2004. http://www.historians.org/ Perspectives/-Issues/2004/0411/0411fi11.cfm. Accessed June 4, 2009.

Goldhagen, Daniel Jonah. *Hitler's Willing Executioners: Ordinary Germans and the* Holocaust. New York: Alfred A. Knopf, 1996.

Hilberg, Raul. *The Destruction of the European Jews.* New Haven and London: Yale University Press, 2003.

Krankenhagen, Stefan. *Auschwitz darstellen: Ästhetische Positionen zwischen Adorno, Spielberg und Walser.* Cologne, Weimar, and Vienna: Böhlau, 2001.

Langer, Lawrence L. *Holocaust Testimonies: The Ruins of Memory.* New Haven and London: Yale University Press, 1991.

———. "Die Zeit der Erinnerung: Zeitverlauf und Dauer in Zeugenaussagen von Überlebenden des Holocaust." In *"Niemand zeugt für den Zeugen": Erinnerungskultur nach der Shoah,* edited by Ulrich Baer, 53–67. Frankfurt am Main: Suhrkamp, 2000.

Lanzmann, Claude. *Shoah.* France: Les Films Aleph, 1985.

Laub, Dori. "An Event without a Witness: Truth, Testimony and Survival." In *Testimony: Crisis of Witnessing in Literature, Psychoanalysis, and History,* edited by Shoshana Felman and Dori Laub, 75–92. New York and London: Routledge, 1992.

Learning Resources. http://www.pbs.org/auschwitz/. Accessed June 4, 2009.

Levi, Primo. *Die Untergegangenen und die Geretteten.* 1986. Munich and Vienna: Carl Hanser Verlag, 1990.

Nichols, Bill. *Introduction to Documentary.* Bloomington and Indianapolis: Indiana University Press, 2001.

Orth, Karin. *Das System der nationalsozialistischen Konzentrationslager: Eine politische Organisationsgeschichte.* Hamburg: Hamburger Edition, 1999.

Oster, Anja and Walter Uka. "Der Holocaust als Filmkomödie: Komik als Mittel der Darstellung des Undarstellbaren." In *Die Shoah im Bild,* edited by Sven Kramer, 249–66. München: Edition text + kritik, 2003.

Rees, Laurence. *Auschwitz: The Nazis and the 'Final Solution'* [U.S. title: *Auschwitz: Inside the Nazi State*]. Great Britain and United States: BBC and KCET, 2005.

———. *Auschwitz: The Nazis and the 'Final Solution.'* London: BBC Books, 2005.

Reichel, Peter. *Erfundene Erinnerung: Weltkrieg und Judenmord im Film und Theater.* Frankfurt am Main: Fischer, 2007.

Spielberg, Steven. *Schindler's List.* United States: Universal, 1993.

Storeide, Anette H. *Arven etter Hitler: Tysklands oppgjør med naziregimet* [*The Shadow of Hitler: Germany and the Confrontation with the Nazi Past*]. Oslo: Gyldendal, 2010.

Sørenssen, Bjørn. *Å fange virkeligheten: Dokumentarfilmens århundre* [*To Capture Reality: The Century of Documentary Film*]. Oslo: Universitetsforlaget, 2001.

Wiesel, Elie. "For Some Measure of Humility." *Sh'ma* 15 (1975): 314–15.

Zimmermann, Michael. "Arbeit in den Konzentrationslagern: Kommentierende Bemerkungen." In *Die nationalsozialistischen Konzentrationslager,* vol. 2, edited by Ulrich Herbert, Karin Orth, and Christoph Dieckmann, 730–54. Frankfurt am Main: Fischer, 2002.

CHAPTER 12

Moving Testimonies

"Unhomed Geography" and the Holocaust Documentary of Return

JANET WALKER

> [T]he lived body is coterminous with place because it is by bodily movement that I find my way in place and take up habitation there.
>
> —Edward S. Casey, *Remembering: A Phenomenological Study*

An older Jewish émigré was asked why he had joined a tour to Auschwitz, Majdanek, the Warsaw ghetto, and the Polish village whence he came. Why would he travel years later from his adoptive home in the United States to these Eastern European sites of killing, sickness, and survival? "'The same reason I did the first time,'" he replied with a shrug, "'I had to'" (Bukiet 129). Or consider an acclaimed special episode of Oprah Winfrey's popular talk show in which her guest is Elie Wiesel and the venue Auschwitz. The two figures walk arm in arm through the camp, their boots crunching on the drifted snow. "When here . . . the professor speaks very softly, allowing silence to have its space," explains Winfrey in voice-over. Then, as the day wears on, she consoles him: "It cannot be easy for you to make this journey." "I wouldn't have done it with anyone," he replies. Perhaps he meant to say he wouldn't have done it with "just anyone." In any case, the statement signals not only Wiesel's appreciation of Winfrey's sensitivity but also the concomitant difficulty and necessity of his presence in that place of death. Conducted on foot and filmed for national and international circulation, this affecting interview constitutes a moving testimony of return.

All around the world people are picking up and traveling to places they expected never to see again, and this powerful impulse to go back to a site of origin or catastrophe, just to visit or for good, is finding eloquent expression in conversation, print, and screen media. Where previous scholars have offered inspiring exegeses of post–World War II exilic memory and return in literature and photography (Bukiet; Gilbert; Jacobson; M. Hirsch; and Hirsch and Spitzer "'We Would Never Have Come'" and *Ghosts of Home,* Kugelmass, Palmer, Suleiman), the current chapter seeks to designate and study a corpus of documentary films that are dramatically shaped by the European visits of Jewish refugees of Hitler's Holocaust to places from which they have previously departed, emigrated, or fled; places where they survived; or places from which they were unwillingly removed or rescued.

Such a "documentary of return" may begin casually when someone grabs a video camera on the way out the door, or more formally with a concept and agreement between producers and travelers. In neither case, though, is the film a mere record of an autonomous itinerary. Rather, as in Jean Rouch's and Edgar Morin's cinema verité creation, *Chronique d'un été* (1960), where various gatherings were held for the purpose of filming the ensuing discussion, so too in each of these film or digital media projects, words and gestures are brought into being, and place itself is enacted.

The filmmaker also travels. Shoshana Felman has observed in her widely recognized and aptly titled chapter, "The Return of the Voice: Claude Lanzmann's *Shoah*," that along with Simon Srebnik's reluctant return from Israel to Poland to testify sur place (as one of two survivors among 400,000 murdered in gas vans), the documentary naturally required the "no less difficult biographical and geographical return (a return in space) of [Claude] Lanzmann" himself for a sustained decade of filming (257).[1] Nor is the viewer left behind. The motion picture itself is "the very synthesis of seeing and going—a place where seeing *is* going" and where the cinema spectator is mobilized for "site-seeing" across a "geopsychic" landscape (Bruno 245, 15–16). It follows, therefore, that the Holocaust documentary of return, by its very premise, represents an over-determined and crucial case of cinema's synthetic seeing/going.

With this activity, the possibility of a shift opens up: from Holocaust testimony studies as a mentally recursive and diasporic paradigm in which verbal and written testimonies are conducted, filmed, and archived after the fact and far from the catastrophic event itself, to testimony as a matter of the here and now. I concentrate, therefore, on filmed, situated testimonies delivered verbally or bodily from a significant site and in the presence of others; for the places to which these (auto)biographical travelers return have persisted all the while. They have their own regional histories, practices, physical situations, and, importantly, current inhabitants.

Physical location matters deeply to the full impact of Holocaust testimonies of return, but so do insights about the psychic dimensions and the
unassimilability of place and occurrence. As Cathy Caruth has written, "The
impact of a traumatic event lies precisely in its belatedness, in its refusal to be
simply located, in its insistent appearance *outside the boundaries of any single
place or time*" or, putting it differently, "*in connection with another place* and
time" (9, 8, emphasis mine). Even as locals and returnees reunite in a "fatal
environment,"[2] this anti-essentializing view of place, hinted at by Caruth
and further developed in the works of critical human geographers, remains
crucial (Rogoff, Tuan; see also Walker "Rights and Return"). The ground of
testimony sur place like exilic space, but not to be conflated with it is always
already "other."

This chapter will proceed with a discussion of some of the ethical complexities of situated testimony, unfilmed and filmed, turning then to the
analysis of two significant, and rhetorically different, Holocaust documentaries of return: *The Last Days* (1998) and *Hiding and Seeking* (2004). In their
respective presentations of bodies and voices along country roads, at the
thresholds of childhood homes, and on sacred ground, these two nonfiction
narratives exemplify the felicities and complications of the mode. Analyzing them, I seek to map the transposition and transmission of Holocaust
testimonies generally, across geographical distance, and into the audiovisual
space of the moving image.

Because I Had To
The Uses and Abuses of Private Journeys and "Holocaust Tourism"

Holocaust survivors may feel an "irresistible" urge to "go home" or return
to the camp (in either case, "to the fire") as part of an ongoing traumatic
response to the shock of forcible removal (Brenner 157, 147). The actual
journey may be an enactment of certain "themes of attachment, loss, reunion,
and return home" (158). It may be experienced as a pilgrimage, however
triumphant ("to celebrate my survival in the place that tried to kill me"),
or, alternatively, "counterphobic" ("I felt empty, cheated . . . The Germans
succeeded in Mannheim. It certainly was Judenrein") (Brenner 156 quoting
Michel 266, 208–9). In their critically insightful and personally generous
essay, Marianne Hirsch and Leo Spitzer use the occasion of their trip back to
her parents' hometown of Chernivtsi (formerly Czernowitz) to explore the
feelings and formations of "nostalgia's complicating other side" (83). "This
ambivalent desire to recall negative experiences at their place of happening,

and to transmit them to sympathetic listeners and co-witnesses," they submit, "is a significant motivation for return journeys" (84).

Those with no personal connection to the Holocaust may also "venture back in time" (Bukiet 128) and place as a form of participation in the collective impulse and effort to memorialize, as hallowed sites, the extermination camps of Eastern Europe. "The March of the Living," started in 1988, along with other organized trips provide "an institutionalized way" for successive generations to commemorate and work through catastrophic past events (Brenner 160).

Deeply experienced by participants, the personal/genealogical trip and the more broadly touristic journey may also produce culturally and sometimes even historically meaningful findings, as when artifacts and long-buried memories (which may lead to further questions[3]) are unearthed on-site. Hirsch and Spitzer report that only in Chernivtsi did Marianne's mother Lotte tell how a soldier came to the door to announce their deportation from the ghetto, and only in Chernivtsi did her father Carl refuse this version of events, insisting, "'Everyone was already outside, we all knew.'" As the authors remark, "[T]his detail, about the soldier, and the discrepancy between the two versions of the story, emerged there on site: we had never heard it before" (88).

The significance of such moments lies not only in what the returnees remember and narrate but also in the physical dimension of return as a particular kind of testimony and contemporary finding. Consider Edward S. Casey's phenomenological insights: "the lived body is coterminous with place because it is by bodily movement that I find my way in place and take up habitation there," and (extending beyond this chapter's epigraph) "[m]oving in or through a given place, the body *imports its own implaced past into its present experience:* its 'local history' is literally a history of locales" (180, 194, emphasis mine). Or, as Joshua Hirsch offers through a filmic example, *Chronique d'un été,* "The past inheres in the relationship between the speaking body situated in a space of memory and the audible and visible signs of memory emanating from and written on the body" (67).[4] The sequence he evokes is the famous one in which Marceline, a concentration camp survivor and part of the filmmaking collective, walks by herself at a distance from the camera and with a hidden tape recorder over her shoulder through the Place de la Concorde and Les Halles—speaking and softly singing her feelings and memories of deportation and return. The "modernist subjectivity" of the passage, Hirsch argues, is distinct from the more traditional voice of the first Shoah Foundation documentary, *Survivors of the Holocaust* (1996), in which interviews are conducted in a "'safe' interior location" (68).[5] "In the testimony of this [earlier] witness," he recognizes, "we discover an archive of the past" (67).

Such "returns in space" may also catalyze encounters that are simultaneously new and seeded with past associations: transferential, we might say, for the play of earlier conflicts that remerge in the context of a current relationship. Pointing to the gestures and comments made by Polish residents of Chełmno when the largely silent Srebnik returned to their midst, noting the prevailing anti-Semitism that must in the past have enabled Jewish genocide, Shoshana Felman explains that "[t]he film makes testimony *happen*— happen inadvertently as a second Holocaust" (267). Or, as Linda Williams elaborates, filmmakers who stage these types of encounters "do not so much represent that past as they reactivate it in images of the present" (17). What I would like to emphasize here are the spatial, bodily, and sometimes, but not always, verbal dimensions of situated testimony for film, video, and digital media: the fact of filmed presence as a kind of a kinesthetic historiography.

This is not to underestimate the revelations made to relatives and other companions on-site without a camera. What I would say, though, is that the perceived indelibility of the filmic and videographic media encourages or exacerbates the testimonial impulse. From Hirsch and Spitzer's discussion of Lotte's observation made for the first time in Chernivtsi and (consequently) disputed for the first time in Chernivtsi, we may conclude that the onus of factual accuracy was, if not imported, then at least enhanced by the presence of Leo Spitzer's video camera. "We have to tell the same story," Carl insisted, for posterity (88). On one level and by its very nature, the project of a return documentary is to occasion testimony, be it spoken, gestural, or silent.

These, then, are some of the intrinsic qualities and productive uses of situated testimony. But the "abuses" alluded to in the section heading are also pertinent because return journeys are undoubtedly open to ethical, as well as practical, challenges. Marianne Hirsch and Leo Spitzer acknowledge that while "affectionate longings for earlier stages and scenes" are complicated, real, and enduring, the feelings and discourses around the return journey still do reveal a propensity for "indiscriminate idealization of past time and lost place that had angered nostalgia's critics" (82–83).

Jack Kugelmass, for his part, critiques the "mythic" meaning of certain "missions" that "begin by visiting Poland (thus entering the abyss of despair) and then conclude by touring Israel (thus experiencing redemption)" for failing to recognize disturbing or contradictory present-day realities (211). Even more pointedly critical of Holocaust tourism or "atrocity heritage," G. L. Ashworth characterizes the oft-stated motive for visiting the sites of concentration camps—to prevent the recurrence of similar genocides—as "global humanitarian propaganda" (363–64). "Victimization as a founding mythology has played a central role in state-building," he opines; "[t]here are . . . dangers inherent in a dominating sense of past injustice [such that it] may not be an ideal paradigm for the guidance of future action (363)."[6] A source of the problem is the co-presence of three communities at odds with one another in the business of Jewish heritage tourism: "the world-wide Jewish community," "the wider Polish nation," and "the existing local inhabitants" (366). Since there are few Jews currently living in the area Ashworth takes as his example (Kraków–Kazimierz), and since the local inhabitants are not middle-class Polish Gentiles but rather people from "among the poorest groups in the city" including many "re-housed migrants displaced from eastern territories lost in 1945," the much-needed urban renewal would have to go far beyond the local economy of restaurants, souvenir shops, information sites, and memorials catering to tourists. "The presence of a resuscitated Jewish heritage," Ashworth submits, "raises not only the question of 'whose heritage?' but also more immediately [and] threateningly 'whose property?'" (366).

Without buying into the animosity of Ashworth's brand of anti-Zionism, we may still recognize the relationship between the redemptive tendencies of some Holocaust narratives and the wider cultural critique of nostalgic fundamentalism. The territorial claims of a village, a people, or a nation may well function as naïve or self-serving; as a form of "restorative nostalgia" (Svetlana Boym's term); or worse, as a rationale for xenophobic nationalism. The affinities among homeland, "ethnic purity," and so-called hereditary rights may be murderous indeed (Marciniak 66, Naficy). But these complexities are all the more reason why it is important not to abandon in the rush for critical footing the historiographic, geographic, and ethical significance of place attachment. Indeed, by virtue of its necessarily spatial and temporal unfolding, and because it engages the bodies and imaginations of literal and armchair travelers, the documentary film or video of return has tremendous potential to stage very tangibly the pulsions and problems of the contested territories of the Holocaust and beyond.

The Last Days

On the very ground where the wheels rolled, Bill Basch, in *The Last Days,* bends forward slightly and mimes grasping a handle to illustrate how he pushed the tumbrel of heaped corpses to the gate of the crematorium compound at Dachau. This and other passages exemplify the documentary's function to inscribe history through bodily movements that simultaneously reenact what was and what continues to be.

Irrupting here and there, out of a film also comprising archival and distant testimonial footage, are two dozen brief sequences depicting visits to Europe by the film's five Hungarian subjects accompanied by their respective family members. These visits, like that of Elie Wiesel to Auschwitz with Winfrey, were made, in large part, to be documented—and I do not mean that pejoratively. For here they are now, productively staged (like all filmed interviews) to bring into being thoughts, words, actions, and encounters that otherwise might have remained unformulated, unexpressed, and unlived. And here they are now for communication to the next generation and for cinematic sustenance beyond the lifespan of Holocaust survivors and refugees. Marianne Hirsch and Leo Spitzer end their essay with the insight that "at the crossroads in Czernowitz, telling and listening became a collaborative endeavor." For their parents Lotte and Carl Hirsch, "'It would not have made sense to return except in this constellation.' . . . 'We would not have come without you'" (93). *The Last Days* and other Holocaust documentaries of return, for their parts, orchestrate a cinematic telling and listening in which it would not have made sense to return without a camera.

In the film and because of the film project, we see Renée Firestone at the Auschwitz archives leafing through a stack of index cards to find the record of her sister Klara's incarceration and death. Obviously anticipated as a significant moment that could be documented as it happened, this sequence captures the quiet shiver of horror when Firestone reaches Klara's card. The film project also enables Firestone to interview the Nazi Dr. Hans Münch about the medical experiments performed on Klara at Münch's concentration camp "clinic." "He was very evasive," Firestone later summarizes, confirming my own impression of the interview.

Lanzmann's explanation of his own research process would seem to apply as well to that of protagonists in documentaries of return, including this one: "If you go to Auschwitz without knowing anything about Auschwitz and the history of the camp, you will see nothing . . . In the same way, if you know without having been there, you will also not understand anything . . . *This is a film from the ground up*" (Chevrie and le Roux 38–39, emphasis mine). With all due respect for the wealth of documentation on industrialized mass murder available at the Auschwitz museum, much of which is effectively geared toward meeting the first-time visitor's need for introduction and explanation, I take Lanzmann's point that extraordinary knowledge is produced from this chemistry of distant or proximate learning and physical gleaning.

Moreover, a film sur place can extend to spectators the benefits or horrified shivers of "site-seeing."

HOLOCAUST documentaries of return are in these ways very valuable cinematic interlocutors in the ongoing effort to fathom Holocaust history. But there is also a manifest tendency in quite a few of them to capitalize on the particular emotional appeal of the redemptive narrative. In *The Last Days*, after having experienced important discoveries with Renée Firestone, we come finally to the moment when she returns to her childhood home. She spots the house and crosses the street. With the film crew trailing, she reaches the gate and presses the handle. "It just doesn't open . . . it doesn't open." She bows her head and cries. Later in the film we will observe her lighting a memorial candle at Auschwitz. For a hopeful ending, *The Last Days* offers up the new and successive generations: the family members of the five protagonists who accompany and witness their journeys and the adult children and grandchildren home in the United States. Bill Basch has brought his son Martin to tour Dachau. In the DVD *Outtakes and Behind the Scenes Footage*, he exacts a promise: "You will bring your children here and they should bring their children."

These are moving sequences, and it is heartening, for many, to witness the return and continuation of a people all but doomed to extinction. But I am cognizant as well of the aforementioned problems posed by the redemptive narrative of return with its "dominating sense of past injustice" and disengagement from pressing, current problems and competing claims to land and property. However viscerally we may feel the pull of ancestral and childhood abodes and the grief of deportation and exile, critical human geography teaches us that neither the territory, nor the map, nor the visitor it guides is a stable entity with a tangible existence apart from assertions and contestations of belonging.

In her aptly titled *Terra Infirma,* Irit Rogoff charts an "unheimlich" or "unhomed geography" where rites/rights of return are not fixed with regard to national, religious, and generational features of the landscape. She advocates a shift away from a "moralizing discourse of geography and location, in which we are told . . . who has the right to be where and how it ought to be so . . . to a contingent ethics of geographical emplacement in which we might jointly puzzle out the perils of the fantasms of belonging as well as the tragedies of not belonging" (3). An art historian by training, Rogoff envisions a space where "political insights, memories, subjectivities, projections of fantasmatic desires and great long chains of sliding signifiers" can hold sway against "concrete coercions" determined by religious and state apparati (7, 4). Contemporary works of art, she believes, may array "alternative strategies" through which we can "review our relationship with the spaces we inhabit" (frontispiece).

So, too, may documentaries of return. Watching such films critically, we may discern how the "tragedies of not belonging" are indeed intercalated with the "perils of the fantasms of belonging." To some extent, *The Last Days* enables this sort of critically fruitful thinking where competing and even irreconcilable territorial claims break a path toward mutual understanding. The film is at its most compelling, I believe, when in addition to affirming the presence of situated bodies, it also physically documents what Howard Jacobson calls the "voluptuous ambition of repossessing nothing" (Jacobson 7, cited in Palmer 248).

Prior to the image of Firestone before her gate, there is a sequence involving Irene Zisblatt's return to her hometown, now in Ukraine. She testifies that she remembers the town as "picturesque and happy." We see a castle on a hill, a man in a horse-drawn cart, and the view from the van as Zisblatt travels along. "I'm hoping that I can find some of the people that I knew before the Holocaust and maybe that I can talk to them." Amazingly, we do witness her reunion with an old woman, Mariska, who remembers Zisblatt's grandparents, father, mother, and Zisblatt herself. "I was most surprised that she remembered me," the latter reflects in voice-over, "I was really afraid that the people were going to be hostile to me. . . ." We cut to an interview with Zisblatt at night, in what is probably the van interior, a spotlight on her face providing dramatic intensity (as well as the illumination necessary to film) as she continues: ". . . that they were going to be accusing me of coming back to take something away from them." Over an image of the countryside: "I was asked in a very nice way, am I planning to take my property and come back to live there? And I said no." Back to the van interior: "I just want my children to know where I came from and I wanted to see my town where I grew up one more time before I die." Cut to Zisblatt on a rural road, pointing out landmarks to her daughter.

This is information we have when we see Firestone before the closed gate and then walking up the road to a former neighbor's walled home. There, Firestone speaks with a man who was a child during the war and his Russian wife. "Your own house; to take someone's house. How could that be?" he sympathizes. His wife continues, evoking the atmosphere of decades of communist rule, the conflicting interests of the current situation, and the physical materiality of witnessing: "There would be a lot to tell. But you know what they say: even the walls have ears." The sequence concludes with

Firestone's understandable and revealing reflection about the doubleness of home: "At that moment I felt very lucky that I will have a chance to go back to the United States, to my home."

Blocked from entry into her former home, suspended between the evidence Auschwitz coughs up and the information withheld, and reversing the direction of return, Firestone's trajectory extends beyond any single point of arrival. Likewise, Zisblatt's return to Polena is successful only because it is a temporary visit that does not involve the repossession of property and because its transposition into film form highlights the rigors (and weirdly fortuitous benefits) of confinement, expulsion, and exclusion. Zisblatt, like Firestone, may have lived a fuller existence unhomed from Ukraine. Here and there among the film's multiple narratives of return, we sense the energy of critical geography: "home" is both a magnetic field that attracts us and a molten extrusion of historical and contemporary, regional and national, economic and political, ethnic, and religious frictions.

Hiding and Seeking

Hiding and Seeking (2004) is explicitly anti-redemptive in its narrative patterning. The trip and its documentation do not take place primarily to interview former neighbors who stood by while Jewish families were taken away, or to mourn and memorialize the deceased, or to commemorate the Shoah, or to celebrate the triumph of the generations. Rather, film and trip were initiated by Menachem Daum (who was raised an Orthodox Jew and remains religiously observant) with the aim to combat religious insularity and xenophobia in the thinking of his own sons and, presumably, in the thinking of some of the film's viewers. His plan is to engage the sons and "us" in the activity of finding and recognizing the family's Polish rescuers. As with Lanzmann's return of the "one-time boy singer" to Chełmno, Daum's actions also entail, therefore, a persuasion and a return. And, like *Shoah*, *Hiding and Seeking* is a "film from the ground up." But in this more recent film, both the grounds for action and the situations of bodies in space have been redefined.

New York–based Menachem Daum with Oren Rudavsky is co-director of this thematically progressive, audiovisually inventive, and thereby semi-autobiographical documentary. The child of a father who survived the Holocaust, Daum has constructed an itinerary that begins with him and his wife Rifka taking leave of their aging, immigrant fathers and traveling from New York to Israel to pick up their two grown sons who live as Orthodox Jews with their wives and children. Together, the family then travels on to Poland, where they go first to the hometown of Menachem's father and then to the farm where Rifka's father, Chaim Federman, along with his two brothers, survived the genocide hidden by a Polish farmer and his family at the risk of their own lives.

Prior to leaving on the trip, Daum asks for a paternal blessing. "Go in peace and return in peace," his wheelchair-bound father pronounces in halting Yiddish, affected perhaps by the lingering results of a stroke. Then, surprising us and maybe his son as well: "I want to go with you." "Where do you want to go?" Daum inquires. "To my home," his father answers. "Where is your home?" "Stevchinka 7." But Daum's father does not make the journey, and his original home is made strange by its presentation in the film.

In the car, driving along in the Polish countryside, Rifka Daum responds to her husband's repeated whistling and humming of the song, "I'm Going Home," with a very definite: "You may be going home. We're certainly not going home . . . This ain't my home." Her point about having been raised elsewhere is emphasized when the group is met with an absence in Daum senior's hometown of Zduńska Wola. The houses and the synagogue that used to stand in the Jewish quarter are gone, and a convenience store among other shops occupies space near Stevchinka 7A. When Daum folds and refolds a paper prayer inscribed with family names and tucks it into the crevice between a telephone pole and its concrete base, this is too much for his younger son. "I'd like to say . . . I think this is nuts," he asserts in direct address to the camera. "I object." "I think this is completely ridiculous. A complete waste of time. Like the film." Indeed, he and his brother look very much out of place in their black clothing, hats, and payes among the Polish young people out on the street.

It is precisely in and through the resistance of the various family members, and in and through the visual evidence of the differences between the Jewish visitors and the presumably non-Jewish Polish residents, that the film reminds us of the area's history of anti-Semitism and, following Rogoff, of the near-inevitability that a given town or region will be multiply inhabited (if not ethnically cleansed). In this and other ways, *Hiding and Seeking* brings to the fore the complicated, spatialized relationships among "the world-wide Jewish community," "the wider Polish nation," "the existing local inhabitants" and the returning Daums. Particular advantage is made of the motion picture's ability simultaneously to ground and to unleash bodies and spaces from one another and, I submit, from an imagined territorial imperative where only certain people belong. Specifically, through the use of voice-over narration and editorial juxtaposition, the film establishes a productive asynchronicity between seeing and hearing (image track and sound track) and a productive spatial noncontiguity (physical presence and absence).

As does his father, Daum's father-in-law remains at home rather than making the trip to Europe. But they both return by generational proxy, and, especially in the case of the latter, Rifka Daum's father Chaim Federman, by filmic means as well. While Federman is home in the United States, the film nevertheless enables the "return of [his] voice." Prior to the trip, he had advised his son-in-law not to go to the farm where he had been hidden, even though Federman acknowledged that the farmer and his family had rescued him and his brothers: "He saved our lives. Otherwise, I wouldn't be here." Still, he rationalized, "they forgot already," and he urged his son-in-law to tell the Polish family that he had died. For one thing, Federman had "promised them the world." For another, he had good reason to be leery of return. After the war, he recalled, "When a Jew came back, they killed him." "I don't know what's going on there today. Better, don't show yourself." But, of course, Menachem Daum and family do make the trip. Over images of the Polish countryside we hear Federman's voice on the soundtrack: "Don't look. Don't stay on the street. You go by car. You stay outside. Better you shouldn't show yourselves." Accompanying images of Daum and one of his sons, in a field in Poland under partly cloudy skies flouting their patriarch's advice Federman's words are heard in haunting voice-over: "I don't like that you should go there."

That Chaim Federman is there, paradoxically, in absentia, and that his absent presence matters, are also conveyed through another sequence, amazing for its condensation of new and old technologies on the filmic windowpane. Pulled over to the side of the road, the Daums, their guide, and their driver peer at the map and a laptop computer open on the hood of the car. Działoszyce, the town, and then, smaller, Dziekanowice, we make out. But how to get there? Menachem Daum reaches his father-in-law back in Brooklyn on the cell phone, and, in Polish retained from childhood, Federman describes, apparently to a local of the area passing by, the landmarks by which the family (and the film crew) might navigate the narrow roads to the farmhouse. We see the Poland end of the conversation and the little silver instrument from which the voice emanates. The call exemplifies Felman's assertion that eyewitness testimony holds an "utterly unique and irreplaceable topographical *position* with respect to an occurrence" (206) (Federman was [once] there; he and he alone among the visitors remembers the way back). At the same time, the call also exemplifies the possibility that that position may be one of distance and difference. Lanzmann is critical of knowing without going and going without knowing. This film somewhat reflexively presents (audio)visual technologies as a means of collaborative, mediated, and, as I will elaborate below, resistant knowing and going that problematizes redemptive narration.

The next sequence is astounding, for the Daums do make it to the home of the Polish rescuers and the very spot on earth where the young Chaim Federman was given shelter, the cradle of the gathered family. The reunion happens very fast on film. First a shot through the front windshield as the car proceeds according to Federman's long-distance directions; then a close-up of Rifka in the car with the countryside unrolling behind her; then a long-shot of a farmyard, a barking dog tied up at the tree. Suddenly the Daums have arrived and it is established that the woman on the path in front of a substantial home with a beautiful flower garden is the granddaughter of the late farmer, Stanislav Matuszcyk. After nearly sixty years, the daughter of Chaim Federman and the granddaughter of Stanislav Matuszcyk inhabit the same patch of ground where their forebears met, and they also inhabit the same filmic shot. As Rifka excitedly questions the woman, "Did [your grand-father] ever tell stories about that he hid three brothers?" the film cuts to the woman's father, Wojciech Mucha (the now-elderly son-in-law of Matuszcyk), rounding the corner of the garden fence, tipping his hat to the visitors with Old World manners. With some prompting, he is able to recall at least two of the brothers' names. "Get your grandmother," says Mucha's daughter to her own daughter, a young person who appears to be in her early twenties. Daum's sons, no longer protesting the ridiculousness of their father's "quest," shake hands with Mucha just before the film cuts back to the fence corner to take in the arrival of Honorata Mucha, daughter of Stanislav Matuszcyk and wife of Wojciech Mucha. Completely bent over, she cranes her neck to greet the group and then rattles off with decisive speed the names of the three brothers. She herself cooked their food, we later learn, and carried it to the barn in a bucket so as not to alert the neighbors to the hidden Jews.

The group then files up the path into the farmyard, halting where the barn once stood and where the brothers secreted themselves in a pit covered over with hay. We see Honorata Mucha from above, her green headscarf with the flowered border bright against the grass in the yard. The bones of her body mark the passage of years; her feet retrace steps of long ago—perhaps kicking up some particle of dust that had lain on the ground these many years—while her gesturing arms conduct the family's testimony. The Ger-mans entered the yard, we learn through the translator. The season was late autumn or winter, so only one layer of hay remained to hide the entrance to the hole. But the family was brave, Wojciech Mucha recalls. The Jew-ish brothers were not found, and everybody survived. Menachem Daum's sons, Tsvi Dovid and Akiva, read a prayer for a "place where one's parents, forebears, torah teacher or nation as a whole were miraculously saved from imminent danger." The dog, tied to a nearby tree, barks incessantly over the words of the prayer while Rifka Daum and her sons are moved to tears. In relation to the film's plot, thrumming with travel and conversation, this is a privileged moment amply illustrating Yi-Fu Tuan's profound insight: "If we think of space as that which allows movement, then place is pause; each pause in movement makes it possible for location to be transformed into place" (6). From undifferentiated *space,* post–Holocaustic Europe such as the travelers perhaps imagined before the journey, the farmyard takes shape as a known and valued place. A year later, inside the house, we pause again when Honorata Mucha smiles over the telephone as she speaks with Federman in New York. "Good health to you," she says. "May you live to be a hundred years."

Bodies exposed to the camera and film exposed to our eyes fix, very tangibly, the historical knowledge of a past event, miraculous or miraculously and exceptionally humane. And yet the film is also open to an alternate architectonics where knowledge circulates semi-autonomously from the physical proximity of people who "were there" at the time of the original events and place. Federman himself did not make the trip. But the filming and the film convey their lessons through the physical transportation of second- and further-generation travelers and also, significantly, through the physical absence, marked by the audio presence, of Federman.

As discussed above, Federman counseled his family not to go. He himself may have been as unwilling as he was unable to undertake the journey. This resistance informs *Hiding and Seeking,* such that the film may be read as countervailing the very materiality of eye-witnessing and mediated-witnessing in which it also revels. We learn from a conversation between the two families that the Polish household took in the Jewish brothers out of pity and with thoughts of future compensation. Back in New York, Chaim Federman had acknowledged, "I promised them the world, [that I can] support them, understand?" Now, the granddaughter of Wojciech and Honorata Mucha questions why the family had never heard a word from the three brothers after the war. Rifka Daum explains that her father "feels bad about it; he regrets that he didn't do more." "We're here to correct that," vows Menachem Daum. And so the Daums apply to Yad Vashem and return to Poland one year later to participate in a ceremony, included in the film, in which the Muchas are presented with the medal for the "Righteous among the Nations." The Israeli Ambassador, himself a Polish Jewish survivor, officiates, and Tsvi Dovid gives a speech thanking and honoring the Muchas and offering a fund for the education of their descendants. He also explains that his grandfather "has literally become paralyzed to act upon . . . an overwhelming sense of insurmountable debt." Rifka's and Menachem's eldest granddaughter, representing the fourth generation, presents flowers to Honorata Mucha and kisses her on the cheek.

Juxtaposed with this sequence (preceding it in the order of the film) is Chaim Federman's admission, with all due self-knowledge, that if the situation were reversed, if Jewish refugees had come to him for a place to hide and he would have had to risk his life to give it, he would have refused. But why, then, hadn't he kept in touch with his rescuers, knowing full well what they did for him? Actually, from a special feature on the DVD, we learn that fifty items of correspondence between Stanislav Matuszcyk and the Federman brothers were discovered in the Muchas' attic a year after the film was finished. This is a correspondence that ended in 1959, that Federman apparently, perhaps symptomatically, forgot and that Matuszcyk apparently never shared with his daughter and son-in-law. Some of the letters allude to attempts to purchase property for the farmer. One letter in particular is quoted by co-director Oren Rudavsky. It is a letter from Federman to Matuszcyk that ends with the following sentences: "How are you without the Jews? Are you better without them?" Federman's words betray anger, a justifiable emotion under the circumstances, many would say. Indeed, it is possible to watch the film and wonder whether Federman's would-be debt wasn't already canceled several million times over by the Polish expropriation of property and lives. The incessant barking where the barn once stood underlines that the Daums are strangers. The sound bothers the nerves and threatens the audibility of reconciliation.

Without utterly suppressing Jewish anger or Jewish difference (the letters may be confined to the special features, but the bow-wow-wow is live action), it is nevertheless the goal of the film to work them through. Near the beginning, Menachem Daum plays for his sons a tape of an Orthodox Jewish leader advocating separation between Jews and Gentiles and a legacy of hatred. Jewish people should "implant in ourselves and in our children, hatred to them," he orates. "Tell our children what the goyim have done to us for 1,900 years." This is precisely the attitude the film is designed to reject. We cannot let the religion be "hijacked by extremists," teaches Daum. And yet Daum includes as the penultimate sequence the response of his younger son, Akiva, heard in voice-over, accompanying a traveling shot of the road through the car windshield as the Daums drive away after their second visit to the farm. "What did you learn, Akivala, from meeting these people?" inquires Daum. "I learned there's some very good people in the world. Some very nice people, and a lot of not nice people. . . . That was the truth. You want to know the truth? You add a few exceptions to the rule. But the general rule of thumb was, you know, to get rid of the Jew was the best thing to do and, um, they'd probably do it again."

Jewish anger is rarer in Holocaust narratives than are sadness and expressions of victimhood. Survivors and refugees generally take and are often ceded the moral high ground. In *Hiding and Seeking,* the situation is more complex and ongoing. The film could have ended triumphantly, with positive lessons learned from the ceremony of the "Righteous among Nations." But Akiva's resistance, like Federman's, is pronounced, and the narrative maintains a purposeful lack of closure. Daum describes the trip to Poland as his "tzavoah" to his children, "a document; sort of an ethical will," through which he has communicated the important values by which he would like them to live. "I think it's like planting a seed," he says, in voice-over narration as he and Rifka along with their grandchildren stroll under a canopy of trees to the edge of a lake. "It can take years and years. But that's my hope." Here, as in *The Last Days,* the succession of the generations is presented optimistically. But *Hiding and Seeking* takes pains to highlight the ethical complexities of religious difference by acknowledging both the humanity of others and the hatred that Jewish religious extremism can harbor. The film itself is a tzavoah, a document through which these hopes and acknowledgments are nurtured.

Menachem Daum responds to his wife's emphatic "this ain't my home" with the characterization of himself as a "wandering Jew." And yet his trajectory is deliberate. As they encounter the generous past actions of the Matuszczk family and, by implication, other non-Jewish people, the Daums' "sentiments come to be mapped as physical transformations" (Bruno 245). In bringing his religiously insular sons from Israel to Poland, Daum reverses the redemptive narrative pathway from the camps of Poland to the Jewish state. "Neither the exilic dream of return to organic connection nor the nomadic celebration of rootless liberty," John Durham Peters writes, "offers quite the best option for living in a world of differences" (39). Agreed. This is precisely why I value the film's presentation of travel by person and by proxy and its use of asynchronous and noncontiguous sounds and images as an innovative, critically productive way of bridging the disjunction between over-zealous assertions of belonging and commemorative rites of resigned expatriation. Through its establishment of an anti-essentializing positionality, *Hiding and Seeking* "teaches the perpetual postponement of homecoming and the necessity, in the meanwhile, of living among strange lands and peoples" (39).

Conclusion

Certain Holocaust documentaries of return tend to further fantasies of home and homeland while avoiding competing claims to physical place and cultural space. But I hope this chapter has shown as well that the Holocaust documentary of return may function as a flexible modality that increases the dimensionality of seeing, going, and being-there beyond any specific narrative trajectory; certain documentaries of return or portions thereof maximize their potential to make "more room for lived space and its movement" (Bruno 245).

Along with the personal histories of survivors and refugees that have been collected by the various Holocaust video archives around the world (and that now contribute to an enormous digital repository), we now have the filmically documented visits or situated testimonies of many "who were there." In the form of built or unbuilt environments, places remain that returnees and their descendents can point to and say, "it is here, right here at this [train] track" (Winfrey anticipating Wiesel's arrival) or "in front of the tree; right here" (on the Mucha farm): this is where it happened.

But, as I have sought to argue here, neither the physical presence of an actual refugee on the soil or pavement that she or he fled or was removed from, nor any proliferation of landmarks, can guarantee the fullness or accuracy of historical detail. In fact, the absence of persons and structures may be particularly telling, as in the case of the ruined synagogue in Zduńska Wola or that of Chaim Federman's failure to write or return. We may take the very instability of the documentary of return as an invitation to read moving testimonies critically and with renewed vigor. The seed is planted in a "terra infirma."

The main aim of this essay, then, is to recognize the radical, historiographic possibilities of the Holocaust documentary of return as a material form of testimony that nevertheless resists a deterministic view of place. By presenting the critically accessible suggestion that "every topography and every text is doubly inhabited by often irreconcilable cultural positions," these texts help "undo the universalism that attempted to bind us all together under the aegis of the dominant" (Rogoff 110–11). However committed to physical propinquity, however engaged with the allure of past haunts—and it is so committed and engaged—the Holocaust documentary of return, as a film or video text on the move, is also beautifully cut out to mediate our experience of testimony and witnessing across the discontinuous geographical spaces and the multiply inhabited places we call home.

AUTHOR'S NOTE: I would like to express my gratitude to Susan Rubin Suleiman for recommending *Hiding and Seeking* as a film that might further my interest in documentaries of return; it did indeed. And many thanks to the editors of the volume for their expert comments on this chapter and their exceptionally generous working method that included inviting geographically dispersed contributors to meet and talk in person.

Notes

1. "I did not want to go to Poland," Lanzmann explained. "I thought that one can talk about this from everywhere, from any place, from Paris, from Jerusalem, from New Haven . . . And I said, 'what will I see in Poland, I will see the nothingness, I will see the absence'" (Felman 256 and 256n36, referencing Lanzmann, "Evening" 4–5). But, of course, he did make the trip and many more. "The Israelis . . . asked me if I would consider undertaking a film about the Holocaust," recounts Lanzmann; "I said yes rather quickly, without thinking very much . . . After I started, it became impossible to stop" (Felman 250, referencing Lanzmann, "Interview" 21).

2. Here I am borrowing Richard Slotkin's phrase from his book title because it calls to mind not only a specific place of genocide but also the mythologizing impulse through which that space is continually reimagined.

3. Elsewhere I have written about the vicissitudes and the "paradox" of traumatic memory; see works cited.

4. The film, Hirsch observes, has not been received "as a significant cinematic representation of the Holocaust" (64), and yet it is significant in this regard for revealing the inextricable connections between "the technical/formal innovations" of cinema verité and "the memory of the Holocaust" and for revealing as well the "impossibility of presenting a snapshot of French society in 1960 without either confronting or repressing the unresolved collective memory of deportation" (64–65). *Chronique d'un été*, Hirsch asserts, "constituted a crucial moment in the development of a documentary discourse of historical trauma in Europe" (65).

5. I would add that in relation to *The Last Days* and other Holocaust documentaries of return of which I speak, Marceline's is a different sort of return, this time from the camp rather than back to it.

6. By "state-building," I assume Ashworth is referring to the state of Israel, and I read his article as implicitly anti-Zionist. In any case, Holocaust tourism in Eastern Europe does seem worth exploring from a critical perspective.

Works Cited

Film and Video

Chronique d'un été. France, dir. Edgar Morin and Jean Rouch, 1960.
Hiding and Seeking: Faith and Tolerance after the Holocaust. United States, dir. Menachem Daum and Oren Rudavsky, 2004.

The Last Days. United States, dir. James Moll, 1998.

Shoah. France, dir. Claude Lanzmann, 1985.

"A Special Presentation: Oprah and Elie Wiesel at Auschwitz Death Camp." *The Oprah Winfrey Show* (United States, syndicated television), season 22, episode 132. Originally aired May 24, 2006. Available on DVD (Harpo Productions, 2006).

Survivors of the Holocaust. United States, dir. Allan Holzman, 1996.

Print

Ashworth, G. J. "Holocaust Tourism: The Experience of Kraków–Kazimierz." *International Research in Geographical and Environmental Education* 11, no. 4 (2002): 363–64.

Boym, Svetlana. *The Future of Nostalgia.* New York: Basic Books, 2001.

Brenner, Ira. "Returning to the Fire: Surviving the Holocaust and 'Going Back.'" *Journal of Applied Psychoanalytic Studies* 1, no. 2 (1999): 145–62.

Bruno, Giuliana. *Atlas of Emotion: Journeys in Art, Architecture, and Film.* New York: Verso, 2002.

Bukiet, Melvin Jules. "Memory Macht Frei." In *Second Generation Voices: Reflections by Children of Holocaust Survivors and Perpetrators,* edited by Alan L. Berger and Naomi Berger, 128–40. Syracuse: Syracuse University Press, 2001.

Caruth, Cathy, ed. *Trauma: Explorations in Memory.* Baltimore: The Johns Hopkins University Press, 1995.

Casey, Edward S. *Remembering: A Phenomenological Study.* Bloomington: Indiana University Press, 1987.

Chevrie, Marc and Hervé le Roux. "Site and Speech: An Interview with Claude Lanzmann about *Shoah.*" In *Claude Lanzmann's Shoah: Key Essays,* edited by Stuart Liebman, 37–49. New York: Oxford University Press, 2007.

Felman, Shoshana. "The Return of the Voice: Claude Lanzmann's *Shoah.*" In Shoshana Felman and Dori Laub, M.D., *Testimony: Crises of Witnessing in Literature, Psychoanalysis, and History,* 204–83. New York: Routledge, 1992.

Gilbert, Martin. *Holocaust Journey: Travelling in Search of the Past.* New York: Columbia University Press, 1997.

Hirsch, Joshua. *Afterimage: Film, Trauma, and the Holocaust.* Philadelphia: Temple University Press, 2004.

Hirsch, Marianne. *Family Frames: Photography, Narrative and Postmemory.* Cambridge, MA: Harvard University Press, 1997.

Hirsch, Marianne and Leo Spitzer. *Ghosts of Home: The Afterlife of Czernowitz in Jewish Memory.* Berkeley: University of California Press, 2010.

———. "'We Would Never Have Come without You': Generations of Nostalgia." In *Contested Pasts: The Politics of Memory,* edited by Katharine Hodgkin and Susannah Radstone, 79–95. London: Routledge, 2003.

Jacobson, Howard. *Roots Schmoots: Journeys among Jews.* London: Penguin, 1993.

Kugelmass, Jack. "Missions to the Past: Poland in Contemporary Jewish Thought and Deed." In *Tense Past: Cultural Essays in Trauma and Memory,* edited by Paul Antze and Michael Lambek, 199–214. New York: Routledge, 1996.

Lanzmann, Claude. "An Evening with Claude Lanzmann." Videotaped and copyrighted by Yale University, May 4, 1986.

———. Interview given by Lanzmann on the occasion of his visit to Yale University. Interviewers Dr. Dori Laub and Laurel Vlock. Filmed at the Fortunoff Video Archive for Holocaust Testimonies at Yale, May 5, 1986.

———. *Shoah: An Oral History of the Holocaust: The Complete Text of the Film*. Preface by Simone de Beauvoir. New York: Pantheon Books, 1985.

Liebman, Stuart, ed. *Shoah: Key Essays*. Oxford: Oxford University Press, 2007.

Marciniak, Katarzyna. "Transnational Anatomies of Exile and Abjection in Milcho Manchevski's *Before the Rain* (1994)." *Cinema Journal* 43, no. 1 (2003): 63–84.

Michel, E. W. *Promises to Keep*. New York: Barricade Books, 1993.

Naficy, Hamid, ed. *Home, Exile, Homeland: Film, Media, and the Politics of Place*. New York: Routledge, 1999.

Palmer, Andrew. "(Re)-Visiting Der Heim: The Amazing Return to the Place You've Never Been Which Isn't There." In *Issues in Travel Writing: Empire, Spectacle, and Displacement*, edited by Kristi Siegel, 245–51. New York: Peter Lang, 2002.

Peters, John Durham. "Exile, Nomadism, and Diaspora: The Stakes of Mobility in the Western Canon." In *Home, Exile, Homeland: Film, Media, and the Politics of Place*, edited by Hamid Naficy, 17–41. New York: Routledge, 1999.

Rogoff, Irit. *Terra Infirma: Geography's Visual Culture*. London: Routledge, 2000.

Slotkin, Richard. *The Fatal Environment: The Myth of the Frontier in the Age of Industrialization 1800–1890*. New York: Atheneum, 1985.

Suleiman, Susan Rubin. *Budapest Diary: In Search of the Motherbook*. Lincoln: University of Nebraska Press, 1993.

Tuan, Yi-Fu. *Space and Place: The Perspective of Experience*. Minneapolis: University of Minnesota Press, 1977.

Walker, Janet. "Rights and Return: Perils and Fantasies of Situated Testimony after Katrina." In *Documentary Testimonies: Global Archives of Suffering*, edited by Bhaskar Sarkar and Janet Walker, 83–114. New York: Routledge, 2009. Reprinted in revised form as "Moving Testimonies and the Geography of Suffering: Perils and Fantasies of Belonging after Katrina." *Continuum: Journal of Media & Cultural Studies* 24, no. 1 (February 2010): 47–64.

———. *Trauma Cinema: Documenting Incest and the Holocaust*. Berkeley: University of California Press, 2005.

———. "The Traumatic Paradox: Autobiographical Documentary and the Psychology of Memory." In *Contested Pasts: The Politics of Memory*, edited by Katharine Hodgkin and Susannah Radstone, 104–19. New York: Routledge, 2003.

Williams, Linda. "Mirrors without Memories: Truth, History, and the New Documentary." *Film Quarterly* 46, no. 3 (1993): 9–21.

PART III

The Holocaust and Others

CHAPTER 13

From Auschwitz to the Temple Mount

Binding and Unbinding the Israeli Narrative

SIDRA DeKOVEN EZRAHI

To Write Poetry after Auschwitz, You Need the Barbarians

John Coetzee's most memorable novel taught us that we are always Waiting for the Barbarians: identifying who and where they are is the best way of defining who we are. Aren't *we* what is left over after the barbarian is subtracted or banished from our social order? But if we succeed, as C. P. Cavafy warns us, "what's going to happen to us without barbarians? / They were, those people, a kind of solution" (18–19).

For those artists, scholars, and politicians who spent most of their professional lives staring at the ashes and the aftergrowths of Nazi Europe, Theodor Adorno's statement—"to write poetry after Auschwitz is barbaric"—established epistemological, moral, and political boundaries. First uttered in 1949 (*Prisms* 34) and revisited many times in subsequent essays, this dictum provided "a kind of solution": the relief of knowing that the barbarians were defined—if not confined—by Auschwitz, and the challenge of engaging in art that was both dangerous and consequential. As in classical rhetoric, the "barbarian" came to exist, "not in himself, but as an idea enabling civilization to define itself" (Goffart 128n63). While the physical borders of postwar Europe were being negotiated, contested, and renegotiated in the context of the Cold War, its cultural and moral boundaries (and forms of trespass) were also being tested. The failures of the past remain the template for the challenges outside one's window.

The focus of this essay is Israel in the aftermath of the Six-Day War, where a similar dynamic evolved into something quite different. In the first part I will argue that the sense of urgency that characterized the Cold War debates in Europe—and the mandate for healing through boundary consciousness, both temporal and spatial—was echoed in, and informed, a robust protest culture in Israel that was triggered by the spoils of the June war and culminated in the last years of the twentieth century. The peace process was more than a series of agreements; it was a new mode of accommodation with both the "barbarians" at the gates and with the "discarded" members of the collective self. It was permeated by the recognition that extraordinary vigilance and mutually recognized borders were needed to prevent one's own traumatized community from turning xenophobic.

The second part of this essay will attempt to show how that culture has been all but defeated by other dormant but deep-seated forces that were also unleashed by the 1967 war and the acquisition of "holy" territory. Sacred stories would come to be conflated with sacred shrines to produce a toxic narrative in which the *shoah* would play an increasing role. For Jews haunted by unburied "martyrs" from Europe and intoxicated by new proximity to the sacred center, a continuum stretches from the biblical *topos* of the *akeda* (the Binding of Isaac, Gen. 22) through Auschwitz to (*back*) to) the Temple Mount in Jerusalem, where the *akeda* "happened"—an arc that is also a circle. In this circle, which radiates out concentrically to endless, borderless vistas, there are only two alternatives: to sacrifice or to be sacrificed.

I am, in effect, defining an historical metanarrative that positions the Holocaust as the Ur-event of modern Jewish history and the *akeda* as the Ur-"event" of Jewish memory. I will outline the process by which this metanarrative congealed, as the four chapters of Israel's history, bookended by war and political assassination (1948–67, 1967–82, 1982–95 and 1995 to the present[1]) evolved from a "Narrative of Strong Borders" consonant with the statecraft of compromise into a "Narrative of Borderlessness" consonant with the stagecraft of the sacred. Each phase entails parallel shifts in the aesthetics, ethics, and politics of memory, representation, and action; the emphasis here is on the last two chapters, stretching from 1982 to the present. We are left, at the beginning of the second decade of the twenty-first century, in a "genocidal" space of sacrifice. The only way out, I will conclude, is by rediscovering a hermeneutic that allows us to read these stories, and these stones, at a distance—to turn our backs, as it were, on the *akeda,* on Auschwitz and on the Temple Mount with their holy and wholly homicidal mandates and, finally, to recapture the narrative of boundaries from the very story that occluded it.

The Narrative of Strong Borders

Before 1967, an obsession with borders prevailed in Israel along with a sense of claustrophobia and deep existential angst, as the Arab countries continued to deny the legitimacy of Israel's existence and as Israel continued to deny responsibility for the expulsion of much of the indigenous population during the War of 1948. In this first stage of statehood, the areas beyond Israel's armistice lines were regarded by its citizens as places not only of barbaric danger but also of desire and occasional suicidal acts of trespass (Alter 249–62). The entire country was a narrow strip of land hugging the Mediterranean coastline—and what the poet Yehuda Amichai later called the "supple and thin-waisted" city of Jerusalem ("The Land Knows," *Yehuda Amichai: A Life of Poetry* 464) was the intersection of Israeli politics and geography, the holy sites temptingly out of reach in Jordanian hands. Maintaining what we might call a kind of "diasporic" distance from the sacred center, Amichai describes the pre-1967 "longing [that] floated overhead in the sky / like ships whose anchors stuck deep in us, / and sweetly ached." Divided Jerusalem was crossed by "crazy people," breached by "enemies," tested by "lovers" ("Songs of Zion the Beautiful," #24, 23 *Poems* 95). But more important than the longing for what was out of reach was the presence of concrete armistice lines that, however tenuous, marked at least the *promise* of containment through physical borders.

The historical timeline echoed the geographical outline, including its blind spots. In an attempt to distinguish between the discarded or murdered past and the utopian present, the chronology of modern Israel somehow managed to incorporate the past into the present: in its quasi-messianic reach and its quasi-therapeutic lexicon, the "phoenix" narrative of Israel's birth—"*mi-shoah le-tekuma*" [from Holocaust to Rebirth]—seemed to preempt prolonged mourning or guilt through action; to swallow the losers, from the victims and survivors of Europe to the Arabs of pre-state Israel, into an epic of heroic sublation. On the surface, it appeared to create a boundary between the past tense and the present in order to strengthen the fledging state without burdening it with a melancholy connection to its memories. But its blind spots were in fact signals of something far more sinister and widespread. In drawing parallels between the occlusion of the *galut* other[2] and of the Arab other in the creation of the New Hebrew self, Amnon Raz-Krakotzkin focuses on a succession of repressive moves in Zionist thought and action ("Bein brit shalom" and "Galut"). Both forms of repression begin, rather naïvely, in the phoenix narrative.

The unlikely victory that ended the war of 1967 inaugurated the second phase in Israel's history, characterized initially by a sense of military invincibility. This was short-lived; the Yom Kippur War of 1973 revealed the cracks in the armor, and the invasion and occupation of Lebanon in 1982 effectively concluded this chapter with the breakdown of the internal consensus over the role of the Israel Defense Forces and the justness of Israel's military posture in the world.

In addition to the evolving discourse on power, a debate on territory came to dominate the post-1967 period. The West Bank would soon come to be designated in the public rhetoric as "liberated Judea and Samaria" and to constitute a new canvas for the Jewish imagination. Over the next four decades, the settlement of this territory would be viewed by growing sectors of the Israeli populace as "sanctified" by biblical texts and postbiblical acts of pilgrimage. The Temple Mount, which had remained the putative but distant *axis mundi* of the Hebrew imagination after the destruction of the Second Temple, became once again a proximate and palpable anchor for cultic Jewish claims, radiating out in concentric circles to other shrines scattered throughout what had been ancient Israel—and to the Land itself (see Inbari; Ezrahi, "To What"). Archetypal memory based in scriptural narratives began to prevail over historical thinking, and mythical claims began to supplant political ones.

The implications of this move were apprehended early on by a cohort of politicians, activists, and artists who constituted the Israeli peace camp and launched vigorous campaigns meant to make the native residents of the occupied territories visible and the territory negotiable. With this exposure, the repressed atrocities of 1948 also began to resurface within the "Green Line" through acts of excavation and representation (see Slymovicz; Grossman, *Sleeping*).[3]

By the mid-1980s, the culture wars had been clearly delineated. In his Hebrew novel *Arabesques* (Hebrew 1986), the Arab Israeli writer Anton Shammas defined—and performed—the competition in the here and now between the "Jew of Time" and the "Arab of Place" (121–22). Shammas's incursion into the hitherto ethnically homogeneous precincts of Hebrew literature[4] was a demonstration of the kinds of delicious ironies and amalgamations that are possible when conflicting identities are demarcated, recognized, and elasticized.

Many other daring acts of trespass by Israeli poets, playwrights, and novelists were undertaken in the public square. Largely informed by the intellectual debates in postwar and postcolonial Europe, they dramatized the ways in which Israelis and Palestinians continue to live in a haunted state. In *The Yellow Wind,* his nonfictional journey through the West Bank, and in *Smile of the Lamb* (Hebrew 1983; English 1990), the first Israeli novel to be set in the territories, David Grossman revealed the places that the apparatus of occupation had kept hidden from the general Israeli population.

The driving force behind this entire enterprise was paradoxical: stealthy border crossings into "closed military areas" by peace groups, echoed in various forms of artistic transgression, were meant to lead to the *creation of legitimate borders* between Palestine and Israel. At the same time, the unburied ghosts from Europe were harnessed in order to eventually retire them to the *pastness of the past.* In Michael Rothberg's words (in regard to Adorno's embrace of the bold transgressions of modernist artists), the "notion of art's barbarity [was] not refuted but *enacted* in order to present the barbarity of the age" (40).

The barbarity of this age was exposed by chipping away at the self-immuring forces of paranoia, election, and collective self-exoneration. A host of theatrical and literary events in the 1980s demonstrated, often in a mechanistic way, how inextricably bound were the Nazi/Jewish and the Palestinian/Israeli self-narrations. The perversities of collective memory were exposed in the first place as a meditation on power and victimization:

> As he waited in front of the new invention,
> Danton said, "The verb *to guillotine*
> (this brand-new verb of ours) is limited
> in the tenses and persons of its conjugation:
> for example, I shall not have a chance to say *I was guillotined.*"
>
> Acute and poignant, that sentence, but naïve.
> Here am I (and I'm nobody special),
> I was beheaded
> I was hanged
> I was burned
> I was shot
> I was massacred.
> I was forgotten
> (But why give an opening to Satan?—
> he might still recall
> that, morally at least,
> for the time being, I've won.)
> (Dan Pagis, "An Opening to Satan")

The grammar of power: exclusive claims to suffering in the passive voice yield (parenthetically, at first) to active projections of responsibility—and, hopefully, to a poetics of empathy that could spur political change. After the breakdown of the consensus on the uses of Israeli military power and the ambitions of Israeli expansionism, the poet Dahlia Ravikovitch led a group of writers who exposed the traditional vocabulary of Jewish suffering to contamination and ambiguation:

> She
> is not your sort.
> She's a Diaspora kind of Jew whose eyes dart around
> in fear . . .
> On the road.
> Caravans pass her by . . .
>
> Once the caravan has crossed,
> night will fall and she'll find her house.
> Her feet stub against the sharp gravel—stones,
> dust soils her dress . . .
> Her eyes are the blue eyes of Khazars,*
> her face a broad face,
> her body the heavy body of a native woman,**
> third generation in the Land of Israel.
> June 4, 1982
>
> *The *Khazars* (the translators' notes explain) were a "Turkic people from Central Asia, commonly believed to have converted to Judaism in the Middle Ages."
> **"*Native.* (Heb. "*mi-bney ha-makom*"). Official code for Israeli Palestinians."

("A Jewish Portrait," *Hovering* 190–91)

In this radical departure from the proprietary rhetoric of representation, it is unclear whether the object of the gaze is Jewish or Palestinian, while all assertions of ethnic purity are upended by reference to those intrusive Khazars. The appearance of the woman in this poem is as generic as the claims that both sides make to the same fear and the same territory.

In an even more blatant act of moral ambiguation, Hanokh Levin's play *Ha-patriot* (*The Patriot*) conflates the iconic Jewish child from the Warsaw

Ghetto and an innocent Palestinian child. Mahmoud, cap on head and hands raised, begs for mercy from an Israeli soldier, Lahav. Pointing a gun at the child's head, Lahav addresses his own mother:

> He will avenge your blood and the blood of our murdered family, as then, mother, when your little brother stood alone in front of the German, at night, in the field, and the German aimed his revolver at his head, and your little brother, trembling with fear, said (and he sings as he aims the revolver at Mahmoud):

> Don't shoot
> I have a mother
> she is waiting for me at home.
> I haven't eaten yet.
> Dinner.
> Don't kill me.
> I am a child.
> I am a human being like you.
> What did I do?
> What difference would it make to you if I yet lived?

This passage was excised from the performances of the play by the censorship that still prevailed in those years as a relic from the British Mandate.[5]

In David Grossman's novel *See Under: Love* (1986), Momik, the young child of Holocaust survivors, renders the Holy Land as a palimpsest in which "Over There"—Nazi Europe and Jewish Europe—shows through the half-erased spaces of Israel–Palestine (62). Going on to meditate, as an adult writer, on the ways in which the poison of Nazism can infect even (especially?) its victims, Momik warns of "the LNIY" (the Little Nazi in You) (262).

During this third phase in Israel's history, the spectral world could be invoked as a warning that each of us carries Pagis's guillotine or Grossman's "LNIY"; writing poetry *nach* Auschwitz meant, therefore, forging a moral universe *after* Auschwitz but *vis-à-vis* the new world created in its wake. Putting the past *behind us* meant first acknowledging and then exorcising, often through dangerous acts of impersonation, our potentially fatal impulse to repeat it—this time as the victors of history. After having been recklessly subsumed into the narrative of Israeli triumphalism, the fate of European Jewry began both to recede into the past as memory—and to inform the present as knowledge.[6]

Walter Benjamin would surely have recognized the protest culture of the last decades of the twentieth century in Israel as a welcome "intervention" in response to a patent "state of emergency," to the "moment of danger," as a daring attempt to "blast open the continuum of history" (257, 262, 255). One imagines that he, and Adorno, would have condoned its various manifestations as a reprise of the very mindset that was not barbaric *precisely because it appeared to be so,* that which "displace[d] and estrange[d] the world, reveal[ed] it to be, with its rifts and crevices, as indigent and distorted as it will appear one day in the messianic light"—analogous to the prose of Kafka, the poetry of Celan, the plays of Beckett in their day (Adorno, *Minima* 274).

Most of the cultural events of the 1980s and 1990s featured elements taken from the repertory of comedy and the grotesque while envisioning a world more fully reconciled. At that point, some thirty to forty years after the liberation of the death camps and some twenty to thirty years after the conquest of the West Bank and Gaza, the function of comedy was no longer constitutive in the *wake* of tragedy ("laughter after . . ."), but hortatory—or "homeopathic"—in the face of a new unfolding tragedy. The novels of Grossman and Yoram Kaniuk (*Adam Resurrected,* Hebrew 1969); the dramas of Yehoshua Sobol (*Ghetto* trilogy 1984–90), Shmuel Hasfari (*Tasmad*), and Hanokh Levin; and the poetry of Dan Pagis and Dahlia Ravikovitch demonstrated—through irony, satire, and the grotesque—the haunting presence of the holocaustal past in the unfolding reality of an Israel perpetually at war. Like Aristophanes' *Lysistrata* in the early fifth century B.C.E. or Chaplin's *The Great Dictator* in 1940, this is comedy in "real time," the comic muse enlisted to speak truth to power. Indeed, coming increasingly to resemble the ancient Athenian amphitheater in the last years of the Peloponnesian wars, the Hebrew stage in the last decades of the twentieth century reflected the ethical power of the comic imagination to recruit the catastrophic past to address the endangered future.

What remains constant in both the constitutive and the hortatory stages of the comic imagination is the demarcation between norm and anti-norm, between civilized self and barbaric other. The bipartite structure of the comic imagination—what Arthur Koestler calls "bisociation" (37) and what I define as the "simultaneity of incompatible worlds, the safe and quotidian with the barbaric and monstrous" ("Acts" 18)—presumes boundaries, even as it violates and attempts to redraw them. Taking as his point of departure Benjamin's "'weak messianic values,'" Dominick LaCapra talks of the "crucial problem of ethics" embedded in acts of transgression as attempts to establish new boundaries—the "relationship between normative limits that you want to affirm and the possibility of transgressing those limits, which is the only way . . . you get a newer normativity" (154). The new normativity in Israel comprised an ethics of empathy accompanied by an aesthetics of trespass and impersonation[7]—and it nearly succeeded.

This process culminated in the Acco Theatre production *Arbeit Macht Frei*. Directed by Dudi Ma'ayan, the five-hour performance included two actors (Semadar Ya'aron-Ma'ayan as "Selma" and Haled Abu Ali as "Mahmoud") who in real life and in their stage personae represented the two repressed "others" in Israel: the Holocaust survivor and the Arab. After a carnival of trespass enacted in every imaginable realm, Selma and Haled end in a naked embrace, their two scarred bodies entwined in an exhausted *pièta*. The play ran from 1991 to 1995, had two cinematic incarnations, and has been widely discussed by Israeli scholars as a cultural watershed (Ezrahi, "Acts"; Bartov; Raz-Krakotzkin, "Galut"; Rokem).

Exploring the ways in which the *shoah* was being projected phantasmagorically but therapeutically onto the Palestinian–Israeli conflict, one was easily convinced, through the mid-1990s, that the resolution of both the haunting past and the embattled present was only a matter of time and of mutually acceptable borders which, once established, would allow—or force—the collective self to recognize, civilize, or resist the barbarians without and within, and to pacify the ghosts from the past (Ezrahi, "Revisioning"). This was based on confidence in the historical ability of Jews to reinvent their culture in the wake of catastrophe (Mintz) as well as on what appeared to be inexorable political developments in the decades that hosted the peace process. The protest movement that began in the wake of the 1982 invasion of Lebanon and the massacre at Sabra and Shatilla was spurred on by the first Intifada (1987–93) and given legitimacy by the Oslo Accords (1993).

But the counter-forces that had been unleashed in the wake of 1967 would largely succeed in derailing this process. Israeli Jews in growing numbers came to refract the Palestinian–Israeli conflict through the prism of the genocidal past not in order to overcome it but to submit to its deadly hold on any claim to the present or the future. Increasingly, the struggles between Israelis and Palestinians became a drama not of this time and not of this place.[8] The early "negationist" impulses in Zionist thought vis-à-vis the victims of Nazi Germany and their culture and vis-à-vis the Arabs on both sides of the non-border became, after 1967, increasingly annexationist. Every Israeli government was complicit in the usurpation of land that began in the early 1970s, but widespread public legitimacy for the enterprise came about through a radical rhetorical shift that touched a very old nerve. From the late 1970s on, led by right-wing governments and the growing religious sector, the unburied European past was summoned for its most public task:

to explain and navigate the conflict in the Holy Land. In her trenchant analysis of the ways in which the absent presence of the *shoah* comes to shape the ongoing debate over borders, Idith Zertal quotes the claim of the "Gush Emunim" [bloc of the faithful] settlers that withdrawal from the territories is "withdrawal to the crematoria" (184–208). The category of holiness conflates the *kedoshim* or martyrs of World War II and *eretz ha-kodesh*—the Holy Land.

The Narrative of Borderlessness

If, from the perspective of 2012, it appears that the culture of protest has been all but defeated, it is largely due to the fact that for forty-four years now *there are no boundaries.* The conquest of East Jerusalem in the Six-Day War turned the lean city of the 2,000-year-old dream into a "noisy old dowager, all of her, / with her gold and copper and stones, / . . . come back / to a fat legal life" (Amichai, "Songs of Zion the Beautiful," #23, 24 *Poems* 95). During what I have delineated as the second, third, and fourth chapters of Israel's sovereign existence, from 1967 to the present, two generations of Israelis have grown up without borders demarcating either where Jews end and Israelis begin or where Israel ends and Palestine begins. Ongoing acts of cruelty against an occupied people take place in an increasingly invisible space, for which the only witnesses are mute, conspiratorial, or muzzled—the Palestinians, the settlers, and the Israeli soldiers (plus a dwindling handful of intrepid journalists and human rights activists).[9]

In March 2004, Hebrew novelist and polemicist A. B. Yehoshua expounded on what it means to be a people without a sense of borders. We are driving ourselves and our neighbors mad, he said in an interview in the daily *Haaretz:* "The moment Israel becomes [undefined] it drives the Jews crazy and drives the anti-Semites crazy; it drives the Arabs crazy and drives the Christians crazy." At the deepest level, he continues, this is a Jewish quirk: "The Jews don't want borders; Jews want everything to be open. So it will be possible to move from here to there. So things won't be defined. And that is exactly why Zionism to me means that we will finally have a border . . . to free ourselves of our *dybbuk* of latching onto other nations, and to regroup in our territory" ("Interview" 10–11). Toward that goal, Yehoshua was one of the early supporters of the "Security Wall" that has, unfortunately, become the parody of a border between Israel and Palestine (see Bitton; Brown).

Indeed, in place of recognized geopolitical borders we now have unilaterally imposed fences, walls, and impassable "gates" planted deep inside

occupied territory; instead of clear, temporal boundaries we have a conflation of there and here, of then and now, fed by deep reflexes of the Jewish
imagination that were never retired. I have already noted that before 1967,
the architects of national memory in Israel had attempted to substitute presence for absence and gain for loss as both the Arabs of Israel and the Jews of
Europe were incorporated into the triumphalist Zionist narrative. But loss
and absence came to overtake the project at the turn of the century. LaCapra
writes that "when mourning turns to absence and absence is conflated with
loss, then mourning becomes impossible, endless, quasi-transcendental
grieving, scarcely distinguishable (if at all) from interminable melancholy"
(69). The "phoenix" narrative of Israel's birth defined a deeply flawed and
hubristic project held in check by the minimal constraints of late national-
ist and colonialist practice. But it would evolve into something even more
insidious: the mandates of a mythical past and the mournful yearning for an
eschatological future would once again, as in the first centuries of the Common Era, overwhelm historical time as primary referent of Jewish memory
and arbiter of Jewish politics.

Empathy and compassion are handicapped when the passage of time is
denied as a major dimension of representation of the cataclysmic past. It is
the essentializers who keep the victims of the *shoah,* the survivors and all
who speak in their name, safe from any implication in the moral challenges
of the present—who, that is, insist on the eternal, haunting *presentness* of
the past. To the already degraded status of the present tense of the Hebrew
verb "to be"[10] are added the reifying and fetishizing acts of memory. The
consequences of "total recall" are far greater, I have argued, than the risk
of repressed memory or amnesia (Ezrahi, "Representing"). If from the outset there were hardly any representations of the Arab–Israeli conflict that
were not obscured by unburied phantoms from "Over There," as the conflict morphed into the *Palestinian*–Israeli conflict, the phantoms hijacked the
moral ground.

This development is consistent with the darker forces that Zionism had
inherited from the deep recesses of the Hebrew imagination. For large sectors of the populace, Israel's enemies are no longer regarded as recalcitrant
human adversaries, or even as barbarians to be vanquished or pacified in
a political conflict, but as new exemplars of the mythological archenemy.
Because of the peculiar claims of "return" and "recovery" of ancient privileges that guided Zionist thinking, because the map of Jewish desire is identical to the map of ancient Jewish memory, the modern Arab in his role
as descendant of Ishmael had long doubled as implacable oriental stranger
and romantic embodiment of the Hebrew self (Ezrahi, *Booking* 22). What

appeared in its early artistic forms as an innocuous and even respectful, though supersessionist, gesture toward the "other brother"—turning colonialist enterprise into one of atavistic self-realization—would become lethal by the end of the century.

It appears indeed that there no longer is an "other," as all rational versions of history—Marxist or Zionist utopian, Enlightened or pragmatic, history constructed entirely of acts of human intervention, built to human scale and unfolding in the present tense—are under full attack. Looking back, one can say that history itself was murdered along with Yitzhak Rabin in 1995. Events leading up to and including the Al Aqsa Intifada (2000) sealed the coffin on the peace process. During this fourth chapter in Israel's history, from 1995 to the present, archetypal thinking has come to prevail, and linear, open-ended apprehensions of Jewish history have been overwhelmed by circular reflexes; the "Palestinian–Israeli conflict" itself is being increasingly referred to by all sides as a "Condition" (ha-matzav), hardly amenable to human resolution.

The moment political conflict gives way to apocalyptic surrender is the most dangerous in the annals of any polity. The modern Jewish apocalyptic has its origins in two biblical prototypes: Ishmael [Gen. 21] and Amalek [Ex. 17, Deut. 25]. If in early Zionist representations of the Arab other in art and literature s/he is the romantic embodiment of the primordial self, in later representations, the Arab is the implacable enemy. When Yasir Arafat was added to the lineage that goes through Hitler back to Amalek, the demonic other was reincarnated. But whether the enemy is identified as the discarded (br)other, Ishmael—whose task it was to handle the estate for as long as it took the chosen one to return and reclaim it—or as the embodiment of the archenemy, Amalek, the result in the context of occupation and religious war is the same: the transformation of historical into archetypal adversaries, the abandonment of political and geographical containment for the expansionist myths of election and divine promise. Effacement is achieved by various mental and physical acts of "ethnic cleansing" or by an ostensibly gentler form of aufhebung. Even the "gentler" mode turns genocidal when the brothers return to the place of sacrifice and sacred narratives come to reinhabit sacred space.

Sacrificing Isaac/Ishmael

The shift from historical to mythical thinking and from political to sacred geography places a particular story and a particular site at the center of consciousness. In the two warring religious traditions, Isaac and Ishmael exchange roles as preferred/discarded brother; the center of each story is a small hilltop referred to in one tradition as Mt. Moriah or the Temple Mount and in the other as Harim al Sharif (Golgotha is but a stone's throw away . . .). If before 1948, Zionism had a profoundly ambivalent approach to the cartography of holiness (Saposnik), and if between 1948 and 1967 the physical distance from the Old City of Jerusalem perpetuated a healthy "diasporic" engagement with the actual sites, after 1967 and the reterritorialization of a literary *topos,* the *akeda* on "Mt. Moriah" would prove to be the biggest obstacle to the viability of political discourse and geopolitical borders. I will conclude by briefly examining the sacrificial claims at the heart of this phenomenon and by arguing that the story-that-won't-go-away contains a secret that could help us out of the impasse to which the engorgement or effacement of the Palestinian other and the annihilating and all-consuming fury of the *shoah* have brought us in this part of the world.

Nearly twenty years ago, A. B. Yehoshua—the same writer who would argue fecklessly for unilaterally constructed borders—tried to exorcise the haunting figure of Isaac on the altar. The last character in Yehoshua's novel *Mr. Mani* (1990),[11] the enigmatic Joseph Mani, lives in Jerusalem in the middle of the nineteenth century and is obsessed with the need to "remind" the "forgetful Jews" (i.e., the Ishmaelites) of their Judaism (337). This same Joseph will soon be killed—whether at the hand of the Ishmaelites or that of his own father is not clear, but what is clear is that this murder is both a "realization" of the *akeda* and a conflation of the story of Isaac and Ishmael—meant to make two murderous stories go away. In interviews after the appearance of this controversial novel, Yehoshua claimed that he had decided to *"annul the sacrifice of Isaac by its fulfillment":*

> When I wrote the "Fifth Conversation" for *Mr. Mani,* we were in the first difficult months of the Intifada, *before we became inured to atrocity, and every dead Palestinian child still caused us sleepless nights.* At the time, I recalled that at the beginning of Zionism, Ben Gurion and President Ben Zvi came up with the peculiar notions that Yosef Mani propounds—*that the Arabs of the country were merely converted descendants of Jews who had remained devoted to the land after the destruction of the Second Temple.* And that perhaps due to their attachment to the land they gave up their loyalty to the faith of their fathers. Yet now we torture our brothers of old with the afflictions of the occupation. ("Mr. Mani and the Akedah," emphasis mine)

Here we meet, explicitly, the Arab other as autochthonous Jewish self, an intensified version of the supersessionist view I outlined above, which

Yehoshua attributes to Ben Gurion and Ben Zvi. It is, perhaps, a way of returning Ishmael to the equation—this time not as the other brother or "cousin" (as he is designated in Talmudic and modern Hebrew), but as an incarnation of Isaac himself. But of the many curiosities in Yehoshua's statement, the most curious is his claim to be the first to try to resolve the *akeda* by realizing or literalizing the *topos* of sacrifice—to annul the sacrifice by its fulfillment. He does not take into account the fact that virtually every invocation of the *akeda* in postbiblical Jewish literature is an *enactment of the sacrifice,* and, therefore, a profound and fatal misreading of the original biblical story. Even the biblical story carries traces of an accomplished sacrifice that may have been overwritten by the redactors of Genesis. The slaughter that didn't take place in Genesis 22, that was interrupted at the last minute by a divine voice, is represented in Christian art and exegesis as the "sacrifice of Isaac," foreshadowing the Crucifixion. But in Jewish literature as well, from Talmudic times to the present, it is the presumed *death* of Isaac that has become a template for Jewish martyrdom (Spiegel).

Modern philosophers have been as mesmerized as writers and artists by this story. Jacques Derrida invokes the *akeda* while standing, as it were, on Kierkegaard's shoulders: "The sacrifice of Isaac is an abomination in the eyes of all, and it should continue to be seen for what it is—atrocious, criminal, unforgiveable; Kierkegaard insists on that. The ethical point of view must remain valid: Abraham is a murderer" (85).

Even as careful and clever a reader as Derrida designates this *topos* as the "sacrifice" of Isaac and labels Abraham's act "murder." He acknowledges the miraculous intervention, but indicates that the ultimate sacrifice, amounting to a kind of suicidal self-denial on the father's part, has already been performed. And, moreover, that it has since become commonplace: "Is it not inscribed in the structure of our existence to the extent of no longer constituting an event . . . *the sacrifice of others to avoid being sacrificed oneself* [?] . . . In the discourses that dominate during . . . wars, it is rigorously impossible, on one side and the other, to discern the religious from the moral" (85–87, emphasis mine).

The sacrifice of others to avoid being sacrificed oneself. The sacrificial space knows only one thing. Taken together, chapters 21 and 22 of Genesis create an echo chamber in which first one brother and then the other is nearly killed—saved at the "last minute" by divine intervention. Some time later, their younger brother from Nazareth comes to the site and is not spared. Thus all their descendants are candidates for murder. "The warring factions are all irreconcilable fellow worshippers of the religions of the Book," continues Derrida. "*Does that not make things converge once again on Mount*

Moriah over the possession of the secret of the sacrifice by an Abraham who never said anything? Do they not fight in order to take possession of the secret as a sign of an alliance with God and to impose its order on the other, who becomes for his part nothing more than a murderer?" (85–87, emphasis mine).

The "secret of the sacrifice of Isaac" is, according to Derrida, "the space separating or associating the fire of the family hearth and the fire of the sacrificial holocaust" (88). That space contracts the closer we come to consummating our physical claims to—that is, domesticating—the sacred center. In the more benign version, as we have seen, one brother incorporates the other; in the more pernicious version, the one annihilates the other. Both versions are being enacted daily on the bloody streets of the Holy Land.

Toward a New Narrative
A Comic Reading of the Akeda

What shapes the riddle of filicide that lies at the heart of all three mono-theisms—the riddle that refuses to disappear or to be resolved—is based, then, on a gross misreading of the constitutive story. The original version is, I submit, theatrical and *comic:* the aborted sacrifice of Isaac is framed in the biblical narrative as a "test," and the murderous act is preempted in classical comic fashion by the appearance of a *deus ex machina.*[12] Different versions of the Hebrew word for laughter, *tz-h-k,* appear twenty-one times in the chapters that frame the story (Gen. 17–22). But even if in modern Hebrew literature the *akeda* has been secularized and nationalized as an internal affair between Israel and its destiny, or its government, or between fathers and sons (Feldman; Kartun-Blum), the *interrupted holocaust*[13] is still deemed inadequate to the task of representing Jewish martyrdom, having been replaced long ago by the tragic, sacrificial version.

In *Sweet Violence: The Idea of the Tragic,* Terry Eagleton argues that the sacrificial and the tragic are inseparable in Western imagination. With Caravaggio's graphic *Sacrifice of Isaac* on its cover, Eagleton's book demonstrates the close relation between the sacrificial figure, the *pharmakos*—Isaac—and tragic figures such as Oedipus, Antigone, and Lear (274–97). At its heart, the ultimate act is still a sacrifice of brothers to the insatiable God on the Mountain.[14] Raz-Krakotzkin has argued that the suppressed temple cult continues to bubble just below the surface of secular Zionism ("Bein"). Idith Zertal has shown how the "process of sanctification ... of the Holocaust, coupled with the concept of holiness of the land, and the harnessing of the living to this two-fold theology, have converted a haven, a home and a homeland into a temple and an everlasting altar" (8).

Dan Pagis was one of the few writers in Israel who, in treating the time/ place of the *shoah,* not only (as we have seen) insisted on the moral equations of power, but also turned his back on both the Temple Mount and the *akeda.* In place of Abraham and Isaac and the covenant of sacrifice, Pagis foregrounds Cain and Abel and the arbitrary, pre-covenantal fratricide of brothers. Cain and Abel are imagined as interchangeable; the Nazis (and, by implication, all demonized enemies of Israel) are humanized and divested of their mythological status while the Jews are stripped of their immunities and their sacrificial designation: "here in this carload /I am eve / with abel my son / if you see my other son / cain son of man / tell him that I" ("Written in Pencil in the Sealed Boxcar"; see also "Autobiography" and "Brothers").

But we have seen that as the millennium turned and the political hold on sacred space congealed, there was no way to disengage from the gravitational pull of the altar, or from the story that "took place" on that altar. I will, therefore, suggest that we can emancipate ourselves from its genocidal grip only if we learn to read it differently. "I am . . . against originary ethics," writes John Caputo, "having lost all contact with the First Beginning and everything Originary" (1–2). His "originary ethics" comes close to what I have defined as the supersessionist logic that loops back to original persons, places, and stories. When Caputo describes "obligation" as replacing "ethics," he too implicitly returns to the story of Abraham and Isaac, and to Derrida and Kierkegaard—though with a possible way out. "For Derrida as for Kierkegaard," he argues, "ethics ought to be sacrificed in the name of obligation . . . Obligation calls, but its call is finite, a strictly earthbound communication, transpiring here below, not in transcendental space (if there is such a thing) . . . [but rather] *wherever* we are, in the middle of the fix we find ourselves in . . . Obligation is . . . the feeling of being bound (*ligare, ob-ligare, re-ligare*)" (ix, 7, 15, 21).[15]

In Hebrew *akeda* literally means *binding.* Returning the story to its original language and action allows binding and intervention once again to preempt sacrifice. Human obligation, the "feeling of being bound," creates *boundaries.* In the *akeda* restored as comedy, the angel appears as human projection to stay the murderous hand:

> ABRAHAM: Isaac, my son, do you know what I'm about to do?
> ISAAC: Yes, Abba, you are going to slaughter me . . .
> ABRAHAM: I am afraid I have no choice . . . I am doing this only as God's
>   messenger.

ISAAC: Of course as messenger, Abba. Get up as messenger and raise the knife as messenger on your son, your only one, whom you love . . .

ABRAHAM: Great, that's really what I deserve at my age. Put all the blame on me if it's easy for you, on your old and broken father who has at his age to climb the mountain with you, bind you on the altar, slaughter you, and on top of everything else to tell your mother everything. You think I have nothing else to do at my age? . . . That's the way you toy with the feelings of one who is about to become a bereaved father? . . .

ISAAC: Slaughter, kind and merciful Abba'le, slaughter me, saintly Abba'le . . .

ABRAHAM: Kill your father, gangster! Just kill him! [CATCHES ISAAC BY THE THROAT] Lie down!

ISAAC: A voice! A voice! I hear a voice!

ABRAHAM: What kind of voice? Lie down!

ISAAC: A voice from heaven!

ABRAHAM: What voice from heaven?! Lie down!

ISAAC: I don't know. It said: "Lay not thy hand upon the lad."

ABRAHAM: I didn't hear a thing.

ISAAC: Your hearing has been bad for some time. Here it repeats, "lay not thy hand upon the lad." . . . Abba, I swear I heard a voice from heaven.

ABRAHAM [AFTER A PAUSE]: Nu, if you say you heard it, you must have heard it. I, as you pointed out, am a bit deaf.

ISAAC: One hundred per cent. You know that for my part I was ready, but a voice is a voice. [PAUSE] You saw yourself that I was okay with this. [PAUSE] Both of us were okay. [PAUSE]. Right, we were both okay? Everything turned out well, Abba, why are you sad?

ABRAHAM: I think about what will happen if other fathers will have to slaughter their sons, what will save them.

ISAAC: A voice can always come from heaven.

ABRAHAM: Nu, if you say so . . .

(Hanokh Levin, *Malkat ambatia* 91, translation mine).[16]

This exchange appears in Hanokh Levin's controversial satirical revue, *Malkat ambatia* (*Bathtub Queen*), first performed in Tel Aviv in 1970. The play, a massive attack on Israel's sacred cows, appeared in the euphoric aftermath of the Six-Day War. Levin's *akeda* remains one of the few comic renderings of this constitutive story in Jewish literature, flanked on one side by Woody Allen and on the other by Franz Kafka.

Allen's prankish God and humorless Abraham replay the drama in its "original" form, with an American eye toward the abuse of power. After the

Lord "stayed Abraham's hand," He blames Abraham for his lack of a sense of humor. "'But doth this not prove I love thee, that I was willing to donate mine only son on thy whim?'" answers Abraham in shame. "And the Lord said, 'It proves that some men will follow any order no matter how asinine as long as it comes from a resonant, well-modulated voice'" (23–24).

Kafka's Abraham, generated after reading Kierkegaard, is, perhaps, the ultimate comic figure for our time: one who cannot obey the call-from-without because he is too embedded and obligated in this world. He may be "prepared to satisfy the demand for a sacrifice immediately" but is simply "unable to bring it off because he could not get away, being indispensable; the household needed him, there was perpetually something or other to put in order, the house was never Ready . . ." (172).

The phantoms of the genocidal past can still be contained, indeed, if household needs take priority, if the present tense is stretched and territory contracted to accommodate temporal and geographical borders and recognized selves and others. I am suggesting, however, that it will take more than a reinstatement of political, "historical" thinking to counter the mythic-apocalyptic turn in Israeli culture. I am offering nothing less than a paradigmatic shift in the hermeneutic as in the political–ethical sphere of regained Jewish sovereignty, a shift as radical as that performed by the Rabbis in the first centuries of the Common Era to cope with the loss of sovereignty. The comic critique can of course break the pathos of mythic thinking that is so dysfunctional for the democratic polity. But in this case, in retiring the supersessionist, apocalyptic impulses, we are also returning to the strictly "literal" construction of the *akeda*—to a comic, bounded, "bisociated" reading of the Abrahamic legacy—and one that, going forward, respects boundaries even when (especially when) it attempts to transgress them for purposes of achieving a "new normativity."

No one on the comic stage dies, no one is dispensable. Even if getting back to a "fundamentalist" reading of Genesis 22 as comedy appears quite daunting, it is, I believe, the only salvation we need.

AUTHOR'S NOTE: For responses to earlier drafts of this essay, I wish to thank the participants in the Berlin seminar on "After Testimony," and the participants in the Van Leer Seminar and Conference on "The *Shoah* and Globalization" (2007–9); for responses to later drafts, I am particularly grateful to Susan Rubin Suleiman, Ronit Peleg, Amos Goldberg, Marianne Hirsch, Michal Ben-Naftali, Sacvan Bercovitch, and Bernard Avishai.

Notes

1. Three of these dates refer to Israel's wars: the 1948 War of Independence, the June war of 1967, and the 1982 Israeli invasion of Lebanon (subsequently called the "first Lebanese War"); 1995 refers to the assassination of Yitzhak Rabin.

2. "*Galut*" is the Hebrew term for Jewish existence in the Diaspora after the destruction of the Second Temple in Jerusalem in 70 C.E. In contemporary Hebrew, *galut* designates the condition of Jews outside the State of Israel, specifically in this instance the Jews of Europe before or after the Holocaust.

3. Early literary mappings of the *nokhahim nifkadim*—the official term for "absent [Arab] presences"—include the stories of S. Yizhar, written before the smoke had cleared from the battles of 1948, and the fiction of A. B. Yehoshua ("Facing the Forest") and Benjamin Tammuz ("The Orchard"). See the afterword by David Shulman to a recent English edition of Yizhar's "Khirbet Khizeh," which highlights the perennial urgency of this classical Israeli text and its biblical intertexts in light of the ongoing violations in the occupied territories (121–22). The Palestinian poet Mahmoud Darwich relates in interviews in *La Palestine comme métaphore* (*Palestine as Metaphor*) that his native village of Birwa was "rayé de la carte dès notre départ forcé" (erased from the map after our forced departure). Admitting that he has not been able to reclaim his "personal patrimony," Darwich sings the collective history of the whole of Palestine (13, 9). But he also speaks (in Hebrew!) of his affinity for Hebrew poets, from H. N. Bialik to Y. Amichai.

4. There seem to be only one or two Arab or Palestinian writers per generation (the poet Salman Masalha and novelist/journalist Sayed Kashua are contemporary examples) who venture into Hebrew territory, but they signal the possibilities of a major cultural meeting ground.

5. From the Program Notes of Levin's *The Patriot*. The echo chamber in which the *shoah* and the Palestinian *naqba* resonate found one of its earliest dramatic expressions in Palestinian writer Ghassan Kanafani's story "Return to Haifa." A central character in that narrative is, through a quirk of fate, the son of "both" *shoah* survivors and *naqba* survivors. Many years after this story appeared, and long after Kanafani's death at the hands of the Israeli military, Israeli writer Sami Michael published *Yonim be-trafalgar* (*Pigeons in Trafalgar Square*), which implicitly continues Kanafani's narrative. See also the Arab Institute for Holocaust Research and Education, run by Khaled Mahameed. "The world will not see our *naqba* before we can feel for their Holocaust," Mahameed is quoted as saying in *The Heart of the Other*, an English language documentary on this institute: http://jerusalemnewyork.com/_wsn/page12.

6. "'When knowledge comes, memory comes too, little by little,'" writes Saul Friedländer, quoting Gustav Meyrink in the epigraph to his Holocaust memoir, *When Memory Comes*. I am suggesting that the process may also be reversed and that knowledge or wisdom comes to supersede memories that confine the individual or the collective to a vindictive, hermetic space. On the "theology" of memory and its implications for ethics and politics in contemporary Israel, see Adi Ophir, 12–50.

7. See also LaCapra's "empathic unsettlement" (78) and Martha Nussbaum, who has been at the forefront of a new discourse that defines empathy and compassion as an insistence on "similar possibilities," a refusal to regard the other as non-human (34–35).

8. *Not of This Time, Not of This Place* is the English title of an ambitious novel by

Yehuda Amichai that probes the haunted life of a young soldier in pre-1967 Israel who returns to his German hometown to search for his childhood love who had been lost in the Nazi inferno; meanwhile, his *doppelgänger,* who stays in Jerusalem, gets blown up when he steps on a mine on Mt. Scopus.

9. In exploring the discourse on the bystanders' indifference during the *shoah*, and its implications for other situations, Carolyn Dean points to the "institutionalized forms of everyday violence that normalize the dehumanization of specific groups of people in ways mostly invisible to others . . . who are not its targets, even when [such violence] takes place right in front of them" (95–97, 101).

10. The present tense hardly exists in classical Hebrew, and in the modern Hebrew imagination, the present—squeezed between the engorged past and the inflated future— has always had a hard time forging its own space. "Between the eve of the holiday and the final day / the holiday itself gets squeezed," writes Yehuda Amichai; "between/ longing for the past and longing for the future / the spirit is ground up as if by two heavy grindstones" ("I Foretell the Days of Yore," #7, *Open Closed Open,* 13).

11. This Mr. Mani is technically the first Mr. Mani, since the novel is a series of one-sided "conversations" that move backward in time. This is not the first time that A. B. Yehoshua explored this subject; see his novella, *Early in the Summer of 1970.*

12. Although construing the *akeda* as comedy is far from common, there are a few biblical critics who have suggested similar directions. See Whedbee, 64–93.

13. The technical Hebrew term for the sacrifice Abraham is commanded to bring is *olah*, the whole-burnt offering, which is translated in the Septuagint as "holocaustum": "Tolle filium tuum . . . Isaac . . . etque ibi offeres eum in holocaustum . . ." Clementine Vulgate, Gen. 22:2. The common Hebrew term *shoah,* used to designate the Nazi genocide of the Jews, is devoid of these sacrificial connotations, but failed to put the brakes on the sacrificial cult that evolved after 1967.

14. Much of the contemporary discourse on sacrificial elements in contemporary culture is a response to the work of René Girard, *Violence and the Sacred.* Eagleton's *Holy Terror* examines the modern manifestations of martyrs and scapegoats; his reading of the "suicide bomber" as expression of a sacrificial impulse touches on the same phenomena I am exploring here: "the terrorist is not the *pharmakos;* but he is created by it, and can only be defeated when justice is done to it" (140). I am insisting on the distinction between the sacrificial victim and what Giorgio Agamben calls *"homo sacer"*—common life that is deemed universally "sacred" and therefore "may be killed but not sacrificed" (114–15). See also Paul W. Kohn.

15. The longer version of this debate over ethics and obligation, with the *akeda* as point of departure, meanders through the philosophy of Emmanuel Levinas and Jean-François Lyotard.

16. In the original stage script, after Isaac asks his father why he is sad, the exchange ends with the following:

> ABRAHAM: I am thinking of the future generations. I wonder what will be when other fathers send their sons to be killed, what will save them?
> ISAAC: It's always possible that God will come and say, "lay not thy hand upon the lad."
> ABRAHAM: But you know that there is no God."
> (*Malkat ambatia,* 1970 stage script, n.p.)

Works Cited

Adorno, T. W. *Minima Moralia: Reflections from Damaged Life*. London: NLB, 1974.
——. *Prisms*. Translated by Samuel Weber and Shierry Weber. Cambridge, MA: MIT Press, 1967.
Agamben, Giorgio. *Homo Sacer: Sovereign Power and Bare Life*. Translated by Daniel Heller-Roazen. Stanford: Stanford University Press, 1998.
Allen, Woody. "The Scrolls." In *Without Feathers*. New York: Random House, 1975.
Alter, Robert. *Defenses of the Imagination: Jewish Writers and Modern Historical Crisis*. Philadelphia: Jewish Publication Society, 1977.
Amichai, Yehuda. *Not of This Time, Not of This Place*. Translated by Shlomo Katz. New York: Harper & Row, 1968.
——. *Open Closed Open*. Translated by Chana Bloch and Chana Kronfeld. New York: Harcourt, 2000.
——. *Poems of Jerusalem*. Bilingual edition. Tel Aviv: Schocken, 1987.
——. *Yehuda Amichai: A Life of Poetry, 1948–1994*. Translated by Benjamin Harshav and Barbara Harshav. New York: HarperPerennial, 1994.
Bartov, Omer. *The Jew in Cinema: From the Golem to Don't Touch My Holocaust*. Bloomington: Indiana University Press, 2005.
Benjamin, Walter. "Theses on the Philosophy of History." In *Illuminations: Essays and Reflections*. Edited and with an Introduction by Hannah Arendt. New York: Harcourt Brace Jovanovich, 1968: 253–64.
Bitton, Simone. *The Wall*. Film, 2005. http://www.wallthemovie.com/.
Brown, Wendy. *Walled States, Waning Sovereignty*. New York: Zone Books, 2010.
Caputo, John. *Against Ethics: Contributions to a Poetics of Obligation with Constant Reference to Deconstruction*. Bloomington: Indiana University Press, 1993.
Cavafy, Constantine P. *Collected Poems*, Revised edition. Edited by George Savidis. Translated by Edmund Keeley and Philip Sherrard. Princeton: Princeton University Press, 1992.
Coetzee, J. M. *Waiting for the Barbarians*. New York: Penguin, 1980.
Darwich, Mahmoud. *La Palestine comme métaphore* [*Palestine as Metaphor*]. Translated from Arabic by Elias Sanbar and from Hebrew by Simone Bitton. Paris: Sinbad, 1997.
Dean, Carolyn. *The Fragility of Empathy after the Holocaust*. Ithaca: Cornell University Press, 2004.
Derrida, Jacques. *The Gift of Death*. Translated by David Wills. Chicago: University of Chicago Press, 1995.
Eagleton, Terry. *Holy Terror*. Oxford: Oxford University Press, 2005.
——. *Sweet Violence: The Idea of the Tragic*. Oxford: Blackwell, 2003.
Ezrahi, Sidra DeKoven. "Acts of Impersonation: Barbaric Space as Theatre." In *Mirroring Evil: Nazi Imagery/Recent Art*. Catalogue of The Jewish Museum (NY) exhibition. Edited by Norman Kleeblatt: 17–38. New Brunswick, NJ: Rutgers University Press and The Jewish Museum, 2001.
——. *Booking Passage: Exile and Homecoming in the Modern Jewish Imagination*. Berkeley: University of California Press, 2000.
——. "Representing Auschwitz." *History and Memory* 7, no. 2 (Winter 1996): 121–54.
——. "Revisioning the Past: The Changing Legacy of the Holocaust in Hebrew Literature." *Salmagundi* (Fall 1985–Winter 1986): 245–70.

———. "'To what shall I compare thee?' Jerusalem as Ground Zero of the Hebrew Imagination." *PMLA* 122 (2007): 220–34.

Feldman, Yael. *Glory and Agony: Rewriting Isaac/Sacrifice in Tel Aviv.* Stanford: Stanford University Press, 2010.

Friedländer, Saul. *When Memory Comes.* Translated by Helen R. Lane. New York: Avon, 1979.

Girard, René. *Violence and the Sacred.* Translated by Patrick Henry. Baltimore: The Johns Hopkins University Press, 1977.

Goffart, Walter. *Rome's Fall and After.* London: The Hambledon Press, 1989.

Grossman, David. *See Under: Love.* Translated by Betsy Rosenberg. New York: Farrar, Straus and Giroux, 1989.

———. *Sleeping on a Wire: Conversations with Palestinians in Israel.* New York: Farrar, Straus and Giroux, 1993.

———. *Smile of the Lamb.* Translated by Betsy Rosenberg. New York: Farrar, Straus and Giroux, 1990.

———. *The Yellow Wind.* Translated by Haim Watzman. New York: Farrar, Straus and Giroux, 1988.

Inbari, Motti. *Jewish Fundamentalism and the Temple Mount: Who Will Build the Third Temple?* New York: SUNY Press, 2009.

Kafka, Franz. "Abraham." In *The Basic Kafka.* Introduction by Erich Heller. New York: Washington Square Press, 1979: 172. From letter to Robert Klopstock, June 1921. *Franz Kafka: Briefe 1902–1924. Franz Kafka/ Gesammelte Werke.* Hamburg: S. Fischer Verlag, 1966: 332.

Kanafani, Ghassan, Barbara Harlow, and Karen E. Riley. *Palestine's Children: Returning to Haifa and Other Stories.* Boulder, CO: Lynne Rienner, 2000.

Kartun-Blum, Ruth. *Profane Scriptures.* Cincinnati: Hebrew Union College, 1999.

Koestler, Arthur. *Insight and Outlook: An Inquiry into the Common Foundations of Science, Art and Social Ethics.* New York: Macmillan, 1949.

Kohn, Paul W. *Sacred Violence, Torture, Terror, and Sovereignty.* Ann Arbor: University of Michigan Press, 2008.

LaCapra, Dominick. *Writing History, Writing Trauma.* Baltimore: The Johns Hopkins University Press, 2001.

Levin, Hanokh. *Ha-patriot* [*The Patriot*]. *Malkat ambatia* [*Bathtub Queen*]. In *Ma ekhpat la-tzipor: satirot, ma'arkhonim, pizmonim I* [*What Difference Does it Make to the Bird? Satires, Revues and Songs I*]. Tel Aviv: Hakibbutz hameuhad, 1987.

———. *Malkat ambatia.* Stage script. 1970 (n.p.).

Michael, Sami. *Yonim be-trafalgar* [*Pigeons in Trafalgar Square*]. Tel Aviv: Am Oved, 2005.

Mintz, Alan. *Hurban: Responses to Catastrophe in Hebrew Literature.* New York: Columbia University Press, 1984.

Nussbaum, Martha. "Compassion: The Basic Social Emotion." *Social Philosophy and Policy* 1 (Winter 1996): 27–58.

Ophir, Adi. *Avodat ha-hoveh: masot al tarbut yisraelit ba-zman ha-ze* [*Working for the Present: Essays on Contemporary Israeli Culture*]. Tel Aviv: Hakibbutz hameuhad, 2001.

Pagis, Dan. "Autobiography," "Brothers," "Written in Pencil in the Sealed Boxcar." In *Points of Departure,* translated by Stephen Mitchell. Introduction by Robert Alter. Philadelphia: Jewish Publication Society, 1981: 3, 5, 23.

———. "An Opening to Satan." *Variable Directions.* Translated by Stephen Mitchell. San Francisco: North Point Press, 1989: 30.

Ravikovitch, Dahlia. *Hovering at a Low Altitude: The Collected Poetry of Dahlia Ravikovitch.* Translated by Chana Bloch and Chana Kronfeld. New York: W. W. Norton, 2009.

Raz-Krakotzkin, Amnon."Bein brit shalom u-vein beit ha-mikdash" ["Between Brit Shalom and the Temple"]. *Teoria u-vikoret* [*Theory and Criticism*] 20 (2002): 387–413.

———. "Galut be-tokh ribonut: le-vikoret 'shlilat ha-gola' ba-tarbut ha-yisraelit" ["Exile within a Sovereign State: Towards a Critique of 'Negation of Exile' in Israeli Culture"]. *Teoria u-vikoret* [*Theory and Criticism*] 4 (1993): 23–55, and 5 (1994): 113–32.

Rokem, Freddie Rokem. *Performing History: Theatrical Representations of the Past in Contemporary Theatre.* Iowa City: University of Iowa Press, 2000.

Rothberg, Michael. *Traumatic Realism: The Demands of Holocaust Representation.* Minneapolis: University of Minnesota Press, 2000.

Saposnik, Arieh Bruce. "Wailing Walls and Iron Walls: The Wailing Wall as Sacred Symbol in Zionist National Iconography." In *1929: Mapping the Jewish World.* Edited by Gennady Estraikh and Hasia Diner. New York: New York University Press, 2010.

Shammas, Anton. *Arabesques.* Translated by Vivian Eden. New York: Harper and Row, 1988.

Slyomovics, Susan. *The Object of Memory: Arab and Jew Narrate the Palestinian Village.* Philadelphia: University of Pennsylvania Press, 1998.

Spiegel, Shalom. *The Last Trial: On the Legends and Lore of the Command to Abraham to Offer Isaac as a Sacrifice.* Springfield, NJ: Behrman House, 1979.

Tammuz, Benjamin. *The Orchard.* Translated by Richard Flantz. Providence, RI: Copper Beach Books, 1984.

Whedbee, J. William. *The Bible and the Comic Vision.* Cambridge: Cambridge University Press, 1998.

Yehoshua, A. B. *Early in the Summer of 1970.* Translated by M. Arad and P. Shrier. New York: Doubleday, 1977.

———. "Facing the Forests." In *Three Days and a Child.* Translated by Miriam Arad. London: Peter Owen, 1970.

———. "Interview." *Haaretz* Magazine (March 19, 2004): 10–11.

———. *Mr. Mani.* Translated by Hillel Halkin. New York: Doubleday, 1992.

———. "Mr. Mani and the Akedah." Translated by Rivka Hadari and Amnon Hadari. *Judaism* (Winter 2001). http://findarticles.com/p/articles/mi_m0411/is_5_49/ai_73180736.

Yizhar, S. *Khirbet Khizeh.* Translated by Nicholas de Lange and Yaacob Dwek. Jerusalem: Ibis Editions, 2008.

Zertal, Idith. *Israel's Holocaust and the Politics of Nationhood.* Translated by Chaya Galai. Cambridge: Cambridge University Press, 2005.

CHAPTER 14

The Melancholy Generation

Grossman's Book of Interior Grammar

DAPHNA ERDINAST-VULCAN

I.

The state of Israel rose from the ashes of the Jewish people of Europe in the most literal and blood-chilling sense, out of a desperate need for communal survival, under the motto "never again." But the first fifteen years which followed the establishment of the state were marked by a "pact of silence" that sealed off the present from the immediate past: the silence of those who knew, and the silence of those who did not want to know; the silence of survivors who could not break through the unspeakable horrors or who desperately tried to protect own their children from that devastating knowledge; and the silence of people who could not face what could not possibly be comprehended, who felt guilty at their own survival and—worst of all—deeply ashamed at the thought of their people who had been—to use the expression current at the time—"led like lambs to the slaughter."

Nowhere is the poverty of our vocabulary more apparent than when we try to articulate the unspeakable. The Shoah, as Yolanda Gampel writes, is "analogous to nothing"; it cannot be "assimilated into the individual's range of inner representations" ("Interminable Uncanniness" 86). In the face of this enormity, when the devastation is so total as to fill up the entire world and extend to its furthest horizons, one can make a case for repression, rather than "working through," as the only viable response. The pact of silence about the Holocaust can also be understood as an unconscious collective strategy of survival through repression: the small Jewish community in Israel could not carry the burden of knowledge; it could not get sucked into the black hole of the Holocaust. It had to create, perhaps to fabricate, the kind of communal identity and myths that would empower rather than weaken it in the struggle for its very existence. And it was thus that the formative years of my own generation, native children of the young state, whose parents were not Holocaust survivors, and who grew into adolescence in the 1960s, were lived in the benign shadow of an overwhelming desire for normality. We were tertiary characters, safely removed from the edge of the gaping abyss. In the implicit hierarchy of testimonial authority, we haven't earned the right to say anything about it. And yet we, too, are a generation of the Holocaust.

We were the lucky ones. Coming back from school, we would sit at the kitchen table with our homework assignments. The radio was always on, a background noise inseparable from the pattern on the formica top of the dining table and the smell of frying onions or scorched eggplants. The lunchtime radio programs were regular and invariable: first came the daily program for "the search of missing relatives": messages posted by Holocaust survivors giving out bare details of their loved ones, in the desperate, mad hope that they had somehow, by some miracle, managed to escape: name, place, and date of birth, and sometimes the names of their parents. The announcements were uniformly laconic: "last seen," "anyone who has any information of the whereabouts," "please get in touch." There were odd-sounding names that recurred in the messages like encoded signals: Warsaw, Bialistock, Lublin; Auschwitz, Dachau, Birkenau. This broadcast was immediately followed by the merry opening tune of "Out on the Town This Evening," an entertainment guide made up of taped pieces of advertised plays, mostly comic dialogues and recorded laughter or applause. Then we heard the one o'clock news bulletin. And then we had our lunch. Life was perfectly normal.

But our post-Holocaust normality could be attained only at the cost of a nearly complete severance of our own identity from that of the Jewish, Diasporic past. In adolescence, we saw ourselves as Israeli rather than Jewish, as natives of the place, brought up on the heroic myths of the reclamation of the land, the struggle for independence, the few-against-the-many. We believed we had discarded 2,000 years of uprooted, Diasporic existence that had come to its inevitable conclusion in the crematoria. After millennia of spiritual existence, we finally had a body and a home. When we thought of our historical heritage, it was the exotic ancient people of the Bible we had in mind, not the human wrecks who had been "there," in what came to be known after the Eichman trial as "the other planet."

Our very entitlement to a generational identity is premised on this distinction, heavily marked and unmistakable, between the Diasporic/Jewish
and the Israeli/Zionist mode of being. This collective, new identity was, to
borrow the cultural diagnosis of Pierre Nora, "a break with and subversion of
the past," a declaration of freedom from the "laws of filiation and the require-
ments of continuity" (515). This symbolic rupture with the past entailed,
as it always does, "a secret acquiescence on the part of the older generation in its own failure, its own incompleteness, its members' own individual self-destruction." It was, in fact, a "drive for fulfillment by proxy," and
a "summons to complete the fathers' work by killing them off" (518). Our
generational self-consciousness was both "imbued with history to its very
core" and "crushed by history's weight" (524), grounded in "a sense of lack,
something in the nature of a mourning," and held together by a "common, a
painful, never-ending fantasy" (525) of giving birth to ourselves.

The cultural transmission of the Holocaust and its literary articulations
were mediated, as Yael Feldman observes, through "mythization, collectiv-
ization, ritualization; in short, all processes that would embed the particular
within the general and surrender the individual to the community—thereby
endowing the narrative with a meaningful, life-affirming closure" (229). It
was the story of heroic partisans and ghetto fighters, a story of resistance and
pride, which was

> the first story we were told—in public ceremonies, in school anthologies,
> in radio programs—and it was clearly exhilarating despite its tragic dimen-
> sions. It told of the victory of the spirit; it was easy to identify with; it was
> protective. Endowing loss and death with meaning, with a purpose, this
> story made our world a good place to grow up in. And of course it was
> totally Hebraic. Everyone in this story spoke Hebrew: the ghetto mother
> singing a lullaby in the shadow of Ponar, the leaders of the Jewish resis-
> tance, and even the Polish underground. . . . The language was the message.
> It was our story: another link in the Hebrew-Israel self-representation,
> emplotted in a tale of a goal-oriented, victorious struggle. (224)

It was only in the 1980s that the tide had turned. Following a series of
ideological crises in the wake of the 1973 War and the Lebanon War in 1982,
Israeli literature broke away from this paradigm of silence, assimilation, and
suppression, and began the process of deconstructing the arch-opposition
between Jew and Israeli. Oddly, perhaps, the break was made by "native
novelists with no personal or direct familial experience of the Shoah," who
"recast the Shoah" in a "new script" in an attempt to release it "from the

shackles of the collective and reclaim it as a subjective experience" (Feldman 234–35, 236).[1] Since the 1980s the Holocaust has become a major preoccupation of Israeli literature and culture, a phantom, or—to use the Yiddish expression—a *dybbuck* that has come back to haunt the collective consciousness (Sicher 56–60).

This eruption of the Holocaust after two decades of virtual silence can be understood as a cultural version of what psychologists recognize as an intergenerational transmission of trauma. The fluidity of psychic borders, evident in studies of the second and third generations of survivors who have the reservoirs of their parents' untold story, has generated terms such as "double realities" (Kestenberg 788), "radioactive identification" (Gampel, "Thoughts about the Transmission" *passim,* and "Interminable Uncanniness" 95), "deposited representations" and "psychological genes" (Volkan and Vamik 258–59, 270–71)—strikingly apt for the description of this collective literary awakening as well. "All children," Yolanda Gampel writes, "act out a scenario of which they have no knowledge, a scenario that is not theirs but, in fact, belongs to the history of their families, and especially of those that have survived the Holcaust" ("Daughter of Silence" 120).[2]

For those of us who were not second and third generation, the trauma was not the stark fact of the Holocaust but the imperative of repression that was transmitted through the split consciousness of our parents, the great divide between the Jewish/Diasporic and the Israeli modes of being. That split may have been necessary for our survival and protection: it enabled us to consign an impossible mourning to collective "memory sites"; it allowed us to sever ourselves from the line of filiation, and granted us an almost normal life. Almost, but not quite. By the mid-1980s it became clear that we, too, were radioactively infected.

II.

Five years after the 1986 publication of David Grossman's *See Under: Love,* the definitive Shoah novel of Israeli literature, Grossman published *The Book of Intimate Grammar,* a story of adolescence in 1960s Jerusalem, spanning several years in the life of Aron Kleinfeld, a bright, sensitive boy, from about a year-and-a-half before his Bar Mitzvah to the age of sixteen.[3] Unlike Grossman's previous work, this novel does not relate to the Holocaust in any obvious way. In fact, the glaring absence of references to this black hole in a narrative that takes place less than two decades after the Shoah might have raised some serious questions as to its historical authenticity: for us, the generation of the 1960s, the very air we breathed was made of those dark invisible particles, oblique and insidious reminders of what, paradoxically but powerfully, had to be forgotten. I would suggest, however, that far from a strategy of avoidance or suppression, what the novel offers is a poignant inscription of a dead end in the brief history of the Jewish people after the Holocaust, a cultural pathology born out of the desperate need for communal recovery and normalization.

The Book of Interior Grammar has been widely read—with some encouragement from the author himself—as a bildungsroman or a kunstlerroman, a "portrait of the artist" as a young adolescent. But Aron Kleinfeld, as his surname implies, does not grow up. He remains as small as a ten-year old, his voice does not break, and he does not go through puberty, right to the very end of the novel. He remains trapped in the body of a little boy, frozen in time. Aron's story is, in fact, an anti-bildungsroman, a story of arrested growth, of non-continuity.

No realistic, medical, or genetic explanation is offered to account for what seems to be an evil spell, a curse that has interrupted the natural process of maturation and growth. At some point the mother relates to it as part of the give-and-take of destiny and offers up the grandmother in exchange for the removal of the curse. Aron, too, sometimes perceives himself as a freak of nature and forms unspoken alliances with other "freaks": David Lipschitz, the slow albino kid who is later discreetly removed and transferred to an institution (32–33, 54); Edna Bloom, the lonely, artistic spinster who plays the piano, fills up her flat with artifacts, statuettes, and reproductions, and finally goes mad; and Lilly, the wild, demented grandmother who dreams of her bohemian youth as a cabaret dancer in Poland, embroiders gaudy, obscenely exotic pillowcases that no one would buy, and obstinately refuses to die.

At the same time, however, Aron is intensely reluctant to grow up. When his mother lovingly talks of his becoming a man, and he is reminded of the promise of the father's shaving kit, "the army shaving kit with the razor and the shaving soap and the little tray he used in the Sinai campaign" passing on to him as a special gift for his coming of age (18), he feels alienated and depressed, "as though she wanted to lock him inside the future and jangle the keys in his face" (24). And so, when his mother despairs of his ever growing up and maliciously turns on him in her brutal but acutely intuitive way, hissing "you're doing this to us deliberately" (49), she is not entirely wrong. It is the central thesis of this essay that Aron's arrested growth is another way of speaking the unspeakable, both a symptom of pathology and a mode of ideological resistance. It is, to put it briefly, a refusal of the kind of suppression that has made it possible for the Jewish people to recreate itself in Israel. To understand this apparent paradox, I would now turn to the metaphychologi-cal theory of Nicolas Abraham and Maria Torok, which hovers—somewhat uneasily, but always suggestively—between psychoanalysis and literature and may offer some insights as to the dynamics of Grossman's novel and to what follows "after testimony."

The epigraph to the novel is a sentence from Rilke's *Letters to a Young Poet:* "Those who live [with?] the secret falsely, wickedly—and there are many of those—lose it only for themselves, but pass it on unknowingly, as one passes on a sealed letter."[4] Indeed, there are many secrets in this novel: the secret of the mentally retarded cousin who had been put away in an insti-tution by her parents (115); the mother's attempts to conceal the demented grandmother, the family's shame (111); the secret history of the father's imprisonment and escape. During the sad Bar Mitzvah celebration, Aron realizes that "everyone knew everyone else's secrets, everyone was a hostage in someone else's hands, at their mercy or in their cruelty. . . . The air was full of tiny darts, phrases waiting to burst with poison, compliments with false bottoms, the caress of secrets shared, and carefully circumvented top-ics" (121).

But these are merely the secrets one would find in any society, skeletons in the cupboard, dirty family linen, secrets born out of the need to keep up appearances and remain within the boundaries of respectability. I would suggest that the kind of secret to which the epigraph alludes, the secret that is unknowingly passed on to others "like a sealed letter," is of an entirely different substance and magnitude, much closer to the concept developed by Abraham and Torok. Rather than a hushed-up fact, or some dark story that may come to light, the secret is "a trauma whose very occurrence and devastating emotional consequences are entombed and thereby consigned to internal silence, albeit unwittingly, by the sufferers themselves. . . . It desig-nates an internal psychic splitting" (Nicolas Rand, Editor's Note on "cryptic mourning and secret love" 99–100). The buried secret relates to a segment of reality that is "untellable and therefore inaccessible to the gradual, assimi-lative work of mourning." This unconscious refusal to mourn produces "a sealed-off psychic place, a crypt in the ego . . . comparable to the forma-tion of a cocoon around the chrysalis" (Abraham and Torok, "'The Lost Object-Me'" 141).[5] This psychic formation is variously called in Abraham and Torok's work "the illness of mourning," "melancholia," "incorporation," or "preservative repression." As we shall see, all of these terms are relevant to our discussion: "The words that cannot be uttered, the scenes that cannot be recalled, the tears that cannot be shed—everything will be swallowed along with the trauma that led to the loss. Swallowed and preserved. Inexpressible mourning erects a secret tomb inside the subject. The objectal correlative of the loss is buried alive in the crypt as a full-fledged person, complete with its own topography" (Abraham and Torok, "Mourning or Melancholia" 130).

Being buried alive, incarcerated in a box, shut up inside a sealed coffin, or imprisoned in a cave are recurrent motifs in Aron's story: the story of a young blacksmith in Armenia who had been buried alive (23), the spy in the suitcase (50); Rabbi Yohanan Ben-Zakai who was smuggled out of Jerusalem in a coffin (39), and—most prominently—the Houdini act, which Aaron often performs for his friends at school parties (37, 44, 50, 54, 91, 98, 107, 148). All of these stories involve the image of enclosure inside a crypt and a fantasy of escape, which is also a fantasy of rebirth. "All through the disaster there had been a comforting aura about him, a corridor of hope, the secret wish of a tunnel from which he would emerge a new and different being, and maybe somewhere, amid the darkness and confusion, a miracle would occur, an invisible hand would reach out and switch the suitcase, and wave a wand and change the secret orders, so that when Aron reached the light he would meet the new him out there" (280).

Aron Kleinfeld is a *cryptophore,* the carrier of a secret made up of unspeakable words. But, like Oscar Mazareth in Gunter Grass's *The Tin Drum,* or Trudy Montag in Ursula Hegi's *Stones from the River* (1995), he carries in his stunted body both the pathology and the potential resistance of an entire generation. Abraham and Torok's theory of the "transgenerational phantom" is, once again, relevant in this context, not only for its account of the unconscious transmission of private trauma, but also in its explanatory potency in relation to the split consciousness of Israeli culture, the form of generational melancholia that has developed as a substitute for the impossible mourning (see Nicolas Abraham's "Notes on the Phantom" 173–75; and Maria Torok's "Story of Fear" 181). Having broken with the Diasporic past for the sake of normality and survival, the native Israeli generation has cut off the line of filiation. Orphaned of its heritage, it has had to give birth to itself, to invent itself. The paradigmatic literary inscription of this autochtonous fantasy is the elegiac opening sentence of Moshe Shamir's semi-autobiographical novel, *Be-mo Yadav:* "Elic was born from the sea."[6] (1). The myth of the young *sabra* is made up of such flimsy stuff: the regime of normality, the protective cocoon of young Israelis, has become a crypt, harboring the phantom of the discarded Jewish self.

Recalling Freud's "Studies on Hysteria" (1895), whose point of departure is the three-way exchange between the psychic, the verbal, and the bodily, Abraham and Torok suggest that the messages between these layers of subjectivity move in both directions, in a process of "dual inscription" ("Conceptual Renewal" 91), allowing psychosomatics or "endocryptic" patients, who "have no way of indirectly evoking the contents of their crypt," to convert the psychic into the somatic ("Self-to-Self Affliction" 163–64). Aron's arrested growth is also a literalization or a somatization of language. The "interior grammar" of the body is the inscription of the psyche. The message, I would reiterate, is not only a private pathology: it is a single-handed challenge to the regime of normality, which seems to operate in collusion with the laws of nature, with the biological and cultural imperatives of intergenerational continuity, sexuality, and filiation. The arrested body becomes a text of refusal.

Aron's fascination with the English present continuous tense, which does not exist in Hebrew, is an obvious instance of this refusal:

> Last year in English class they learned the present continuous. Aron was thrilled, I am go–eeing, I em sleep–eeing. You don't have that *eeng* tense in Hebrew. . . . It was like being in a glass bubble. . . . And inside you feel private, intimate, and the people watching you, pressing their faces against the bubble, wonder what's going on; they stand on the outside looking in, puzzles and sweaty and filthy, and again he asks himself what it will be like when his bar mitzvah comes around in a year and a half, will he start growing those stiff black hairs all over. . . . and he vows that even when he's big and hairy some day, with coarse skin like Pap and other men have. . . . he will still whisper, at least once a day, I am go–eeng; I am play–eeng; I am Aron–eeng; and that way he will always remember the individual Aron beneath the generalities. (36–37; see also 92)

Being an individual, being himself—as opposed to the collective law-abiding subject—is also linked to the refusal of filiation and of the progression of time and the inevitability of growth and decline. Time itself is out of joint.[7]

Aron's vision of himself is shadowed by recurrent images of a sleeping boy, a curled-up fetus, a cocooned chrysalis. Forced by his mother to try on the outgrown clothes of his cousin Giora (who has matured into an all-Israeli, tall adolescent), he looks at himself in the mirror and has a vision of "little white boy, so white he was almost blue" sailing "out into a craggy moonscape," and of the fetus from science lab floating in formaldehyde, "slowly decomposing and blinking its tadpole eyes" (48).

As his friends grow up and lose interest in make-believe, spy games, and escape acts, Aron is left behind, trapped in his stunted body. He curls up around himself and whispers at the imagined urging of Gideon's voice: "No, no, I can't come yet. . . . You see, I'm going away for a while, I'm entering the chrysalis phase of my disaster, Aroning into a cocoon" (108). At the close of the novel, he will curl up in a fetal position inside an old derelict refrigerator, in a final gesture of refusal. Although Grossman himself has claimed in interviews that this is a prelude to a rebirth of the artist, this last scene, with everything that has led to it, is much more powerfully suggestive of suicide. Aron's last Houdini act, performed with no audience, literally puts the lid on the escape fantasy. The cocooned self is invariably a stillborn (Abraham and Torok, "Self-to-Self Affliction 21, 48), a buried phantom that cannot come to light.

The ostensible normality of the "model family" is questioned at the very beginning of the story, at the first intimation of Aron's "curse." On the same evening when he is told to try on last year's old boots and has to face his mother's dismay as she realizes that he has not outgrown them, Aron discovers in one of his parents' drawers a stack of pornographic cards covered with greasy finger marks, which he suspects of having been put there by some unknown spy, traitor, or an enemy agent. The family supper scene turns into a nightmare in Aron's mind: "From the pantry he watched them sit down to supper, reflecting how cozy the kitchen was at times like this, with everyone eating and talking at once, but the wistful scene dissolved before his eyes, and an arctic fog descended, full of ghoulish apparitions, naked bodies, tangled limbs, a dog on top of a woman; he suddenly felt the blood drain from his hand as he picked a boot up and reached into the lining with its smell of old fur" (26). As the familiar domestic scene becomes a terrifying inferno, the *heimlich* turns into the *unheimlich*. The Freudian Uncanny makes its first appearance.

Most readings of the novel have focused on the nearly monstrous figure of the mother, who ruthlessly controls her family in what seems like a crude parody of the proverbial Jewish mother. I would suggest, however, that the question of paternity, inversely related to any paternal presence in the lives of the boys in this perfectly normal neighborhood, is far more significant in this text. Unlike the literally or virtually absent parental figures in the lives of his friends (Gideon's father, who forms an odd alliance with Aron, is probably a latent homosexual and seems to be indifferently passive when his wife is drawn into an affair with their lodger; and Zacky's father works in Africa and is away throughout his son's adolescence, while his wife entertains other men), Aron's father is almost unbearably present in his son's life, but cannot form a bond of paternity with him. Their alienation is profoundly temperamental: the father, who has managed to escape his imprisonment in the Russian taiga and survive against all odds, is an all-masculine, intensely physical, and inarticulate character, who has nothing but contempt for intellectuals and artists—"inallactuals," as he mockingly calls them (4, 16–17, 69)—and what he sees as their inherent weakness. The son—artistic, musical, wildly imaginative, and intellectually curious—is both incomprehensible and disappointing for this man, who sometimes acts as a surrogate father for Zacky, the "normal" boy (13, 22, 63).

This is not only a personal and temperamental opposition. Both of Aron's parents are themselves orphans who have managed to survive by their wits (310), and the history of the family begins with the anecdote of the mother as a young woman who had sold her father's cherished prayer book—the Venice Machzor—in order to feed the starving refugee into a virile manhood and turn him into the father of her children (137). The meaning of this transaction goes far beyond that of the family: it is deeply rooted in the equation of Zionism with the "normalization" of the Jewish people. The father's disdain of bookishness and art; the mother's prohibition on the use of Polish and her censorship of the father's past (135, 220); the parents' refusal to replace Aron's broken guitar or let him take music lessons (112, 219); the consignment of books to the storage loft (112, 128)—anything associated with the Jewish, Diasporic identity, anything that smacks of spirituality, art, and learning, is perceived as an obstacle to survival and suppressed under the regime of normality.

The complicated relationship between Aron and his father is played out in the sea:

Papa was a terrific swimmer, you could always tell he was in the water by his powerful kicking and splashing and the pranks he played, like diving down and attacking their card friends. . . . Aron was very careful never to go in the water while Papa was there, he had secretly decided that only one of them should be in the water at a time; besides, he suspected pap liked to piss in the sea, and even when Aron came out and sat on the sand, he felt as if Pap's piss had followed him; and once, in the middle of a tranquil swim, far away from the crowd, just him and the open sky, he had a sudden apprehension that something was chasing him, he knew it couldn't be, that he was imagining things, but still he felt it slithering beneath the waves; at first he thought Papa was down there, trying to scare him, which made him panic and kick and splash and swallow water, but then something rough and rubbery circled his waist like a sinewy arm, or the trunk of a giant elephant, trying to pull him down, and when he crawled up on the shore, he knew he hadn't imagined it, that something very strange had happened in the sea. . . . and he searched for Papa but couldn't see him, he was reading

the paper under a beach umbrella, and he didn't even look up when Aron
shuffled over wrapped in a towel and sat shivering beside him and said,
It was just a cramp, and when Papa didn't answer, Aron sobbed and said,
It could have happened to anyone, but still papa wouldn't look at him, he
merely rolled over with his face in the paper. (44–45)

An echo of this near-drowning scene is later evoked when, during his last
vacation in Tel-Aviv, Aron talks his cousin Giora and his friends into building a raft, which sinks right away: "the children bailed out and scrambled
ashore, looking stunned and devastated. There was one scary moment, when
Aron and Giora were sucked into an eddy together, and Aron was almost
sure Giora had pushed him down to save himself. The wind blew cold, and
the children shivered. No one actually blamed him outright, but Aron felt as
though a big hand had just snuffed out the candle in his darkened cell" (47).
He will later go back to this episode in his mind, time and again, and wonder
whether this was not "the beginning of everything" (47, 66, 117). The recurrence of this scene, being held under water in the grip of a stronger man—
first the father and then the grown-up, all-Israeli cousin—is telling: when we
recall Elic, the paradigmatic *sabra,* who was "born from the sea," it appears
that Aron's near-drowning scene is indeed "the beginning of everything."

When Aron's friends and cousin discover sex and seem to be obsessed
with nothing else, Aron remains oblivious, wondering about the meaning
of those signs and signals that seem to be part of an alien language (63–65).
His realization of his parents' sexuality hits him like lightning: "In a flash
he understood: Papa's hand reached out of the waves, dripping with tangled
seaweed. They were unmistakably his father's hand's dangling ape-like at
his side, and now he imagined them stroking his hair, tending to the fig
tree, leaving greasy fingerprints on the pictures . . ." (69–70; see also 118). In
the ensuing fight with Giora, Aron is beaten up. Going back to Jerusalem,
past the rusty auto wrecks left by the roadside to commemorate the heroes
of the War of Independence, he is sick and imagines that the other passengers on the bus accuse him of "being disrespectful to our valiant dead,"
of not being patriotic. The proximity of these incidents—the realization of
his father's sexuality, the painful defeat in the fight with Giora, the sense of
alienation from the communal national ethos—is not only temporal. When
Aron finally gets home, he realizes that the plans his parents had made for
his grandiose Bar Mitzvah—the ritual coming of age—have been put aside
(60, 83–84).

But this is not a paradigmatic, oedipal situation. Significantly, the father
is portrayed as a potential healer of almost supernatural powers on more

than one occasion. He saves a blind kitten and brings it back to life by feeding it gently and patiently through a dropper (87); he tries to heal the sick fig
tree by cleaning its sores and rubbing the scars with a medicinal ointment for
seven days (9–15). And finally, in one of the most powerful and longest episodes in this novel, he is chosen by Edna to demolish the walls of her dainty,
virginal flat, to awaken her into a sensual life (128–217). Edna—a feminine
counterpart of Aron—is a "wisp of a woman, floating embryonically in her
sac of skin," hungrily looking at the powerful body of the father, and then
falling asleep, "winding around herself as though she had no bones," sucking
her thumb "with a dreamy, faraway look on her face" (135, 140). She is forty,
and desperately alone. The demolition of the walls is her last gift to herself in
an attempt to cross over the threshold to a normal life, from sterile, hyper-
refined gentility into a bodily existence. Aron's father, bull-like and virile,
becomes a savior figure (144).

Throughout these healing episodes, the father is perceived as distinctly
un-Jewish. Seen from the back when he is up on the fig tree, he is a giant with
"hefty legs," a "thick neck" and a "fleshy nape." The adjective used by Grossman to describe the back of the father's neck—untranslatable, perhaps—is
"*aarel*," which means "non-Jewish" and literally—"uncircumcised" (17; in
the original Hebrew 22).[8] Indeed, there are scattered suggestions in the novel
that he might, in fact, have been born to a non-Jewish father. When the
half-demented grandmother tells her grandchildren of her bohemian life
as a cabaret dancer and her many "cavaliers" before the war in Poland, she
seems to be quite vague about the paternity of her son whom she calls Mau-
ritzy, after a particularly dashing Polish officer (76). "Back in Poland he was
strong . . . the Polacks never guessed he was a Jidovksy" (76–77). And Edna's
perception of this man, who is so powerfully sensual and masculine, is satu-
rated with pagan, mythical allusions (142, 144, 162, 175). The association of
the father's healing powers and his non-Jewish, corporeal quality is a distinct
echo of the conception of Zionism as a project of healing the extraterrito-
rial, disembodied, and uprooted Jewish people; of making them normal, like
other people.

During the drama that develops between the father and the two women,
the intense erotic rivalry between the mother and Edna takes the form of a
feeding competition, as they stuff the father in turns with a variety of meat
dishes and heaps of exotic delicacies. In the midst of this Rabelaisian drama,
Aron, the vegetarian, is badly constipated and sleeps through the afternoons,
as if hibernating. He seems to be suspended, curled up on bed with his swol-
len belly, his "little pregnancy," waiting to give birth to himself (187–89), or
to a spectral twin (222). At the rage of his parents at his refusal to eat "so that

he can grow up to be normal" (201), Aron "shuts his ears from inside, Aron-ing slowly down, till suddenly they're speaking a language he doesn't under-stand" (201). Having the meat forced down his throat, he imagines himself as a martyr, acting out the recurrent scenario of Jewish history.

In the regime of normality, the freaks are defeated. Edna's flat is entirely demolished, and Edna herself, finally out of her virginal chrysalis, but demented rather than liberated, is turned into a catalyst for a rekindling of the erotic bond between the parents. As Edna is led away from the ruins of her flat, Aron's mother is pregnant again, and Aron listens as she anxiously interrogates the demented grandmother about the family history: "Leibaleh's brother, what's-his-name, the one you told us about who was killed by the Germans, remember? . . . The one you said there was something wrong with, do you remember what it was? What? Show me by nodding. Was he, *eppes,* deaf? Was he epileptic? If yes, nod; was he crippled from polio? Was he a midget?. . . . An albino?. . . . Feeble-minded?" (326). This interrogation takes place as the mother is unraveling Aron's sweater so that she can reuse the wool for another knitting project, perhaps for the baby who will take Aron's place, who will eat meat, grow up normal, and perpetuate the family line (318).

Aron's suicide, his final cocooning of himself, follows after the eve of Independence Day, a time of collective celebration, when he finds himself amidst the dancing crowds, at the lowest ebb of his own isolation. It is also, significantly, the eve of the 1967 War, the Six-Day War, which was perceived at the time as a glorious victory of the few-against-the-many—the culmina-tion of the *sabra* myth—and which turned out to be a tragic turning point in the short history of Israeli society. For Aron, at this moment of collective unity, everything is falling apart (298). His parents have given up on him. His friends have gone ahead and grown up, leaving him behind.

Losing all hope for a miraculous metamorphosis that would make him normal, Aron now knows "from the pangs in his heart and the coded com-munications, the idiom of his most intimate grammar, that this was no tem-porary delay, it was becoming, God forbid, the thing itself, and just as he had felt *chosen* somehow before his problem started, now he felt chosen, too, same difference, which gave his disaster a dark and twisted logic: it was *his* disaster, out of which he had been fashioned" (303). The Jewish, Disaporic echoes of this interior, private monologue are loud and clear, and the land-scape of Aron's mind at that moment of final resignation is a post-Holocaust landscape: "the tender boy, misty and white, fades out as he slithers over the chilly ash-or-frost-dabbled earth, creeping cautiously over the crimpled ter-rain and the pearly-gray craters" (307).

III.

Abraham and Torok's metapsychological theory begins with a distinction between Ferenzi's concept of "introjection"—a working-through of loss in a process of "naming," a transition from the lost object to its linguistic, semiotic or symbolic representation—and their own concept of "incorporation," which moves in the opposite direction, through the literalization of language in "oral-cannibalistic and anal-evacuative processes" (Torok, "The Illness of Mourning and the Fantasy of the Exquisite Corpse" 111), a de-metaphorization of both food and excrement (Abraham and Torok, "Mourning or Melancholia" 131–32). When words fail, an imaginary thing is inserted into the mouth (128–29). The relevance of this description to the Kleinfeld's household, endlessly preoccupied with what goes in and out of the body—with food, constipation, diarrhea, gaining and losing weight—is obvious, literal, and concrete (260).

But if melancholia, the "illness of mourning," is a loss of language, a somatization and literalization of meaning, the cure may be found in an inverse process of re-metaphorization that would recover the power of words. This is where the metafictional aspects of the novel take over (somewhat heavy-handedly, perhaps). For Aron, the innocent narrator, is both a scapegoat and an authorial figure, a potential writer who takes on the deadly task of making the silence speak. No wonder, then, that the father flies into a rage when Aron innocently provides the term "salt cellar" as a correction of the father's "whatsit." The eruption of physical violence is, in fact, a response to what this inarticulate, intensely corporeal man intuitively perceives as the ultimate gesture of defiance: the missing word is the son's only weapon, but the challenge is real enough (200–202, 224).

At a moment of intense pain, Aron remembers the tiny piece of golden thread given to him by his demented grandmother as though it were a precious family heirloom (58–59). The grandmother, too, is a freak of nature, an artist who refuses to be domesticated and civilized by the mother (74, 80). She, too, has resisted the laws of time and nature and remained obstinately alive, "clogging up the bowels of the death" (204). The golden thread is gone. It is merely a word now, but still—in Aron's mind—a token of resistance to normality.

The question is whether that mouth could manage a word like "thread," and Aron pictures a golden thread shining in the sunlight, dripping honey, like a guitar string still aquiver with the melody a moment after it was strummed. Threa-d, murmurs Aron with fine-drawn lips, with deep devotion, threa-d, like a string plucked out of his depths, lyrical and sweet, but airy too, and hazy like the halos around those people in his negatives, and he can easily slip through any crack, through a needle's eye. He tilts his head, eyes shut, lips parted like the mouth of an urn, uttering "Thread," like the whistle of the wind, gentle but cutting, and he smiles to himself: Papa can't get in, like a thread with a knot at the end. (225)

The last-ditch recovery of the magic of words and their power climaxes in a moment of pain and release, as Aron injures himself with the potato peeling knife and—still bleeding—empties himself on the kitchen floor violently and uncontrollably in front of his horrified parents. At the moment of release, he feels that he is "giving birth to himself, a small, beloved, stinking self; rid at last of the horrible anguish, the harsh dark secret, not his own, he had been forced to keep inside" (226–27). It is—to return to Abraham and Torok—the secret of what cannot be named and mourned, because if it were, "the whole world would be swallowed up in this cataclysm," whose emergence in words may lead to madness ("The Topography of Reality" 158, 159–60). But the golden thread, now turned into a word and thus into an emblem of continuity, becomes an erotic gift:

> Certain words, if you know how to pronounce them in a special way, not from the outside but as though you were calling their names, right away they turn to you, they show you their pink penetralia, they purr to you and they're yours, they'll do anything you want; take "bell," for instance, he rolls it over his tongue as though tasting it for the first time ever, "bellll," or "honeysuckle," or "lion" or "legend" or "coal" or "melody" or "gleam" or "velvet," melting on his tongue, sloughing off their earthy guises, till suddenly there is red heat, a cinder of memory spreading its glow as it slowly disappears into his mouth, for *Lo, this hath touched thy lips, and thine iniquity is taken away, and thy sin is expiated.* (225)

The last line of this interior monologue is a passage out of Aron's Bar Mitzvah text, a verse from the book of Isaiah, where the prophet's mouth is touched by burning embers so that he can speak out in the name of God. This is, at long last, the rite of passage though blood, pain, and fire. With the re-empowerment of language, Aron, whose stunted body has borne the inscription of cultural pathology and challenged it, and who is about to die in a few pages, has finally come into his legacy of word-magic and prophecy. His authorial surrogate will take up this legacy, and—to misquote Adorno— go on to rattle the cage of normality.

Notes

1. For discussions of this break with the Diasporic past, the need to assimilate the Holocaust into the Zionist ethos of a heroic struggle, and the collective translation of the trauma into the terms of homecoming and renewal, see Yael Feldman, Sidra DeKoven Ezrahi, and Ephraim Sicher.

2. Significantly, Gampel resorts to the Freudian conception of the "Uncanny"—located somewhere between psychoanalysis and literature—in her discussion of the intergenerational transmission of the trauma.

3. As indicated by the title of this essay, I take issue with the English translation of Grossman's Hebrew title and will therefore use the familiar translation only in italicized references to the English title of the book, but modify it in the body of my own text.

4. For some reason, the epigraph does not appear in the English translation of the novel.

5. In a comprehensive study of Israeli Holocaust literature, Iris Milner cites Abraham and Torok, noting the recurrent motif of entombment (hidden boxes, enclosed spaces, cellars) in novels written by second-generation writers. I would suggest, however, that Milner's reading of the secret—as an event or a story that is concealed and may come to light—involves some reduction or simplification of Abraham and Torok's theory, whose point of departure is precisely the non-substantive quality of the secret, its being unrepresentable by definition.

6. Like Uri, the protagonist of Moshe Shamir's best-selling 1947 novel, *Hu Halach Ba-Sadot* (*He Walked though the Fields*), Elic is an ideal-type *Sabra*. Both of these literary characters were the much-sung heroes of Israeli collectivity during the first decade after the establishment of the state.

7. Aron's Rip Van Winkle fantasy (34), his imaginary transportation to the time zone of America (112), and the poignant passage when he casts himself into an imaginary future as a prisoner in the frozen taiga of Russia—as his father was—remembering his own childhood, are additional instances of the same time loop.

8. I am grateful to Emanuel Berman, who has pointed out that the use of this seemingly odd adjective to describe the back of the father's neck reinforces the suggestion of Aron's disgust with his parents' sexuality.

Works Cited

Abraham, Nicolas. "The Shell and the Kernel: The Scope and Originality of Freudian Psychoanalysis." 1968. In *The Shell and the Kernel*, 79–97.

———. "Notes on the Phantom: A Complement to Freud's Metapsychology." 1975. In *The Shell and the Kernel*, 171–76.

Abraham, Nicolas and Maria Torok. *The Shell and the Kernel: Renewals of Psychoanalysis*, edited, translated, and with an Introduction by Nicholas T. Rand. Chicago and London: The University of Chicago Press, 1994.

———. "The Lost Object-Me: Notes on Endocryptic Identification." 1975. In *The Shell and the Kernel*, 139–56.

———. "Mourning or Melancholia, Introjection versus Incorporation." 1972. In *The Shell and the Kernel*, 125–38.

———. "Self-to-Self Affliction: Notes of a Conversation on 'Psychosomatics.'" 1973. In *The Shell and the Kernel*, 162–64.

———. "The Topography of Reality: Sketching a Metapsychology of Secrets." 1971. In *The Shell and the Kernel*, 157–61.

Ezrahi, Sidra. "Revisioning the Past: The Changing Legacy of the Holocaust in Hebrew Literature." *Salmagundi* 68 (Fall–Winter 1985–86): 245–70.

Feldman, Yael. "Whose Story Is It, Anyway? Ideology and Psychology in the Representation of the Shoah in Israeli Literature." In *Probing the Limits of Representation: Nazism and the "Final Solution,"* edited by Saul Friedländer, 223–39. Cambridge, MA: Harvard University Press, 1992.

Gampel, Yolanda. "A Daughter of Silence." In *Generations of the Holocaust,* edited by Martin S. Bergmann and Milton E. Jucovy, 120–36. New York: Basic Books, 1982.

———. "Thoughts about the Transmission of Conscious and Unconscious Knowledge to the Generation Born after the Shoah." *Journal of Social Work and Policy in Israel.* Special Issue, *Holocaust Trauma: Transgenerational Transmission to the Second Generation* 5–6 (1992): 43–50.

———. "The Interminable Uncanniness." In *Psychoanalysis at the Political Border: Essays in Honor of Rafael Moses,* edited by Leo Rangell and Rena Moses-Hrushovsky, 85–98. Madison, CT: International University Press, 1996.

Grossman, David. *The Book of Intimate Grammar.* 1991. Translated by Betsy Rosenberg. New York: Farrar, Straus and Giroux, 1994.

———. *See Under: Love* (1986). Translated by Betsy Rosenberg. New York: Farrar, Straus and Giroux, 1989.

Kestenberg, Judith S. "Psychoanalyses of Children of Survivors from the Holocaust: Case Presentations and Assessments." *Journal of the American Psychoanalytic Association* 28 (1980): 775–804.

Milner, Iris. *Kirei Avar* [Hebrew title translated as *Past Present: Biography, Identity and Memory in Second Generation Literature*]. Tel Aviv: Am Oved, 2003.

Nora, Pierre. "Generation." In *Realms of Memory: Rethinking the French Past* (1992), under the direction of Pierre Nora, vol. I, edited and with a Foreword by Lawrence D. Kritzman, translated by Arthur Goldhammer, 499–531. New York: Columbia University Press, 1996.

Shamir, Moshe. *Be-Mo Yadav* [*With His Own Hands*]. Merhavyia: Sifriat Poalim, 1951.

———. *Hu Halach Ba-Sadot* [*He Walked through the Fields*]. Merhavyia: Sifriat Poalim, 1947.

Sicher, Ephraim. "The Burden of Memory: The Writing of the Post-Holocaust Generation." In *Breaking Crystal: Writing and Memory after Auschwitz,* edited by Ephraim Sicher, 19–90. Urbana and Chicago: University of Illinois Press, 1998.

Torok, Maria. "The Illness of Mourning and the Fantasy of the Exquisite Corpse." 1968. In *The Shell and the Kernel,* 107–24.

———. "Story of Fear: The Symptoms of Phobia—The Return of the Repressed or the Return of the Phantom." 1975. In *The Shell and the Kernel,* 177–86.

Volkan, M. D. and D. Vamik. "Intergenerational Transmission and 'Chosen' Traumas." In *Psychoanalysis at the Political Border: Essays in Honor of Rafael Moses,* edited by Leo Rangell and Rena Moses-Hrushovsky, 257–82. Madison, CT: International University Press, 1996.

CHAPTER 15

Fractured Relations

The Multidirectional Holocaust Memory of Caryl Phillips

MICHAEL ROTHBERG

In the concluding lines of André Schwarz-Bart's novel *A Woman Named Solitude* (*La mulâtresse Solitude,* 1972), the narrator recalls the "humiliated ruins of the Warsaw Ghetto" while describing the site of a failed Caribbean slave revolt (*Woman* 150). Schwarz-Bart, who died on September 30, 2006, was a French Jew of Polish origin who lost his family in the Nazi genocide and who remains best known for his novel of Holocaust and Jewish history, *The Last of the Just* (*Le Dernier des Justes,* 1959). In the wake of the surprising success of that prize-winning novel, Schwarz-Bart, in collaboration with his Guadeloupian wife Simone Schwarz-Bart, set out on an ambitious, multivolume project to write a comparative fictional history of blacks and Jews in diaspora. Only sections of that project were ever published—besides *A Woman Named Solitude* there is the co-authored *Un Plat de porc aux bananes vertes* (1967)—but the questions Schwarz-Bart's work raises echo to this day.[1] What happens when different histories of extreme violence confront each other in the public sphere? Does the remembrance of one event erase others from view? When memories of colonialism bump up against memories of the Holocaust in contemporary multicultural societies, must a competition of victims ensue?

Many discussions of collective memory today are based on a zero-sum logic in which the evocation of one group's history is said to block other groups' histories from view. In typically provocative fashion, the literary critic Walter Benn Michaels presents a sharp version of this argument in a discussion of the political significance of the United States Holocaust Memorial Museum. Evoking the perspective of certain African Americans allegedly frustrated by the absence of commemoration of their traumatic history on the Mall in Washington, Michaels asks if "commemoration of the Nazi murder of the Jews on the Mall [might not be] in fact another kind of Holocaust denial" (289–90). Analogizing collective memory to the occupation of real estate, Michaels assumes that both memory and the public sphere are defined by a logic of scarcity: in this scenario, too much Holocaust memory entails not enough memory of other histories. Although few people would put the matter in such controversial terms, many other commentators, both inside and outside the academy, share the understanding of collective memory articulated by Michaels. I contrast this model of *competitive memory* with a theory of *multidirectional memory* that redescribes the public sphere as a field of contestation where memories interact productively and in unexpected ways. By making visible an intellectual and artistic counter-tradition that bucks the dominant zero-sum game and links memories of genocide and colonialism, I reveal how the public articulation of collective memory by marginalized and oppositional social groups provides resources for other groups to articulate their own claims for recognition and justice.[2]

In this essay, I focus on the novels and travel writing of Caryl Phillips, prime literary examples of multidirectional memory that help reveal some of the crucial narrative strategies through which such memory takes shape. The author of a dozen books in the last twenty years, Phillips was born in the Caribbean, grew up in England, and now lives much of the time in the United States, although he travels regularly across the globe. His aesthetic concerns refract that geographic displacement and range between past and present, old world and new, and black and Jewish themes.[3] In his fiction Phillips seeks, like Schwarz-Bart, to "people" history's abysses through risky acts of imagination, and, like his predecessor, he does so through an anachronistic aesthetics that explores links between seemingly disparate times and places. Nevertheless, the lessons Phillips draws from the past are more ambiguous than those espoused by Schwarz-Bart. In Phillips's oeuvre, the frontier between victim and victimizer is never as clear as it is in Schwarz-Bart's. Scrambling the forms of historical comparison he finds in Schwarz-Bart, Phillips's works situate blacks and Jews not only outside or at the margins of Europe, but also inside, at the center.

Those works also lead us to pose a question central to the investigation of Holocaust literature "after testimony": they force us to ask what narrative forms correspond to and express the work of intercultural remembrance. Paying particular attention to intertextuality and the fragmentation of narration, I argue that Phillips's project is not to establish an equation between black and Jewish history, or even strictly parallel histories, as can be found in Schwarz-Bart. Rather, Phillips uses what Rebecca Walkowitz has called an "anthological" aesthetic to highlight both similar structural problems within those histories and missed encounters between them. Through his particular juxtaposition of blacks and Jews in a transnational narrative frame, Phillips alludes to Schwarz-Bart's oeuvre in order to decompose it; he thus produces a fractured form of relatedness characteristic of the Holocaust's multidirectional legacies in a globalized, yet unevenly developed, age. His narrative strategies strike at the roots of competitive understandings of memory by revealing all histories as beyond appropriation and outside the logic of the zero-sum game.

Mediated Identifications
The European Tribe

Fifteen years after Schwarz-Bart conjured the ruins of the ghetto from a site of Caribbean trauma, Phillips also wrote about visiting Warsaw. In his 1987 travel report *The European Tribe,* he tells of a yearlong journey through the Europe of the mid-1980s that included a stop in Poland. Phillips writes from a Europe different from the one Schwarz-Bart abandoned for Guadeloupe, yet his sense of both the racist legacies of the past and the foreboding of the racial and ethnic violence of the near future seems to echo the French writer's insights.

The European Tribe provides various keys to understanding Phillips's investment in the Holocaust. At the most explicit level, a chapter titled "Anne Frank's Amsterdam" brings together black and Jewish experience through a model of identification. Here Phillips describes the inspiration for his first fictional work:

> I was about fifteen when Amsterdam first began to fascinate me. There was a programme on television, part of the *World at War* series, which dealt with the Nazi occupation of Holland and the subsequent rounding up of the Jews. . . . One thing I could not understand about the programme was why, when instructed to wear the yellow Star of David on their clothes, the Jews complied. They looked just like any other white people to me, so who would know that they were different? As the programme progressed my sense of bemused fascination disappeared and was supplanted by my first mature feelings of outrage and fear. These yellow stars were marking them

out for Bergen-Belsen and Auschwitz. I watched the library footage of the camps and realized both the enormity of the crime that was being perpetrated, and the precariousness of my own position in Europe. The many adolescent thoughts that worried my head can be reduced to one line: "If white people could do that to white people, then what the hell would they do to me?" (66–67)

Phillips refers here to *Occupation: Holland, 1940–1944,* the eighteenth of twenty-six episodes in *The World at War* British TV series, and possibly to *Genocide,* the twentieth episode, both of which first aired in March 1974. The passage is dense with multiple acts of looking that indicate different levels of narration and focalization: the narrator looks back at his teenage self as that younger self watches a television film constructed out of diverse sources of archival and postwar footage. Phillips's staging of race and visuality moves beyond the face-to-face encounter with racism famously depicted by Frantz Fanon in *Black Skin, White Masks* into a world characterized by multiple layers of mediation: the fifteen-year-old migrant child in England does not directly *face* the racist gaze, but *looks on* as the flow of a television program concatenates archival imagery with postwar narration and interviews.[4]

In order to comprehend the complexity of this viewing scene, it is important to be aware of the sources of the imagery in these two episodes of *The World at War*. *Occupation* begins with the narrator reading quotations from Anne Frank against the backdrop of color shots of contemporary Holland, but it then goes on to draw on a mixture of archival images and present-day "talking heads" interviews. The episode's themes are ones that will indeed come to haunt Phillips's oeuvre: complicity and resistance. It includes images produced by the Nazis themselves, including the famous footage of deportation from the transit camp Westerbork, also used in Alain Resnais's *Night and Fog,* and stills from the extermination camps; selections from propaganda films such as *The Eternal Jew;* and interviews with eyewitnesses (including, on the one hand, survivors, and, on the other hand, relatives of former Dutch Nazis). Two weeks later, the *Genocide* episode adds rare footage of mass executions and well-known scenes of bulldozers burying masses of emaciated corpses, which were taken on liberation by Allied soldiers and also featured in *Night and Fog*. While the Nazi footage might be more or less assimilable to the racist gaze of which Fanon speaks, the interviews and Allied footage raise different types of problems involving the framing of testimony and the depiction of abject victimization. Most significant in Phillips's account, though, is the representation of the viewer's relationship to these images of extreme racialization: it is simultaneously decentered and decontextualized, not only by the overlap of non-synchronous perspectives staged in the film, but also, more importantly, by the fact that the viewer is a black child from the former colonies in a post-Imperial metropolis whose response to the images fluctuates between identification and distanciation.

Yet it is precisely the film's lack of sense for the young Phillips—its depiction of victimization at the limits of understanding and its mobilization of contradictory perspectives—that proves productive, that produces a writing subject. Musing on the film leads the young Phillips to produce his first fictional work: a short story about a young Dutch boy in occupied Amsterdam who resists wearing the yellow star. Ultimately, during "resettlement" to the east, the boy escapes from the cattle car and is saved when "the sunlight shining on his yellow star . . . attracts a kindly farmer's attention" (*European Tribe* 67). Phillips later writes of this story, "The Dutch boy was, of course, me" ("On 'The Nature of Blood'" 6). This phrase echoes a key moment in *Occupation* in which the Dutch survivor Rita Boas-Koopman narrates the deportation of her young brother to the extermination camps in the east. She describes how, fearing for his life, she gave him her coat and boots; as he walked away from her, she reports, "He looked like me." In Phillips's telling, his first significant exposure to the Holocaust—an exposure importantly mediated by televisual images—takes place on the cusp between "adolescent thoughts" and his "first mature feelings." Through a process of identification, the history of the Holocaust helps to form Phillips as an adult subject and as a writer. At this moment of his youth, Phillips's relationship to Jewish history carries the hallmarks of what Diana Fuss, following Freud, has called the "obviousness" of identification, its "predicat[ion] on a logic of metaphoric exchange" (1, 5): "The Dutch boy was, of course, me." Such a logic, while understandable from the perspective of a fifteen-year-old boy, might be considered to carry the danger of appropriation, the full-scale metaphoric substitution of one identity or history for another. The unmarked echo of Boas-Koopman's words in Phillips's "mature" reflections signals the ongoing risk of that appropriation.

But *The European Tribe*, like *Higher Ground* and *The Nature of Blood*, the novels that emerged from it, also demonstrates a more complex logic, one that reminds us that, for Freud, identification is much more ambivalent and indirect than the simple process of metaphoric substitution. In fact, the identificatory processes at work in both the travel book and the novels are more strongly metonymic than metaphoric. This more complex notion of identification is captured in Eve Sedgwick's assertion, "The paths of allo-identification are likely to be strange and recalcitrant": "to identify *as* must always include multiple processes of identification *with*" (59, 61). The paths and multiple processes in Sedgwick's formulation correspond to the metonymic displacements that underwrite Phillips's approach to the otherness of Jewish history and the Holocaust. Tracing those paths of displacement reveals the stakes of identification in these texts. Metonymic identification is both enabled and made necessary by the deficit of representations of black suffering in the England of Phillips's youth. As he also writes in *The European Tribe,* "The bloody excesses of colonialism, the pillage and rape of modern Africa, the transportation of 11 million black people to the Americas, and their subsequent bondage were not on the curriculum, and certainly not on the television screen. As a result I vicariously channeled a part of my hurt and frustration through the Jewish experience" (54). At stake, in other words, is less the will to take the place of the other than the desire to map out the uncanny geographies of diasporic life; Phillips's diasporic subject shares spaces and histories with *various* others without developing a sense of being at home in that terrain. In Phillips's work, metonymic identification helps to capture the contingent contiguities of diasporic experience and its necessarily multiple locations and syncretic cultures.

Not only is Phillips's interest in the Nazi genocide revealed in *The European Tribe,* but also an ongoing fascination with the figure of Othello and the history of Venice. Following this intertextual route returns us to the Holocaust, but in a more roundabout way. Phillips's visit to Venice forms something of a turning point in his travel book: "I saw only one other black man in Venice. He looked nothing like Othello. . . . How did Othello live in this astonishing city? Sixteenth-century Venetian society both enslaved the black and ridiculed the Jew" (45). While Phillips is clearly interested in the common experience of racism suffered by blacks and Jews in Europe, this chapter is nonetheless called "A Black European Success." Despite the obvious irony, that title tells us something about what is important for Phillips: not simply the existence of a hatred that can turn genocidal, but the productive presence of racial others in the midst of Europe. Venice is a significant choice, not only because of the two relevant Shakespearean figures it conjures up—Othello and Shylock—but also because of its place in the world economy of its day. Indeed, for the sociologist Giovanni Arrighi, the Venetian city-state stands as "the prototype of the leading capitalist state of every subsequent age" (84). Othello's presence in the early modern Italian city thus represents a historical mirror for Phillips's own condition as a "black European success" who now lives in two of late modernity's global cities, New York and London.

But Venice also has further significance because it was the location of the first Jewish ghetto and indeed of the origin of the word "ghetto." In the twentieth century, the concept of the ghetto has provided one of the most salient links in the identificatory chain connecting blacks and Jews. The lexical connection also leads Phillips to explore those other ghettos, the ghettos established by the Nazis as part of the genocidal destruction of the Jews of Europe. The associations fostered by *The European Tribe* are not simply grounded in a metaphoric identification of racism against Jews with racism against blacks, although this link is not excluded. Nor are many of the historical associations of a sort that would be accepted by the discipline of history. Rather, this travel book leads us to identify a metonymic chain of multiple identifications that works through more accidental associations of history, geography, and literary reference and puts anachronism to work. Shifting from a metaphoric to a metonymic conception of identification helps to bring the mediated nature of Phillips's historical references to the fore: the Holocaust arrives via a television documentary; Venice is as much a literary space (Shakespeare's Venice) as it is a geographical place.

Phillips's more recent fictional work continues to chart this new imaginative terrain. As the references to school curricula, canonical literature, and television programming in *The European Tribe* indicate, the project of diasporic mapping undertaken by Phillips involves an engagement with multiple forms of textual culture and the appropriation and reconfiguration of dominant narratives. Such acts of engagement and appropriation, however, are not meant to render history or identity as entities that can be "owned," either by individuals or by groups. Phillips's reconfiguration of dominant narratives signals that multidirectional exchange takes place beyond the forms of cultural ownership that motivate competitive struggles over the past.

Missed Encounters
Higher Ground

In *Higher Ground,* his first novel after the publication of *The European Tribe,* and in *The Nature of Blood,* Phillips returns to related historical terrain in order further to fracture the lines of identification. Phillips's "Jewish" novels have received mixed reviews, with detractors asserting (as in the title of one review) that "black is not Jewish" and proponents lauding Phillips's "attempt to mix different cultures and traditions into a diverse whole."[5] In contrast to these positions, I argue that Phillips's project is not to establish an equation between black and Jewish history, but rather to highlight both similar structural problems within those histories and missed encounters between them. Despite moving toward a more fractured form of relatedness, however, the fictional texts still maintain the sense of urgency that lies behind black–Jewish identification in the earlier travel report.

Higher Ground consists of three disconnected, novella-like parts. The first is narrated from the perspective of an African man who works in a slave fort as a go-between and translator. The second is made up of letters from Rudi Williams, an African American man discovering the philosophy of Black Power while imprisoned during the late 1960s for having stolen forty dollars during an armed robbery. The novel concludes with the story of Irene, a Polish Jewish refugee in England, who seems to have lost her family in the Holocaust and who struggles with madness and depression. *Higher Ground*'s three separated stories bleed into each other and suggest a desire for contact across identities and histories. Most relevant here, Rudi deploys Nazi- and Holocaust-inflected figures in an attempt to make sense of his situation, while Irene yearns for a connection with Louis, a sympathetic but distant Caribbean immigrant. Yet, despite the different desires for contact evinced by these characters, the novel ultimately stages a series of missed encounters. Although Bénédicte Ledent has shown that common themes and problems cut across the three sections of the novel (54–79), I argue that what unity the novel has derives primarily from what is absent, both within and between the sections: that is, its unity is a function of traumatic ruptures and missed encounters instead of "positive" presences.

The theme of the missed encounter is established in the first section, "Heartland," set during the slave trade. The narrator, an African collaborator with the British, seeks to carve out a zone of normality within a situation of radical extremity and violence. After falling in love with a village girl who has been abused by the governor's deputy, the narrator smuggles the girl (as he calls her) into the fort and attempts to lead a "domestic" life within this site of inhumanity. His plans are doubly foiled, first when one of the soldiers discovers the presence of the girl and takes advantage of her and the narrator's vulnerability; second, when the soldier betrays them and lands them in the slave hold. Shipped to America, the narrator ends up as one of "the prime nigger heathens" on the auction block, "resigned to the permanence of [his] separation" from the girl. In the last lines of the section, he recognizes that his "present has finally fractured; the past has fled over the horizon and out of sight" (*Higher Ground* 60). The narrator finds himself displaced and fractured by history, but his experience makes him neither innocent victim, nor heroic resistor, nor martyr. Hence, I disagree with Bryan Cheyette's assertion, in an otherwise excellent essay on Phillips, that the "construction of an endless victimization of both the Jewish and black minorities" characterizes

Phillips's oeuvre (60). Rather, those minorities tend to occupy an in-between space characterized by complicity and moral ambiguity.

The narrator's missed encounter with his beloved—inevitable given his misrecognition of his place in history—finds its echo in the succeeding sections. Rudi, the letter-writing protagonist of part two, "The Cargo Rap," is no collaborator with oppression, but he similarly misconceives his place in history. To be sure, as a working-class African American man, he is certainly a victim of the same system of racialization that in an earlier phase claimed the life of the narrator of "Heartland." Yet his attempts to carve out a place for himself in history—attempts made from the none-too-spacious confines of a maximum-security prison cell—leave him even more imprisoned. In letters to his family and the few strangers who take up his cause, Rudi frequently figures himself in the place of Holocaust victims. In a letter to the president of his "Defense Committee," Rudi introduces himself as serving "one to life in a concentration camp of their [the State's] own choice" (92). In prison, which Rudi refers to on several occasions as "Belsen" (69, 84, 145), Rudi suffers tortures that, he suspects, closely resemble those inflicted in Nazi Germany (72).

Rudi's references to the Holocaust ultimately serve neither the interests of history nor those of his own liberation. Although Rudi uses the "opportunity" of prison to read important works of black, anticolonial, and leftist resistance, all of which he recommends to his family in self-righteous and didactic terms, he ultimately succumbs to madness and despair. His last letter, written to his mother after she has already died, demonstrates that overidentification with victims of the Holocaust is premised on an anachronistic reading of African American history. Here, as in his opening letter, Rudi imagines himself a slave; but while the opening letter uses the language of slavery metaphorically, in his confused state the metaphor is literalized: "Dear Moma, / The overseer has a horse named 'Ginger.' The plantation is wide and stretches beyond the horizon. . . . The master is cruel, but nobody 'knows' him better than his slaves. There is strength in this" (172). Besides importing a sly reference to Hegel, Rudi's final letter demonstrates a complex, but ultimately self-defeating, logic of identification; his identification with Jewish victims is premised on a prefigurative identification with slaves that founds his identity in the first place. While such identifications can provide sources of selfhood that allow for survival and resistance, they also can lead into polarized and static discourses. Such discourses replay narratives of trauma so insistently that they become structural features in the present instead of historical legacies that are susceptible to working through. If, then, "Rudi's recurrent references to Nazism . . . reinforce his dehumanisation by echoing the holocaustic horrors that suffuse the last story" in the novel, as Ledent has argued (65), this is so in a different sense than intended. Phillips's point, I would argue, is that part of the horror lies in the very "recurrent references"—not because Rudi is doing violence to Jewish history in loosely appropriating it to his own situation, but rather because he is doing violence to himself by trapping himself in a rhetoric of absolute victimization that ultimately eliminates all agency.

In "Higher Ground," the third part of the novel, the Jewish immigrant through whom the story is focalized also remains trapped in the past, but for quite different reasons. In contrast to Rudi, who contributes to his own entrapment through overidentification with African American as well as European Jewish history, "Irene" is overwhelmed by the split that marks her life, a split that inheres in her very name, or what she calls "the Irene-Irina-Irene-Irina-Irene-Irina-Irene problem" (183). Sent from Poland to England on a *Kindertransport*—a transport of Jewish children away from the Nazi threat—the young Irina soon becomes Irene, "for English people were too lazy to bend their mouths or twist their tongues into unfamiliar shapes" (183). Phillips highlights the ensuing split by referring to his protagonist as Irina during flashbacks and as Irene for the period after her move to England. Separated from her family, whom we are led to believe have been murdered by the Nazis, and assimilable into English society only at the cost of losing part of her identity, Irene is trapped into an unhappy marriage and then suffers a breakdown that sends her to a psychiatric hospital for ten years. The present of the novel finds her living in a rooming house and working in a library, but falling back into madness and about to be sent back to the hospital. Her persistent foreignness seems to draw her close to Louis, a brand-new West Indian migrant suffering in the alien English landscape. The logic of the story seems to be leading toward contact and bonding across black and Jewish differences—a supposition reinforced by the novel's use of colonial discourse to describe Irene's condition, as Ledent has shown (68), as well as by shifts in focalization between Irene and Louis, which seem to promise a melding of imaginative horizons. But once again the novel turns away from such a redemptive possibility; black and Jewish histories do not actually intersect but approach each other and then veer away asymptotically. Although drawn to Irene, Louis has already decided to return home to the Caribbean: "She touched him, but he knew that he must steel himself and step out into the crisp, sweatless, fresh, cold, white, snowy night . . . Then at dawn he would return to the men's hostel and take his bag and his leave. It was probable that this woman would extend and demand a severe loyalty that he could never reciprocate. Not now. Sorry" (216). Louis refuses—or at least defers indefinitely—Irene's offer of contact and solidarity and leaves Irene "for ever lost without the sustaining love," waiting for the nurse to take her back to captivity in the hospital (218).

Although thematically unified in its exploration of forms of imprisonment, displacement, and racialized violence, *Higher Ground* refuses redemptive closure and easy analogy across histories and identities. Even as it encourages readers to search for links between the various stories staged in the novel, the narrative discourse also keeps them isolated from each other, a point we find allegorized in the missed encounter between Irene and Louis, where shifts in focalization finally signal alienation of one from the other. In the final story, differences of gender, social status (refugee vs. migrant), ethnicity, and nationality overrule the commonalities that nonetheless draw the two characters together. Victimization proves not to be the best grounds for solidarity because processes of victimization take multiple, contradictory forms and erode the bases of selfhood necessary for relationship with others (as illustrated by Rudi's descent into fantasy and Irene's madness). In addition, as the case of the narrator of "Heartland" demonstrates, possessing the status of the victim does not grant immunity from complicity or prevent the occupation of other subject positions, such as collaborator. In the fragmented stories of *Higher Ground,* the position of victims is revealed as unstable and shifting, and therefore not susceptible to the construction of facile linkages.

Intertexuality and Stratified Minoritization
The Nature of Blood

In *The Nature of Blood* Phillips refashions the materials of *The European Tribe* and *Higher Ground,* as well as many other texts, into a fictional narrative that spans 400 years and links Nazi Germany, fifteenth- and sixteenth-century Italy, and contemporary Israel. The novel focuses primarily on Eva Stern, a young German–Jewish woman who survives the death camps before succumbing, like Irene, to madness after the war and a tragic end in England. The novel also presents us with Eva's uncle Stephan, a doctor who leaves Europe before the war and is part of the Jewish underground in Palestine; he also shows up many years later in Israel. Interwoven with the story of the Sterns is a chronicle-like account of a fifteenth-century Venetian ritual murder case and a first-person narrative by none other than Othello. All of this is recounted in a fragmented text characterized by rapid shifts in perspective, a dense intertextual fabric, and alternation between carefully constructed historical milieus and deliberate anachronism.

Working from the same chain of associations that stands behind the interlocking histories of blacks and Jews in *The European Tribe, The Nature of Blood* extends the earlier book's exploration of diasporic identity. What is most striking about the novel is the narrative form that exploration takes. The novel employs more than a dozen different narrative voices and shifts perspective several dozen times. It also mobilizes a markedly interdisciplinary set of cognitive genres, from the clinical diagnosis of Eva's doctor in England to interpolated dictionary definitions of key terms such as "ghetto" and to the disturbingly blasé historical voice of the chronicle-like ritual murder case. Characterized by discontinuity between multiple forms of knowledge and multiple forms of violence, *The Nature of Blood* testifies to the existence of new possibilities for thinking the relatedness of the unrelatable.

How can we make sense of the juxtaposition of histories in *The Nature of Blood*? Like *The European Tribe,* with its staging of two different forms of identification, the novel also contains two different logics of comparison. On the one hand, the title, *The Nature of Blood,* gestures at a commonality that links the different stories as essentially the same. A transhistorical racist imaginary obsessed with purity of blood seems to unite the various Jewish and black victims across time. This sense of commonality is reinforced by certain textual echoes that link the stories to each other—as when the Jews of fifteenth-century Portobuffole recite the same prayer while being burned at the stake as the Jews who arrive at a Nazi camp (155, 164), or when Eva's suicide echoes Othello's. Were this logic to dominate, the novel would risk reproducing the racist discourse that it obviously seeks to contest. But, on the other hand—and whether intentionally or not—the differences between the stories ultimately overwhelm the apparent similitude suggested by the title. The novel's primary focus is not the simple binary between perpetrators and victims of racist violence. Instead, the novel emerges as an exploration of ambivalent modes of belonging and exclusion in which accidental contiguity plays a greater role than correspondence of historical essences.

The first word of *The Nature of Blood* is "between," and indeed the novel begins in the interstices, in a liminal zone between geographies and histories. The opening scene takes place between the end of the war and the beginning of a new era. It is set on the still-contested island of Cyprus, between Europe, Africa, and the Middle East, in camps established by the British for refugees refused entrance into Palestine. Stephan, the doctor, is talking to Moshe, a young survivor of the camps.

> Between us a small fire sputtered. . . . The new kindling snapped, and the flames rose higher and illuminated the boy's face. He spoke quietly.

"Tell me, what will be the name of the country?"

"Our country," I said. "The country will belong to you too."

The boy looked down at the sand, then scratched a short nervous line with his big toe.

"Tell me, what will be the name of our country?"

I paused for a moment, in the hope that he might relax. And then I whispered, as though confessing something to him.

"Israel. Our country will be called Israel." (3)

In this scene, Phillips describes the moment of transition when a collective "we" is being formed, a new nation imagined and named from a non-national space. The narrative begins between the waning days of one colonial regime and the establishment of a new state that will be perceived as independence and homecoming by some and as occupation and displacement by others.

While the novel quickly leaves behind twentieth-century Cyprus, the tensions of place and time evoked by this opening persist. Indeed, we return to Cyprus in the second half of the novel when Othello sails there in order to counter the Ottoman Empire's threat to Venice. It becomes clear at this point that, as in *The European Tribe,* Othello's position in the novel is double. He has certainly been marked out as "alien" in Venice and has suffered because of it, but he is also portrayed as driven by a will to assimilate and a willingness to be exploited in the fight against other, more "dangerous," outsiders. Upon arrival in Cyprus, Othello finds that the Ottoman fleet has drowned in a storm, allowing Othello to reflect on his situation there: "This island of Cyprus, to which fate had deposited me safe in both body and mind, would serve as the school in which I might further study the manners of Venice, before eventually returning to the city to embark upon my new life. However, my first action as both General and Governor was to order that revels should commence within the hour to celebrate both the drowning of the heretical Turk and the happy and fortuitous marriage of their commanding officer to fair Desdemona" (166). The conjunction of death and marriage does not seem to bother Othello or distract him from his revels. By suggesting that the consolidation of Othello's identity as "black European success" takes place through possession of a "fair" prize, through the mimicry of normative manners, and through the fatal disappearance of another "foreign" group, Phillips initiates a critique of minority consciousness under diasporic conditions. Phillips's work, in other words, does not simply celebrate diasporic consciousness. Rather, the contingent association of the two Cypruses allows Phillips to probe the formal problems of the diasporic subject who is ambiguously situated between home and exile. The historical palimpsest of the still-contested island of Cyprus provides an imaginative space for rethinking the ways that binary relationships—such as self/other, victim/perpetrator— can become transformed into more complicated configurations such that new figures come into view: the other of the other, the victim of the victim.

Yet, *The Nature of Blood* also makes clear, there is a limit to the logic of assimilation and complicity. While both Stephan and Othello represent ambiguous minority figures caught between racialized exclusion and the demands of state and empire, Eva, the surviving victim of the Nazi camps, comes to embody a more radical history of annihilation as well as the problems of narrating such a history. Phillips attempts not to write "parallel" histories of minoritization but rather to bring into view a "stratified" map of difference, to adopt the terms of critical race theorist Susan Koshy, in which the accidental contiguity of some experiences is matched by the incommensurability of others.

Other than its end in suicide, Eva's story is quite unlike Othello's, but, like Othello, Eva is more a product of the literary imagination than she is a historical figure. Although a greater portion of the novel is narrated in Eva's voice than in any other, her depiction is still ultimately indirect. The Holocaust sections are, for example, scattered with intertextual borrowings from accounts of Holocaust survivors, such as Primo Levi and Elie Wiesel, and from other Jewish writers, such as Cynthia Ozick. The indirection of the novel's account of the genocide becomes even more marked as Phillips nears the center of the disaster. When Eva enters the cattle car that will transport her to the death camps, the narrative switches from first to third person and then back (155, 163). As the train approaches and then enters the camps, the narrative and, implicitly, Eva's consciousness start to fragment into a collection of dispersed voices:

> The boxcar was near the locomotive, so Eva was able to listen to the engine die. Silence. The world remained silent. And then, some hours later, a roar and a shudder, and once again the locomotive tugged against the weight of the train. . . . A long-drawn-out whistle. Then a loud crash and a judder. The darkness began to echo with barked orders. Then the doors to the boxcars roll open. . . . Already, a loudspeaker is blasting instructions to remove all clothing. Remove artificial limbs and eyeglasses. Tie your shoes together. Surrender any undeclared valuables and claim a receipt. Children go with the women. Where are we? The thin and the handicapped, this way, please. All gold rings, fountain pens, and chains. Roll up. Where is God? Where is your God? . . . A uniformed adolescent kicks an old man. Then he laughs. The old man stops and stares. I am your father. He reloads his

weapon. I am your father. Each time he fires the young man laughs louder.
(161–62)

In this passage we see the dark inversion of the scene of identification in *The European Tribe*. Here, mediation and intertextuality do not create possibilities for identity formation and solidarity but instead index dehumanization. Even as the narrative discourse suggests that this passage might be taking place within the frame of Eva's consciousness, it undermines the unity and "authenticity" of that consciousness by bringing together a mixture of materials that could not have been accessible to Eva. The references, for example, to the Yiddish title of Wiesel's memoir (*Un di Velt Hot Geshvign* [*And the World Remained Silent*]) and to the archetypal questioning of God and the father/son conflicts that mark that memoir do not so much call upon authoritative survivor testimony as stage the collapse of all (patriarchal) authority in the face of an inhuman, genocidal machine. The narrative's dispersed voices correspond to the disembodied voice of the loudspeaker and its command to disassemble an already artificial body. There is, of course, an implicit and perhaps appropriate modesty in Phillips's approach. He does not attempt to portray realistically a scene he can never know; thus, the ultimate site of horror, the gas chamber, is portrayed in a distanced and an a-subjective third-person voice ("The process of gassing takes place in the following manner" [176]). Most crucially, Phillips's generalized intertextual approach to history accomplishes two things at the level of form: it evokes a mode of narration that refuses to gloss over the disruption it portrays, and it opens itself to the global circulation of memories beyond competition and identitarian conflict.

The novel's indirect, intertextual technique is thus not simply a matter of playful postmodern pastiche. Rather, this indirect mode gestures toward another crucial feature of the diasporic condition shared by blacks and Jews: at the limit, diaspora frustrates all forms of metaphoric identification because it is rooted in, or—better—uprooted by, traumatic history.[6] While, as Cathy Caruth suggests, trauma may provide "the very link between cultures," that link is premised on an initial violence that installs loss at the origin of diaspora (11). Loss—which Dominick LaCapra helpfully distinguishes from absence—is related to the specificities of historical trauma (43–85). Any metaphoric identification with specific losses will always perform a kind of violence. But Phillips's strategy is to juxtapose particular losses—such as those of Eva and Othello or those of Jews of the fifteenth and twentieth centuries—through indirect invocation. This indirect, metonymic form of reference to unrepresentable extreme violence not only is a mark of the contingencies of diasporic geographies but also signals the disruptions of traumatic history.

That history in its "presence" is significantly "lost" and definitively unrecoverable, but its effects register nonetheless.[7]

The disruptions of traumatic history indexed by *The Nature of Blood* become particularly clear through comparison with what may be the novel's most significant unremarked intertext: Schwarz-Bart's *The Last of the Just*. Like Phillips, Schwarz-Bart links the medieval and modern persecution of Jews. Yet, *The Last of the Just* presents that link as a thousand-year genealogical "biography" of the Levy family that unfolds in a continuous chronicle of pogroms, persecutions, and autos-da-fé. Such a continuous narrative form cannot fully acknowledge the traumatic losses that call it into being—it risks becoming a version of what Eric Santner has called "narrative fetishism," as, in fact, the more disjunctive narrative of *A Woman Named Solitude* also suggests. Acknowledging the force and form of discontinuity, Phillips deconstructs—takes apart and reconfigures—Schwarz-Bart's first novel, maintaining the contact between different histories of persecution without rendering them as pieces of a totalizable collective biography. This resistance to narrative fetishism also helps explain the foregrounding in *Higher Ground* of missed encounters, one of the forms in which trauma "appears," according to Lacanian psychoanalytic accounts.

While in *The Last of the Just* Schwarz-Bart draws on the unfolding temporality of the chronicle, Phillips can be located within the multi-temporal space of an "anthological" aesthetic, to draw on terms developed by Rebecca Walkowitz. Walkowitz situates Phillips's oeuvre within an emergent category of self-consciously global works that she names "comparison literature." As she notes, Phillips is suspicious of claims to uniqueness, yet he remains "engaged with debates about *historical* distinctiveness, such as whether the Holocaust can be usefully compared to other examples of racism and genocide" (537). Engaged in this dialectic between distinctiveness and comparison, Phillips turns especially to the form of the anthology: "Phillips's novels and nonfiction works are like anthologies in that they sample and collate stories of racism, slavery, European anti-Semitism, and recent violence against immigrants. But unlike other anthologies, which create a single series, Phillips's books tend to promote various microseries within them. In addition to collating the lives of several migrants, his books also represent the life of any single migrant, including their author, as yet another collated account" (539). The infinite regression of the microseries—the fact that each element of the series is itself defined by another series ad infinitum—distinguishes Phillips's aesthetic of anthological collation from both the linear history of *The Last of the Just* and the parallel histories evoked at the end of *A Woman Named Solitude*.

Conclusion
Multidirectional Memory and the Work of Narrative

Common to multidirectional memory and Phillips's narrative discourse is a rejection of the proprietary relationship to the past. Although Phillips's works sometimes seem motivated by a desire to collapse historical particularity, they ultimately reveal that desire to be part of a larger movement of exchange between dispersed histories and memories that preserves particularity without fetishizing difference. That exchange is multidirectional not only because of its crosscutting transnational and transhistorical scope but also because it avoids the traps of competitive victimization, cannibalizing appropriation, and aggressive abjection of the other's story. Such avoidance derives in turn from concrete narrative strategies that collate stories "anthologically" without smoothing over their jagged edges.

Phillips's fragmentation of perspective, his montage of media and modes of discourse, and his sometimes playful, sometimes serious intertextual allusions constitute radical acts of depropriation, in which, as Timothy Bewes writes, characters are rendered "incapable of speaking 'authentically,' on their own account or in their own voices" (43). According to Bewes, Phillips consistently deploys clichés and "ventriloquism" instead of individualized, "realist" voices in order to enact "the systematic evacuation of every discursive position that might claim freedom from implication in colonialism" (46). While Bewes correctly stresses the complicity in colonialism that marks much of Phillips's work, the implications of Phillips's narrative depropriation are even more far-reaching: Phillips's intertextual aesthetic also produces complicity *between* different histories and sets the stage for the articulation of multidirectional memory. Rejecting "ownership" of the past at the level of form as well as at the level of content, while simultaneously tracking our ongoing and inevitable implication in history, Phillips treats the past as a shared heritage of cultural memory. Wandering anachronistically through the ruins and traumas of modernity, he forces readers to confront the common legacies of violence that persist beyond the age of testimony.

Notes

1. For a more detailed consideration of Schwarz-Bart's work, see Rothberg, *Multidirectional Memory*. The present essay is a revised version of my discussion of Caryl Phillips in that book. I am grateful to the editors of this collection for their helpful comments and to Stanford University Press for permission to reprint.

2. For a full discussion of the contrast between competitive and multidirectional

memory, see the introduction to Rothberg, *Multidirectional Memory*. For a contrasting scholarly articulation of competition as the essence of disputes over historical victimization, see Chaumont.

3. For other critical works that helpfully describe these and other aspects of Phillips's oeuvre in the texts I discuss, see Cheyette, Dawson, Ledent, Whitehead, and Zierler, "Caryl Phillips" and "'My Holocaust Is Not Your Holocaust.'"

4. For a discussion of Fanon that considers race and visual culture in relation to both colonialism and the Holocaust, see Rothberg, "In the Nazi Cinema."

5. The reference to the book review comes from Zierler's account of the critical reception of Phillips in "Caryl Phillips," 936–37. The second quotation comes from Cheyette, 63.

6. For more on intertextuality, trauma, and memory, see Rothberg, "Dead Letter Office."

7. Such indirect reference bears a resemblance to what, in a discussion of Holocaust memoirs, I have called "traumatic realism." See Rothberg, *Traumatic Realism,* chapters 3 and 4.

Works Cited

Arrighi, Giovanni. *The Long Twentieth Century: Money, Power, and the Origins of Our Times.* New York: Verso, 1994.

Bewes, Timothy. "Shame, Ventriloquy, and the Problem of the Cliché in Caryl Phillips." *Cultural Critique* 63 (2006): 33–60.

Caruth, Cathy. "Trauma and Experience: Introduction." In *Trauma: Explorations in Memory,* edited by Cathy Caruth, 3–12. Baltimore: The Johns Hopkins University Press, 1995.

Chaumont, Jean-Michel. *La concurrence des victimes.* Paris: La Découverte, 2002.

Cheyette, Bryan. "Venetian Spaces: Old–New Literatures and the Ambivalent Uses of Jewish History." In *Reading the "New" Literatures in a Postcolonial Era,* edited by Susheila Nasta, 53–72. Cambridge, UK: D. S. Brewer, 2000.

Dawson, Ashley. "'To Remember Too Much Is Indeed a Form of Madness': Caryl Phillips's *The Nature of Blood* and the Modalities of European Racism." *Postcolonial Studies* 7, no. 1 (2004): 83–101.

Fanon, Frantz. *Black Skin, White Masks.* Translated by Charles Lam Markmann. New York: Grove Press, 1967.

Fuss, Diana. *Identification Papers.* New York: Routledge, 1995.

Genocide: 1941–1945. Episode 20 of *The World at War.* Written by Charles Bloomberg. Directed by Michael Darlow. London: Thames Television, 1974.

Koshy, Susan. "Morphing Race into Ethnicity: Asian Americans and Critical Transformations of Whiteness." *boundary 2* 28, no. 1 (2001): 153–94.

LaCapra, Dominick. *Writing History, Writing Trauma.* Baltimore: Johns Hopkins University Press, 2001.

Ledent, Bénédicte. *Caryl Phillips.* Manchester: Manchester University Press, 2002.

Michaels, Walter Benn. "Plots against America: Neoliberalism and Antiracism." *American Literary History* (Summer 2006): 288–302.

Occupation: Holland, 1940–1944. Episode 18 of *The World at War.* Written by Charles Bloomberg. Directed by Michael Darlow. London: Thames Television, 1974.

Phillips, Caryl. *The European Tribe.* 1987. Boston and London: Faber and Faber, 1992.

———. *Higher Ground: A Novel in Three Parts.* New York: Viking, 1989. 60.

———. *The Nature of Blood.* Boston and London: Faber and Faber, 1997. 3.

———. "On 'The Nature of Blood' and the Ghost of Anne Frank." *CommonQuest* (Summer 1998): 4–7.

Rothberg, Michael. "Dead Letter Office: Conspiracy, Trauma, and *Song of Solomon*'s Posthumous Communication." *African American Review* 37, no. 4 (2003): 501–16.

———. "In the Nazi Cinema: Race, Visuality and Identification in Fanon and Klüger." *Wasafiri* 24, no. 1 (March 2009): 13–20.

———. *Multidirectional Memory: Remembering the Holocaust in the Age of Decolonization.* Stanford: Stanford University Press, 2009.

———. *Traumatic Realism: The Demands of Holocaust Representation.* Minneapolis: University of Minnesota Press, 2000.

Santner, Eric. "History beyond the Pleasure Principle: Some Thoughts on the Representation of Trauma." In *Probing the Limits of Representation: Nazism and the "Final Solution,"* edited by Saul Friedländer, 143–54. Cambridge, MA: Harvard University Press, 1992.

Schwarz-Bart, André. *Le Dernier des Justes.* Paris: Seuil, 1959.

———. *The Last of the Just.* Translated by Stephen Becker. New York: Atheneum, 1960.

———. *La Mulâtresse Solitude.* Paris: Seuil, 1972.

———. *A Woman Named Solitude.* Translated by Ralph Manheim. New York: Bantam, 1974.

Schwarz-Bart, Simone and André Schwarz-Bart. *Un Plat de porc aux bananes vertes.* Paris: Seuil, 1967.

Sedgwick, Eve. *Epistemology of the Closet.* Berkeley: University of California Press, 1990.

Walkowitz, Rebecca, "The Location of Literature: The Transnational Book and the Migrant Writer." *Contemporary Literature,* Special Issue, "Immigrant Fictions" 47, no. 4 (2006): 527–45.

Whitehead, Anne. *Trauma Fiction.* Edinburgh: Edinburgh University Press, 2004.

Zierler, Wendy. "Caryl Phillips." In *Holocaust Literature: An Encyclopedia,* Volume II, edited by S. Lillian Kremer, 934–37. New York: Routledge, 2002.

———. "'My Holocaust Is Not Your Holocaust': 'Facing' Black and Jewish Experience in *The Pawnbroker, Higher Ground,* and *The Nature of Blood.*" *Holocaust and Genocide Studies* 18, no. 1 (2004): 46–67.

CHAPTER 16

Hiroshima and the Holocaust

Tales of War and Defeat in Japan and Germany—
A Contrastive Perspective

ANNE THELLE

All narratives need to address the issue of beginnings and endings. During her adventures in Wonderland, Alice is given the advice "begin at the beginning, continue until you reach the end, then stop." This seems simple enough, but what is a beginning? Where does a story really start? At what point can one become aware of the fact that an event constituted a beginning? Can one truthfully tell the complete story of a single event? Brian Richardson notes that when used about fictional narrative, beginnings are "provisional concepts, inherently unstable, typically elusive, and always capable of being rewritten" (124–25). Beginnings, narrative theory has taught us, are structured by the end to come and are thus always chosen in hindsight. Not surprisingly, then, endings in narrative have received far more attention by theorists than beginnings. It is "the last stage in a plot that confers meaning upon that story" (Carrard 62), thus enabling us to categorize it as either a comedy or a romance, a tragedy or a satire. Consequently, the ending holds a stronger sway over the ordering of the narrative than the beginning. In discussions of historical narrative, too, endings have received more attention than beginnings. In his analysis of narratives of World War II, Philippe Carrard observes that historians are always aware of their narratives being "open-ended" and thus write their narratives with the knowledge that new events and new insights can emerge to demand that the story be rewritten. However, says Carrard, historians seem to display a "lack of self-reflexivity" (73) when it comes to the nature of their narratives' beginnings. Historical narratives, he points out, are not only open-ended; they are also "open-begun" (76). What strategies do historians rely on to launch their account, and do historians reflect on the arbitrariness of their stories' beginnings?

Contrasting with German narratives of war, this essay will examine the narratives of one apocalyptic ending, the bombing of Hiroshima, as these narratives are conveyed in contemporary Japan. I will focus on the story of Japan's war as it is told in Hiroshima and its memorial sites—the Peace Memorial Museum and the Peace Park with its monuments. Narratives of Hiroshima, the essay will show, make assumptions about both the story's beginning and its ending, thus privileging some elements while repressing others. A significant constituent element of my method will be to use strategic comparisons between narratives about Hiroshima and German narratives about the bombing of German cities during the war. When it comes to the memorialization of the Second World War, Japan offers an interesting contrast to Germany, since both countries' story of war share many parallels while at the same time representing important differences in the historical record. These similarities and contrasts can in turn provide useful insights in our understanding of narratives' importance in our collective remembering of historical events. As I will show, in order to understand how narratives affect our memory of historical events, it is important to scrutinize not just the narrative's end but also its beginning.

There are three major parallels between the two countries' war experience. First, both Japan and Germany were principal aggressors of the war. Second, both countries experienced heavy Allied bombing aimed at civilian sites, resulting in large-scale destruction of major cities. Finally, Japan and Germany are linked also through their association with the two major tropes for catastrophe in the twentieth century: the Holocaust and Hiroshima. With these links, then, both countries can be said to hold the dual roles of victim and perpetrator during the war. And yet the manner in which these dual roles are dealt with in the respective countries' narratives of war, and thus in their collective memories, are fundamentally different. Let us start by taking a closer look at these historical parallels, before putting the telling of their historical tales closer under scrutiny.

First the association to catastrophe: as an instance of atrocity, Hiroshima is often linked to the Holocaust with the conjunction "and"—Hiroshima and Auschwitz, the atomic bomb and the Holocaust. In his comprehensive study of A-bomb literature, John Treat notes that "subsuming now as they do all other sites of mass murder," the names Hiroshima and Auschwitz "are terms that symbolize a reduction of history into two names no longer merely places but ideas, tropes of a new fact within the human condition: a condition compromised by our ability, in a mater of respective hours and seconds, to eliminate whole ghettos and cities of people" (9). However, there is an obvious imbalance in this relationship between Hiroshima and the Holocaust and in their respective associations to Japan and Germany. For one, in Hiroshima the Japanese were victims of atrocity, while Germany's relationship to the Holocaust is one of perpetrators of violence. And second, whereas the experience of the atomic destruction of the city of Hiroshima is a uniquely Japanese experience, the Holocaust certainly does not "belong" to Germany in any similar fashion.

More appropriately, perhaps, Japan and Germany are joined by the same conjunction, "and," in their wartime role as principal aggressors, as *enemy* of the Allied forces. In the Pacific, it was Japan that started the aggressive expansion against its neighboring countries, and it was Japan that brought the United States into the war through its surprise attack on Pearl Harbor on December 7, 1941. In common with Germany, Japan too faced at the war's end responsibility for atrocious crimes against humanity committed during the war years. The Nanjing Massacre, where Japanese troops in the course of a few December days in 1937 mutilated, slaughtered, and raped tens of thousands of Chinese civilians is no doubt the most famous example, but it was by no means an isolated event. Japanese soldiers were responsible for similar incidents throughout China, as well as in Korea, the Philippines, and the Pacific Islands. Though in no way as systematic or anywhere near the scale of the Nazi extermination camps, these actions by the Japanese exemplified a brutalization justified by a similar belief in national superiority.

While the bombing of Hiroshima and Nagasaki is the culmination of a prolonged effort to put an end to Japanese aggression through so-called morale bombing, Germany too had already been subjected to such bombing by the Allies for many years before the war's end. Almost all major cities were targeted, and many experienced more than 50 percent destruction. Estimated death tolls in Germany range from three hundred to more than five hundred thousand, and the burned-out rubble of German cities in the end measured several hundred million cubic meters (Vees-Gulani 2). In Japan, too, most major cities were destroyed, and the death toll on account of bombing by conventional bombs far exceeds that of the two atomic bombs. It is estimated that more than half a million were killed by firebombs across Japan, and at least five million were left homeless. In Tokyo alone, Allied bombing killed more than one hundred thousand civilians and left more than one million homeless. As a historical event, Hiroshima could just as well be coupled with Dresden or with other cities subjected to Allied bombing.

Considered as a memorial site, then, Hiroshima offers both a parallel and a contrast to memorials of the Holocaust. Yet in the telling of this particular historical event, it seems difficult to provide a balanced picture: the focus—depending on who is telling the story—tends to be either on *victimization* (Hiroshima as apocalyptic catastrophe) or on *war responsibility* (Japan as perpetrator). The controversy at the Smithsonian offers illustrative examples of the dual nature of the narrative and of the consequences of choosing one over the other. For the anniversary commemorating the fiftieth anniversary of the end of World War II, the Smithsonian National Air and Space Museum decided to organize an exhibition displaying the Enola Gay aircraft together with other exhibit items related to the dropping of the bomb on Hiroshima. The exhibit plans caused immediate reactions, with criticism coming both from war veterans and from academics and peace organizations. The curators' original plan to combine the exhibit of the bomber aircraft with items from Hiroshima displaying the destructive force of the bomb was met with fury by war veterans. A commemorative exhibition of the war's end, they said, should display the Enola Gay with pride and should therefore not include negative perspectives. The museum subsequently altered their plans, suggesting instead the incorporation of information about Japan's military invasions and colonial atrocities as a background for America's decision to drop the bomb. But once again, the plans were met with protests, this time from historians and peace activists. After a long debate, the commemorative exhibition was cut down to a bare minimum, with the airplane displayed virtually on its own, stripped of any historical commentary.

Among the elements scratched from the exhibit plans were details about the discussions among U.S. leaders and military commanders regarding the decision to use the atomic bomb; information and photographs showing Japanese atrocities in Asia; items and photographs demonstrating the material and human devastation caused by the bomb; and information about subsequent development of nuclear weapons and the rise of the atomic age. The story of the Smithsonian exhibition has often been cited as a prime example that demonstrates how sensitive historical narration is and how difficult it is to tell the final events of a story unless one at the same time also has a clear picture of how one should envision its beginning. In Japan, the memorialization of Hiroshima has to a great extent focused on the story of Japanese victimization. In the following I will first outline how two parallel stories—the bombing of Dresden and the bombing of Hiroshima—have followed divergent paths. Next, I will identify and discuss some significant forces that have shaped the dominating story of Hiroshima.

The focus of my analysis will be sites of memory—museums, monuments, and commemorative ceremonies. In his influential study of Holocaust memorials, James E. Young points out how memorials of World War II seem to become increasingly more prominent the further the historical events recede in time. Testimonial accounts have been written, but the witnesses of the events of the war are decreasing in number and will soon be gone altogether. Hence the public memory of this time is now instead "being molded in a proliferating number of memorial images and spaces," memorials that evoke the past "according to a variety of national myths, ideals, and political needs" (1). Memorials represent events and experiences of the past, but perhaps more importantly they reflect "the current lives of their communities, as well as the state's memory of itself" (1–2). By looking at the way history is presented through memorial sites and monuments, then, one can come closer to an understanding of the way in which a given community seeks to preserve the memory of its past. This can be described as "cultural memory," as Mieke Bal does in her influential essay on the topic. Memory, she writes, is both a cultural phenomenon and an individual one, and cultural memorialization should be viewed "as an activity occurring in the present, in which the past is continuously modified and redescribed even as it continues to shape the future" (vii).

Along with many others who have explored the subject of cultural memory, Young and Bal focus on the experience and the memory of the Holocaust, and particularly on the various processes for memorialization that have taken place in Germany. Since the end of the war Germany has engaged in a thorough process of remembering and accounting for its misdeeds. Like "a massive tongue, seeking out, over and over, a sore tooth" (Buruma 8), the war in Germany is remembered on TV and radio, in schools and museums. Again and again, their crimes are rehearsed, reenacted, and remembered. Memories of war in Germany, writes Ian Buruma, are accompanied by a sense of being *betroffen*. To be *betroffen,* Buruma explains, indicates a sense of guilt and shame, perhaps even embarrassment. "To be *betroffen* is one way to 'master the past,' to show contriteness, to confess, and to be absolved and purified" (21).

The focus in Germany on wartime responsibility is reflected also in the way the country remembers its own victims. In her analysis of the literature of wartime bombing in Germany, Vees-Gulani points to what has been generally regarded as accepted truth in Germany: "one cannot write responsibly about the bombings without also writing about the Holocaust" (4). Writing about German victimhood after World War II, she points out, has always been intertwined with a deep sense of guilt and remorse, so much so that the topic has been avoided by many. It has even been claimed by some that Germans need to build their identity on the past of the Third Reich and that the country "can remain a successful democracy only if the memory of the past is kept alive in order to avoid repeating the same mistakes" (54). Overall, in representations of war in Germany there is a strong sense of purpose relating to owning up to past iniquities and facing the crime of the Holocaust.

Considering the brutality of the war Japan waged on its neighboring countries, one might expect that the narratives of war memories in Japan would be accompanied by a similar sense of guilt and remorse. After all, the military tribunal held in Tokyo after the war had received broad press coverage, making the many acts of war crimes committed by Japanese during the war known to the public. However, when the story of war is told in Hiroshima, the story is first and foremost a story of victimization. How could a nation responsible for brutal crimes against humanity and an aggressive war of expansion end up in its own eyes only as a victim? One could offer the simple, obvious answer to this question: the Japanese, and in particular the people of Hiroshima, see themselves as victims of World War II because they were, indeed, victims. When civilians become a target in a war, they will always be victims. And surely the survivors of the infernos caused by the firebombs and the two atomic blasts have every right to convey the horrors of their experience. Isn't their narrative of victimization understandable?

Yet the issue is not so simple. A comparison with the German experience of wartime bombing will show just how complicated the dual role of victim and perpetrator can be. In Germany, it is the story of the extermination camps, and of German responsibility, that have come to the fore, in particular since the "explosion of critical self-examination" (Moeller 15) began in the late 1960s. In face of the enormity of the Nazi crimes, other stories of the past—the memories of German victimization—have since stood in a complicated relationship to public memorialization of wartime responsibility and to the feelings of shame and guilt that accompany the acknowledgment of such responsibility.

In February 2005, when the city of Dresden ventured to commemorate the sixtieth anniversary of the Allied bombing of the city, the plans were met with riots and protests both from the extreme right and from the left. The anniversary, and the attempt to commemorate it, writes one journalist, "unleashed an anguished response from Germans unsure whether they should cast themselves as victims or continue silently to shoulder the blame for wartime atrocities" (Connolly). The ceremonies themselves were disrupted by demonstrators from both extremes: while the right wing wanted Dresden's victims to be recognized as victims of "mass murder," the left wing called for a tearing down of the Frauenkirche church under slogans such as "no tears for krauts."

Some months later, on August 6, 2005, the city of Hiroshima held its annual Hiroshima Peace Memorial Ceremony in memory of the bombing of the city. This ceremony has been conducted every year since the end of the war, on the morning of August 6. The ceremony itself follows a fixed pattern, starting with a reading of new names to be added to the register of fallen A-bomb victims, addresses by the mayor of Hiroshima and representatives from the Japanese government; then one minute of silence at precisely 8:15, followed by the sounding of the peace bell, the reading of the peace declaration, the releasing of doves, and peace songs by schoolchildren. The 2005 ceremony was not much different from the one held the year before, or the following year, with public addresses calling for world peace and expressing hope that the suffering the people of Hiroshima had been subjected to would never again be experienced by mankind. While the ceremonies in Dresden were disrupted by demonstrators from both political extremes, the sixtieth anniversary of Hiroshima was followed by an international gathering of "Mayors for world peace." In Germany, the story of civilian suffering seems inseparable from the story of responsibility for the Holocaust. One rarely speaks of one without also speaking of the other. Conversely, in Japan it seems that the story of Hiroshima has been given a place of its own, independent of the story of Japanese guilt and aggression.

Many forces were at play in the shaping of the two countries' narratives of war. However, two elements in particular can account for the very different directions the two narratives have taken: the degree to which military and political leaders were forced to take responsibility for their crimes and the "rhetoric of peace" that seems to have dominated the dissemination of the story of the destruction of Hiroshima. Let us first take a look the nature of the war trials in the two countries, especially the position of the nations' political leaders before and after the war. These two elements are closely linked. As Ian Buruma puts it, "Germany lost its Nazi leaders, Japan lost only its admirals and generals" (63). The American occupation forces in Japan decided to keep the emperor as the nation's symbolic head, and as a result quite effectively blocked any possibility for the nation to take full responsibility for its wartime aggression. Many of its military leaders were tried, convicted, and executed, but their leader remained in place—albeit with his powers significantly weakened, as he was forced to publicly denounce his god-like status. "The fact that Hirohito not only escaped punishment for his participation in this war of aggression and destruction, but appeared to take no responsibility whatsoever for any of his actions, made it hard for anyone else in Japan to acknowledge truthfully what they themselves had done during the conflict" (Rees 143). Japan has often received well-deserved criticism for failing to unequivocally own up to its crimes committed during its many years of aggression toward its neighboring countries, and the results of this can still be seen today in the form of strained political relationships between Japan and its Asian neighbors.

Still, the nature of the war trials and the emperor's lack of responsibility cannot adequately account for the different directions the narratives of war have taken in Germany and Japan. The most important factor is the shaping of the narrative of the atomic bomb, as it was created both in the United States and in Japan. This narrative endowed the bomb, paradoxically, with a positive meaning for having ushered forward Japan's surrender, thus saving the many lives a prolonged war would have cost. At the same time, the narrative lauded the leaders of both countries—President Truman and Emperor Hirohito—as great men who secured peace for their people and for the world. Although the story of the atomic bomb is certainly incorporated into the two countries' national histories in very different ways, they share a remarkable number of elements, and both stories embrace a surprisingly similar rhetoric of peace and heroism.

In the Japanese narrative, the emperor is made the hero, the one who took action and accepted the American demand for surrender. For, even after the devastating effect of the bomb was made known, Japanese military leaders were not ready to give up their fight. The meeting of The Supreme Council of Japan thus reached a deadlock, with three members opting for an immediate surrender—still with the condition that the emperor be retained—while the other three wanted to include three more conditions in their terms of surrender: Japan's right to disarm her own soldiers, the right to conduct her own war trials, and a limitation of the forces of occupation. In the end it was the emperor who, stepping out of his apolitical role, broke the deadlock and spoke up for an acceptance of the Potsdam declaration and of the demand for Japan's surrender. In the Japanese narrative, the emperor's decision is presented as a "divine intervention," one that saved Japan and the Japanese people from utter destruction: without the emperor's benevolence, more Japanese lives would have been lost. The emperor, the narrative stresses, understood the significance of the bomb's message and interpreted it wisely, for the best interest of his subjects.

The American narrative too casts its leader into a heroic role: Truman's decision to use the bomb is presented as a "sacred moment in American history," with the bomb being a "benevolent weapon that ultimately saved millions of lives" (Igarashi 22). In this narrative the history of the bomb itself, and of the processes involved in the development of this powerful weapon, are all but erased. Here, as in the Japanese version, history is simplified into a story of one man's great decision.

Although these two narratives are told from diametrically opposite points of view, they share a larger point: because of one man's heroic act—President Truman in the American version, Emperor Hirohito in the Japanese—lives were saved. Ultimately, the lesson of both of these narratives gives the atomic bomb one essential role only: the bomb ended the war. Truman and Emperor Hirohito were the agents who deciphered the message of the bomb. It is not difficult to recognize how both the United States and Japan, and not least their postwar relationship, depended on a narrative that cast the bomb into such a positive role. Only by endowing the bomb with the power to end the war could its devastating effect be given meaning, and thus only could the "sacrifice" of the peoples of Hiroshima and Nagasaki be made comprehensible. "It was not the destructive power of the bomb per se," writes Igarashi, "but rather the narrative that 'the bomb ended the war' that brought the war to its denouement" (24). The bomb becomes what brought peace to the Pacific, and through the bomb, Japan goes from being the United States' starkest enemy to becoming its closest Cold War ally.

With these narratives, Hiroshima is transformed into a city of peace, and the atomic bomb into a harbinger of that peace. Japan's story of the Second World War thus takes a very different path from German narratives of war, although the raw material from which those narratives are constructed could very well have led to narratives that are quite similar. What are the consequences of the Japanese narrative? In my opinion, two major factors continue to shape the way the story of Hiroshima is told and passed on to future generations. The first is the inseparable link created between the bomb—and the city of Hiroshima—and a concept of peace, even world peace. The second is a redefining of the belief that the bomb brought to an end a conflict that existed solely between the two countries of Japan and the United States, a belief that omits all other narratives of war in the Pacific in the process.

Let us look at the second point first. In the introductory chapter to an anthology of studies of the Asia–Pacific War(s), the editors write that Pacific War memories have been "systematically silenced by global, national, and masculinist narratives of the major warring powers" (Fujitani, White, and Yoneyama 3). Histories of the war, they point out, have a tendency to limit its temporal scope to 1941–45, having the war start with the attack on Pearl Harbor and end with the atomic bomb dropped on the two cities of Japan. Thus the account of the war is rendered in a "framework of a binary clash between Japan and the United States and its allies" (6), ignoring the fact that, for Japan, the conflict started as early as 1931, when Japanese forces invaded

Manchuria. It is precisely because of this dominating framework that Japan continues to be cast as a victim of World War II, while all the narratives of Japanese aggression are pushed into the background: "other lands and peoples are simply background or, more precisely, battlefields for the clashes of the great powers" (6). As long as the narrative of the Pacific War as a binary clash between major powers is allowed to dominate, these other stories will remain in the background.

The rhetoric of peace that surrounds the dissemination of the Hiroshima story is equally responsible for allowing these "minor" stories to remain minor. Ever since the very first commemorative ceremony was held at Hiroshima's epicenter only two years after the bomb wiped out the city, the focus of the memorialization of the bomb has been on a didactic message of peace. Understandably, this focus was encouraged by American occupation authorities. The focus on peace, and on the A-bomb as somehow a harbinger of that peace, was important to the American occupation, not only in order to make their presence more acceptable to the Japanese public but also because the linking of the bomb to peace became an important element in the Cold War rhetoric upon which America built its postwar supremacy. As Lisa Yoneyama has pointed out, "The textual production of Hiroshima as the A-bombed city that revived as a Mecca of world peace thus helped disseminate the view that the world's peaceful order was attained and will be maintained not by diplomatic efforts or negotiations, but by sustaining a menacing military force and technological supremacy" (20).

With the focus on peace, the message of the A-bomb is redefined as one with a universal appeal. Thus, Hiroshima, and by association all of Japan, becomes a beacon to the world. Redefined as a master code for catastrophe in the twentieth century, the subject remembering Hiroshima, through slogans such as "never again Hiroshima!" is all of humanity, whose remembering is expressed through a notion of universally shared emotions and sentiments unlimited by cultural boundaries and united in what Yoneyama has coined "nuclear universalism" (15). This sentiment is reflected, for example, in the commitment to peace prepared for the commemoration ceremony at the sixtieth anniversary: "we renew our determination to carry on the quest of the hibakusha [A-bomb victim], to continue telling the world about the horrors of nuclear weapons, to learn and pass on the Hiroshima story, until we build a world at peace" (Hiroshima Peace Memorial Ceremony). In the coupling of the experience of Hiroshima to world peace, the city's symbolic role as the site for the birth of the nuclear age becomes something over and above the specific, historical Japanese situation. The peace rhetoric of Hiroshima effectively pushes the specific Japanese context—the stories of

Japanese aggression—into the background, into oblivion. Thus the symbolic function of the apocalyptic ending dictates the beginning of this war narrative.

From the moment one steps off the train in Hiroshima, one is met by the city's focus on the message of peace: the main east–west avenue is called *Heiwa-ôdôri* (Peace Boulevard), and at the center of the city one finds the Peace Park and the Peace Memorial Museum. The power of the peace rhetoric is mirrored in the Peace Park both in rather subtle and in more explicit ways. Two illuminating examples are the construction and architecture of the park itself and the Children's Peace Monument located centrally in the park. Both elements in their own way contribute to the one-sided focus of the A-bomb's memorialization in Hiroshima, and either implicitly or explicitly they give voice to a narrative that casts Japan in the heroic role as messenger of peace, thereby covering over Japan's aggressive warfare and militaristic past.

The Peace Park is located at the heart of Hiroshima, at the epicenter of the atomic blast. Standing in front of the cenotaph at the southern end of the park, with one's back to the Peace Memorial Museum, one can enjoy the simple but elegant symmetry of the park's main elements. However, most visitors to the park, myself included, are unaware of the background for the park's design—a design that embodies a direct link to Japan's militaristic history. According to the historian Inoue Shôichi, Lisa Yoneyama explains, the Hiroshima Peace Park's stylistic origin can be traced back to a "nearly identical ground plan that had been adopted three years before Japan's surrender as part of a grand imperial vision, the Commemorative Building Project for the Construction of Greater East Asia" (Yoneyama 1). Both plans were designed by the architect Tange Kenzô, though under very different circumstances and for very different purposes. In 1942 the first plan proposed a "grandiose Shintoist memorial zone" at the foot of Mount Fuji, dedicated to the celebration of the Greater East Asian Empire. Yoneyama has traced the similarities between this planned park and the Hiroshima Peace Park. The parallels are striking—in shape, placement of buildings, entrance, and the "worshipping line" running from the main buildings to the central commemorative monument, with the Atom Bomb Dome functioning as the contemporary version's main point of worship.

The connection of these two plans, through the architect himself and through the many similarities between the two designs, is obvious enough to those who are aware of the Peace Park's history. But most visitors are not. What then is the significance of the connection? Doesn't the symbolism of the park work well enough within its present set of signifiers? There is a great beauty to the way in which the arch over the central cenotaph frames the bombed-out iron structure of the Atom Bomb Dome, with the eternal flame burning between the two points of vision. Every time I visit the park, I am moved by the simplicity and beauty of its architectural design. Why should it matter where the plans for the park originated? The answer is obvious: the design and structure of a commemorative space—a monument, park, or museum—is never innocent. In his study of Holocaust memorials, Young remarks that memory "is never shaped in a vacuum; the motives of memory are never pure" (2). Therefore, he continues, when speaking of monuments one needs to take into consideration not only the monument's exterior, but also such elements as the time and place it was conceived, its actual construction within its political and historical realities, its final finished form, and its place in national memory (14). Only then can one begin to grasp the multiple meanings it generates. Speaking for myself, the knowledge of the park's origin has planted a seed of resistance enabling me, on subsequent visits, to take a step back and to reflect on the problematic relationship of Japan's war responsibility to Hiroshima memories.

Combined with the origins of the architectural design, the choice of architect becomes an integral part of the park's meaning production. When the planners behind the Hiroshima Peace Memorial Park chose Tange, with his design so strikingly similar to the plans developed for the commemoration of the Japanese Empire, a link—intentional or not—was established between the ideology of the "Greater East Asia War" and Hiroshima's contemporary celebration of peace. Tange's design, which once was hailed as the vision that best represented the sublime objective of the Greater East Asia Co-Prosperity Sphere, could, it seems, be redefined only a few years later as a symbolic representation of a city's, and a country's, prayers for peace. Although Tange's name is mentioned in tourist pamphlets, the story of the design's origin is not. The connection, Yoneyama points out, is thus important on two levels: on the one hand, it embodies the continuity between imperial prewar Japan and peaceful postwar Japan; on the other hand, it demonstrates how this continuity remains largely unrecognized: "Hiroshima memories have been predicated on the grave obfuscation of the prewar Japanese Empire, its colonial practices, and their consequences" (3).

The amnesiac relationship to Japan's recent colonial past, so illuminatingly exemplified through the park's design and construction, is further enhanced through the emphasis that Hiroshima's monumental form places on peace and on victimization. In particular, this emphasis is visible in the manner in which the stories told through the park's museum and through its monuments tend to move from a focus on individual suffering to a collective call for peace. Let us pause for a moment on one of the most famous stories of individual suffering: the story of Sadako. Sadako's story is first and foremost told through the monument raised for all child victims of the A-bomb, the Children's Peace Monument (also called the Tower of a Thousand Cranes). The monument, a bronze statue depicting a young girl holding a huge paper crane in her outstretched arms, was raised in 1958 by Sadako's classmates. But who was Sadako? Sasaki Sadako was two years old the day the bomb fell on Hiroshima; ten years later she fell ill from leukemia, also known as the Atom Bomb Disease, due to her exposure to radiation from the bomb. While in hospital, she learned that folding one thousand paper cranes was a symbol for good luck and long life, and she decided that if she managed to fold so many, she could survive. Sadly, she died less than a year after she first fell ill. Inspired by her strong will to live, Sadako's classmates wanted to do something to honor her and all other children who became victims of the atomic bomb, and they set about collecting money in order to raise a monument to her memory. Through the monument, and through the Sadako story, the paper crane has become a symbol not only for the suffering of the people of Hiroshima but also for peace and the fight against nuclear weapons. Every day, new paper cranes are donated by visitors and placed at the foot of the monument. More than any other story, the story of Sadako demonstrates the erasure of the line between individual and collective suffering.

Of all the children who were killed by the atomic blast, why did Sadako, a girl who died a decade after the explosion of an illness that children succumb to every day around the world, become singled out for this symbolic role? Maybe it was a matter of timing.

At the time Sadako became ill, the American occupation had ended, and the censorship on writing anything that could be conceived of as a criticism of the occupation authorities was lifted, allowing room for a freer discussion of the atomic bomb. Furthermore, the international political climate of the 1950s—the Korean War and American tests of nuclear weapons in the Pacific—gave rise to peace movements and antinuclear movements across the globe. After a Japanese fishing boat was caught in the fallout from the nuclear testing on the Bikini Atoll in 1954, the Japanese public's interest in the damage from the atomic bomb gained increased momentum. When Sadako died in 1955, antinuclear movements and peace organizations in many countries had already begun to turn their eyes toward Hiroshima. Sadako's classmates' movement to build the monument thus became a part of this larger peace movement in Japan.

Today, the story of Sadako has become one of the best known victim stories from Hiroshima, and monuments to her memory have been erected throughout the world. The monuments, in addition to books and films, are accompanied by websites where one can find information about Sadako, learn how to fold paper cranes (which one is encouraged to send to Japan), and join forums such as "Peace Club" and "Kids Peace Plaza." In the Kids Peace Plaza one is guided through activities such as "talking about peace," writing "letters to Sadako," and observing the "peace studies presentation room." Sadako's death thus is transformed from the death of a young girl—a friend, classmate, and daughter—into the death of a beacon for peace and hope for the whole world.

The same pedagogical and didactic message of peace that can be seen in the story of Sadako is present also in the Peace Memorial Museum itself. The overall message and purpose of the museum is presented to the visitor at the very beginning of the exhibit, where one is met in large print across the first wall: "Having now recovered from that A-bomb calamity, Hiroshima's deepest wish is the elimination of all nuclear weapons and the realization of a genuinely peaceful international community" (Hiroshima Peace Memorial Museum). Step by step, the museum proceeds to guide the visitor through exhibits that will help him or her reach that awareness. The museum exhibit unfolds like a narrative, starting with exhibits showing Hiroshima before the war, followed by information on the development of the bomb and the Manhattan Project. Next, after taking the visitor through facts about the destruction of Hiroshima and "the nuclear age," there is an exhibit called "the path to peace." Here the visitor is presented with the "spirit of Hiroshima" and explanations of how this spirit has fostered "the unwavering hope for the abolition of nuclear weapons and the realization of lasting world peace" (museum pamphlet). Although Japan had inflicted great pain on its neighboring countries, the text reads, it must "find a way to make our mutual pain a positive gift for the future" (museum exhibit text). According to the narrative of the museum, then, there is a natural progression from the development of the bomb via destruction to the "path to peace." Presenting this narrative's development, the exhibit clearly seems to be downplaying Japan's responsibility for the war, and thus serves to condone the lack of official public apologies in Japan. In the final part of the museum the visitor is confronted with the individual fates of bombing victims and their stories of suffering. The exhibits include melted glass, burned clothes and school lunches, and twisted scraps of metal, accompanied by stories about young boys and girls who lost their lives in the inferno of flames. In the museum's narrative, it is not the apocalyptic ending of the atomic blast that constitutes the narrative's ending but the rise to awareness and a call for world peace. This overall message frames both the museum's beginning and ending, and all exhibits are interpreted within this framework. The information that the exhibit includes about Japan's expansion and militaristic rule is downplayed in favor of the "path to peace" that Hiroshima later followed.

Despite the intrusive pedagogy, it is hard to leave Hiroshima's peace museum without being moved, without feeling that the people of Hiroshima were unjustified victims of war. Incontestably, they were; civilians always are. And yet I always leave the museum with mixed feelings. Naturally the survivors of Hiroshima must be allowed to tell their stories, and their stories must be treated with respect. Still, there is something undeniably self-righteous about the way Hiroshima poses as a city of peace. And, as I have tried to show, there is something fundamentally problematic in the way the story of Hiroshima is told there. As long as the stories of individual suffering are brought to the forefront, I believe they will continue to overshadow other accounts of Japan's war. James Orr acknowledges that the "Hiroshima and Nagasaki bombings privileged the Japanese nation with an exclusive claim to leadership in the global ban-the-bomb movement and provided the country with its first powerfully unifying national myth after defeat" (7). But Orr also points out that alongside the atomic bomb victim exceptionalism that started in the 1950s, Asian suffering and Japanese wartime aggression have been a "vital concern of both progressives and conservatives in many discursive fields, including war victimhood" (175). In Hiroshima, however, the *Peace* Park and the *Peace* Memorial Museum, already in the choice of names, establish from the outset a focus and a purpose that perhaps blind the visitor to critical accounts that certainly exist in historical and political discourse.

The memorialization of the atomic bombs in Hiroshima today, then, lacks the self-reflexive scrutiny that has ridden German memories of war. For while new "countermonuments" in Germany display "the torturous complexity of their nation's relationship to its past" (Young 27), Hiroshima as memorial site seems unable to reflect any similar complexity. Perhaps "the most stunning and inflammatory response to Germany's memorial conundrum is the rise of its countermonuments: brazen, painfully self-conscious memorial spaces conceived to challenge the very premises of their being" (27). One example is Jochen Gerz and Esther Shalev-Gerz's Monument against Fascism in Hamburg, which was unveiled in 1986. This monument, a 12-meter-high pillar of aluminum, was designed to challenge memorial conventions by itself being, gradually over the course of a number of years, lowered into the ground, and thus in the end vanishing completely from sight. "As if in mocking homage to national forebears who planned the Holocaust as a self-consuming set of events—that is, intended to destroy all traces of itself, all memory of its victims—the Gerzes have designed a self-consuming memorial that leaves behind only the rememberer and the memory of a memorial" (31). But while the Hamburg monument was shrinking, Hiroshima's monuments seemed to be "growing," with new names being added yearly to the cenotaph and donations of paper cranes piling up around the Children's Peace Monument.

Yet it is important to acknowledge the existence of counter-narratives also in Japan and the difficulties they have faced in their struggle to be heard. One such narrative can be found in the peace park itself, not far from the Children's Peace Monument, although one needs to read between the lines in order to truly take in its counter-message: the cenotaph for Korean victims of the atomic bomb. This monument, the explanatory plaque tells us, is raised in memory of Korean colonial subjects who had been forcefully brought to Japan and who subsequently lost their lives in the atomic blast. It was not until 1999 that this monument was included in the park, having initially been given a space *outside* the Peace Park. With its short explanatory note, this monument implicitly tells the story both of Japanese colonialism and of postwar discrimination. What name one gives the war also reflects how one wishes to frame the major historical events: rather than referring to the war as the Second World War or the Pacific War, for example, an increasing number of people in Japan now refer to the war as the "fifteen year war," thus acknowledging a different start for the narrative. Furthermore, there have always been voices in Japan—political, academic, and journalistic—that have attempted to counter and to criticize what became the dominating story of war. Sadly, however, some of these voices have been met by intimidating opposition. For example, when the mayor of Nagasaki, Motoshima Hitoshi, suggested in 1988 that the emperor bore responsibility for the war, a right-wing fanatic attempted to assassinate him. Others who have spoken openly of their wartime crimes have been met by so much harassment from the political right that they have had to move from their homes (Chang 213–14).

Despite the existence of counter-narratives, there is no doubt what narrative has been allowed to dominate the dissemination of the Hiroshima story in Hiroshima: the story of the major powers. This story has in turn become completely intertwined with the narrative of postwar peace. Igarashi has called this narrative the "foundational narrative" of United States–Japan postwar relations and points to how their respective versions of the story have served the interests of both nations, in a sense exonerating them from wartime guilt. In the case of Japan, the narrative "managed to cloak Japan's defeat in the guise of strategic necessity and concern for humanity at large" (20), thus providing the Japanese wartime leadership with a "narrative that could explain away the tension created by its acceptance of defeat" (20). For the United States, on the other hand, this narrative transforms the atomic bomb into "a benevolent weapon that ultimately saved millions of lives" (22).

Concluding, I concur with James Young's observation that "once we assign monumental form to memory, we have to some degree divested ourselves of the obligation to remember." Hiroshima—with its park, museum, and monuments—continually appeals to our obligation to remember. However, the monumental form that the story of Hiroshima has to a great extent taken gears our remembering toward one interpretation and one story. This essay has attempted to explain the very different directions the memorialization of war has taken in Germany and Japan, despite the existence of considerable parallels, by examining the structure and creation of Hiroshima's narrative. I hope to have shown that how we remember a historical event depends not only on how we understand the story's end but also on how we envision its beginning. In choosing a narrative's beginning, one is to a great degree also determining which parts of the story are to be included and which are to be left outside of the narrative. One major consequence of such choices can be the erasure of other important elements of historical record. Comparing Germany and Japan is one way of examining, and understanding, the different roads the dominating narrative of aggression and defeat can take, and the dissimilar ways in which the roles of victim and perpetrator can be incorporated into national narratives. More importantly, the comparison can teach us something about the consequences narrative choices have for the creation of collective identity-forming narratives.

Works Cited

Bal, Mieke. "Introduction." In *Acts of Memory: Cultural Recall in the Present,* edited by Mieke Bal, Jonathan Crewe, and Leo Spitzer, vii–xvii. Hanover and London: University Press of New England, 1999.

Buruma, Ian. *The Wages of Guilt: Memories of War in Germany and Japan.* 1994. London: Phoenix, 2002.

Carrard, Philippe. "September 1939, Beginnings, Historical Narrative, and the Outbreak of World War II." In *Narrative Beginnings: Theories and Practices,* edited by Brian Richardson, 63–78. Lincoln: University of Nebraska Press, 2008.

Chang, Iris. *The Rape of Nanking: The Forgotten Holocaust of World War II.* New York: Penguin Books, 1997.

Connolly, Kate. "Horror of Dresden Bombing Divides." *Telegraph.co.uk.* http://www. telegraph.co.uk/news/main.jhtml?xml=/news/2005/02/10/wdres10.xml&s. Accessed October 10, 2007.

Fujitani, T., Geoffrey M. White, and Lisa Yoneyama. "Introduction." In *Perilous Memories: The Asia-Pacific War(s),* edited by T. Fujitani, Geoffrey M. White, and Lisa Yoneyama, 1–29. Durham and London: Duke University Press, 2001.

Hiroshima Peace Memorial Ceremony Program. The City of Hiroshima, August 6, 2005.

Igarashi, Yoshikuni. *Bodies of Memory: Narratives of War in Postwar Japanese Culture, 1945–1970.* Princeton: Princeton University Press, 2000.

Moeller, Robert G. *War Stories: The Search for a Usable Past in the Federal Republic of Germany.* Berkeley: University of California Press, 2001.

Orr, James J. *The Victim as Hero: Ideologies of Peace and National Identity in Postwar Japan.* Honolulu: University of Hawai Press, 2001.

Rees, Laurence. *Horror in the East: Japan and the Atrocities of World War II.* London: DaCapo Press, 2001.

Richardson, Brian. "A Theory of Narrative Beginnings and the Beginnings of 'The Dead' and *Molloy.*" In *Narrative Beginnings: Theories and Practices,* edited by Brian Richardson, 113–26. Lincoln: University of Nebraska Press, 2008.

Special Exhibition 5.http://www.pcf.city.hiroshima.jp/virtual/VirtualMuseum_e/eshibit_e/exh0107_e/esh0. Accessed October 28, 2007.

Treat, John Whittier. *Writing Ground Zero: Japanese Literature and the Atomic Bomb.* Chicago: University of Chicago Press, 1995.

Vees-Gulani, Susanne. *Trauma and Guilt: Literature of Wartime Bombing in Germany.* Berlin and New York: Walter de Gruyter, 2003.

Yoneyama, Lisa. *Hiroshima Traces: Time, Space, and the Dialectics of Memory.* Berkeley: University of California Press, 1999.

Young, James E. *The Texture of Memory: Holocaust Memorials and Meaning.* New Haven and London: Yale University Press, 1993.

CONTRIBUTORS

DAPHNA ERDINAST-VULCAN is Professor of English at the University of Haifa, Israel, and Editor-in-Chief of the Haifa University Press. She is the author of *Graham Greene's Childless Fathers* (1988); *Joseph Conrad and the Modern Temper* (1991); and *The Strange Short Fiction of Joseph Conrad* (1999), and has recently completed an interdisciplinary study, provisionally titled *Between Philosophy and Literature: Bakhtin and the Question of the Subject.*

SIDRA DEKOVEN EZRAHI is Professor of Comparative Literature at the Hebrew University of Jerusalem. Her work ranges from explorations of literary and cultural representations of the Holocaust to studies of the Jewish configurations of exile and homecoming. She was a featured speaker at the Chicago Humanities Festival and the Jewish Arts Festival in New York. She is the author of *By Words Alone: The Holocaust in Literature* (1980) and *Booking Passage: Exile and Homecoming in the Modern Jewish Imagination* (2000). She received a Guggenheim fellowship for her current project "Jerusalem and the Poetics of Return."

ANNIKEN GREVE is Professor of Comparative Literature at the University of Tromsø, Norway. She has published articles in Norwegian and English on theoretical issues ranging from philosophy of language and philosophical anthropology to issues in narrative theory and methodology.

JEREMY HAWTHORN was born in England in 1942. Since 1981 he has been Professor of Modern British Literature at the Norwegian University of Science and Technology, Trondheim. He has published three monographs and a number of articles on the fiction of Joseph Conrad and has edited Conrad's *Under Western Eyes* and *The Shadow-Line* for Oxford World's Classics. Other publications include *Cunning Passages: New Historicism, Cultural Materialism and Marxism in the Contemporary Literary Debate* (1996); *A Glossary of Contemporary Theory* (4th edition 2000); and *Studying the Novel* (6th edition 2010).

MARIANNE HIRSCH is the William Peterfield Trent Professor of English, Comparative Literature, and Gender Studies at Columbia University. She is Vice President of the Modern Language Association of America. Most recently, she co-authored, with Leo Spitzer, *Ghosts of Home: The Afterlife of Czernowitz in Jewish Memory* (2010). Her other publications include *Family Frames: Photography, Narrative, and Postmemory* (1997) and the forthcoming *The Generation of Postmemory: Visual Cultures after the Holocaust*. She has edited and co-edited a number of books, including *The Familial Gaze* (1998); *Teaching the Representation of the Holocaust* (2004); and the forthcoming *Rites of Return*.

IRENE KACANDES is the Dartmouth Professor of German Studies and Comparative Literature at Dartmouth College. Author of *Daddy's War: Greek American Stories* (2009) and *Talk Fiction: Literature and the Talk Explosion* (2001), she has also co-edited three volumes: *A User's Guide to German Cultural Studies* (1997); *Teaching the Representation of the Holocaust* (2004); and a special issue of *Women's Studies Quarterly* on "Witness" (2008). Author of articles on German and Italian cultural studies, narrative theory, feminist linguistic theory, Holocaust studies, memory and trauma studies, and life writing, her current research focuses on generational memory and the Second World War. Kacandes is recipient of a Fulbright Full grant, a SONY grant, a fellowship at the United States Holocaust Museum and Memorial, and a Friedman Family fellowship.

JAKOB LOTHE is Professor of English Literature at the University of Oslo. His books include *Conrad's Narrative Method* (1989) and *Narrative in Fiction and Film* (2000). The author of numerous essays, he has edited or co-edited several volumes, including *Franz Kafka: Zur ethischen und ästhetischen Rechtfertigung* (2002; with Beatrice Sandberg); *The Art of Brevity* (2004, paperback 2011); *Literary Landscapes* (Basingstoke: Palgrave, 2008); *Joseph Conrad: Voice, Sequence, History, Genre* (2008; with Jeremy Hawthorn and James Phelan); and *Franz Kafka: Narration, Rhetoric, and Reading* (2011; with Beatrice Sandberg and Ronald Speirs). During the 2005–6 academic year he was the leader of the research project Narrative Theory and Analysis at the Centre for Advanced Study, Oslo.

PHILIPPE MESNARD is Professor of Comparative Literature at the Université Blaise-Pascal in Clermont-Ferrand, France. He is also Director of the Fondation Auschwitz in Brussels, member of a committee at the Fondation pour la Mémoire de la Shoah in Paris, and director of a program at the Collège International de Philosophie in Paris. His most recent books are a biography of Primo Levi, *Primo Levi: Le passage d'un témoin* (Paris: Fayard, 2011); *Primo Levi: Una vita per immagini* (Venise: Marsilio, 2008); and *Témoignage en résistance* (Paris: Stock, 2007).

J. HILLIS MILLER taught for many years at The Johns Hopkins University and then at Yale University before going to the University of California at Irvine in 1986, where is he now UCI Distinguished Research Professor. He is the author of many books and essays on nineteenth- and twentieth-century English, European, and American literature and on literary theory. His recent books include *Zero Plus One* (2003); *Literature as Conduct: Speech Acts in Henry James* (2005); the *J. Hillis Miller Reader*

(2005); *For Derrida* (2009); and *The Medium Is the Maker: Browning, Freud, Derrida and the New Telepathic Technologies* (2009). In 2011 he published *The Conflagration of Community: Fiction before and after Auschwitz.* Both *Reading for Today:* Adam Bede and Middlemarch and *Theory and the Disappearing Future: On de Man, on Benjamin* (co-authored with Tom Cohen and Claire Colebrook) are due in 2012. Miller is a fellow of the American Academy of Arts and Sciences and a member of the American Philosophical Society. He received the MLA Lifetime Scholarly Achievement Award in 2005.

JAMES PHELAN is Distinguished University Professor of English at The Ohio State University. He is a founding member of Project Narrative at OSU and the editor of the journal *Narrative* and co-editor (with Peter J. Rabinowitz and Robyn Warhol) of the Theory and Interpretation of Narrative series at The Ohio State University Press. He has also edited or co-edited several collections, including *Joseph Conrad* (2008; with Jakob Lothe and Jeremy Hawthorn); *Teaching Narrative Theory* (2010; with David Herman and Brian McHale); and the Blackwell *Companion to Narrative Theory* (2005; with Peter J. Rabinowitz). Phelan has written extensively about the rhetorical theory of narrative, especially in *Worlds from Words* (1981); *Reading People, Reading Plots* (1989); *Narrative as Rhetoric* (1996); *Living to Tell about It* (2005); and *Experiencing Fiction* (2007). He has collaborated with David Herman, Peter J. Rabinowitz, Brian Richardson, and Robyn Warhol on *Narrative Theory: Core Concepts and Critical Debates* (2012).

MICHAEL ROTHBERG is Professor of English and Conrad Humanities Scholar at the University of Illinois at Urbana-Champaign, where he is also Director of the Holocaust, Genocide, and Memory Studies Initiative. His work has been published in such journals as *American Literary History; Critical Inquiry; Cultural Critique; History and Memory; New German Critique;* and *PMLA,* and has been translated into French, German, and Hungarian. His latest book is *Multidirectional Memory: Remembering the Holocaust in the Age of Decolonization* (2009), published by Stanford University Press in their Cultural Memory in the Present series. He is also the author of *Traumatic Realism: The Demands of Holocaust Representation* (2000) and has co-edited *The Holocaust: Theoretical Readings* (2003) and *Cary Nelson and the Struggle for the University: Poetry, Politics, and the Profession* (2009). His current project, "Citizens of Memory: Muslim Immigrants and Holocaust Remembrance in Contemporary Germany," is being supported by an ACLS Collaborative Research Fellowship (2011–12).

BEATRICE SANDBERG is Professor in German Literature, the German Department, University of Bergen, Norway. She has published widely on Swiss literature, Franz Kafka, the twentieth-century novel, and national and cultural identity. Co-author (with Ronald Speirs) of *Franz Kafka* (1998), she has edited or co-edited a number of volumes, including *Fascism and European Literature* (1991); *Franz Kafka: Zur ethischen und ästhetischen Rechtfertigung* (2002; with Jakob Lothe); *Autobiographisches Schreiben: Grenzen der Identität und der Fiktionalität* (2006); *Meldungen aus Norwegen 1940–45* (2008); *Familienbilder als Zeitbilder: Erzählte Zeitgeschichte bei Schweizer Autoren vom 18. Jahrhundert bis zur Gegenwart* (2010); and *Franz Kafka: Narration, Rhetoric, and Reading* (2011; with Jakob Lothe and Ronald Speirs).

ANETTE H. STOREIDE is currently Associate Professor of German at the Norwegian University of Science and Technology, Trondheim. She wrote her dissertation on the autobiographical writings of Norwegian survivors of the Nazi concentration camp Sachsenhausen, and she has worked at the Memorial Site Sachsenhausen. Her publications include *Tidsvitner: Fortellinger fra Auschwitz og Sachsenhausen* (*Time's Witnesses: Narratives from Auschwitz and Sachsenhausen*) (2006; co-edited with Jakob Lothe) and *Arven etter Hitler—Tysklands oppgjør med naziregimet* (*The Shadows of Hitler: Germany and the Confrontation with the Nazi Past*) (2010).

SUSAN RUBIN SULEIMAN is the C. Douglas Dillon Professor of the Civilization of France and Professor of Comparative Literature at Harvard University. Her books include *Authoritarian Fictions: The Ideological Novel as a Literary Genre* (1983); *Subversive Intent: Gender, Politics, and the Avant-Garde* (1990); *Risking Who One Is: Encounters with Contemporary Art and Literature* (1994); *Crises of Memory and the Second World War* (2006); the memoir *Budapest Diary: In Search of the Motherbook* (1996); and several edited volumes, including most recently *French Global: A New Approach to Literary History,* co-edited with Christie McDonald (2010). In 2009–10, Suleiman was the Shapiro Senior Scholar-in-Residence at the Center for Advanced Holocaust Studies of the U.S. Holocaust Memorial Museum in Washington, DC.

ANNE THELLE has an MA in English literature and a PhD in Japanese literature, both from the University of Oslo. She has also studied Japanese language and literature at Ritsumeikan University in Kyoto. She is currently Associate Professor of Intercultural Communications at the Norwegian Military Academy, in addition to holding a postdoctorate fellowship in Japanese studies at the University of Oslo. Previous publications include *Writing as Negotiation: Nakagami Kenji's Kiseki and the Power of the Tale* (2010) and *Japan—solens opprinnelse* (*Japan—Origin of the Sun*) (2000).

JANET WALKER is Professor of Film and Media Studies at the University of California, Santa Barbara, where she is also affiliated with the Feminist Studies and Comparative Literature Programs and the Environmental Media Initiative of the Carsey-Wolf Center. Her published writings in the areas of feminist historiography, documentary film, and trauma studies have been published in journals including *Screen* and *Continuum,* and she is author or editor of books including *Westerns: Films through History* (2001); *Trauma Cinema: Documenting Incest and the Holocaust* (2005); and *Documentary Testimonies: Global Archives of Suffering* (with Bhaskar Sarkar, 2009). Walker lectures internationally and co-directs a local community project, *Video Portraits of Survival,* to create expressive videos and archival material from the testimony and encounters of refugees and rescuers of the Holocaust. Her current project is a book about documentary, geography, and environment.

INDEX

THEORY AND INTERPRETATION OF NARRATIVE

James Phelan, Peter J. Rabinowitz, and Robyn Warhol, Series Editors

Because the series editors believe that the most significant work in narrative studies today contributes both to our knowledge of specific narratives and to our understanding of narrative in general, studies in the series typically offer interpretations of individual narratives and address significant theoretical issues underlying those interpretations. The series does not privilege one critical perspective but is open to work from any strong theoretical position.